A Reader's Guide to
Fifty Modern British Poets

Reader's Guide Series
General Editor: Andrew Mylett

Shakespeare and His Contemporaries
Marguerite Alexander

Fifty British Novels 1600–1900
Gilbert Phelps

Fifty American Novels
Ian Ousby

Fifty Modern British Poets
Michael Schmidt

Forthcoming

Fifty British Plays 1660–1900
John Cargill Thompson

Fifty European Novels
Martin Seymour-Smith

Fifty American Poets
Peter Jones

Fifty Modern British Novels
Andrew Mylett

Fifty British Poets 1300–1900
Michael Schmidt

Fifty Modern British Plays
Benedict Nightingale

A Reader's Guide to
Fifty Modern British Poets

by Michael Schmidt

Heinemann – London
Barnes & Noble – New York

Heinemann Educational Books Ltd

LONDON EDINBURGH MELBOURNE AUCKLAND HONG KONG
SINGAPORE KUALA LUMPUR NEW DELHI IBADAN NAIROBI
JOHANNESBURG KINGSTON PORT OF SPAIN

First published 1979 by Pan Books as
An Introduction to Fifty Modern British Poets
in the Pan Literature Guides Series
First published in this casebound edition 1979

ISBN (UK) 0 435 18810 0
ISBN (USA) 0–06–496110–9

Library of Congress Number 79–53438

Published in Great Britain by
Heinemann Educational Books Ltd
22 Bedford Square, London WC1B 3HH
Published in the U.S.A. 1979 by
Harper & Row Publishers, Inc.
Barnes & Noble Import Division

Printed and bound in Great Britain by
Richard Clay (The Chaucer Press) Ltd,
Bungay, Suffolk

Contents

Preface 7

Thomas Hardy 13
A. E. Housman 27
Rudyard Kipling 35
W. B. Yeats 44
Charlotte Mew 57
Walter de la Mare 64
Edward Thomas 69
Wyndham Lewis 79
T. E. Hulme 88
D. H. Lawrence 94
Edwin Muir 102
Edith Sitwell 109
Elizabeth Daryush 115
T. S. Eliot 121
Isaac Rosenberg 134
Hugh MacDiarmid 140
Wilfred Owen 148
David Jones 156
Robert Graves 166
Austin Clarke 173
Edmund Blunden 181

Edgell Rickword   186
Basil Bunting   193
Stevie Smith   200
Patrick Kavanagh   207
William Empson   213
John Betjeman   220
Louis MacNeice   225
W. H. Auden   233
Roy Fuller   244
George Barker   251
R. S. Thomas   260
C. H. Sisson   266
Dylan Thomas   278
David Gascoyne   285
Charles Causley   291
W. S. Graham   297
Keith Douglas   305
Edwin Morgan   314
Donald Davie   321
Philip Larkin   330
Michael Hamburger   339
Elizabeth Jennings   346
Christopher Middleton   353
Charles Tomlinson   360
Burns Singer   369
Thom Gunn   376
Ted Hughes   383
Jon Silkin   392
Geoffrey Hill   398

Bibliographies   408
Index   427

Preface

A preface to a book of fifty introductory essays is almost superfluous – except as it forewarns the reader of the author's intentions and gives due notice of his biases. In conformity with other books in this series, and with my own predisposition as a reader of poetry, rather than describe 'movements' and 'trends' I have taken fifty individual modern poets and attempted to provide summary biographical details, a description of the scope and nature of their work, and some critical comment on what I see as its salient features. Where space has permitted I have drawn analogies and contrasts between the poets, suggested something of their contemporaries, and identified their mentors as my ear detected them.

I took as my youngest poet Geoffrey Hill (b. 1932). It would have been a disservice to more recent writers to provide an introductory essay when the body of their significant work is still small: such descriptions would have been out of date in two or three years. At the other extreme, I included only those poets some of whose work was written in 1900 or later. I therefore omitted Gerard Manley Hopkins, though his readership was not found until this century. Where his formal experiments or his vision seem to influence later poets – David Jones and Elizabeth Daryush, for example – I have tried to indicate the points of affinity.

Had I been able to include sixty poets, I should have added essays on Robert Bridges, Arthur Symons, John

Masefield, Siegfried Sassoon, Norman Cameron, Henry Reed, Seamus Heaney, Alun Lewis, Peter Scupham, and Roy Fisher. It would, however, have been difficult to go further. Indeed, fifty genuinely durable poets are too many to expect from any century. It is unlikely that the work of more than ten of the poets considered here will be read in the next century. Yet they should be important to us, now.

This book does not attempt to chronicle reputations. Its purpose is to point in the direction of the best British poetry of this century and to trace, in the work of some lesser writers, techniques and critical tendencies which became or are still to become assimilated into our tradition. I have placed some emphasis on 'modernist' writers whose toe-hold in British poetry is – in some readers' minds – neither secure nor particularly British. T. S. Eliot, himself the outstanding modernist poet, through his later work helped deflect modernism and its acceptance in Britain. But the significant modernism of writers such as Hugh MacDiarmid, David Jones, C. H. Sisson, Donald Davie, Charles Tomlinson, and Geoffrey Hill is thoroughly in keeping with a distinctively British adaptation of those traditions which Eliot was himself, early on, instrumental in articulating.

It is worth remarking that what still strikes many readers as the most original, perhaps even the most *contemporary*, poetry of this century, is the work of poets writing in the first quarter of it, when revolutions of technique and form and a remapping of poetic subject matter were problems of urgency. Eliot, T. E. Hulme, MacDiarmid, Edward Thomas, and on a lesser scale Wyndham Lewis, Charlotte Mew, D. H. Lawrence and Isaac Rosenberg, still have about them an alerting freshness which few of their successors possess. These may not all be among the best poets of the century, but they are explorers, and the problems they created and resolved have proved the perennial problems of serious modern writers.

Developing in the same period were the Georgians, including Walter de la Mare and, later, Robert Graves and Edmund Blunden. Taking their cue from Hardy, Housman, and Masefield, they were radical not in their approach to technique or form but in their attempt to expand poetic subject matter and adapt new experiences to the old forms. War was among the experiences they had to accommodate. Like the poets associated with the more rigorous Imagist movement, these writers passed through a Georgian discipline and went on to develop in their own distinctive ways.

In the 1930s, with the rise of W. H. Auden and the poets associated with him – Louis MacNeice, Stephen Spender, C. Day Lewis, and others – there was a return to more traditional forms; the political and lyric poetry of the poets of the early 1930s is occasionally inventive in technique, experimenting with alliterative patterns, rhythms, and rhymes – the surface of the poem. But they learned their formal lessons from Hardy, not from Eliot.

The term 'Apocalyptic Poetry' came to be applied not only to the founders of 'The Apocalypse', Henry Treece, J. F. Hendry, and G. S. Fraser, but to poets more distantly associated with the group, even to Dylan Thomas, W. S. Graham, George Barker, and others. It describes more an attitude to the poetic vocation than to the art of poetry. Short-lived as it was in the late 1930s and early 1940s, several of the poets associated with it wrote in sympathy with the 1930s poets' political commitments but were not attracted to their techniques. The younger poets resorted to various styles, notably subjective versions of surreal rhetoric, though again none of them was *formally* radical except David Gascoyne, whose commitment to surrealism was, for a time, critically wholehearted.

The 1940s were not sterile years, however. The achievement of individual formalism by poets such as Keith Douglas, R. S. Thomas and Charles Causley was notable. These poets' work in no way suggests a movement; each developed to a degree in isolation. But 'The Movement' of the early 1950s – including Donald Davie, Thom Gunn and Philip Larkin – consolidated its energies against the much-publicized Apocalyptic excesses, countering them with a severe advocacy of reason, irony, and traditional forms.

Briefly it gained the ascendancy. Like the important movements of the past, it was in part a strategic grouping of writers with similar distastes and similar objectives; as they developed, the best of them moved beyond the prescriptive discipline of their early work towards more individual styles.

Prompt reactions discredited The Movement. A. Alvarez's anthology, *The New Poetry* (1962), which included work by Movementeers, diagnosed the 'gentility principle', chastised the narrow range of British poetry as Alvarez saw it, and suggested obliquely – but in a manner that later critics and poets simplified and dogmatized – that discipline, form, reason, measure, were in effect incompatible with sincerity, that true poetry could be made today only from extreme experience, that to engage a naked experience naked language was necessary, that formal perspective produces untruth, that truth is communicated only as language, in its very processes, apes the extremity of experience and response. The subjectivity implicit in this position contributed to many of the excesses of the 1960s, the development of confessional verse, and the cult of self-dramatizing 'authenticity'. It helped make for the atmosphere which was so congenial to facile poetry, the most extensive anthology of which – Michael Horovitz's *The Children of Albion* (1969) – Alvarez was himself quick to condemn.

No significant poetic movements arose during the 1960s and in the 1970s the positive disarray has continued. The poet – and the reader – has a multiplicity of choices open to him. The reader now asks, not how a poem conforms to certain prescribed rules, but how it achieves wholeness within the system of values it proposes, within its chosen form. He can accept the rich plural literature of our century for what it is. The outstanding poets of this century have, for the most part, developed outside movements, regardless of the taste of their immediate audience or the noises of the critics. They have measured themselves not against their contemporaries but against their masters.

The chief temptation threatening the modern poet, it

seems to me, is public professionalism, the tendency to capitalize on the identity of 'being a poet', believing that the profession validates the work. When a man says 'I am a poet' as another man would say 'I am a coal miner' or 'I am a bank clerk', he has put his vocation in danger. Poetry, unlike verse, is not as readily mined as coal, nor as manageable as bank notes. Poetry is the one literary vocation which cannot be made into a career. A poet may become a journalist, a teacher, a painter, a civil servant, a road sweeper. In doing so he enriches his art, while in 'being a poet' merely, he impoverishes it. For the poet must recognize the actual effects his work may have, must exist in a wide pattern of social relationships – not as an entertainer before an audience but as a man working among men and responsible to them. Michael Roberts wrote, 'The poetic use of language can cause discord as easily as it can cure it. A bad poem, a psychologically disordered poem, if it is technically effective may arouse uneasiness or nausea or anger in the reader.' Any serious reader – and any serious poet – will agree. The poet must be alert to the consequences of his ideas as the poem contains them. For if he is a good poet, his ideas have consequences. The making of poetry may be a gratuitous act; but in its gratuity it cannot afford untruth or forfeit responsibility. The poet is 'professional' only with regard to his art.

My own first point of access to a poem is the rhythm, the work's 'residual magic'. I am biased in favour of the poet who speaks with his own voice, avoiding easy rhetoric, posturing, and deceitful irony. I respond to poetry whose didactic edge is carefully experiential, not exhortatory, cajoling, or condescending; a poetry that engages experience, whatever its intensity, and that apprehends the formal challenge each experience raises. It is my conviction that – again in Michael Roberts's words – 'primarily poetry is an exploration of the possibilities of language'. All poetry, however obliquely, is didactic, but seldom baldly so. The best poetry eludes paraphrase. What the poem says is implicit in *how* it is speaking.

The reader will, I trust, make allowances in his reading for the author's confessed biases and for the brevity of the essays, and will forgive the necessary incompleteness of an introductory approach. It is in a sense his task to complete the book.

Michael Schmidt

Acknowledgements

I wish to express my particular gratitude to Val Warner, Andrew Mylett, David Wright and Robert Nye for their assistance in bringing this book to final form, and to several of the poets included who generously supplied me with information. I should like to dedicate the book to Brian Cox and Alan Young.

Thomas Hardy (1840–1928)

I am I
And what I do I do myself alone.

Robert Louis Stevenson visited Hardy in Dorset in 1885, thirteen years before Hardy's first collection of poems appeared. He saw 'a pale, gentle, frightened little man, that one felt an instinctive tenderness for, with a wife – ugly is no word for it! – who said "Whatever shall we do?". I had never heard a human being say it before.' Stevenson took away a vivid impression of Emma Hardy, but only a feeling of sympathy for the 'little man', her husband, already a widely acclaimed novelist. Even at that time the label of 'pessimist' had been affixed to him; it was only a few years before he was stigmatized for 'immorality' in *Tess of the d'Urbervilles* (1891) and *Jude the Obscure* (1896) and gave up prose fiction altogether in favour of verse.

Thomas Hardy was born in Bockhampton, Dorsetshire, in 1840. His father was a builder and a skilful musician, two accomplishments Hardy also acquired. His mother, who deemed herself socially superior to her husband, had ambitions for Thomas, and he received the best education his family could afford, studying in Dorchester and later at King's College, London. Articled as an ecclesiastical architect from 1856 to 1861, he became a specialist in the Gothic revival and a competent draftsman. Architectural imagery, and a persistent preoccupation with perspective, come into his poems. From 1862 to 1867 he worked in London at an architect's office and became a prizeman of the Royal

Institute of British Architects. During this period he wrote the earliest of the poems which he was ultimately to collect in *Wessex Poems* (1898). In 1870 he began his career as a novelist.

From his early years he had performed verse experiments and exercises. He attempted to translate Ecclesiastes into Spenserian stanzas – a project he fortunately never completed, though he uses Biblical imagery, subject matter and rhythms naturally in many poems. He mused continually on poetry, defining and redefining it, thinking in terms of poems, developing his craft. Some of his early poems he turned into prose and used as descriptive passages in his fiction. Later they were translated back to verse.

A number of his critical opinions are provident and – if we take into account the literary milieu of mid- and late-Victorian England – radical. His comments – sometimes wry asides, sometimes observations on literary criticism, often on creative writing generally – are at their best aphoristic. 'My opinion is that a poet should express the emotion of all the ages and the thought of his own.' 'My opinion is': all of Hardy's opinions emerge from his experience as a prose and verse writer.

In 1887 he wrote, 'I begin to feel that mere intellectual subtlety will not hold its own in time to come against the straightforward expression of good feeling.' As a poet, he set out to show 'the other side of common emotions'. 'The business of the poet . . . is to show the sorriness underlying the grandest things, and the grandeur underlying the sorriest things', bringing opposites and contrasts into controlled tension. 'To find beauty in ugliness is the province of the poet.'

Out of such a programme comes a specific poetic style. 'The whole secret of living style and the difference between it and dead style, lies in it not having too much style . . .' In dealing with 'the other side of common emotions', the style must grow out of the commonness. The language must correspond in register to the subject matter: a rustic plot will demand simple diction; a poem on the loss of the

Titanic will involve a more developed and consciously literary rhetoric. The language must finally be subtle enough to contain the 'beauty' *and* the 'ugliness'. This is an important view of poetic tension: some poems – 'The Man He Killed', for example – state one thing ('quaint and curious war is') but in the dramatic hesitations of syntax, the indecision of the speaker himself, whose emotions are in conflict with his statement, contradict eloquently what they seem to say.

Hardy, refuting Matthew Arnold's strictures on provincialism, wrote, 'A certain provincialism of feeling is invaluable. It is the essence of individuality, and is largely made up of that crude enthusiasm without which no great thoughts are thought, no great deeds done.' In many of his critical statements Hardy appears to be justifying himself with considerable candidness: 'Poetry is emotion put into measure. The emotion must come by nature, but the measure can be acquired by art.' One of his ambitions was to write a handful of poems worthy of inclusion in a good anthology. Even when he speaks of other writers, he responds to virtues their works share with his. In commenting on Anatole France, he highlights 'the principles that make for permanence' – 'the value of organic form and symmetry, the force of reserve, and the emphasis of understatement, even in his lighter works' – all Hardyesque qualities. What he quotes from other writers illuminates his own work: from Browning, 'Incidents in the development of a soul! Little else is worth study'; from Leslie Stephens, the poet 'should touch our hearts by showing his own'. Illumination falls, too, on what Hardy wanted his poetry to be. The poems both exceed and fall short of his aspirations for them.

In 1874 Hardy married Emma Gifford, the daughter of a parson whose church in Cornwall he helped to 'improve'. The first two years of their marriage were apparently happy. But Emma and her husband gradually disagreed. She grew increasingly distressed by criticism of his 'moral tone', by his public agnosticism, by his long absences in London, and even by his 'social inferiority' to her. Though there is little evidence that Hardy ever behaved badly to her, his gallantry became formal, endurance replaced love, and more than thirty-five years of unhappiness elapsed before Emma died. Her death ironically occasioned the greatest of Hardy's poems, the elegiac verses of 1912–13, and others that came later. On her death, his mind flooded by recollections of their happy years, he experienced remorse for his part in the decades of hostility. Thus he wrote his great love poems not at the age of thirty, when he was courting, nor at the age of thirty-four, when he was happily married, but in 1912, at the age of seventy-two, when death had done what life had failed in.

They are poems of guilt as much as love. They lament not the death of Emma but the squandering of love. She died suddenly, and the first elegy expresses recrimination as well as guilt:

> Never to bid good-bye,
>   Or lip me the softest call,
> Or utter a wish for a word, while I
> Saw morning harden upon the wall,
>   Unmoved, unknowing
>   That your great going
> Had place that moment, and altered all.

The alteration was devastatingly simple. Emma, in dying, denied Hardy the chance to atone for his part in their un-happiness. She had rendered the past hard, unalterable:

> Well, well! All's past amend,
>   Unchangeable. It must go.
> I seem but a dead man held on end
> To sink down soon . . . O you could not know
>   That such swift fleeing
>   No soul foreseeing –
> Not even I – would undo me so!

He forgives her in this stanza, in the broken syntax of loss. What has been lost becomes clear in the great poems that followed, gradually assimilating the experience. There are twenty-one poems in the final sequence 'Poems 1912–13' (the first eighteen are the original and essential sequence), and they proceed from the immediate apprehension of loss to a kind of stoical acceptance. After Emma's death, in 1914 Hardy married Florence Dugdale, who had long been his amanuensis. With her he revisited a number of places where he had stayed with Emma in their happy years.

Poems came from these 'revisitings': 'Beeny Cliff: March 1870–March 1913', 'At Castle Boterel', 'St Launce's Revisited', and 'Where the Picnic Was'. Emma, in turn, revisits him as the 'hauntress' in a number of poems, and when he employs so poignant a ghost, the verses acquire an intensity he seldom achieved before. 'The Voice' is among Hardy's few unflawed poems, opening with the lines:

Woman much missed, how you call to me, call to me,
Saying that now you are not as you were
When you had changed from the one who was all to me,
But as at first, when our day was fair.

Three stanzas of this fluent, basically monosyllabic, powerfully nostalgic cadence are arrested in the final quatrain. Fancy deceives no more, it gives way to the unmitigated reality of isolation:

Thus I; faltering forward,
Leaves around me falling,
Wind oozing thin through the thorn from norward,
And the woman calling.

The sequence originally appeared in *Satires of Circumstance* (1914). Its emotional veracity points up a wilful element in the other *Satires*. What has often seemed in the earlier poems a predisposition to pessimism here becomes an actual, emotive experience.

The syntax of Hardy's early poems is full of inversions and often hard to comprehend. Nonetheless, there is little development – except in deftness – throughout his poetry. The themes of nature's indifference or hostility, lost or thwarted love, and Time, are developed again and again.

Many of his poems are organized in a similar way – working through a plot to an unexpected conclusion, like verse fables.

In the *Life* Hardy says, 'The world does not despise us; it only neglects us.' In his poem 'Neutral Tones' he evokes nature's neutrality, the lack of correspondence between the objective and subjective worlds. This view means that tragedy is impossible in Hardy's world. There is guilt: 'hid from men / I bear that mark on me.' There is a strong sense of responsibility for others. But the dominant theme is always human unfulfilment in time.

Whereas Wordsworth's past contains the lost childhood, the infant 'trailing clouds of glory' gradually evolving into impoverished man, and Tennyson's past is an idealized world of order, Hardy's vision is of a past not idealized but *unrealized*, a past that was full of potential, when 'everything glowed with a gleam' – but 'we were looking away'. The past with its wide range of choices is placed beside the present that those choices have impoverished. What *is* stands juxtaposed, implicitly or explicitly, to what might have been.

Death is a central theme in the poems. Hardy chooses situations where death watches life or life death. In almost every poem death, or a sense of ephemerality, is present. 'I rose up as my custom was' – the poet gets out of his grave to go visit friends. In 'Channel Firing' the dead sit up and comment on the futility of their lives, of war, of faith, the foolishness of God, the shapelessness of the future. In other poems Hardy seeks out ghosts or old people and talks with them or makes them talk.

Frequently there is a difficulty of tone in Hardy's poems. Humorous poems are interspersed with the decidedly serious, and at times Hardy leaves the poem apparently suspended between seriousness and humour, with haunting effect. 'Transformations' is one of his best short poems, revealing the 'other side of common emotions'. He is writing about a graveyard, but the poem presents us with no image of decay. Instead, Hardy celebrates *life* with such imaginative force that the graveyard is altered into something new, generative, unexpected. Man is resurrected in flowers. The language contributes to a central image of growth and nourishment:

Portion of this yew
Is a man my grandsire knew,
Bosomed here at its foot.

In turning the noun 'bosom' into a verb, the suggestions of nourishment and protection are heightened. Reciprocity, warmth and love are implied. In three lines the chilling associations of the churchyard are dispelled. The theme is carried further in the next triplet:

This branch may be his wife,
A ruddy human life
Now turned to a green shoot.

Man and wife are united in the yew, consummated in death. Her 'ruddy life' suggests the red bark of a damp yew tree.

These grasses must be made
Of her who often prayed
Last century, for repose . . .

Another life finds consummation in death, a prayer is answered. Repose is found in manifest nature: she has become part of it. Then comes the powerful image:

And the fair girl long ago
Whom I often tried to know
May be entering this rose.

There is an erotic element in the triplet, the rose carrying its conventional symbolic value, the verb its sexual overtones. Through the rose – someone he knew – the poet himself relates to the graveyard.

The line that casts doubt on the tone of the poem is, 'So they are not underground . . .' There seems an implicitly comical effect, 'look, we have come through – in flowers'. The poem continues, heightening the imagery of growth with 'nerves' and 'veins', 'the growths of upper air'. But the question of tone remains tantalizingly unresolved.

Death is seen here as congenial, generative, reducing metaphysical considerations to the physical churchyard vegetation. Life gets life. Other graveyard poems are less positive in tone, for example 'Rain on a Grave', 'Voices Growing from a Churchyard', and 'Drummer Hodge'. Nature, however, absorbs the dead here too.

Hardy seems best able to appreciate natural objects without any sense of metaphysical content – as objects, not symbols. He may long for religious faith and the certainty and community it brings, but he is 'outside, prayer denied', and he finds little comfort in religion, except in its artefacts. His ghosts are seldom meant to be more than revelatory illusions. They bring no gothic horror from the grave, but simply reports of failure in life – and afterlife. 'Death's inviolate halls' don't let real souls go. Nor will Hardy romanticize objects in nature. 'Shelley's Skylark' is a poem in which he grants the bird power to make a song which might throw men into ecstasies – but the creature is not immortal. It is now a dead knot of bones and feathers somewhere. Hardy is saying, 'Hail to thee, blithe bird! Spirit thou never wert.' His 'Darkling Thrush' is a real bird too, growing old, but still singing. Its song does not make the poet ecstatic, but rather accentuates his grief. There is no romantic certainty, only the concession of a possibility, as tenuous as that expressed in 'The Oxen'.

Hardy's habit of juxtaposing past and present experiences is more than merely dramatic technique. When newly-weds are about to consummate their marriage, a street musician plays a tune which, for one of them, conjures abruptly the recollection of a past love, and suddenly their rapport is destroyed. Dormant memory destroys relationships. Memory and desire are in continual tension, but memory is usually the more powerful. Hardy's refrain is that each individual is ultimately sealed within the particulars of his own biography, that he can never communicate or share himself fully with another. There is an implicit and universal alienation between individuals; it is impossible to progress beyond a certain limited intimacy. Hardy says that Shakespeare will 'remain at heart unread eternally'. So will every man.

While isolation is the cause of unfulfilment, it seems irremediable. Memory invades and disrupts the present unpredictably. God himself – the God of Hardy's child-hood – like the ghosts, appears as a memory to accentuate his despair and isolation. The darkling thrush expressing joy confirms sorrow. Life becomes 'a thwarted purposing'.

The past is clarified only as the present reveals what we have missed and lost. In one poem an old lady lives wilfully in the past: 'Past things retold were to her as things existent, / Things present but as a tale.' He cannot join her. In the elegies to Emma, the past, rich with potential, is juxtaposed with the present, too. But the world of memory is more complete:

Nay: one there is to whom these things,
That nobody else's mind calls back,
Have a savour that things in being lack,
And a presence more than the actual brings;
To whom today is beneaped and pale,
    And its urgent clack
    But a vapid tale.

The present, caught in the fleeting image of the train, barely suggested in 'urgent clack', is flattened by 'vapid tale' which corresponds to it rhythmically and syllabically, but which in its different sound and sense destroys the urgency. Things in memory are vivid and disrupting to the individual largely because they are so private, like tasting food ('savour'), and not to be shared.

Hardy called himself an 'evolutionary meliorist' when he was accused of wilful pessimism. He quoted the line from his 'In Tenebris ii': 'If way to the better there be, it exacts a full look at the worst.' The 'satires' will teach us not to make the same mistake twice, or not to repeat the errors others have made. But there is in Hardy's notion of time and memory something that no evolution will ameliorate: the individual's isolation within his own memories. The world might become, as he seems to urge in the late novels and in some vivid poems that would have startled his late-Victorian audience ('The Christening' and 'A Wife to Another', for example), more tolerant and hence more tolerable. But the individual condition would hardly improve. Hardy's social optimism is fully balanced by his psychological pessimism.

In a sense Hardy's poems are didactic. He speaks of them as the 'application of ideas to life'. But he is not a philosopher – he presents 'a series of fleeting impressions I have never tried to coordinate'. It is wrong to look in the work for systems or myths: there are none. The poems are 'unadjusted impressions', though they build on certain central themes.

They were written by a man responsible for many novels. Some novelistic elements are developed in the poems. The drama of incident is strong; the matter is drawn from a wide range of experience; the language is in various registers, from the rustic and dialect to the highly literary. But, while the novels sketch in the background, the poems generally take setting for granted. Unlike Kipling, who has to establish a setting before his poem can evolve, Hardy takes location as implicit. In most of the poems, Hardy's plots are not imposed but rather seem to emerge naturally from the subject matter and the tones of the speaker. We are seldom engaged by the character of the speaker himself: it is the situation that attracts us. Hardy does not confuse short story form with poetic form as Kipling sometimes does. His poems move beyond the range of brief fictions, avoid over-particularizing.

His style is original but not particularly idiosyncratic. He uses a wider range of traditional rhymed forms than any other modern English poet. His *oeuvre* amounts to almost a thousand poems, some of them in extremely inventive forms. *The Dynasts*, his epic verse 'drama', reveals most of his stylistic skills and weaknesses. The poem appeared in three successive volumes (1904, 1906, 1908). It is written 'in three parts, nineteen acts, and a hundred and thirty scenes', largely in verse, about the wars with Napoleon. Covering the action of ten years (1805–15), shifting to and fro between

England and the Continent, and concluding with Waterloo, it is an account of 'The Human Tragedy' – not only of heroes and generals but of common men, and a chorus of 'phantom intelligences'. The central fact of the poem is Napoleon's isolation, which causes his downfall.

As early as 1882 Hardy had conceived the poem. He noted down, 'Write a history of human automatism, or impulsion – viz., an account of human action in spite of human knowledge, showing how very far conduct lags behind the knowledge that should really guide it.' Twenty-two years later he published the first part of his mammoth poem. It is doubtless the *summa* of Hardy's thought, but Hardy is not a thinker of much consistency, and the burden of the poem is borne far better with real economy in fine short poems – 'The Man He Killed' or 'In Time of the "Breaking of Nations" ', for example – than in the lumbering mechanical development of *The Dynasts*. It fails because of its structural defects. The 'phantom intelligences' are not poetically realized. The best parts of the poem relate the thoughts and preoccupations of common people in clear particularity, with the simple diction of speech.

In many of his poems there are the invented words – nouns turned into verbs, words made negative that are usually positive, and so on. In a short poem, 'Thoughts of Phena: at news of her death', the following invented or archaic words appear: 'unsight', 'enray', 'enarch', 'disennoble', and 'up-brimming'. Hardy uses odd epithets – 'aureate nimb', for instance – and a sense of ghostly musing is conveyed in words of spectral quality, suggesting meaning but not containing it, unfamiliar but comprehensible. This poem, with no imagery as such, defines clearly through a deft use of negatives. It deals in thoughts, not pictures. It is a poem of 'unsight'.

Hardy is capable of unfortunate inventions: 'stillicide' and 'cohue' are two such words, though when he invents – or borrows from Dorset usage – the perfect word 'unhope' at the end of 'In Tenebris i', we can forgive the less felicitous inventions. He is also capable of writing grotesque lines, with the comic effects of unresolved syntax or sentimental twaddle. In one poem he writes, 'While her great gallied eyes through her hair hanging loose . . .' In a set piece composed for a charity, he evokes the 'frail human flowerets, sicklied by the shade'.

Hardy is the first essentially twentieth-century poet. He was intellectually of this century, well read in Darwinian thought, acquainted with Einstein's work, caught between the new scientific approach and the old religious dogmas and values, conceiving his moral function as 'interfusing' essential religion, stripped of superstition and dogma (and, by the way, godhead) with scientific rationality. But it was not this, or solely his ideas about Time and the individual, that have made him 'the most far-reaching influence, for good or ill . . . in British poetry of the last fifty years', as Donald Davie has called him. It is more his approach to craft and subject-matter that illuminated the way for others.

Davie writes, 'Hardy has the effect of locking any poet whom he influences into a world of historical contingency, a world of specific places at specific times.' Place for Hardy is 'enghosted' with echoes. History becomes inherent in place. Order and sequence are part of Hardy's world. Poetry detects order and expresses it. It is not the function of the poet to project order. He makes the real world more accessible. He does not posit an alternative world.

Davie also speaks of the 'cunning irregularity' of Hardy's technique and its attraction for later poets. Many of Hardy's early critics felt the poems lacked 'technique'. The rusticity was seen as naïvety or faulty craft. Lytton Strachey spoke of 'the gloom . . . not even relieved by a little elegance of diction'. But this want of 'elegance' is essentially original, in the way Wordsworth's was in the *Lyrical Ballads*.

Ford Madox Ford said that Hardy 'showed the way for the imagists' – an important observation made by an editor and friend of the imagists. In two ways particularly he affected them. His direct language, sharing the quality of speech, must have stood out sharply against the poised literary perfection of Robert Bridges, the rhetorical tub-thumping of Kipling, and the rugged, picturesque aestheticism of the Georgians. The other and perhaps more important example Hardy set the imagists was of the power of juxtaposition in poetry, showing the way two incidents, images or plots can 'interfuse' one another. Ezra Pound wrote of his poems, 'Now *there* is clarity. There *is* the harvest of having written twenty novels first.'

Davie points out how the irony in Hardy's poems, as in Housman's, is different from the more common concept of irony in this century: 'The older poets do not recommend irony as a secure or dignified stance from which to confront reality, rather it is the stance of reality as it confronts *us*. Their irony is cosmic, where an Auden's is provisional and strategic.' When Hardy writes of 'life's little ironies' the ironies are inherent in 'life', not in the poet's approach to life. This sets Hardy apart from many poets who have learned serious lessons at his knee.

Another quality which has drawn writers of the middle of the twentieth century as it did writers of the nineteenth is Hardy's lack of sentimentality. Lionel Johnson commended the 'primitive savour' of his work, the 'earthy charm', but more emphatically stated, 'He is among the least sentimental of writers.' It was a quality which drew W. H. Auden as well.

But Auden particularly admired Hardy's 'hawk's vision, his way of looking at life from a very great height . . . To see the individual life related not only to the local social life of its time, but to the whole of human history . . . gives one both humility and self-confidence.' He added, 'Here was "modern" rhetoric which was more fertile and adaptable to different themes than any of Eliot's gas-works and rats' feet which one could steal but never make one's own.' The very faults in Hardy make him a good teacher. His followers do not imitate his techniques but perceive in the way his poems work and fail to work what problems of form and subject matter he was grappling with. Hardy clarified in his poems many of the modern poet's problems. No generation of serious writers since the turn of the century has written in ignorance of Hardy. In one way or another, most of the substantial writers of the last seventy-five years have acknowledged their debt to him.

When Robert Graves visited him at Max Gate, the house he built for himself near Dorchester, and where he died in 1928, Hardy said, 'All we can do is write on the old themes in the old styles, but try to do it a little better than those who came before us.' It is an extraordinarily modest statement for the man who brought English poetry forward, unpretentiously and irreversibly, into the twentieth century.

A. E. Housman (1859–1936)

The blazing pier of diamond flawed
In shards of rainbow all abroad.

Though some modern critics have dealt harshly with Housman, he remains among the most widely read twentieth-century poets. Readers find the pastoral nostalgia bitter-sweet, melodious, memorable; composers including Vaughan Williams and Butterworth recognized excellent *lieder* texts in the poems. What many modern critics look for – grittiness, real hearts on imaginary sleeves – they do not find in Housman. His formal conservatism and thematic repetitive-ness leave them cold. They prefer the raw imperialism of Kipling or the authentic pastoral of Hardy to the poised narrowness of Housman.

Alfred Edward Housman was born in 1859 in Fockbury, Worcestershire. His comfortable, conservative, middle-class background was congenial to the development of an interest in literature, which matured into a passion for classical studies. He seems to have enjoyed escaping into the country-side for walks. The eastern horizon of these childhood outings was Shropshire.

His education was conducted at Bromsgrove, Worcester, and then at Oxford. His university career included impress-ive achievements and failures. He became an outstanding textual critic, so single-mindedly involved in his texts that he omitted to mug up his ancient history and philosophy and – under severe emotional strain – failed to take even a pass degree. He went down and entered a Civil Service job in the Patent Office.

After ten years there (1882–92) his classical achievements earned him a Professorship of Latin at University College, London, where he worked from 1892 to 1911. There he published his first collection of poems, *A Shropshire Lad* (1896). In 1911 he became Professor of Latin at Cambridge, a post he held until his death in 1936. His editions of Manilius, Juvenal and Lucan reveal his brilliance as a scholar; his acerbity in critical debate and his passion for accuracy made him something of a terror to his professional colleagues.

A Shropshire Lad achieved for Housman wide and almost immediate fame as a poet. The book answered, in its expressions of frustration and futility and in its traditional voice, the same needs that Tennyson's *In Memoriam* had answered two generations earlier. It was twenty-six years before Housman published another collection, called simply *Last Poems*. This was followed, as 'last poems' sometimes are, by *More Poems*, a collection issued in 1936, shortly after the poet's death. A few poems have since been appended to the *oeuvre*, but the *Collected Poems* is remarkably slim for a poet who reached the age of seventy-seven. Its thinness is manifest in various ways. Though all the work was assembled by a mature man – his books appearing when he was thirty-seven, sixty-three, and seventy-seven – there is a nagging adolescence about the content, a lack of formal and linguistic development, and a tendency to become self-imitative, not only echoing earlier themes but even redeveloping earlier phrases and imagery.

Housman's attitude to poetry was expressed most controversially in his lecture 'The Name and Nature of Poetry' which he delivered in Cambridge in 1933. In it he condemned the 'difficult' poetry of the metaphysicals, much in vogue at the time, and by implication discredited most of the new poetry of the century. Poetry for him was not so much an intellectual as a physical experience – both in the composition and in the reading. And the effect of the poem has more to do with music, rhyme, and emotional direction than with *meaning*. His theories grew out of his own practice, not out of an assessment of modern poetry, and signify primarily as they relate to his own work. At the time, however, this severe oracle roused the critic I. A. Richards, who left the lecture muttering, 'Housman has put the clock back thirty years!' And indeed his attitudes and his poems in various ways resemble those of some of the poets of the Rhymers' Club.

His poems are certainly not argumentative, but rather metaphors for emotions. They can be parodied, their forced pessimism at times becomes sentimental, and not infrequently the expression is convoluted and banal. His various admirations – for the Greek Anthology, Heine, Kipling, Arnold, Wordsworth and others – did not imbue him with power to think in verse. Though an atheist, he is often ambivalent in his use of religious imagery and – like Hardy – seems frequently to acknowledge a malignant deity, calling him, 'whatever brute or blackguard made the world'. *Thought* engages only the surface of his poems, it edits, while he lets emotion hold the depths – often distressingly unchecked. His classical concern with surfaces yields some coy circumlocutions.

Now, of my threescore years and ten,
Twenty will not come again,
And take from seventy springs a score
It only leaves me fifty more.

He is saying that he is young only once, and that life is brief. In another poem he has a peculiar way of telling us that the lads found and picked a quantity of daffodils: 'And home at noonday from the hills / They bring no dearth of daffodils.' The parodies of Housman which many – including Ezra Pound – have attempted are not nearly as amusing as Housman's self-parodies.

For Housman, the pastoral is always a literary pastoral. A real lad or milkmaid lost in one of his landscapes would recognize little but the flowers. This is part of the late nineteenth-century heritage which Housman, like Kipling, Hardy, Daryush, and to some degree Yeats, brought into the twentieth. Housman's was a more modern temperament than Kipling's, but less so than Hardy's. His choice of subject matter defines him. He elects for himself what Hardy was elected *by*, the pastoral. It would be better to speak of Hardy as 'rural' rather than 'pastoral'. For all of Housman's use of place-names and his ruddy lads and lasses, his debt to Theocritus, Horace, Virgil, and other classical poets of the pastoral genre is greater than his debt to Shropshire or to living farmhands and soldiers. Most of the forms he uses, too, are variations on one form: the rhymed quatrain.

And yet there is a haunting authenticity in the movement of the poems. One might attribute this to his frustrated homosexual passion which helped to withdraw him into the world where his poems exist, and also intensified his expression around an emotional core. His homosexuality is certainly an element in his pessimism. Perhaps it is the selfish tenderness of the pessimism that makes the poems poignant; and the precise, condensed language and clear rhythms make them memorable. To Housman, his poetry was 'a morbid secretion, like the pearls in an oyster'. He would often conceive a stanza whole, sometimes a whole poem, and write it out in almost a final draft. At other times part of a poem would come easily while another part would demand from him an agony of concentration and numerous drafts and redrafts. Sometimes a phrase appears in his notebooks and is lost sight of for years, to emerge later in a poem. He usually composed when depressed or ill. Great bouts of creativity were followed by long gestating vacancies.

All of Housman's poems work together, thematically and formally, almost as a sequence. The *Collected Poems* add up to a sort of pre-emptive elegy – not for things lost but, more melancholic, for things never attained. There is no emotional or physical fulfilment to look back on, no trumped-up theological consummation to look forward to. Youth had lacked the self-awareness to recognize the urgency of self-fulfilment, while age must muse wryly that, had youth made its choice, a different anguish would nonetheless have ensued. The predicament is that of classical tragedy. Given the moral orthodoxies in which Housman was reared, to act out a homosexual passion had its destructive consequences; and yet to sublimate it had the very real consequence of blighting his life. The retrospective desire prompts some of the best poems:

Here dead lie we because we did not choose
 To live and shame the land from which we sprung.
Life, to be sure, is nothing much to lose,
 But young men think it is, and we were young.

In another poem he writes, 'But he that drinks in season / Shall live before he dies.' Housman missed that season.

As John Sparrow noted, we cannot conveniently label Housman's verse: 'it is classical and it is romantic; it is simple and it is sophisticated; it is derivative and it is original.' The forms are classical, the content romantic; the forms are simple, the content at times sophisticated; the forms are derivative and the content original. Housman is a classical poet with a romantic temperament. The world to which his romanticism is confined confronts him, as it does Hardy, with teeming paradoxes and its inscrutable irony. He writes from a personal apprehension of this, but when he tells us that his verse with its sad and 'narrow measure spans / Tears of eternity, and sorrow / Not mine, but man's', he is guilty of partial deception – whether self-deception or not it is hard to tell. He realizes in other poems that his is a specific suffering, that the mass of others are more or less content, if not happy, in ignorance of the under-lying irony.

Those poets of this century whose distinctive mood is pessimistic seem often to be the tautest formalists – Hardy, Housman, Daryush, Larkin and Hill, for example. They are also impersonal writers, expressing a negative vision without direct recourse to autobiography. The inability to find objects for authentic commitment makes them elect a self-contained, effective form of statement, larded with negatives, setting off the darkness with a deeper darkness, confronting chaos with formed fragments. They bear torches like Lawrence's gentians, which radiate darkness, not light. The form is a hard thing, a stay, in a world of flux with no revealed order and no inherent structure, on which projected orders are recognized as nothing more than projections.

Housman's poems often begin in apparent optimism and cheerfulness, but they seldom end so. The traditional ballads – among the most effective literary ballads of this century, deeply rooted in a knowledge of the Border Ballads – reveal his dramatic sense of peripeteia: for example, 'Farewell to barn and stack and tree' and 'The Carpenter's Son'. There is also drama, bordering on melodrama, in some of his recurrent situations: the man committing suicide, the man hanged, the soldier dying gratefully. The still nullity of the grave, 'the nation that is not' as he calls it more than once, is peopled by the multitude at last released from passion:

Lovers lying two and two
  Ask not whom they sleep beside,
And the bridegroom all night through
  Never turns him to the bride.

In the last five lines of the poem from which this stanza comes, five negatives appear: *not*, *nothing*, *never* and *no*, four prominent characters in Housman's morose apocalypse. The poet vainly tries to escape his world by fancy. In one poem he gazes at pure reflections on water, longing for that other world, until he perceives a face looking back at him with the same discontent and longing.

The poems are most effective when he casts his anguish into historical perspective. The anguish is seen to recur, but the man who suffers is bound to the final community of the dead. When Wenlock Edge is fretted by wind, the poet stands where a Roman soldier stood when Uricon was a city.

'Tis the old wind in the old anger,
  But then it threshed another wood.

Then, 'twas before my time, the Roman
  At yonder heaving hill would stare:
The blood that warms an English yeoman,
  The thoughts that hurt him, they were there.

The recurrence is inevitable, 'The tree of man was never quiet: / Then 'twas the Roman, now 'tis I.' By implication, he consoles himself with oblivion: 'Today the Roman and his trouble / Are ashes under Uricon.'

Soldiers are the principal actors in the poems. The Shropshire Lad enlists and is wounded and killed all over the Empire, responding to each fate with much the same resignation. Soldiers inhabit the poems even when they are unseen, 'drumming like a noise in dreams'. The noise is constant though the dream changes.

There are other drummings, too. Wordsworth's cadence is present in a passage which reverses Wordsworth's meanings: 'The troubles of our proud and angry dust / Are from eternity, and shall not fail.' The lines from the *Prelude* come to mind: 'Our destiny, our nature, and our home / Is with infinitude, and only there . . .' The drumming of Browning can be heard in the lines:

How one was true and one was clean of stain
  And one was braver than the heavens are high,
And one was fond of me: and all are slain . . .

Inevitably this recalls the climax of 'Childe Roland to the Dark Tower Came':

How such a one was strong, and such was bold,
And such was fortunate, yet each of old
  Lost, lost! one moment knelled the woe of years.

Man's 'immortal part' is his skeleton, 'the steadfast and enduring bone'. When we read this – and the long chronicle of vain deaths and frustrations – Pope's 'Epistle', in which he described 'this long disease, my life', suggests itself. Housman, however, had no Dr Arbuthnot, no consolation but the eventual darkness. He responded with passive resignation, while Pope – with strong social commitments – exhibited satirical passion. Still, nostalgia for the shire where, in sadness, 'homely comforters I had', is occasionally a consolation, though usually it works as an irritant, heightening the present frustration. It is 'the land of lost content'. Housman has no peer in this century for evoking the ambivalent contents of the past, the ambivalent bourn of the future, and the present diseased with longing both for the past which cannot be relived and for the future death which, when it comes, will render him insentient, will not even be apprehended as relief:

Into my heart an air that kills
   From yon far country blows:
What are those blue remembered hills,
   What spires, what farms are those?

That is the land of lost content,
   I see it shining plain,
The happy highways where I went
   And cannot come again.

Rudyard Kipling (1865–1936)

We have served our day.

Joseph Rudyard Kipling was born in Bombay in 1865. His father was a talented teacher of sculpture at the Bombay school of art, and later curator of the museum at Lahore. His mother was the sister of Lady Burne-Jones and of Stanley Baldwin's mother. His background was intellectually lively and socially privileged.

As a young child he was under the care of an Indian nurse and with her attention grew proficient in Hindustani as well as English. His 'below stairs' experience of the Raj never left him. When he returned from England a sahib, he was still not fully assimilated into the Colonial world.

At the age of six he was packed off to England for his education, first to the home of an elderly evangelical relative in Southsea. The miserable time he spent there was relieved by occasional visits to the Burne-Jones establishment near Brighton. From the lonely unhappiness of this life he moved in 1879 to the United Services College, Westward Ho!, in Devonshire, a minor public school. There he began writing verses. The experience of these early years influenced much of his later fiction.

His first book was a collection of poems, privately printed in 1881: *Schoolboy Lyrics*. The next year, aged seventeen, he returned to India and served on the staff of the Lahore *Civil and Military Gazette*, contributing articles and poems. In 1889 he became foreign correspondent for the Allahabad *Pioneer* and began extensive travels to China, Japan, America,

Australia and Africa. His experience as a correspondent trained him as a close observer and gave him various insights into Indian life and problems. The feeling that Kipling is a writer with inside information – about the Army, India, and other subjects – is largely due to his journalistic training. So, too, is his accuracy of detail and his public tone.

The light verses he wrote for his newspapers were collected in *Departmental Ditties* (1886), a successful book which reached an English audience; and when Kipling arrived in London in 1889, he found he had a reputation there. He met the leading writers of the time and was fêted by them. Greater success was awaiting him when, in 1892, *Barrack Room Ballads* appeared, containing many of his best-known poems. Hymns, music-hall songs, ballads and public poetry lay behind his verse. With his eye fixed on his audience he developed his demotic Cockney dialect, he experimented with forms and mastered the traditional metrical long line as no poet since has done. Even at this stage his failures came when the skilful technique betrayed inadequate ideas, when a poem had no intellectual or emotional necessity and was merely an entertaining exercise.

In 1895 Kipling refused the poet laureateship after Tennyson's death. This was the first of several honours he turned down. In later years, for example, he would not accept the Order of Merit, and when his remains finally came to rest in Westminster Abbey in 1936, they were untitled.

Kipling married an American and lived in Vermont on her family's property from 1892 to 1896. The unsuccessful American experiment produced a vein of anti-American sentiment in Kipling that appeared in some later productions, a distaste for extreme forms of democracy and a renewed sense of the values of the empire.

His war reports during the Boer War were brilliant, for he was an outstanding correspondent by profession. But in 1902 he retired – to Burwash in Sussex – and lived there for most of his remaining thirty-four years. In his retirement, ob-

serving from a distance rather than reporting on actual
happenings, a gradual melancholy beset him. The relentless
themes of duty, sacrifice and devotion were elicited particularly in the First World War, in which his son died. But in
Kipling's late stories there is a rich allusiveness, an unparaphrasable quality we would more readily associate with
poetry than prose. It was in the late stories that Kipling's
double vocation – verse and prose writing – merged in
fictions of original, difficult power.

In Kipling as in Hardy, those who wish to can find a
poetry from the turn of the century without traces of poetic
weariness, without the rhythmic overemphasis of Swinburne,
the esoteric qualities of Symons, or the twilight of early
Yeats. Plain speaking was his hallmark, nowhere better
illustrated than in his 'Epitaphs of the War'. Almost any of
these brief, uncompromising last words illustrates the height
of his skill, the toughness and yet the humanity of his vision.
'The Coward' is the best of them:

I could not look on Death, which being known,
Men led me to him, blindfold and alone.

His most famous epitaph has the same epigrammatic con-
cision; few talents this century have been given to epigram,
a form more difficult to master – for it demands pure content
and direct expression – than longer, more discursive forms.

If any question why we died
Tell them, because our fathers lied.

This bald, concise style does not dominate Kipling's work.
But it reaches its finest development in the poem 'The Way
Through the Woods'. The poem has the movement of
speech, a subtle, pensive development:

They shut the road through the woods
Seventy years ago.
Weather and ruin have undone it again,
And now you would never know
There was once a road through the woods
Before they planted the trees.

There are a few poems of comparable power and directness in quiet rhythms. 'The Runes on Weland's Sword' is one such poem, gnomic but resonant.

The completeness of Kipling's experiences – of the Raj, where he knew well the Indian and the Colonial; of England, where he was insider and outsider – gave him a kind of aloofness even when he pretended to be familiar. It also contributed to the impersonality of his writing, an unwillingness to dwell on subjective experiences. The death of his son may be suggested in 'My Boy Jack', but it is a poem of general loss. Impersonality is, however, generally accompanied by certain thematic obsessions, a forcing of the poems into particular meanings, celebrating certain virtues and chastising certain vices.

Thus the opinions and preoccupations attributed to the soldier and the 'lower' classes – and indeed the terms in which Kipling has them express themselves – are sometimes the opinions another class ascribes to them; the personae in the dramatic monologues and ballads often appear as journalists' caricatures, forfeiting completeness and authenticity to authority, for an effect of easy resonance. There is an unintentionally satiric element even in his most serious ballads.

Kipling's ambition to achieve an 'irrefutable prose statement', as C. H. Sisson calls it, means that the poems often end on a specific effect, not a general effect. Background, setting, tones and accents of voice are more important than the integrity of the poetic statement. Where in Hardy's *Satires of Circumstance* the background is implicit, in Kipling it is made explicit and often dominates the foreground. He had to define the context through his speakers before he could wrest from them the poem he wanted.

There is often, therefore, an uneasiness in reading Kipling. The poems, once one has grasped their meanings or been cudgelled with them, seem better than their meanings – as though the communication of the meaning was merely an excuse for something else; and yet, because the meanings are so bluntly present, because they coordinate that 'something else', it is bound to them, it has no autonomy. T. S. Eliot points out that Kipling is, to begin with, a ballad maker, that we do not defend him against charges of obscurity but of 'excessive lucidity', that 'people are exasperated by poetry which they do not understand, and contemptuous of poetry which they understand without effort'. And yet there is obscurity in Kipling – not in his meanings but in his motives. Eliot makes another valuable point: Kipling's use of language in poetry differs little from his use of language in prose. The verse is structured in rhythm and has rhymes, but the statements it carries, and the way it carries them, are in most cases analogous to his prose craft.

Kipling owes certain debts to Browning for his dramatic monologues, to Swinburne for his rhythms (though he uses them to different ends), to the pre-Raphaelites, to the Bible. But the ballad and the short story are his main determinants as a poet. Despite his formal inventiveness, and the fact that he is not repetitive, achieving considerable rhythmic subtlety and employing slant rhymes and other devices with skill, he is a public poet first and last. His work develops not stylistically so much as thematically. Eliot sees his development as a shift from 'the imperial imagination into the historical imagination' – from geography and the present to history and the sources of and analogies for the present. There is a shift, too, from early concerns with the branches of empire – India and the army principally – to a concern with the heart of empire – England, and Sussex in particular. He pursues imperial responsibilities home.

Kipling wrote many sorts of poem. His ballads are either narrative, with a plot and often dialogue; or dramatic monologues. He writes topical poems, occasional verse, sometimes 'hymn-ballads' such as 'Ave Imperatrix', celebrating Queen Victoria's escape from an assassin's attempt in 1882. Eliot praises his hymn writing, stressing the extreme poetic objectivity necessary for this mode. And Kipling writes prophecies as well. Later in life he translated Horace with lucid directness, and throughout his life he was a satirist and parodist. *The Muse Among the Motors* shows the breadth of his literary parodies. Chinese, Greek, and Latin poems, the *Rubáiyát*, Middle English, Shakespeare, Donne, Wordsworth, Emerson, Longfellow, the Brownings, Clough, and many others are parodied – they write about the motor car. 'The Idiot Boy' is a parody of Wordsworth's 'Lucy' poems:

He went alone, that none might know
    If he could drive or steer.
Now he is in the ditch, and Oh!
    The differential gear!

In the poems, the poet normally introduces the idea in the first stanza and repeats or decorates it as he goes on. He does not develop it. This is characteristic of the *Barrack Room Ballads*. The developing drama is in the plot which serves to illustrate the idea. In the dedication to *Barrack Room Ballads* he promises us poems about 'such as fought and sailed and ruled and loved and made our world'. 'Our' world is England's: Kipling is a poet who does not lend himself to translation. In the same dedication he describes the sort of man he admires, the man who 'had done his work and held his peace and had no fear to die'. In the subtle 'Sestina of the Tramp-Royal', written in the quasi-Cockney dialect Kipling devised for his rustics, his man speaks out:

Speakin' in general, I 'ave tried 'em all—
The 'appy roads that take you o'er the world.
Speakin' in general, I 'ave found 'em good
For such as cannot use one bed for long,
But must get 'ence, the same as I 'ave done,
An' go observin' matters till they die.

This is the 'trail that is always new' of 'The Long Trail', and the mood of optimistic acceptance and openness dominates.

Kipling is fascinated by machinery. 'McAndrew's Hymn' – about an engineer in love with engines which he regards almost as icons – is full of raucous good humour, with a frightening undercurrent of suggestion. It is far more success-ful, being cast dramatically, than 'The Secret of Machines', a later poem. McAndrew is a budding futurist, a romantic about steamships, power and progress, and a verse Brunel, all at once. The poem, with its vast geographical scope, its consideration of commitment, and its humour, is fine entertainment, owing a formal debt to Browning.

'The "Mary Gloster" ' is another dramatic monologue, spoken by a man who has made his fortune in shipping. Lying on his death-bed, he addresses his silent son, much in the manner of Browning's bishop ordering his tomb. There is a startling, spare lucidity and roughness about the dying man's crude but evocative language, about his ambition for sea-burial, his sentimentality tempered by toughness and pragmatic good sense. The poem has the power and cogency of a short story intensified by deft use of long lines and rhythms.

'The Vampire' and 'Harp Song of the Dane Woman' suggest Kipling's more mysterious balladic vein. The 'Harp Song' begins,

What is a woman that you forsake her,
And the hearth fire and the home-maker,
To go with the old grey widow-maker?

The 'widow-maker' is the sea. The other poem, never specifying its meaning, evokes the fool who prayed 'to a rag and a bone and a hank of hair'. There are a number of poems charged with mystery, usually of a cruel nature, suggesting sometimes a revulsion from sex. They seem to be as much about death and sexual uncertainty as about vampires and Danish women.

Kipling's political and prophetic poetry is at once his most popular and most unpopular. At times he seems himself to have disliked the political vein, writing 'The Fabulists 1914–18' with a degree of personal bitterness lending power to the public statement:

When desperate Folly daily laboureth
    To work confusion upon all we have,
When diligent Sloth demandeth Freedom's death,
    And banded Fear commandeth Honour's grave—
Even in that uncertain hour before the fall,
Unless men please they are not heard at all.

But despite his misgivings about democracy, Kipling celebrates England and English institutions powerfully. 'A Song of the English', which attracted various parodies, is a psalmodic poem, full of Biblical cadences in a strictly rhymed form. 'Fair is our lot – O goodly is our heritage!' he says. After five introductory stanzas he presents 'a song of broken interludes', a song 'of little cunning'. The songs are essentially dramatic narratives of England's relations with the sea, the empire, and the duties of the present to those who died in making the empire. Kipling praises the virtues of severity, resistance, strength, silence, undemonstrativeness, and loyalty. He is at pains here and elsewhere to alert the English at home to their responsibilities for the empire. He does this most powerfully in 'The Islanders'. 'The Dykes', a later poem, dramatically laments irresponsibility. 'All that our fathers taught us of old pleases us now no more.' The exhortation to 'Take up the White Man's burden— / Send forth the best ye breed' comes in a poem which tends to prophetic satire, not simplistic jingoism. The responsibility the burden imposes, the reluctance of those who are ruled, the conceit and deceit of administrators, are all conveyed in it.

Everywhere in Kipling's work we are confronted by his formidable skills. Though he did not write many fine lyrics, few lyric writers could achieve his balladic effects. In 'The Ballad of East and West' his aptitude with long lines is superbly revealed: 'There is rock to the left, and rock to the right, and low lean thorn between, / And ye may hear the breech-bolt snick where never a man is seen.' The lines are long but the control of internal rhyme and rhythmic variations, alliteration and assonance keeps them from rambling. Kipling is striving for a natural and expressive style which can deal with the surface of reality in such a way as to suggest the depths, without damaging the surface. 'The Benefactors', a poem which opens with a parody of Landor, proceeds to question the usefulness of art in confronting reality:

And what is Art whereto we press
　Through paint and prose and rhyme—
When nature in her nakedness
　Defeats us every time?

It is the nakedness Kipling is after. It resides in part in his choice of rhythms. Using popular rhythms, from the music halls, for example, the poet approaches a natural – at least a popular – poetry. 'Bobs' can be sung to the tune of 'She'll be Coming Round the Mountain'. 'Danny Deever', 'Fuzzy-Wuzzy', 'Tommy', 'Gunga Din' and 'Mandalay' have the lilt and verve of a music-hall turn. Others have marching rhythms. 'Natural' expression includes humour, a quality in which Kipling's early poems abound.

He was an innovator from within tradition, developing rhythms, inventing forms, in pursuit of a poetry which instructed as it entertained. Many of his themes will annoy readers with the experience of the Second World War behind them, particularly his suggestion of the racial superiority of the English over those they ruled, his stress on 'the Blood' that binds the English, his occasional paternalism and condescension to the colonized people. But Kipling also wrote *Kim*. As in the case of Hardy, his critics have forced on him a crude consistency of thought which he in no way reveals. Hardy is no more a thoroughgoing pessimist than Kipling is a thoroughgoing racist, sadist, protofascist, or feudalist – all terms his critics have applied to him. Each poem aspires to consistency and truth to *itself*. But the poet is neither philosopher nor politician. As an epitaph for the journalists killed in the First World War Kipling inscribed, 'We have served our day'. This is what he did, in a day when journalism was not merely a job but a vocation.

W. B. Yeats (1865–1939)

...Between extremities
Man runs his course.

Yeats's life is a complex of chance meetings, chance influences, intellectual inconsistencies, a dramatic sequence of
public and private conflicts played out in a personality
which was essentially simple. His work, for all its development, *is* consistent at a deep level. The same themes recur in
1887 and in 1939, the same voice speaks them, though his
symbols change as he moves from passivity to passion.

He was born in Dublin in 1865. His father, John Butler
Yeats, was an accomplished painter, and his mother, Susan
Pollexfen, was a member of an old Anglo-Irish family that
Yeats liked to consider aristocratic. The Anglo-Irish background – Protestant in religion, yet guardedly Republican in
sentiment – was characterized by strongly held and hotly
debated opinions on various topics, not least art and
literature.

Yeats's childhood was spent largely in London, where his
parents moved in 1867. They lived off the income from
family lands in Kildare until 1880 when the Land War put
an end to it. In 1875 Yeats entered the Godolphin School in
Hammersmith and visited Ireland only during the longer
school vacations, when he stayed with the Pollexfens in
Sligo. His first poetic impulse may have been to change the
name of his toy yacht from 'Sunbeam' to 'Moonbeam'. It
was a decisive act.

In 1880 the Yeatses moved back to Dublin and until 1883 William attended The High School in Harcourt Street. Then he entered the School of Art. The first of his verses were published in 1885. This early work was shown to Gerard Manley Hopkins, then stationed in Dublin, who described the poem in a letter to Coventry Patmore as 'a strained and unworkable allegory about a young man and a sphinx on a rock in the sea . . . but still containing fine lines and vivid imagery'.

Fatefully, in 1886 Yeats attended his first seance. His passion for spiritualism and magic was already far advanced, and whatever the ghosts said to him on that occasion increased his enthusiasm. His passion for things Irish was developing too, and he read Irish poetry and the Gaelic sagas in translation. He began criticizing the Anglo-Irish. In 1887, a resolute Irishman, he moved back to London, met William Morris (who found the early poems agreeable) and became a Theosophist.

In London Yeats was active in literature and politics. One particular event stands out: in 1889 he fell in love with the fiery Republican who was to haunt him for the rest of his life: Maud Gonne. His biography from 1889 until Maud Gonne's marriage, and then after her divorce until Yeats's own marriage, is punctuated by the words, 'Yeats proposed to Maud Gonne', with the implicit, 'was refused'.

In 1891 Yeats became associated with the Rhymers' Club – a group of poets who met regularly at the Cheshire Cheese pub in London and discussed poetry. Lionel Johnson and Ernest Dowson became close friends of his at this time. Johnson was among his instructors in philosophy. Arthur Symons, the outstanding poet-critic of the 1890s, was a frequenter of the Club. Yeats shared rooms with him in 1895. Symons opened up European literature for him, pointing him towards the work of Mallarmé, Calderón, San Juan de la Cruz, and others. Unlike the Rhymers who – except for John Davidson – practised an aesthetic of 'art for art's sake', Yeats came to feel that 'literature must be the expression of conviction, and be the garment of noble emotion, and not an end in itself.' Though he developed away from them, he acknowledged his debt to the Rhymers: 'Poets with whom I learned my trade, / Companions of the Cheshire Cheese . . .'

Blake and Shelley were early influences on his writing. With Edwin Ellis he prepared an edition of Blake's poems (1893). These poets' beliefs and sentiments affected him more deeply than their techniques. He may have learned some of his grandiloquence from them and Blake showed him the way to a symbolic idiom. But their view of the poet's identity, social function, and imaginative scope most attracted him.

London and Paris were his meccas at this time. In Paris he met and encouraged the dramatist John Synge. In 1896 he met Lady Gregory and in succeeding years spent time with her at Coole Park in Ireland, studying Irish folklore. In 1897 they began together seriously planning for the Abbey Theatre which opened in Dublin in 1904. Yeats wrote many of his verse plays for it. Indeed, the Abbey exercised his patience, rhetoric, and spleen for many years and helped to modify his naïve social idealism to quasi-aristocratic scorn.

In 1908 his *Collected Works* were issued in eight volumes. He was forty-three, a poet of established reputation, a dramatist and prose writer, a lecturer at home and abroad. He felt drained of energy. He had reached the end of his first period of creative activity.

Critics have laid insufficient stress on the effect Ezra Pound had on Yeats's development. He met Pound in 1912, and Pound was often with him from then until his death, an intimate friend who acted as best man at his wedding and witnessed his will. Pound entered Yeats's life when Yeats's early style was played out, the way forward unclear. From the time of his acquaintance with Pound, a new particularity and concreteness enters the verse. The change is not merely in the approach to content but to diction as well. Pound probably did not suggest the development but rather advised Yeats in rewriting the poems, bringing out tendencies implicit in Yeats's style.

In 1913 Yeats was awarded a Civil List Pension and in 1915 he refused a knighthood. In 1917 he bought his 'castle' in Ballylee – near Coole Park and Lady Gregory. It was little more than a broken tower and cottages, but it seemed to Yeats replete with legendary resonance. The year 1917 was an active one. It included three proposals of marriage to three different women. The last asked accepted, and at the age of fifty-two Yeats was married.

In 1923 he was awarded the Nobel Prize for literature. Later he became a Senator in the Irish Parliament. But his health began to deteriorate. In 1924, suffering from high blood-pressure and respiratory problems, he repaired to Sicily, where he visited the Byzantine mosaics and was enthralled by them. In his illness he entered his most intensely creative period, composing *The Tower* poems and their sequel. His friends' deaths, his own slow weakening, the political turmoil of Ireland and Europe, were tensions affecting him. His greatest loss was the death of Lady Gregory in 1932. His elegy to her is heroic and tender.

He took practical steps to retain his sexual youth, subjecting himself in 1934 to the Steinach operation. Spending more and more of his time in the congenial climate of the south of France, he died in 1939 and was buried at Roquebrune. His body was returned to Sligo and re-interred there in 1948.

Yeats seems to have been obsessed more with the idea of the great *poet* than the great *poem*. Poetry was a mode of identity, and the poems often point back to the poet. He works towards an irrefutable art, evanescent, mysterious, hermetic, which yields up its content fully only to the initiate. Art is a defence of the self. He takes his cue from the Irish bards, aligning himself finally with the dwindling aristocracy. In 'Coole Park and Ballylee, 1931' he writes, 'We were the last romantics – chose for theme / Traditional sanctity and loveliness.' This attitude led to his sense of being embattled in a world hostile to art. 'My poetry is generally written out of despair,' Yeats reports. 'Like Balzac, I see increasing commonness everywhere, and like Balzac I know no one who shares the premises from which I work.' That 'like Balzac', conscious identification with great writers of the past, is characteristic. He is a myth-maker from the self. The autobiography he eventually treats us to is never pure. Pure reality withers him. Hence he fails to understand psychology, to recognize causal relationships. His eye is always on *effect*, which partly explains his political and social naïvety. The reluctance of the Irish people to accept his or his friends' art – at the Abbey, or at the Art Museum – soured his political optimism. Despite his antagonism to bourgeois interests, as a Senator he voted with peers, bankers, lawyers and businessmen against the representatives of the working classes. Many of his poems develop the theme – notably 'Upon a House Shaken by the Land Agitation' and 'To a Wealthy Man who Promised a Second Subscription to the Dublin Municipal Gallery if it were Proved the People Wanted Pictures'.

One of Yeats's early ambitions was to reconcile the courteous Protestant heritage with the martyred, unmannerly Roman Catholic tradition in Ireland, towards a political end. Yet he did not want his poetry to become merely local to Ireland. 'I thought we might bring the halves together if we had a national literature that made Ireland beautiful in the memory, and yet had been freed of provincialism by an exacting criticism, a European pose.' Later he wrote of political poetry, 'All literature created out of a conscious political aim in the long run creates weakness by creating a habit of unthinking obedience. Literature created for its own sake, for some eternal spiritual need, can be used for politics. Dante is said to have unified Italy. The more unconscious the creation the more powerful.' It was not a new Ireland Yeats was prophesying. First he celebrated the ancient, and then the moribund, apparently heroic aristocracy.

Yeats craved mystery. In an extravagant moment he claimed he could believe in all that has ever been believed – the onus of disproof is on the unbeliever. This impulse towards the unknown led Yeats to hermetic pursuits. And yet his ideal worlds are – like his vision of the past – strangely materialistic and literal, even when illuminated by moonlight. They arc this world made better, more heroic and powerful, disencumbered of old age and other human disabilities, but perceptible and rewarding to the five senses. Out of his desire to give form to the mystery, and his inability to give it form except in terms of the images of our shared world, grew his interest in literal notions of communication with other regions, with the dead.

To develop systems of order within the mystery, he evolved a pseudo-geometry, a system of gyres, lunar phases, degrees of subjectivity and objectivity. Thus his conscious desire for conceptual order complements his desire for mystery. He was, after all, an admirer of the eighteenth-century Anglo-Irish writers Swift, Burke, Berkeley and Goldsmith, whose solidity and cogency he craved. Fortunately his theories, elucidated at length in *A Vision* (1925), are not of crucial importance to an appreciation of the poems.

His beliefs and systems did help him to externalize certain inner conflicts. From 1909 to 1911 he was intimately busy with the spirits. He discovered Leo Africanus, his spiritual opposite, and they corresponded: that is, Yeats wrote him letters to which he (through Yeats) replied. Leo helped him to a kind of self-knowledge. The self-clarification is expressed in several poems, notably 'Hic et Ille', a dialogue which Pound nicknamed 'Hic et Willie'. The poet, to find himself, had to find the image of himself, by opposites.

Opposites supply the constant tension throughout Yeats's work. He runs his course between extremities: spontaneity versus craft, laughter versus seriousness, mask versus face, spiritual excitement versus sexual agony. The poems set out to bring into tension and retain in tension contrasts or opposites. The dominant tension is between Leda and Lethe, love and death. Yeats wrote that 'sex and death are the only things that can interest a serious mind'. Certainly his best poems are those written in the expectation of death, with the joys of physical passion still agitating him.

From the outset, Yeats had two stylistic impulses in his

writing: the highly developed cadenced style of shadows and mystery; and a stark, phrased, concrete style, concerned with precise images. His development is in the shifting balance between the two styles, as they reflect the changing nature of his ambitions and passions. The early poems, rooted in Celtic myth, full of abstracted emotion, are dominated by the first style. In his middle period, where the poems draw on biographical and local particulars, the emotions become more specific and the two styles are brought into a not very satisfactory balance. The final period is characterized by a more stark, precise and spoken style, the poems based on biographical and local particulars, but now with a specific emotional and intellectual content. Naturally in each period there are poems which foreshadow the later development or re-echo the earlier.

In the early poems Yeats's symbolism is evasive, its function to depersonalize the poems. In the later poems it becomes a probing instrument. But even those symbols drawn from life in *The Tower* have meanings ascribed to them. The meanings do not emanate from the objects in their particular context. In his middle and late poems Yeats frequently explicates his symbols within the poem for fear we should miss their significance. In 'A Prayer for my Daughter' we read the very unsuccessful final explanation, 'Ceremony's a name for the rich horn, / And custom for the spreading laurel tree.' This is the inherent weakness of his basically arbitrary symbolism. The early symbols, the rose for example, tend to humanize the ideal. The later symbols, the mask in particular, tend to idealize the human. Yeats's early attempt to draw the numinous and the mysterious into his early symbols changes to an attempt to make what is crudely human into something numinously heroic, sanctified and mysterious.

The poetry is always heard, not overheard. It is a poetry of all but social evasion. There is little intimacy about Yeats. Richard Ellmann, Yeats's finest critic, has written that his 'mastery seems almost excessive' at times, bordering on 'overmastery'. Late in life Yeats recognized the evasiveness of his symbolism, the tendency of his poetry to turn away or inward, and in the desperate intensity of the late poems he tried to remedy this. But his main weakness as a poet is his imperfect sense of generality, his willingness to plump out a truism as truth. As his mastery increased, his art became less truthful. But his main concern is not – until the last poems – truth, but the myth house where he can become a principal tenant, with a rhetoric in which it is his voice that we hear casting its spell, and where real men are reduced – or, in his mind, enlarged – to masks and figures useful to the myth, regardless of the human reality they had. If he assumes a mask, so must they. The great poem, 'In Memory of Major Robert Gregory', falsifies by oversimplifying, by masking the persons of Lionel Johnson, John Synge, and George Pollexfen. He adapts parts of them, selectively, like a caricaturist.

While Hardy's sense of the individual's isolation is based on memory (accidents of biography make us utterly distinct), Yeats's sense of isolation is based on self-consciousness. The person is aware of his otherness, aware that others are casting him in different roles. Hence he assumes masks, constructs the myth. Everything, too, observes itself. The poems continually refer back to the poet. In 'The Indian to his Love', Yeats writes, 'A parrot sways upon a tree, / Raging at his own image in the enamelled sea.' The only experiences powerful enough to dispel self-consciousness are sexual love and the apprehension of death.

In the early collections *Crossways* (1889) and *The Rose* (1893), the poems are of mood rather than distinct emotion. Yeats later referred to their 'unmanliness'. The Rose was a useful symbol. Crucified, it suffered with the sufferer. It hung upon the cross of Time. It carried its traditional symbolic meanings, but in the early poems it came to symbolize Ireland and Maud Gonne as well: 'Red Rose, proud Rose, sad Rose of all my days!' It is able to carry, albeit prescriptively, considerable meaning for the poet.

These poems express a peculiarly unimpassioned passion: trumped-up romantic sentiment. Yet there is an impression of almost classical control:

Rose of all Roses, Rose of all the world!
The tall thought-woven sails, that flap unfurled
Above the tide of hours . . .

The popularity of 'The Lake Isle of Innisfree' is partly due
to the fact that it is a romantic theme treated in a fully
romantic idiom.

The impression of control is produced primarily by Yeats's
predominant use of intransitive verbs, participles, and 'to be'
constructions, especially in the shorter lyrics. Thus there is
a static effect around the nouns. The intransitive verbs are,
in a sense, the classical element, stilling the romantic noun
content. Though the rhythms flow, the images and symbols
suffer from a strange inertia. In 'The Pity of Love' and 'The
Sorrow of Love' Yeats holds back the transitive verbs to
good effect, deploying them carefully at the climax. But the
general effect of the intransitive verbs, so at odds with the
rhythms, is one of passivity and dream.

In the Seven Woods (1904), Yeats's worst book of poems,
marks a transition. The poems are coldly made. In 'The
Ragged Wood' one noun, for instance, carries a burden of
adjectives and one prepositional phrase: 'that sliding silver-
shoed / Pale silver-proud queen-woman of the sky . . .' It was
six years before the next book came, years spent working in
the theatre, writing plays, and reconsidering his diction. *The
Green Helmet and Other Poems* (1910) shows him grown more
supple, but still the poetry is essentially statuesque, static
through intellectualized emotion, verbally intransitive.
Though emotion suggests the questions, the intellect shapes
them and their implicit or explicit replies. Yeats had still to
learn his own lesson: 'The more unconscious the creation
the more powerful.'

Responsibilities (1914) was published two years after Yeats
and Pound became friends. Pound's influence may be felt in
the Chinese dedicatory couplet, but more in the new taut-
ness, the way ideas are realized not by moralizing symbols
but in the symbols themselves. There is a new authority in
the public tone he adopts in some of the poems. He experiments with the severe satire of the bardic poets when he

assaults bourgeois philistinism and chastises the misled working classes. He contrasts the art patrons of the Renaissance and the Renaissance audience with the boorish, penny-pinching public servants, the unresponsive public. He apprehends that the jingling of the till has superseded in sweetness the strummed harp of the bard. In 'September 1913' he laments, 'Romantic Ireland's dead and gone, / It's with O'Leary in the grave.' All the Irish heroes and martyrs had given their lives to produce a pusillanimous bourgeois order:

> What need you, being come to sense
> But fumble in a greasy till
> And add the halfpence to the pence
> And prayer to shivering prayer until
> You have dried the marrow from the bone?

'Come to sense' is a carefully loaded phrase. 'Sense' without mystery is to Yeats the basest sterility. Scornfully he adds, 'For men were born to pray and save.' In a later poem, 'The Seven Sages', he defined the Whiggery he so detested:

> ... What is Whiggery?
> A levelling, rancorous, rational sort of mind
> That never looked out of the eye of a saint
> Or out of a drunkard's eye.

Responsibilities is full of beggars, hermits, outcasts, people whose gifts are rejected, whose sacrifices were vain. Men should be responsible to the heroes and patriots, respect what they earned for the present – and the future. The new vigour of the verse is reflected in the precision and concreteness of the imagery, the apparently more real passions the poems express, and in the active verb forms. 'The Mountain Tomb' is a poem full of active verbs – a poem of activity, the early, unmanly, passive voice purged. Anger and disillusion broke up the dreamer's style.

The Wild Swans at Coole (1919) is Yeats's first great collection of poems. The 'Wild Swans' inhabit Lady Gregory's aristocratic park. They are natural and beautiful, passionate, powerful, and most significant, they return, they have a noble permanence. 'That crowd, that barbarous crowd' are the antagonists. 'In Memory of Major Robert Gregory' reveals Yeats's subtle sense of poetic organization. He sets out to recall 'the friends that cannot sup with us'. He begins with Lionel Johnson, a social recluse too learned for this world. He calls up John Synge, a recluse too, dedicated not to scholarship but to social observation. The third ghost is George Pollexfen, a horseman and a withdrawn observer of the stars. The Major, an active man and an artist, embodies the virtues found singly in the other ghosts. 'Soldier, scholar, horseman, he'. He is a Renaissance man. The poem achieves its climax by a progression through great men to the great man, the subject of the poem. The poem is marred by the incompleteness with which the ghosts are presented and by an overuse of the word 'all' – it occurs with the word 'entire' over fourteen times. But 'all' is a favourite word with Yeats, an encompassing verbal gesture.

He considers also the possibility of modern heroism. 'An Irish Airman Foresees his Death' calls up a pilot motivated by no social or religious commitments, but rather by 'a lonely impulse of delight' – a sufficient motive for heroic action in a spiritually impoverished world.

In *The Wild Swans at Coole* the poet begins to age rapidly. The mythologized autobiography is powerful because the 'I-myth' replaces the baseless 'we-myth' of the earlier poems. Yeats begins to stress the unique individual experience. 'To a Young Beauty' is perhaps arrogantly self-aggrandizing and 'The Scholars' smacks of undue scorn. But he can be scornful of himself as well. In 'Lines Written in Dejection' he laments the passing of magic, the lunar vision, and accepts willy-nilly the 'embittered' and 'timid' sun. He expresses a craving for simple rustic readers – 'the wise simple man'. In 'The Fisherman' he seems to crave a reader who is like his own idealized youth:

Before I am old
I shall have written him one
Poem maybe as cold
And passionate as the dawn.

As a poet Yeats reworked his poems relentlessly, sometimes starting from a prose draft and turning it into verse. The care which went to the writing of 'The Fisherman' is invisible. The poem has a natural spoken quality only slightly marred by the access of rhetoric. The art has successfully concealed art. Humour and ribaldry are more readily admitted to the poems, more convincingly expressed.

Michael Robartes and the Dancer (1921) includes, as well as the famous poems 'Easter 1916', 'The Second Coming', and 'A Prayer for my Daughter', 'Solomon and the Witch', one of Yeats's most effective expressions of the theme of self-consciousness and its dispelling (for good or ill) in love:

Maybe the bride-bed brings despair,
For each an imagined image brings
And finds a real image there.

Throughout this collection, especially in the anthologized poems, Yeats handles his verbs with cunning. 'The Second Coming', raw and visionary, with political and religious overtones, like the Byzantium poems that followed, cannot be paraphrased. It is in 'a language not to be betrayed'.

'Sailing to Byzantium' appeared in *The Tower* (1928). In it, an old man rejects, as he is rejected by, the sensuous world of youth, ephemerality and the natural cycles. He travels to the 'Monuments of unageing intellect', to Byzantium – where art arrests change but, in arresting it, transforms it into something other. There he wills himself transformed, freed of human passions and the body, that 'dying animal'. He wills to be assumed 'into the artifice of eternity'. A powerful intellectual passion animates the poem. 'The Tower' itself is one of Yeats's finest long poems, exploring the theme of age. His self-mythologizing is bardic, suggesting the poet is mad, his task is to make others mad. In this collection Yeats settles finally for a less tentative statement of the artist's predicament. 'Ancestral Homes' and the first section of the 'Meditations in Time of Civil War' recall the stately aristocratic homes commissioned by bitter, angry men to be built in order to express sweetness, gentleness, and the civilizing qualities. What if the house does not have the *power* of its sweetness? What if art, finally, is passive, in time of civil war itself affected without affecting? These questions burn at the centre of Yeats's political poems. Sato's sword is laid beside the pen and paper. The overriding perception is that hate is more powerful than love: hate leads to action. 'Among School Children' examines the fate of hope, faith, and love. It also suggests, in the famous closing lines, that form and content, action and actor, are ideally inseparable. The perceived ideal rises out of an accurate presentation of the real.

Three collections were published after *The Tower*: *The Winding Stair and Other Poems* (1933) including 'Words for Music Perhaps' and 'A Woman Young and Old'; *A Full Moon in March* (1935) and *Last Poems* (1936–9). Death and love are the dominant themes. The well-known 'Crazy Jane' sequence, full of the wit, pathos and passion of Yeats's later years, and 'Byzantium', the culmination of the sequence and of his hermetic idiom, are a large part of the achievement of the later books. But the outstanding poem of Yeats's last years was 'The Circus Animals' Desertion'. In search of an authentic theme, he rejects (as he has been deserted by) the 'masterful images'. He recognizes his evasions, the price of his 'overmastery'. The decision to begin again is powerfully expressed by one for whom there had already been so many beginnings. This time the quest was for the maskless, naked 'I'. From the power of the language we can surmise that this, far from being a denial of the heroic ideal, is the most heroic act of all:

> Now that my ladder's gone,
> I must lie down where all the ladders start,
> In the foul rag-and-bone shop of the heart.

Charlotte Mew (1869–1927)

But everything has burned, and not quite through.

It is difficult to understand why Charlotte Mew has so few readers today. She merits them. Thomas Hardy spoke of her as 'the least pretentious but undoubtedly the best woman poet of our day'. De la Mare, Harold Monro and John Masefield, among others, championed her work. But – apart from a few anthology pieces – her life's work of sixty poems is hardly known at all.

She was born in London in 1869 into a moderately well-to-do family. Her father was an architect. He had come to London and married his boss's daughter. She, a petite, apparently pampered Victorian lady, was very much one for keeping up appearances. Even when financial hardship hit the Mew family, she insisted on maintaining a front of gentility. When rooms were let to lodgers, the dark secret was kept from all but the most intimate friends.

Charlotte, enjoying the education of a Victorian lady, was taught no skills and never went – in formal education – beyond the Lucy Harrison School for Girls in Gower Street. Her home was not particularly literary. She confessed that she had never learned the laws of punctuation. Her friend Alida Monro regularized the punctuation of her poems.

Her father took his family responsibilities lightly, and when he died – she was twenty-nine at the time and still living at home – he left almost nothing to his family. Charlotte and her sister Anne (her closest companion) and their mother began to suffer in the battle to keep up appearances – indeed to survive. Anne was an artist, specializing in furniture restoration. Charlotte could teach. The anguish of earning a subsistence plagued them permanently. Charlotte, in the year of her death, through the good offices of Masefield, de la Mare and Hardy, was awarded a Civil List pension – but it came too late to do her any good.

Charlotte had a further brother and sister. Both had suffered acute mental instability and were placed in asylums. There seemed to Charlotte and Anne to be a taint of mental illness in their family, and each vowed never to marry lest the malaise be handed on. This decision was prompted as much by inclination as by conscience. Charlotte's most famous – though not her best – poem, 'The Farmer's Bride', tells the story of a country marriage where the bride refuses to be touched, much less possessed, by her husband. The stair – an image which recurs frequently in her poems – separates man and wife for good:

> She sleeps up in the attic there
> Alone, poor maid. 'Tis but a stair
> Betwixt us. Oh! my God! the down,
> The soft young down of her, the brown,
> The brown of her – her eyes, her hair, her hair!

Her aversion to the farmer is as intense as his desire for her.

Charlotte's early travels – to northern France particularly – impressed her deeply. Many of her poems are set in France. Others are set in the city, but several take place in the English countryside, which she always saw as a visitor, often, it seems, her eyes directed by the pastoral poets she most admired, notably Hardy.

She reached the peak of her poetic powers between 1909 and 1916 when – in her forties – she began writing verse with confidence. Her short stories, which had appeared widely before this time, came now with more originality and fluency. She seemed ambitious, despite her intense reticence, to express something difficult and urgent, the nature of which she herself did not completely understand. Given the hardships she had experienced, her emotional nature, and her educational background, it is miraculous that – after the unpromising start with her early prose romances – she did not choose to write about a fantastic, escapist world. Instead, she began to develop a prose style that engaged reality at its most intense; and from this style it was only a small step to her poetry. The rhythms of her verse were present in her mature stories.

Communication in her best stories is by gesture, facial expression, or through symbols – conversation is always secondary to *how* it is said. The ordering of the images is more expressive than the story itself. Hence later, in her poems, the forms are of crucial importance. There is as much eloquence in the disrupted, dramatic syntax, the long fluent line, the rhythmical emphasis and the quality of the objects rendered, as in the plot and explicit statement of the poem, if it has one.

When she was writing her best poems, Alida Monro, wife of Harold Monro, the poet, publisher, and manager of the Poetry Book Shop, read her work in a magazine. She invited Mew to a reading at the Shop and later arranged for the publication of her two books, *The Farmer's Bride* (1916) and *The Rambling Sailor* (1929) which appeared posthumously. It is largely from Alida Monro's memoir that we glean the little biographical information we have about Charlotte Mew.

A letter Charlotte wrote to a friend tells us much about her mode of composition and her ideas of form. She is writing about 'In Nunhead Cemetery' (note the punctuation – in dashes): 'The last verse which you find superfluous is to me the most inevitable – (and was written first) – being a lapse from the sanity and self-control of what precedes it – the mind – the senses can stand no more – and that is to express their failure and exhaustion.' She explains that she does not write the poem straight out: she assembles it, fits it together. The artistry is in the organization. The content, when under sufficient emotional pressure, must violate form, if the poem is to be true. We will look in vain for formal perfection in her work: form is servant, not master. The emotional content elbows out the form, or pulls it in. This is deeply subjective poetry, resonant and vivid because of the physical veracity of the observations, the speaking quality of the voice, and the poet's intense response.

Her review of Emily Brontë's poems brings us a little closer to her notion of form. She has been compared with Emily Brontë, but apart from their shared intensity, the comparison does damage to the integrity of each. They differ as much in their use of forms as in the quality of passion they convey. Charlotte Mew begins by remarking that Emily Brontë's forms are 'curiously deficient'. 'They are melodies, rather than harmonies, many of a haunting and piercing sweetness, instinct with a sweeping and mournful music peculiarly her own . . . Everywhere, too, the note of pure passion is predominant, a passion untouched by mortality and unappropriated by sex.' Mew's own poems aim at a *harmonic* effect – in other words, the combining of various elements in a single phrase or rhythmic passage, an opacity; the poetry is built of phrases, not of cadences, even in the long lines; and each phrase draws together elements – sometimes conflicting – from several registers of human sensation and emotion. It is not a poetry of developing thought but of developing emotional experience in a physical world. And nor can we find much sweetness in Charlotte Mew. Her own poems are everywhere instinct with mortality, the lament for the passing of beauty, passion, things and people loved; and there is a profound sensuality about all her poetry and explicit sexuality about some of it. It is the *impure* passion, longing for purity (usually conceived in religious imagery – she was much drawn to Roman Catholicism, though she was never converted) since it cannot achieve any earthly permanence.

Mew's early poems explore religious suffering (in the form of martyrdom), punishment, death, sorrow, loss and love. There is one poem full of misanthropic humour, 'Afternoon Tea'. But the others, occasionally witty, are of a generally dramatic and elegiac tone. Recurrent images – the stair, the rose, red petals, dreams, and hair – relate the poems to one another. They seem to illuminate one another. The traditional material is heightened and made strange by her peculiar physicality of response.

It was with 'Poems from France' that she established her own voice. 'The Fête' was her first outstanding poem. A boy in a French school experiences the fair – and love. His dramatic monologue ends with an expression of loss – loss, in effect, of purity, innocence, some intangible:

All my life long I shall see moonlight on the fern
  And the black trunks of trees. Only the hair
Of any woman can belong to God.
The stalks are cruelly broken where we trod,
  There had been violets there,
    I shall not care
As I used to do when I see the bracken burn.

The pain and loss implicit in intense pleasure are conveyed in the extremely complex verse form. The same power of expression characterizes 'Madeleine in Church', Mew's main achievement – uneven but powerful. It too is a dramatic monologue, of a hundred and forty lines, spoken by a woman who fails to re-establish religious faith after a life of intense sensuality. The printer first entrusted with the task of setting the poem returned the manuscript, solemnly declaring it was blasphemous.

'Madeleine' reminds us of Mary Magdalen, whose redemption was made possible only by the physical being of Christ. 'She was a sinner, we are what we are: the spirit afterwards, but first the touch.' The poem is about 'the touch', the inability of the individual – without personal, incontrovertible revelation – to believe in anything beyond the physical world. Christ, she avers, cannot understand the profound darkness of her soul. She tries to explain herself to Him:

  We are what we are: when I was half a child I could not sit
Watching black shadows on green lawns and red carnations
burning in the sun
            Without paying so heavily for it

That joy and pain, like any mother and her unborn child were
almost one.
                    I could not bear
          The dreams upon the eyes of white geraniums in the dusk,
                The thick, close voice of musk,
          The jesamine music on the thin night air,
     Or, sometimes, my own hands about me anywhere.

Her materialism is not intellectual but an emotional disposition which cannot comprehend the metaphysical. 'We
are what we are' recurs as a refrain. She asks God, 'If it is
Your will that we should be content with the tame, bloodless
things.' The poem is a celebration as much as a lament. She
laments the ephemerality of those physical experiences which
seem all-important, and yet as she laments she relives and
celebrates. The power of the poem is in the ambiguous way
she at once prays to and rejects Christ, in her ambivalence
towards her own life. 'If there were fifty heavens God could
not give us back the child who went or never came.' She
cannot accede to Christ:

     Oh! He will take us stripped and done,
     Driven into his heart. So we are won:
  Then safe, safe are we? in the shelter of His everlasting wings—
  I do not envy Him His victories, His arms are full of broken things.

For Madeleine, and indeed for Mew, if we can trust the
evidence of the poems, the world is too richly physical to
allow belief in anything beyond the power bodies and objects
and their mute attraction have over the mind and heart:
'the spirit afterwards, but first the touch.'

There are occasional echoes in her work – of Browning,
Hardy, and others – but 'influences' are transmuted by her
own voice. With Hardy she shares some themes – for
instance, the unalterability of past experience, memory, and
its effect on the present; ephemerality of the passions, regret,
the difficulty of sustained love. Heaven is not 'to come' but
in the past, in youth and its spent intensities. The future is
merely a termination of possibilities, one by one, a putting

out of candles. 'I remember rooms that have had their part /
In the steady slowing down of the heart.' It is a difficult,
unredeemed vision, thoroughly materialistic: her pseudo-
mystical stair leads to a physical place. Refusing the
Christian heaven in 'Not for that City' she defines the stair:

And if for anything we greatly long,
It is for some remote and quiet stair
    Which winds to silence and a space of sleep
    Too sound for waking and for dreams too deep.

'Things that kill us seem / Blind to the Death they give,' she
wrote in 'The Quiet House', a poem she reckoned to be her
most subjective. In it the physical imagination is sharpened
to a degree unprecedented even in 'Madeleine in Church':

Red is the strangest pain to bear;
In Spring the leaves on the budding trees;
In Summer the roses are worse than these,
    More terrible than they are sweet:
    A rose can stab you across the street
        Deeper than any knife:
    And the crimson haunts you everywhere—
Thin shafts of sunlight, like the ghosts of reddened swords have
struck our stair
As if, coming down, you had spilt your life.

Charlotte Mew's sister Anne died in the winter of 1927. The
loss weakened the poet, and she was taken to a sanatorium.
She entrusted to Alida Monro the copy Hardy had taken in
his own hand of her poem 'Fin de Fête'. She bought some
disinfectant and drank it. When her death was reported in
the local paper, she was identified as 'Charlotte New, said to
be a writer.'

Walter de la Mare (1873–1956)

A self there is that listens in the heart
To what is past the range of human speech,
Which yet has urgent tidings to impart—
The all-but-uttered, and yet out of reach.

There are nearly nine hundred pages of de la Mare's *Collected Poems*. It is surprising that a poet devoted to quietness, the ineffable, whose poetic terrain is the 'limbo' between dream and waking, should have found so many subjects for a poetry as limited in scope and diction as his. His dreams are not Freudian or Biblical, his waking includes little of the modern world. His idiom is the traditional language of late romanticism, his forms are adapted from the English pastoral tradition. On what, then, can the critical claims that he is 'a poet of major proportions' be based?

Walter John de la Mare was born in 1873 in Charlton, Kent. His family was of Huguenot extraction. Educated at St Paul's Choir School, he showed a flair for editing when he founded the *Chorister's Journal*. When he was seventeen he became a clerk in the London offices of the Standard Oil Company, a position he held for eight years.

When he left in 1898 to undertake the life of a creative and freelance writer, he had contributed stories to periodicals under the name 'Walter Ramel', an anagram for his own name. He used the pseudonym for his first collection of poems, *Songs of Childhood* (1902). He settled in Taplow, near London, and assembled his prose fantasy *Henry Brocken* (1904) and his second collection, *Poems* (1906). A Civil List pension, awarded him in 1908, eased his financial worries and further facilitated his creative activity. Later on, he was among the beneficiaries of Rupert Brooke's will, which advanced him further towards self-sufficiency.

The publication of *The Listeners and Other Poems* (1912) established him as a popular poet, and he continued to write principally brief, lyrical pieces (with the major exception of 'Winged Chariot' [1951], a long poem) until his death in 1956 at the age of eighty-three. At his death, honoured with the Order of Merit, the Companion of Honour, and a number of awards, he had published fifty volumes of verse, stories, essays and novels. He was also a popular anthologist.

De la Mare's dream world has some affinity with Coleridge's in 'The Ancient Mariner' and 'Kubla Khan', with Poe's, and with Lear's and Carroll's nonsense worlds. In his work, dream poet and fantasist combine and a delicate vision is presented, full of nostalgia for childhood. Randall Jarrell, the American poet and critic, described de la Mare's as 'the world of the child as it seems to the grown-up', where innocence and ignorance are neighbours, where much of the waking life partakes of the unreality and formlessness of dream, and where language is inadequate to engage the complex vision. In de la Mare, 'the forlorn hope is always the purest hope'. There is never any chance of the poem *saying* what it has to say – it attempts to contain the images and rhythms which will convey the meaning just beyond language, or to measure the silences.

De la Mare uses the ordinary vocabulary of romanticism, and for all his formal skills and elegance there is often a homely quality about the verse, with its terse phrasing. He uses abstractions *ad nauseam*: reason, memory, the heart, woes, good, wisdom, happiness, ugliness, wickedness, time, innocence, and so on. Like Hàrdy, he thinks in terms of these abstractions. He employs, particularly in the early poems, conscious archaisms. Though these disappear from most of the later work, there is little development of technique. He becomes more skilful, his late poems apprehend death memorably. But the voice does not change and his themes, though they become obsessive, cannot be said to evolve. He is poetically impersonal, and yet his resolutely traditional style is readily recognizable as his own.

The uniqueness of the poems is entirely thematic. A thematic personality emerges more powerfully than if he had written confessional verse. The unreality with which the poems deal – or the reality beyond language – *is* his reality. In expressing his world, he perfects a genre where cruelty, nonsense, mystery, fantasy and love exist together as constituting and complementary aspects of his world. But his limitations are clear. His and our realities hardly coincide, and where they do he is exploring only a limited range of our common experience. Yet within that range he is powerful, he gives us a poetry of wisdom before knowledge. He is the conscious poet of the unconscious – though in no facile psychological sense. To him 'unconscious' means inarticulable, the limbo in which language, to have power, can be used only connotatively.

Facts for him have little authority. He speaks of 'shaggy Science nosing in the grass', and yet he senses an affinity between science and poetry. Each is devoted to the mystery. In the powerful poem 'Shadow' he is concerned with what is implicit in, and yet not apparently part of, experience: 'The loveliest thing earth hath, a shadow hath, / A dark and livelong hint of death . . .' He reverses the image of the shadow cast by the living, which implies death, to the image of those elements within life which are irreducible by death: the self, the soul. In 'Even in the Grave', death says, 'Even in the grave thou wilt have thyself.'

Standing often as 'a dreamer in a dream / In the unstirring night', the poet listens. Most of his poems include darkness in some form, and solitude and stillness, where he moves between the mundane world and what, in 'Sleep', he calls 'the enchanted realm of dream'. Enchantment is the process by which he would penetrate to meanings otherwise unsayable. When, in his most famous poem, 'The Listeners', he hears 'their silence answering his cry', he has been answered by the mystery. It is silence that, in waves, rolls back towards the house when the horseman goes. In the poem, de la Mare is at once with the horseman and with the Listeners, defining neither, but witnessing their meeting.

De la Mare's achievement is a language of directness and simplicity which suggests experiences beyond its meanings. His language also evokes continuities in a refined manner. In 'All That's Past' he laments,

> Oh, no man knows
> Through what wild centuries
> Roves back the rose.

And the drama within the stillness he creates can be intense – expectation and desire await something ever more about to be: 'Speak not – whisper not; / Here bloweth thyme and bergamot,' he writes in 'The Sunken Garden'. The simplicity of the poem 'Alone', with its refrain which leaves everything of importance said, though it gives no particulars, haunts the reader. Like 'Good-bye' it is a poem notable for its resigned serenity:

> Alas, my loved one is gone.
> I am alone.
> It is winter.

One of de la Mare's most effective symbols is that of the woman wearing a veil in daytime, making a little night about her face where the features exist as suggestion, not definition. She is a mystery, an absence.

His prose writing develops the same themes as the verse, but the verse is more direct. 'The Burning Glass' suggests his creative purpose:

> No map shows my Jerusalem,
>   No history my Christ;
> Another language tells of them.
>   A hidden evangelist.

When there is humour in the poems it is gentle and does not disrupt the stillness. D. H. Lawrence praised his 'perfect appreciation of life at still moments', and Edmund Blunden in his elegy, 'A Poet's Death', calls him 'A light of other days.' This unfairly restricts his achievement for, despite his romantic idiom and his lack of technical originality, thematically de la Mare is timeless. It would be difficult for any poet to fuse the two worlds de la Mare did in 'The Song of Shadows' with anything like his accuracy and unerring rhythms. From the Campion-like world of music and mystery, the poem focuses on a physical image whose mystery – the mystery of the actual, the known – exceeds the mystery of the unknown:

Sweep softly thy strings, Musician,
    The minutes mount to hours;
Frost on the windless casement weaves
    A labyrinth of flowers . . .

Edward Thomas (1878–1917)

I should use, as the trees and birds did,
A language not to be betrayed . . .

When, in April 1917, Edward Thomas was killed by the blast of a shell before Arras, the American poet Robert Frost wrote to Helen Thomas, the poet's wife, 'Who was ever so completely himself right up to the verge of destruction, so sure of his thought, so sure of his word?' If this was true of Thomas, then both Helen and Frost were in large part responsible.

Thomas's life, though intensely active, was not full of incident. The three crucial events in his life gain significance in retrospect. The first was his meeting with Helen Noble in 1894. This led to his virtual marriage when he was still an undergraduate at Oxford. While she provided him with an emotional and practical mainstay, marriage also brought him a family. Having published his first prose book while at Oxford, he decided to become a freelance writer. He followed this vocation for twenty-two years, preparing hundreds of book reviews, compiling anthologies and editions, and writing over thirty prose books on subjects ranging from the countryside to tourist guides, from literary criticism to short stories, biographies, autobiographies, and an autobiographical novel.

Then, in 1912, he met Robert Frost. Frost pointed out passages in Thomas's nature writings and urged him to attempt them in verse. For the four years that his friendship with Frost continued, he gained confidence and composed poems. In August of 1914 he wrote to his friend Eleanor Farjeon, 'I may as well write poetry. Did anyone ever begin at thirty-six in the shade?' His taste had always been for poetry. He set about writing the fewer than a hundred and fifty poems that constitute his complete *oeuvre*.

In 1915 Thomas enlisted in the Artists' Rifles, was made a map-reading instructor and promoted the next year to Second Lieutenant. Army service freed him from financial worry and the responsibilities of freelancing and gave him a formal, disciplined existence where he could write his poems. Helen Thomas saw his enlisting as a sort of surrender, but for the poet in him it was a decisive act.

Philip Edward Thomas was born in 1878 in Lambeth, London, the eldest of six sons. His parents were of Welsh descent and he felt an affection for Wales, though his landscape was the south of England, especially Wiltshire, Kent and Hampshire. He attended St Paul's School, Hammersmith, and went to Jesus College, Oxford. In 1897, when he was nineteen, his first prose book, *The Woodland Life*, was published. He was already living with Helen Thomas, and they were married in 1899. Their children were born in 1900, 1902, and 1910. They lived in Kent and then in Hampshire. Between 1910 and 1912, driven by financial necessity, Thomas wrote no fewer than twelve of his prose books. He suffered a mental breakdown in 1911 and contemplated suicide.

The prose of Edward Thomas is usually dismissed by his critics – considered only in its direct relation to the poems. But Thomas, in his way, was one of the most percipient literary critics of his time. He was among the first reviewers to appreciate Frost's work; he also recognized Ezra Pound's achievement in *Personae* which he reviewed in 1909. Throughout his mature prose there are passages of criticism and descriptive writing which merit attention in themselves.

Thomas began writing prose in the shadow of Walter Pater, and his early work is poised, poetical, and cold – a gap exists between style and voice. As more demands were made on his time, he began to write more fluently. In a letter to Eleanor Farjeon he said he was 'trying to get rid of the last rags of rhetoric and formality which left my prose so often with a dead rhythm'. It is significant that prose and verse rhythms are early concerns of his criticism. Ironically, after his passion for Pater had passed, he was commissioned to write a book about him. It proved to be one of his best critical studies. He takes Pater to task in these terms: 'Unless a man write with his whole nature concentrated upon his subject he is unlikely to take hold of another man . . .' Swinburne had been another of his favourites. With similar irony, when his love for Swinburne had dwindled, he was asked to write a book on him. Of Swinburne's vocabulary he says, 'The words . . . have no rich inheritance from old usage of speech or poetry, even when they are poetic or archaic or Biblical. They have little variety of tone . . . The blank verse changes and does everything but speak.' He reacted against the one-dimensional, unresonant quality of Swinburne's vocabulary, as against the studied, dead rhythms and the artifice of Pater.

An attitude, indeed a critical stance, towards poetry can be deduced from Thomas's criticism. He draws a distinction between Reality and Realism – the style that attempts 'reality' imitates the proportions and rhythms of nature, while the 'realist' style concentrates on reproducing detail. He condones the former and, in his poetry, practises it. But he is always pragmatic in his approach to new work, as to form, assessing it on its own terms first, and his taste encompasses Doughty as well as Frost.

In a book review, he wrote, 'The worst of the poetry being written today is that it is too deliberately and not inevitably English.' In his Pater book he extends this argument. 'Only when a word has become necessary to him can a man use it safely; if he try to impress words by force on a sudden occasion, they will either perish of his violence or betray him.' And in an obituary review of Rupert Brooke, the point is taken further. 'He did not attain the "Shelleyan altitude" where words have a various radiance rather than meaning.'

These ideas were crucial to Thomas's own eventual poetic development. Both his poems entitled 'Words' develop the ideas. In poetry, Thomas is asking for a vocabulary which is one with the poet's normal usage, which does not employ poeticisms or words which the author must force into service. In effect, the 'Shelleyan altitude' he speaks of means that the best poetry is unparaphrasable, self-justifying and self-contained, the words exist not merely in denotative relationships but more richly and truly in connotative relationships. He clarifies the point finally in another review. 'The important thing is not that a thing should be small, but that it should be intense and capable of *unconsciously symbolic significance*' (my italics).

Natural rhythms are extensions of the natural vocabulary. Thomas wrote to a friend about Frost's 'absolute fidelity to the postures which the voice assumes in the most expressive intimate speech.' His instinctive grasp of form is best expressed in his analysis of Richard Jefferies's essay structure: 'Even if it were all nightmare, the very truthfulness of the agitated voice, rising and falling in honest contemplation of common sorrows, would preserve it, since it is rarely given to the best of men to speak the truth. Its shape is the shape of an emotional mood, and it ends because the emotion ends. It is music, and above, or independent of, logic.' So in the poems it is a truth instinctively apprehended, not a truth intellectually understood, that we should look for.

If we contrast Frost's with Thomas's approach to what is similar subject matter, the nature of Thomas's vision becomes clearer. Unlike Thomas's rustic peasants, Frost's have prejudices but no traditions – they seem without roots in their landscape. Thomas's peasants are extensions of a landscape and a history, instinct with a native wisdom and humanity we look for usually in vain in the more competitive and untrusting characters of Frost's poems. Formally, Thomas's poems are more subtle than Frost's early work. Frost used archaisms, and the iambic regularity contributes to the poems' monotonous quality. Thomas wrote poems of variable line length, many of them not metrically or syllabically regular but purely stressed in rhythm. He seldom chose a prescriptive form: the experience determined line length, rhythm, and extent. Even his sonnets are irregular. Thomas is most subtle in his line endings. A poem's rhythm may seem to indicate a direction of development which, at the beginning of a new line, unexpectedly changes: the syntax and the line endings are counterpointed. The effect is to shock us deeper into the experience. In the following passage, the lines ending in 'might' and 'beautiful' illustrate the effect:

The rich scene has grown fresh again and new
As Spring and to the touch is not more cool
Than it is warm to the gaze; and now I might
As happy be as earth is beautiful,
Were I some other or with earth could turn
In alternation of violet and rose,
Harebell and snowdrop, at their season due,
And gorse that has no time but to be gay.

The reversal of sense in the words I have italicized, and the tension of the rhythm straining our expectation in one direction, while the syntax inexorably and deftly goes in another, creates a powerful resonance.

The 'I' of Thomas's poems is usually the poet himself. If he adopts a persona (he occasionally uses 'the child' as speaker) he places the persona's words in quotation marks to avoid confusion. Frequently the 'I' is not present at all, the poem exists with the speaker implicit only in the rhythms. He refuses to deflect his voice through a mask. The theme of solitude is conveyed by the authentic speaking voice. In 'Melancholy' he writes, 'if I feared the solitude / Far more I feared all company . . .' In 'That Girl's Clear Eyes', the isolation of the individual in the sealed, unbreachable world of personal experience he cannot ever fully communicate or share, is expressed:

Every one of us
This morning at our tasks left nothing said,
In spite of many words. We were sealed thus
Like tombs.

The poems are located very much in Thomas's experience.

His most powerful effects are achieved when he contrasts the clearly visualized external world and the more tenuously revealed inner world. The vividness of Thomas's evocations of nature is not the vividness of an internal but of an external landscape. It clarifies the internal without being displaced by it. Thomas often locates a poem in a season, sometimes in a specific place. The experience is thus anchored in time and on the map. He is much concerned with names and naming and, in poems such as 'Adlestrop' and 'Old Man' which explore the distance between the name and the thing named, with the inadequacy of names. The external and internal worlds coexist, the name and the thing named, and in their coexistence and the distance between them the resonance of the poems is achieved. 'A gate banged in a fence and banged in my head,' one of the poems says. The experiences confirm one another.

Thomas's favourite time setting for the poems is the period of transition: twilight, the point of change between seasons, or the present rendered vivid as the point between the past and future, one felt as history, the other as potential. The poetry is of transitions between emotions as well – the almost dark and the almost light, the almost lost and the almost found. The poem 'Interval' is specifically about the point of transition:

Gone the wild day:
A wilder night
Coming makes way
For brief twilight.

'The Thrush' is more subjective:

And April I love for what
It was born of, and November
For what it will die in,
What they are and what they are not ...

This is Winter, seen from either end.

To get closer to the truth of a thing, Thomas sometimes

strengthens the simile in order to transfer our attention from the thing described on to what it is compared with. The effect is Wordsworthian – 'The cataracts *sound their trumpets* from the steep.' The trumpet image is stronger than the image of the cataract. Thomas does this with powerfully evocative effect: 'The swift with wings and tail as sharp and narrow / As if the bow had flown off with the arrow.' In another poem he evokes 'all the clouds like sheep / On the mountains of sleep'. The 'clouds like sheep' come from de la Mare's poem 'Autumn'. But Thomas takes the image further. The implications of such strong comparisons are always controlled to make us aware of what Thomas called 'unconsciously symbolic significance'.

Thomas uses various spatial perspectives to express a whole experience. We see things from two or three perspectives. In 'The Watcher', a man in an hotel looks out at a horse and carter by a ford. He is in turn watched by 'stuffed fish, vermin, and king-fishers' in a glass case within. He stands, sealed off by glass, between the living natural world and the artificially preserved nature. 'Thaw' is another poem in which perspective provides the central tension. The poem takes place in the period between seasons:

Over the land freckled with snow half-thawed
The speculating rooks at their nests cawed
And saw from elm-tops, delicate as flower of grass,
What we below could not see, Winter pass.

The rooks' and our own perspectives are contrasted. They 'speculate' – both look and prognosticate. The word is used in its richest sense, including etymology. The elm-tops become the rooks' lawn – and since the tops of the elms are first to renew, the rooks are seeing spring, while we below are still in winter. Thomas often reverses perspective to emphasize an emotion: 'a poor man of any sort, down to a king,' he writes, or in another poem, 'The clay first broke my heart, and then my back; / And the back heals not . . .'

Few of Thomas's poems are without birds, and several have the names of birds for title. It is the sound, 'A pure thrush word', and the flight that most attract him. Another recurrent image is of rain and storms which wash clean, alleviate tension, and are sometimes correlative with tears. Though Thomas wrote only a few war poems, images of war and conflict occur frequently, though fully integrated into a personal rather than a public utterance. Perhaps his most memorable image is that of roads, paths, lanes. He praised Hardy for his sense of roads and their importance, how they connect people even when they are far apart. Thomas says, 'This is an imaginative fact.'

Roads go on
While we forget and are
Forgotten as a star
That shoots and is gone.

'If' and 'as if' in Thomas's poems suggest a world of similarities parallel to the real world: it may be the internal world, or the world of the past, or some possible future. *Seeming* runs parallel to and grows out of the observed *being*. The world of seeming is conveyed also by a deft use of negatives. Thomas often describes or states what is *not* the case. He can thus convey what could be or what has been, as well as what is. A complex use of explicit and implicit negatives occurs in 'Old Man'. Musing on the flower called 'Old Man' and 'Lad's Love' (and also 'Traveller's Joy'), out of the complexity of memory and sensuous recollection he says:

I have mislaid the key. I sniff the spray
And think of nothing; I see and I hear nothing;
Yet seem, too, to be listening, lying in wait
For what I should, yet never can, remember:
No garden appears, no path, no hoar-green bush
Of Lad's-love, or Old Man, no child beside,
Neither father nor mother, nor any playmate;
Only an avenue, dark, nameless, without end.

'Nameless' implicates the past, 'without end' the future. While Hardy is obsessed with what the mind remembers, how memory and the past impinge upon the present, Thomas is obsessed by what is forgotten, or only half-remembered. 'I can remember much forgetfulness', Hart Crane says – each thing forgotten is a loss, since the missing experience could enrich the present:

All lost, as is a childless woman's child
And its child's children, in the undefiled
Abyss of what will never be again.

'The past is the only dead thing that smells sweet', he writes. He remembers not *what* he has forgotten, but *that* he has forgotten.

Perhaps the most original aspect of his art, after the rhythm, is his control of diction – especially verb tenses. His mind engages a complex experience totally in the following passage, where the tenses suggest various time scales:

Just hope has gone for ever. Perhaps
I may love other hills yet more
Than this: the future and the maps
Hide something I was waiting for.

When, in the first seven lines of 'The Glory', he wishes to convey complete peace, he withholds the main verb until the eighth line, giving an impression of the bustling peace of nature. In 'The Green Roads' he devises a couplet stanza form where the first line of each couplet ends with the word 'forest', and the second has an internal rhyme and is end-stopped. The form grows out of the repetitive syntax. The effect is like that of the paths themselves, suspended, without apparent origin or destination.

We would have to look to the best of George Herbert's poetry to find in English a more direct, unparaphrasable speaking voice, a poetry built of words that are totally natural to the speaker. The lucid, self-contained quality of Thomas's language and vision is best conveyed in the conclusion of one of his poems, 'I Never Saw that Land Before':

I neither expected anything
Nor yet remembered: but some goal
I touched then; and if I could sing
What would not even whisper my soul
As I went on my journeying,

I should use, as the trees and birds did,
A language not to be betrayed;
And what was hid should still be hid
Excepting from those like me made
Who answer when such whispers bid.

Wyndham Lewis (1882–1957)

> to be busily balking
> The tongue-tied Briton – that is my outlandish plot!

Thomas Hardy, who had reason to know, wrote that poetry 'is not at bottom criticized . . . as a particular man's artistic interpretation of life, but with a secret eye on its theological and political propriety'. This largely explains the neglect into which Wyndham Lewis's prose and poetry have fallen. T. S. Eliot called him 'the greatest prose master of style of my generation'. C. H. Sisson praised his 'appreciation of the role of the human mind' in our century, and has written the most sensitive account of his verse yet undertaken. But, until recently, very few critics have attended to Lewis's poetry.

This is largely because Lewis, the enemy of subjectivity, irrationality, and affectation, took a fatal step in 1931. He published a book called *Hitler* which described the programme of National Socialism and guardedly approved it. It was not a prophetic book. It tried to read the facts, for Lewis was an intellectual and not a visionary. In the context of the 1930s, however, this was an act of literary suicide. He was not refuted by argument. There were *ad hominem* attacks and then, in a literary milieu dominated by public-school Marxists, busy praising Stalin and the other Revolution, came the more deadly form of attack: Lewis was ignored.

Lewis himself, in 1937, wrote a book called *The Hitler Cult*, an account of the tragic development of Hitler's programme. Lewis was no 'fascist', not even in the sloppy sense that word is used by student activists. He saw the wrong conclusions of his earlier work and rethought his position. It made no difference to the critics' attitudes towards his work. His contemporaries, when they came to reject their Stalinism, were in the majority. Their recantations were accepted – indeed, recanting gave them a higher moral tone.

Percy Wyndham Lewis was born aboard his father's yacht off Amherst, Nova Scotia, in 1882. His father was an American – a 'professional idler' as Lewis characterized him. He separated from Lewis's mother when the boy was eleven. He and his mother went to England. He had a governess and was sent to various British public schools, finally to Rugby. He did not distinguish himself academically.

From Rugby he went to the Slade (1898–1901). He was known there as 'a poet' and wrote Petrarchan and, later, Shakespearean sonnets (Shakespearean were easier). To his ear his sonnets were so Shakespearean that, he recalled, he confused them with the bard's. After the Slade he went to mainland Europe and lived in Paris and elsewhere for several years. He called Paris his University. In 1909 he returned to London, his father's allowance having been discontinued, and began to try to make a living as a painter.

Ford Madox Hueffer (later Ford Madox Ford) published his stories in The *English Review*, and in London he met Pound, Hulme, Gaudier Brezska and other literary and graphic artists. In 1910 his first published poem, 'Grignolles (Brittany),' appeared in *The Tramp*. It is printed in a large typeface – fifty-two lines of painterly, colloquial quatrains, unlike anything else he wrote, untouched by satire, with a gaunt beauty about it:

Grignolles is a town grown bald
    With age; its blue naked crown
Of houses is barer than any hill,
    On its small hill; it is a grey town.

It was twenty-two years before Lewis's only 'collection' of poems, *One Way Song*, was published. Between these two events Lewis was inexhaustibly active. With Pound he established 'Vorticism' – a movement in painting and literature – and published *Blast*, a periodical which ran for two issues. After his sojourn in France, Lewis was well-acquainted with French painting and was perhaps the first English painter to understand the lessons of Cubism. In *Blast*, his and Pound's aim was to shake what they considered the conservative British into some recognition that art was in need of renewal from intellectual and experiential founts; that lazy sentimentality and hackneyed forms were inadequate to the mechanized age. Lewis was after an art that engaged the modern experience at all points. 'We stand for the Reality of the Present – not the sentimental Future or the sacripant Past,' the Vorticist manifesto proclaimed.

Lewis's main literary contribution to *Blast* was the Vorticist 'drama' – *The Enemy of the Stars*. It takes the form of an intellectual and physical combat, in a sort of heightened imagistic prose, between Hanp, a violent and dull-witted modern everyman figure, and Arghol, the reasoner, the imaginative intellectual, widely travelled and experienced. The conflict is clumsy and intense, with explosive stage directions. The battle prefigures the later, more achieved prose satire of *The Childermass* and *The Apes of God* and the verse satire of *One Way Song*. It is the battle of the artist, the man of integrity, in a world of consumers and sham artists. Hanp wants dreams, but Arghol holds up a mirror to him. Hanp murders Arghol, then commits suicide. In other words, society compromises or kills the artist, and in so doing kills itself.

Blast was the destructive phase of Lewis's work – an attempt to wipe the smug public-school grin off the face of the Academy, in effect to purge English art of introverted irony and renew extrovert wit. After he completed *Tarr*, his first novel, Lewis enlisted in 1917 and went to France, where he served for about seven months. He became an official War Artist for the Canadian War Records Office and his sketches, exhibited in 1919, were regarded as among the most original produced. They have the power of his writing: forceful and true to the endurance of men turned into instruments of war.

After the war, through magazines (*The Tyro* and *The Enemy*) and in a number of books, Lewis grew into the great satirist of his day, and into an original philosophical and political thinker. *The Art of Being Ruled*, his most important political work, appeared in 1926; *Time and Western Man*, a philosophical exploration of his obsessive theme, in 1927. His first major novel in the trilogy which came to be known as *The Human Age*, *The Childermass*, was published in 1928, and his devastating satire on the Sitwells and the literary coteries of the day, *The Apes of God*, struck London in 1930. Thus systematically Lewis made his position on politics, philosophy and society clear. In so doing he collected a large tribe of enemies, all eager for a pretext to attack him – including Roger Fry and the whole of Bloomsbury, the Royal Academy, Romantics, aesthetes, Sitwells, and others.

In the mid- to late-1920s poverty began for Lewis. It was to nag him for the rest of his life, later compounded by blindness. With the publication of *Hitler* in 1931, he reached the nadir of his fortunes. In 1932, suffering from studied neglect, he composed *One Way Song*. 'What has befallen me, or rather my books,' he wrote in *The Writer and the Absolute*, 'proves what is my contention: namely, that the mid-twentieth-century writer is only nominally free, and should not fail to acquire a thorough knowledge of the invisible frontiers surrounding his narrow patch of liberty, to transgress which might be fatal . . . Four or five hundred years ago it was the religious Absolute which was the writer's problem. Today it is the political Absolute.'

Throughout Lewis's work there is a distinction between what Goethe calls 'puppets' and 'natures' – those men who follow clockwork patterns and are entirely conditioned, cogs in the giant machine; and those who are unpredictable, intellectually alive, and creative. Lewis scorned the former, yet they are accommodated in his vision. His position was that of the man 'in the crowd but not of the crowd', the outsider and eventually the enemy. His art exalts space above time and rejects the historical man-centred art which had grown out of romanticism. Lewis was supremely interested in surfaces, the 'behavioural patterns and the ideas that drive the man-machine', as Robert Chapman says in his study of Lewis: the eye, the outside, space, as opposed to the ear, the inside, and time.

His fiction and poetry are a literature of ideas. 'We fight first on one side, then on the other, but always for the same cause,' Lewis wrote. *One Way Song* argues thus with itself, urging one idea, then a conflicting idea, with equal passion. C. H. Sisson calls it the 'most subtle piece of argumentation put into English verse in the twentieth century', and continues, 'He writes from a great fulness, but he is driving all the time into emptiness, or into "the boiling starry cold".'

Wyndham Lewis's didacticism is usually a sequence of questions, not answers. He is a teacher rather than an instructor. His teaching is, however, uncompromising. He rejects the 'dark' impulses and writing derived from the unleashing of the unconscious or the sham unconscious. Aware of the power of the unconscious, he feels its expression is finally subjective and uncommunicable. D. H. Lawrence was one of his *bêtes noires*.

Another important aspect of Lewis's writing, as of his painting, is his refusal to imitate the wholeness of nature. He breaks it up, shuffles the objects or ideas, juxtaposes them so they question or cancel one another out. Thus in fictional characterization he will focus on one aspect of character, fragmenting the whole, so that the data he gives serve as clauses in an overall idea or pattern. As I. A. Richards said, it is an art always sharply in focus, but the perspective changes continually, even bewilderingly. There is an analogy between his technique and Brecht's dramatic technique of *verfremdung*. We are not allowed to identify with character, with the human drama. Our attention is transferred on to the drama of ideas. There is, as Pound says, a 'hyper-daylight' trained on the ideas. Nothing in the poems is concealed. Structure is bared, with the syntactical inversions dictated by rhythm, the auxiliary verbs padding out a cadence, the forced rhymes, and the strongly colloquial speaking voice. Hugh Kenner called it 'rattle-trap verse'. The poetry is in the condensed nature of the statement and argument, the intensity of rhythm, and the surprising intricacy of its development.

His writing is never impersonal: there is always a defined speaker within the machine of the idea, making it work and showing how it works. He usually uses two voices, carrying on an argument which is not expository but exploratory. The dialogue may be between the teacher and the implicit objections of the class, or between the poet and the implicit objections of the reader. Lewis calls into being an imaginary reader, with whom he converses, anticipating this reader's objections. He seems to exchange and enlarge ideas with us. We are engaged in his dialogue.

One Way Song was originally to be called *The Song of the Fronts*. Lewis saw it as operating 'in a no-man's-land of my own making between prosody and prose'. It is in five sections. The first, 'Engine Fight Talk', suggests the immediacy of art and questions the poetry that is in love with history. The second, 'The Song of the Militant Romance', attacks the pseudo-romantics who breathe on the glass, who obscure the poem and believe they have made it profound. The third section, 'If So the Man You Are', is a confessional and devastatingly satirical account of his own fate at the hands of the literary KGB of his day, and a powerful evocation of the fatuity of bourgeois liberalism. The fourth part, 'One Way Song', sets up the mock-positive vision of the one-way artist, eyes for ever fixed on the future, never glancing to left or right, denying what is behind by ignoring it. The 'Envoy' which closes the sequence summarizes the themes and achieves an uncharacteristic apologetic tenderness. There is, however, nothing tentative about the poem. Its principal shortcoming is its unmitigated, aggressive masculinity. It is pugilistic satire.

The poem brings into the scope of its satire autobiography, literary, political and social orthodoxies and a variety of speaking voices. It compels thought and purges passivity.

Truth, plainly revealed, is the object of the satire. In *Men Without Art* Lewis wrote, 'We can . . . write *satire* for *art* – not the moralist satire directed at a given society, but a metaphysical satire occupied with mankind.'

In 'Engine Fight Talk' an instructor addresses an unruly class about the art of the new:

And I sketched them the Flying Scot –
proudest and bravest of trains—
In bold chalk outlines bodily, with black alphabet of smoke,
And I drew beside it the World, with grey chalk for where it rains,
And for where it's hottest, red. I looked up. Nobody spoke.

The drama is compelling. So, too, is the way in which mechanical imagery is used metaphorically: 'Slowly across my chest / I drew my strong serge walls', or later, 'I could see them biting their fingernails behind the breastwork of their cribs'. A timid student states the theme: can a time-bound art – the art of Shakespeare, Browne, or Pound – mean anything? The answer is no and yes. The teacher speaks of the *cleverness* of resorting to 'the sweetmeats of the ages, the bon-bons that are Fancy's bread'. This is what Arghol refused to do in *The Enemy of the Stars* – asked for a dream, he held up a truthful mirror.

The third poem, 'If So the Man You Are', provides a cumulative experience and is probably the peak of Lewis's verse writing. The man of integrity speaks, rejecting aestheticism, effeminacy, and other intellectual and social 'vices'. A long sequence of lines begins 'I'm not', followed by a sequence beginning, 'The man I am . . .' 'I am the man to shun Hamlet's soliloquy', he declares at the climax of the early part. The speaker is perversely out of step with fashion. He attacks the safety-in-numbers attitude of those who have effectively ostracized him. In the middle of the poem, The Enemy enters, '(cloaked, masked, booted, and with gauntlets of astrakhan)'. Lewis presents himself as his enemies saw him, 'a great professional Outcast of the Pen'. This is Mister Enemy who speaks eighteen of the thirty-four cantos of the section. He asks,

What is it that men fear beyond everything?
Obviously an open person. Bring
One of us 'truthful ones' too near, their nests
Would be unfeathered.

He is one of those 'whose tongues are clean'. There is considerable pathos in his self-satire:

All that I know is that my agents write
'Your Hitler book has harmed you' – in a night,
Somewhat like Byron – only I waken thus
To find myself not famous but infamous.

To punish him, 'unmentionability' has been invented 'as a new order of the Dead / Who yet exist . . .' The financial effects on his royalty earnings are grimly stated: 'Withhold from him all sources of supply / Infallibly that art-man comes to die.' The satire is most telling when he draws the analogy between the wars individuals wage against one another, or groups wage against individuals, and the wars nations visit upon each other's heads. The most vivid image in the poem, where laughter is impossible, evokes the consequences:

we know the invisible prison
Where men are jailed off – men of dangerous vision—
In the impalpable dark cages of neglect.

Cruelty and insensitivity are characteristic of the age: 'We are a little age, where the blind pygmy treads / In hypnotized crusades against all splendour.'

The fourth section, intellectually the most taxing, uses Swift's technique of *reductio ad absurdum*, and notes its debt to Swift. 'Creatures of Fronts we are – designed to bustle / Down paths lit by our eyes, on stilts of clockwork muscle . . .' Later he writes wryly,

A god in front, behind, a vacant lot,
A nomansland for trashbins, a nirvana:
But on your street-front sprouts a proud symbolic banana.

A great hypothetical philosophy is erected and dismantled. In the 'Envoy', he speaks his purpose finally:

These times require a tongue that naked goes,
Without more fuss than Dryden's or Defoe's.

T.E. Hulme (1883–1917)

I was bound
Motionless and faint of breath
By loveliness that is her own eunuch.

Thomas Ernest Hulme has earned himself an enigmatic reputation in modern poetry. T. S. Eliot described him as 'the author of two or three of the most beautiful short poems in the language'. Michael Roberts, the outstanding modern verse anthologist, admired his work and developed many of Hulme's ideas. But the modern reader will consider Hulme more in the light of his thought than of his poetry. The handful of poems Hulme wrote are indeed 'beautiful' in Eliot's sense, but though they amply illustrate Hulme's critical beliefs, they are peripheral, where his thought is central to any serious consideration of modern poetry.

He was born in 1883 at Gratton Hall, the family home, in Endon, Staffordshire. In 1901 he went up to Cambridge as a scholar to read Mathematics. In 1904 he was sent down suddenly for unspecified disturbances. He tried a course in Biology and Physics at University College, London, commuting to Cambridge to attend Philosophy lectures. Impatient of authority, he deserted this course as well and left England in 1906, taking a cargo boat to Canada. There he experienced on 'the flat spaces and wide horizons of the virgin-prairie of Western Canada' the 'necessity or inevitableness' of verse. He sensed the 'chasm' between man and God, 'the fright of the mind before the unknown'.

He returned to Europe in 1907 and studied in Brussels

with the philosophers Henri Bergson and Jules de Gaultier and the critic Remy de Gourmont. In 1908 he arrived back in London and founded the short-lived 'Poets' Club', a convivial discussion group. His next club did not have a name. It met at the Eiffel Tower Restaurant in Soho. There, in company with F. S. Flint, Edward Storer, Ezra Pound, and perhaps Wyndham Lewis, among others, he read out his poems, explaining his theory of the 'image' in poetry. His ideas were largely derivative – of Bergson, de Gourmont, de Gaultier, and others – but he was an enthusiastic assimilator and proseletyzer. In 1911 he published a series of essays on Bergson, and in 1912 the 'Complete Poetical Works of T. E. Hulme' were published in January in *New Age* and again in April as an appendix to Pound's collection, *Ripostes*. Hulme's actual collected poems – and there were only very few – were published in 1960 in A. R. Jones's *The Life and Opinions of T. E. Hulme*. As well as the poems and essays, Hulme published translations of Bergson and Sorel. *Speculations* and *Notes on Language and Style*, collections of fragments and notes, were published posthumously. He planned many further works before he fell in action in 1917.

Because he had not been academically trained in literature and his early interests were in mathematics, philosophy, and the sciences, Hulme was an outsider in the literary milieu he chose. It needed such an outsider to diagnose the infirmities of British poetry and to suggest remedies. He reacted most passionately against the facility of the nineties poets and the vapidity of much of the 'new' verse of the day. He and his friends began discussing Japanese tanka and haiku, *vers libre*, and 'poems in a sacred Hebrew form'. They countered prolixity with precise brevity, they refuted the vacuous rumblings of their contemporaries with the vivid whisper of the image. Flint recalled that much of the discussion was about the craft of poetry, that the French symbolists, notably Laforgue, influenced them. In essence, Hulme insisted on 'absolutely accurate representation and no verbiage'.

The international and historical models Hulme chose, and

his rejection of romanticism, were aspects of his wider beliefs. He, like Wyndham Lewis, rejected the man-centred world-view, and vehemently repudiated the principle of continuity. This principle is so prevalent a preconception, informs so many of our institutions and beliefs, that we tend to feel it describes reality, where in fact it is simply one way of conceptualizing it. We tend, because we are conditioned to believe in continuity, to draw back from the gaps and jumps in nature and between ourselves and nature. Hulme posits the *discontinuity* between various realms of thought, the possibility of creating new forms of relationship. The 'image' in this context means that things not normally related can be brought together into a significant relationship; that relationships independent of normal ideas of continuity and of logic can be resonant. This was perhaps the nature of the imagist revolution which Hulme catalysed, though he did not contribute to the Imagist anthologies or participate in their polemics. The Imagists stressed that poetry communicates metaphorically, not logically.

Hulme's programme was for a neo-classical poetry: free to make associations regardless of ideas of continuity; accurate and hard, intellectual, precise, and pessimistic, for man is small, an animal, and fallen. These beliefs converge and mature differently in Eliot and Lewis.

In a lecture in 1914 Hulme argued against metre in poetry. 'It enables people to write verse with no poetic inspiration, and whose mind [sic] is not stored with new images.' Metre is a facilitator, poetry is not a facile art. Metre and the rhetoric it implies can take over and puff out a poem, can indeed not only impose a lax diction but also deform ideas, if unskilfully handled. Hulme suggested that the unit of significance in the poem was not the word but the phrase or the sentence, and that the poet should consider the effect of the whole poem, not local felicities. *Vers libre* therefore had great attraction for him and his followers.

Hulme rejected romanticism largely because of its optimism and the belief in progress. He saw man as 'a fixed and limited animal whose nature is absolutely constant. It is only by tradition and organization that anything decent can be got out of him.' Thus, though temperamentally antagonistic to authority, Hulme suggested an authoritarian ethic. The new classical poet knows he is made of clay, physically and perceptually finite. 'He may jump, but he always returns back; he never flies away into the circumambient gas.'

Hulme reintroduced into English poetic thought distinctions he had learned from Bergson (and could have learned from Coleridge) between intellect and intuition. Intellect analyses and is the language of prose; but intuition, the language of poetry, places the artist 'back within the object by a kind of sympathy and breaking down . . . the barrier that space puts between him and his model.' The model, the object, is what the poet sets out to evoke in the image. Implicit in this is a rigorous suppression of the personality. And Pound's famous dictum, 'Make It New', comes from Hulme as well, who took from de Gourmont the idea that language is constantly nearing extinction, shedding its resonance, and must be regularly injected with a stock of new metaphors.

'Thought', says Hulme, 'is prior to language and consists in the simultaneous presentation of two different images.' This was Pound's definition of the image: 'that which presents an intellectual and emotional complex in an instant of time'. It was not a new idea, but it had not before been made the basis of a doctrinaire poetics. It had been regarded before as simply one aspect of the complex thing men call poetry. Coleridge had defined it in the *Biographia Literaria*. 'It has been observed before,' he wrote, 'that images, however beautiful, though faithfully copied from nature, and as accurately represented in words, do not of themselves characterize the poet. They become proof of original genius only as far as they are modified by a predominant passion; *or when they have the effect of reducing multitude to unity, or succession to an instant*; or lastly, when a human and intellectual life is transferred to them from the poet's own spirit' (my italics). Despite the romanticism implicit in Coleridge's statement, it defines better than Hulme or Pound could both what an image isn't and what it is, what it cannot do and what it can. Coleridge's definition comes in a broader consideration of the language and scope of poetry than Hulme envisaged. It was not prescriptive or programmatic but deductive from the best examples Coleridge had available. The fact that Hulme's and Pound's teaching started a *school* of poets reveals how some of the outstanding creative critics of poetry in our century have lost the wide perspective Coleridge possessed, have been reduced by metaphysical doubt and innate pessimism to programmatic reform, prescriptive orthodoxy. Pound escaped from it – his art extended his theories. But Hulme was killed in 1917.

Hulme's poems 'Autumn' and 'City Sunset', both published in 1909, have the distinction of being the first Imagist poems. 'Autumn' is the better of the two:

A touch of cold in the Autumn night—
I walked abroad
And saw the ruddy moon lean over a hedge
Like a red-faced farmer.
I did not stop to speak, but nodded,
And round about were the wistful stars
With white faces like town children.

The poem is one of observation; but the two images are fused: the sky-scape and the human faces. The moon becomes a farmer, the stars *town* children. The poem both humanizes the sky-scape and etherializes the landscape.

In 'Images' one of the poems reads, 'Old houses were scaffolding once and workmen whistling.' It juxtaposes two aspects of the same thing, past and present, and the effect is more resonant than much strictly Imagist poetry because it has a time context, it does not exist (as the earlier poem does) in a perpetual present. William Empson wrote that Imagist poetry is poetry that has lost the use of its legs – it does not move, it does not generally evoke time sequence, existing only in space. This is one way in which it rejects continuity. It is a poetry committed to the image, not to the context of the image. It has no conscience beyond artistic perfection.

Hulme escapes Empson's stricture occasionally, when he tries to humanize, or belittle, nature. In these poems we feel he is perhaps less than true to his doctrines. 'The Man in the Crow's Nest' is one such poem:

Strange to me, sounds the wind that blows
By the masthead, in the lonely night.
Maybe 'tis the sea whistling – feigning joy
To hide its fright
Like a village boy
That trembling past the churchyard goes.

As in 'Autumn', nature is brought down a peg or two. The poem possesses a quiet, dramatic eeriness, partly due to the rhymes. Its syntactical precision is impressive, and when the poet speaks, in the last line, of the boy as 'that' rather than 'who', he effects a subtle depersonalizing even there.

D.H. Lawrence (1885–1930)

What have we lost in the west?
We who have gone west?
There is no answer.

D. H. Lawrence was the only poet who contributed poems
to the Georgian anthologies edited by Edward Marsh *and* to
the Imagist anthologies edited by Amy Lowell. In his early
writing, two different voices could be heard. One, dramatic,
tending to narrative and interposing moral comments, was
effectively Georgian, though its presence in Marsh's staid
anthologies highlights the passion of Lawrence's apprentice
work. 'Seven Seals' and 'Snake' which Marsh included,
were the closest he came to publishing erotic verse.

The poems chosen for the Imagist anthologies were terse,
direct images, presented without moralizing. 'Green' appeared in 1915:

The sky was apple-green.
The sky was green wine held up in the sun.
The moon was a golden petal between.

In another poem Lawrence wrote, 'The street-lamps in the
twilight have suddenly started to bleed.' His confidence in
the power of the clear image to convey his emotion grew as
he moved away from a received formal style he mastered
only crudely towards a more personal and sometimes vatic
idiom.

It is interesting to trace the development through the

Collected Poems. In effect, it is the gradual evolution of a personal voice, regardless of traditional forms, determined more by certain emotional and intellectual predispositions which came to dominate his writing. The germ of his mature style is present from the outset: he develops by disencumbering himself, and some of his best poems were achieved in the period just before his formal emancipation was complete. He was able to emancipate himself largely because poetic theory and poetic precedent held little authority over him. The present emotion had to find its own form, each image required unique articulation.

David Herbert Lawrence was born in Eastwood, Nottingham, in 1885, the fourth child in his family. His father was a coal miner, his mother a former school teacher who came to despise her often drunk, sometimes uncouth husband. The tension between his parents is evoked in the poem 'Discord in Childhood': 'Outside the house an ash-tree hung its terrible whips.' Inside, the disputing voices rose and fell. Lawrence founded his emotional security in his mother, and their relationship proved emotionally ambiguous for him, inhibiting his later relationships with women. His background was full of contradictions: between his father's resolute working-class attitudes and his mother's hankering after middle-class values; between the rural and industrial landscapes that coexisted around him; and the sexual and moral obligations which often seemed – in those early years – at odds. A further complication in his childhood was the diagnosis of a lung infection which – in 1930 – was to kill him.

From local council school he gained a scholarship to attend Nottingham High School. At the age of sixteen he began work as a clerk in a surgical appliances firm at 13s a week. He soon left to become a pupil teacher in Eastwood and later in Ilkeston. At eighteen, he went to University College, Nottingham. Afterwards he taught school uncommittedly until 1912, principally in Croydon, Surrey. 'How can I answer the challenge of so many eyes?' he asks in one poem. Teaching pupils who evinced little desire to learn irked him, and the situation led to emotional strain. The death of his mother in 1910 – after which he wrote some elegies, including 'Sorrow', 'Brooding Grief' and, in a different vein, 'Piano', left him worn out and near despair.

In 1911 his literary career began to take shape. A friend sent some of his stories to Ford Madox Hueffer who included them in the *English Review* and handed on his first novel, *The White Peacock*, to Messrs Heinemann, who undertook to publish it. It duly appeared, and in 1912 Lawrence gave up teaching and travelled abroad for the first time.

Though he had written a number of poems, primarily in rhyming forms, the style was far from mature. The early work is full of abstractions, forced rhymes and weak auxiliaries. Some of the poems are obsessed with mere physicality. 'Virgin Youth', for instance, a poem which he later revised to accent the erotic element, is a hymn to frustration. Frustration is a dominant theme, reflected unintentionally in the flawed and frustrated forms. 'Monologue of a Mother', 'Cherry Robbers', and other poems of the period are tentative in expression, if not in content. The power of the early poems was in the evocative imagery, the painterly vision. There is an adolescence about much of the early writing, a quality that did not disappear – indeed, in *Nettles* (1929) and in many other late poems there is an immaturity of sentiment and thought, an occasional pettiness, entirely contradictory to the very last poems and the animal and flower poems.

His self-discovery and fulfilment involved Lawrence in running away with Frieda von Richthofen, the wife of a distinguished Nottingham professor, in 1914. Together they travelled widely, and though their relationship was turbulent, it was sustaining. Had it not been, Lawrence would hardly have braved the difficult years that followed. His novel *The Rainbow* was confiscated and banned, and in the same year he was forced with Frieda to leave their home in Cornwall. They were thought to be German spies. Lawrence began to feel persecuted. These pressures contributed to the development of his least successful poetic veins: satire and apocalypse.

After the First World War, Lawrence travelled widely, writing travel books, reviews, introductions, novels, and poems, and painting. He went to Italy, Australia, New Zealand, the South Seas, California, Mexico, and New Mexico. In 1926 he was back in Italy, and he spent his last four years travelling through Europe trying to retard the progress of his tuberculosis. He died in a sanatorium in Vance, in the south of France.

Lawrence's achievement as a poet is overshadowed by his achievement as a novelist. His poems explore some of the themes of his prose fiction, but where the novels concentrate on relationships between people, the poems look into the relationship of the individual and the given world and into those states of mind which exist, subjectively, apart from relationship. The poems complement the fiction.

There are, however, at the outset, a number of love poems. His first collection, *Love Poems and Others* (1913), explores his relationship with his mother, with his first love, and his second. They were written guiltily, 'as if it were a secret sin', because they were autobiographical. He distinguishes between two sorts of poems: those written by his 'demon' and those composed by a more conscious hand. He will tamper with the latter, clarifying them later in life. But the former are final and irrevocable.

In 1913 Lawrence wrote to Edward Marsh that he saw his poems in spatial rather than temporal or rhythmic terms, more 'as a matter of movements in space than footsteps hitting the earth'. The poems worked free from prescriptive metres and followed first conversational rhythm and later a Biblical or incantatory rhythm which Whitman's example helped him to achieve. 'It all depends on the *pause*,' he wrote to Marsh, 'the lingering of the voice according to feeling – it is the hidden *emotional* pattern that makes poetry, not the obvious form.' From the outset he eschewed the traditional Georgian sense of balance and rhythm. He neither depersonalized nor de-fused experience, in the Imagist manner.

Later he called for a poetry of 'the immediate present',

where 'there is no perfection, no consummation, nothing finished', an open-ended poetry. The word 'consummation' is illuminating, suggesting that his poems build towards a deferred climax. He acknowledges Whitman as the master poet of the 'present', a writer whose poem has neither beginning nor end – and this, Lawrence reminds us, does not imply that he has no past or future. The voice of the 'present' tends to be rhapsodic, celebrating 'the urgent, insurgent Now', the 'instant present'.

Free verse is essential, in Lawrence's view, to poetic utterance. A poetry without preconceived metre, stress patterns or syllable count, which is articulated by 'the whole man', expressing his passions, conflicts, and contradictions is the voice of integrity. Lawrence does not see free verse as finally *un*free because ultimately subjective in the way he uses it. Subjectivity, the wilful ascription of significance to certain words, images or rhythms, is his principal limitation.

But the undeniable strength of achieved free verse is that the poet cannot trust traditional poetic diction. He must slough clichés and develop a fresh language, find new wine for new bottles. Lawrence tells us that in free verse 'we look for the insurgent naked throb of the instant moment'. And we are to expect 'no satisfying stability, satisfying to those who like the immutable'. The 'pure present' is a realm, he says, we have never conquered. And he, too, fails to conquer it, for there *is* a stability in his poems – certainly not 'satisfying' much of the times. It is not merely the stability of the moralist who often asserts meanings. It is also a stability of language, a predictability of rhythmic phrasing within a poem.

In a way, like Blake, Lawrence has pre-empted his readers' misgivings by acknowledging all the faults in his writing and classing them as necessary virtues. The poet James Reeves writes of Lawrence, 'He had not the craftsman's sense of words as living things, as ends in themselves. Words were too much means to an end.' And so they were. Lawrence would have said, 'so they should be'. In his perceptive study, Reeves adds, 'He can seldom have conceived a poem as a whole before he sat down to write it. It grew under his pen.' There is an analogy between the form of some of his poems and 'the musical impromptu', a 'series of loosely connected variations'. Even the recurrent formal flaws Lawrence would have presented as virtues.

The famous *Pansies* (1928) – Lawrence once referred to them as 'rag-poems' – are named after the flower, but the title contains too the implication of *pensées anglicées*. The verb *panser* comes to the poet's mind as well, 'to dress or soothe a wound'. Each 'pansy' is 'a true thought, which comes as much from the heart and genitals as from the head'. *Pansies* are the closest Lawrence came to developing his own form. That it is inadequate to all but the statement of an image or an opinion – without the compression or memorability of an epigram, though it claims the authority of that form – implies the limitations of his formal imagination in verse. But when he allows the image to shape the form, as in the animal poems, or when he lets the rhythm take hold, as in 'The Ship of Death', questions of form become irrelevant.

The precision he briefly learned from imagism makes a poem such as 'Baby Running Barefoot' powerful, keeping it free of sentimentality and cliché. But he could write such Georgian waffle as, 'The first white love of youth, passionless and in vain'. We know he was alluding to real experience, described more fully in *Sons and Lovers*. But he is encumbered by a hackneyed diction. The authenticity of the emotion does not guarantee the poetry. It was in 'Snap Dragon', a poem about the same experiences, that he suggested the latent powers that later matured in the animal poems and the poems of death. 'Snap Dragon' is technically marred. Its loosely rhyming form demands that the poet interpose numerous 'did' auxiliaries to plump out the measure; and he forces the rhyme. Yet the flaws accent a tone of tentative innocence. Something of the quality of 'Snap Dragon', with its troubling eroticism, carries over into the other love poems, particularly the imagist 'On the Balcony' and the Georgian 'A Youth Mowing'.

He wrote a number of political poems. In 'Now It's

Happened', with considerable political and poetic naïvety, he chastises the Russian Revolution, its betrayal of the great Russian artists of the last century. In 'Hibiscus and Salvia Flowers' he chides left-wing demonstrators in Sicily, ostensibly because they pluck beautiful flowers and plug them in their churlish button-holes, but also because he despises egalitarianism, the despotism of the crowd.

In the animal poems he finds natural forms in his free verse – forms that answer the images. 'The Mosquito' erratically alternates long and short lines, attacks and retires. The same process occurs in 'Bat', and in 'Snake' the sinuous and the darting lines complement one another.

'Snake' explores the experience of a man finding himself guilty of the Fall, attempting to kill the dark angel, the serpent, visiting his water trough, suggesting in its movements, shading, and self-contained confidence another world. Lawrence, with the animals, would step into their world – with the snake he does not manage to, but later, in his best poem, 'Bavarian Gentians', he does enter the dark, promised world. In 'Snake' he observes fascinated, attacks, and then laments. The snake, as an image, hovers between reptilian, human and divine. For a moment its drinking reminds him of a cow drinking, but it ascends by stages to be god-like. As the snake unfolds its meanings, the man reveals himself in the terms he applies to it, and eventually in his instinctive response to it and its withdrawal into the 'dreadful', the 'horrid black hole'. As he hurls the log of wood, the snake reverts to being snake; the man becomes that limited victim of the Fall:

And so I missed my chance with one of the lords
Of life.
And I have something to expiate;
A pettiness.

The completely colloquial humour in the animal poems further recommends them. In 'Tortoise Family Connections' the baby tortoise is portrayed:

Wandering in the slow triumph of his own existence,
Ringing the soundless bell of his presence in chaos,
And biting the frail grass arrogantly,
Decidedly arrogantly.

In a prose passage Lawrence writes, 'Man cannot live in chaos. The animal can. To the animal all is chaos, only there are a few recurring motions and aspects within the surge.' He presses back towards chaos, to subject himself to the animals' element. The outstanding artist, he urges, will see things *in* chaos.

'The Ship of Death' braves the dark and unknown. It is one of a number of dark poems. The images he calls up are suspended, isolated, within a powerful cadence like an incantation. Unlike most of Lawrence's poems, 'The Ship of Death' is memorable in its actual phrases. 'We Have Gone Too Far' is in the same vein – it has a cadential intensity, like rhapsodic keening and – triumphantly – celebration. This is the world of 'Bavarian Gentians', where the flowers radiate darkness as a torch does light. The poet does not draw back but embraces the experience wholeheartedly, and to powerful effect.

Lawrence's poetry raises more questions – about the nature of poetic form and diction, the relationship of poet and poem, and poetic integrity – than it answers. It has a wide range, a flawed magnificence. The adolescent attitudes which dominate his didactic poems, the small-mindedness of some of his satires, are balanced by the insight and accuracy of the animal poems, the intensity of some of the love poems, and the relentless power of the poems of death.

Edwin Muir (1887–1959)

All things grown
Homeless and whole

Muir's poetry is characterized by its verbal restraint, the economy of vocabulary, the sparsity of imagery, and its narrow technical range. Muir rejected the felicitous style that draws attention to surface effects, distracting the reader from what it says on to how it says it. He did not seek to charm. He excluded even verbal wit from his technical armoury. The poems are without pretence and generally without humour. Images, myths, and a matrix of central themes recur, giving his whole work a strict unity despite its technical development. We read repeatedly of the road, the journey, the labyrinth, Time and the returns it brings, of characters from Arthurian romance, classical legend, the Bible, and elsewhere. Despite his restricted range, Muir has come to be regarded – with MacDiarmid – as the outstanding Scottish poet of the first half of this century.

Born in the Orkneys in 1887 into the family of a tenant farmer, his early childhood haunted his later life. The community he lived in was not competitive. In its patterns and concerns it was untouched by the modern world. In his *Autobiography* (1954), an outstanding book that illuminates the poetry, he writes, 'The Orkney I was born into was a place where there was no great distinction between the ordinary and the fabulous; the lives of living men turned into legend.' It was an informing memory to Muir. In 'The Myth', he wrote,

My childhood all a myth
Enacted in a distant isle;
Time with his hourglass and his scythe
Stood dreaming on the dial.

The bucolic idyll was soon shattered.

My youth a tragi-comedy,
Ridiculous war of dreams and shames
Waged for a Pyrrhic victory
Of reveries and names . . .

His father was evicted from his tenancy and the family
moved to the slums of Glasgow. By the time Muir was nineteen, his father, mother, and two of his brothers were dead.
The losses and hardship of the new life contrasted painfully
with his Orkney childhood. It took him years to fit the two
halves of his early life together.

Working at menial clerical tasks, he gradually educated
himself – thoroughly, learning about Scottish, English and
German literature and philosophy. In 1918, he published
his first book, *We Moderns*, a collection of epigrams, aphorisms, and brief essays, cruelly satirical and totally unlike his
later work. This and another book, written under the spell
of Nietzsche and relating to his political concerns, were false
starts for the future poet.

When he married Willa Anderson in 1919, he was not yet
a poet. But his reading of the German poet Heinrich Heine's
balladic satires and of Scottish ballads helped him in the
writing of his collection *First Poems* (1925), published by the
Hogarth Press when he was thirty-eight. Muir was never a
young poet. Two of his ballads were in Scots, to which he
returned infrequently in later years.

In London, he earned his living as a reviewer and translator. In later years, with his wife, he translated Kafka's
novels among many other projects. He worked for the
British Council in Edinburgh during the War, and afterwards in Prague (1945–8) and Rome (1948–50), where his
poetic vision matured. Later he became the head of an adult

education college near Edinburgh, and was Charles Eliot Norton Professor for a year at Harvard. His writings include a biography of John Knox, critical work, the *Autobiography*, poems and translations. He died in 1959.

The central event in Muir's mythology is the Fall, re-enacted in his own life, when his family left the Orkneys for Glasgow. In the poem 'The Fall' he cannot remember the earlier world. Time is to blame. Though he is fallen and deprived, Muir does not seem to accept *moral* implication in the Fall. It is something that happened to him, not the result of choice or an aspect of his Adamic nature. Hence it seems to be a Knocking Down rather than a Fall, and the religious implications of his writing are complicated by this attitude. 'I build me Heaven and Hell,' he writes, 'to buy my bartered Paradise.' To reclaim imaginatively and morally what is past, he must artificially create dramatic paradoxes. Muir chooses his myth for the form it will give to his own experience – in order to generalize the subjective. But when he takes a myth, he does not take it whole – he borrows only those aspects which answer to his needs. There is no key to his myths, they are not open to allegorical interpretation. This is the Kafkaesque element in all his mythography. The effect of Kafka may be felt in poems such as 'The Interrogation' and 'The Border', poems which seem to demand explanation but are finally inscrutable, unparaphrasable.

The brutal discontinuity in his early life led to emotional tensions, and he underwent psychoanalysis. In 'The Journey Back' he writes, 'Seek your beginnings, learn from whence you came / And know the various earth of which you are made.' This poem in seven parts is among his most original pieces, sustained throughout despite technical flaws, including a certain prolixity. The sections are in different forms, seven aspects of the process of untying the past, which includes the death of the 'self'. Many of Muir's poems take the journey back. In 'The Transfiguration' the Christian myth is lived in reverse, un-lived, left undone. The same process occurs in 'The Stationary Journey' and, less subtly, in 'The Unfamiliar Place'. The return is a 'journey', the 'journey' is a metaphor for the life of man. The basic questions are simple: what are our origins, our destinations, and – in the later poems – how can we coexist. The journey is more pilgrimage than quest, requiring faith and hope without a firm object, until the later poems when the Christian myth is irresolutely accepted without the trappings of dogma. Fable and legend are archetypal, underlying all our experiences, sharing a common reality. Our actions are re-enactments, and this platonic notion was affirmed in 'I Have Been Taught', probably his last poem:

And now the time grows shorter, I perceive
That Plato's is the truest poetry,
And that these shadows
Are cast by the true.

From the *Collected Poems* which he edited shortly before his death Muir omitted all those – including some of his last and best – which could be considered devotional Christian poems. He never accepted fully a solving dogma, though he adopted what he could of faith. In the Crucifixion and Resurrection he perceived the only possible solution to the terrible pattern of recurrences which obsessed him. He was nearly sixty before he purged himself of the terror that there might exist 'no crack or chink, no escape from Time'. During his stay in Rome he emerged from the labyrinth of the 'common dream'. 'The Labyrinth' celebrates his emergence, out of the maze of temporal phenomena. The 'real world' is Platonic, visionary, with purpose, contrasted to this world, the apparently inescapable labyrinth. Only in a dream did he approach the 'real world' – and only once – but that illumination was sufficient to assure him it existed. 'One Foot in Eden' is pervaded by the transfiguring vision.

The Platonic vision corresponded with his Orkney experience: there the literal world and the world of signs coexisted. Despite the subjectivity of Muir's quest, by his own terms the poems are objective accounts. If all experience is recurrent, the expression of even the most subjective process in mythologized terms has its objective application. Muir's vision of inevitable recurrence makes his poetic task one of comprehension and acceptance.

Muir never developed complete technical confidence. Wordsworth exercised a strong influence over his early work and may have retarded Muir's finding his own voice. Muir's debt to him is linguistic, thematic and philosophical, for Wordsworth, too, in 'the stationary blasts of waterfalls', for example, perceived the constant static forms and the fluid content. But Muir has none of Wordsworth's experiential particularity. His moods seem to precede the poem – not to emanate from an experience but to go in search of a structure to convey them. Muir's poetry is sparse in particular imagery.

Through his adaptation of myths, Muir escaped Wordsworth's influence. Yeats stepped into Wordsworth's place, and from Yeats Muir never fully escaped. 'Reading in Wartime' is a thirty-nine line single sentence poem, resonant with Yeats, not Muir. It fails because it lacks compression, the big sentence falls into smaller sentences, the syntax is arbitrary. Even Muir's last poem, 'I Have Been Taught', bears the impress of Yeats. The influence was verbal – Yeats's rhetoric was irresistible, though Muir disliked Yeats's wilfulness, his intellectual mysticism, illogicality, and the arbitrariness of his systems. In the end Muir is engaged by reality, however obliquely he may come at it. He is incapable of aestheticism. His poems excavate and unveil. He wrestled with Yeats's theme of time, but in his own terms, and resolved recurrence finally in apocalypse.

Mythologizing had its dangers. Once Muir started, he could not get away from myth. Myth tends to simplify rather than clarify moral problems, and in his best poems Muir presents complex experience through revised myth. Some critics see Muir's mythologizing as 'refracting' experience, refusing to engage it directly. But Muir is interested in the general forms underlying experience. Many of his titles are introduced by the definite article – 'The Myth', 'The Fall', and so on, at once particularizing and making archetypal the image, symbol, or myth. Muir feels he is engaging experience at the deepest level, not evading it. He has trouble, however, in the later poems rendering the terrible experience of nuclear holocaust. No myth will accommodate it. In 'The Day before the Last Day' he reflects before the event on what will occur – unsuccessfully.

The reason may be that, in Edwin Morgan's words, 'What Muir felt most deeply and expressed most movingly was the sense of aftermath.' In his dramatic monologues his model is Tennyson, not Browning. We do not enter the poem in mid-activity; the speaker speaks *after* the event. Muir's first experiment in dramatic monologue was the 'Chorus of the Newly Dead' (1926), a poem he rejected from his *Collected Poems*. The 'chorus' of voices speaks from conflicting points of view, aspects of Muir's own early indecision, and tries – without success – to externalize his tensions. His later monologues are less stylized.

From the earliest ballads the argument is Time. In 'The Mountain' he writes, 'If I could / I'd leap time's bound and turn and hide / From time in my ancestral wood.' Since evasion won't work, he considers escaping to the future. 'Double delusion!' He must begin from experience in Time. The outstanding early 'Ballad of Hector in Hades' dramatizes a childhood experience, of being chased in complete terror. Here the myth works, and Muir evokes the fleeing warrior and his trailing spear with vivid points of detail and psychological realism: in panic, certain details impress themselves unforgettably on the memory. In other early poems myth desiccates and stylizes the experience. The impersonality can seem sterile. But in a poem such as 'Horses', starting from the real animals, Muir's leap into myth seems inevitable. 'Those lumbering horses' embody myth, 'The furrows rolled behind like struggling snakes.'

Poetic argument comes alive, too, in the internal debate of 'Variations on a Time Theme'. The tension between the continuous and the apparently discontinuous personality, between indifference and commitment, is developed. In 'Troy' he achieves a dramatic mythological poem. An old warrior, who has survived in the sewers of the destroyed city, fighting against the rats, is dragged out by robbers. He witnesses the aftermath:

> Troy like a burial ground
> With tumbled walls for tombs, the smooth sward wrinkled
> As Time's last wave had long since passed away.

The old man is tortured for information he cannot give, then killed.

Muir is one of the few modern poets whose abstractions carry authority. In 'The Human Fold', for instance, his meanings are elusive, but we feel the sense of the abstract words: they adhere to the allusions, are implicit in the legendary matter, or in the religious matter of the later poems. 'What I shall never know / I must make known,' he writes. He is a poet of recapitulation who finds universal analogies between great and small, between common experience and his own experience. 'The Late Wasp' is a fine example of this. The poet is visited at his breakfast table each morning by a wasp. As the year draws on, the creature becomes emblematic – in its fate – of the general fate:

You and the earth have now grown older,
And your blue thoroughfares have felt the change;
They have grown colder;
And it is strange
How the familiar avenues of the air
Crumble now, crumble; the good air will not hold,
All cracked and perished with the cold;
And down you dive through nothing and through despair.

Edith Sitwell (1887–1964)

Man must say farewells
To parents now,
And to William Tell
And Mrs Cow . . .

Edith Sitwell was born in Scarborough, Yorkshire, in 1887,
the eldest child and only daughter of the eccentric Sir
George Sitwell – a baronet of long pedigree – and Lady Ida.
Sir George was a less than sympathetic father; and Lady Ida
was by no means enthusiastic about her daughter's curious
beauty or her lack of taste for convention. Edith Sitwell
inherited her father's eccentricity. One of her best prose
books is about *The English Eccentrics* (1933). She also inherited her mother's pride. For one who flouted convention,
she managed to surround herself in later years with various
ceremonies rigorously observed, exchanging social convention for strict laws of decorum that whim and a sense of self-
importance dictated.

  She and her brothers Osbert and Sacheverell relished
their childhood holidays at Renishaw Hall in Derbyshire.
'Colonel Fantock' celebrates those periods:

  Dagobert and Peregrine and I
Were children then; we walked like shy gazelles
Among the music of the thin flower-bells.

The poem is 'beautiful' in the poised romantic aestheticism
of her early manner, evocative and careful in its sound

qualities, outlandish in its delineation of character. The poet confesses, 'I always was a little outside life.' She also stresses her brothers' and her own uniqueness: 'We all have the remote air of legend.' The holidays gave her 'a taste for the grand and picturesque'.

Educated – in her words – 'in secrecy', she had the good fortune to have a governess with an unconventional taste for Rimbaud and the French Symbolist poets. She read them closely, adopting from them the idea of 'synaesthesia' or 'transmutation' in poetic imagery, presenting things seen in terms of smell or taste, sounds in terms of colour, inter-changing the senses.

In 1914, Edith, aged twenty-seven, descended on London. There she spent much of the remainder of her life until her death in 1964. There, too, in 1916 she edited and published *Wheels* – an *avant garde* periodical whose aim was to startle the bourgeoisie, and more generally to prompt a recon-sideration of the diction and scope of poetry. Her attacks on philistinism and conservatism were implicitly revolutionary, but they were waged from the palace and not from the slums. She was then, and she remained, a thoroughly aristocratic Bolshevik.

In 1924 *The Sleeping Beauty*, an autobiographical sequence of poems, appeared. It was in this year too that Edith Sitwell's most popular poems – the *Façade* sequence (1922) – were set to music by William Walton in one of the most apt marriages of words and music in this century. Many readers find *Façade* Edith Sitwell's outstanding contribution to modern poetry – rhythmically and verbally inventive, full of humour and complex intellectual passion.

With *Gold Coast Customs* (1929), she moved away from her playful aestheticism and, in satirical terms, commenced her denunciation of the corrupt, frivolous Mayfair life, juxta-posing it with the savage rites of West African tribes. Her long interweaving of polite society's and cannibals' customs, where Lady Bamburgher is her satirical butt, is impres-sionistic and imprecise. There are moments of near felicity:

But Lady Bamburgher's Shrunken Head,
Slum hovel, is full of the rat-eaten bones
Of a fashionable god that lived not
Ever, but still has bones to rot...

But the rhymes are painfully – not effectively – forced. Her 'virtuosity', which she calls attention to in her self-criticism, is here in abeyance. This is poetry in the grand manner without intellectual or technical distinction. Anthropological naïvety is only one of its faults. It ends in revolutionary prognostication:

Yet the time will come
To the heart's dark slum
When the rich man's gold and the rich man's wheat
Will grow in the street, that the starved may eat;—
And the sea of the rich will give up its dead—
And the last blood and fire from my side will be shed.
For the fires of God go marching on.

The language is wrenched into service. The Christ-pose the poet assumes in the penultimate line, and the banality of the last, further weaken the poem. It marks the end of her experimental period.

Gold Coast Customs was followed by ten years' poetic silence. Financial hardship, the necessity to write prose and to care for a dying friend, kept her from the Muse. She wrote many prose volumes, notably a study of Pope that marked the beginning of a serious reassessment of his work. Her prose is always rapid, engaging, careless, and she draws unashamedly – sometimes word for word – from the work of other writers.

After ten years' hardship she returned to verse. The later poems are no longer experimental. Some – notably 'Invocation' – are extraordinarily elegant. The themes of age and waiting are developed – and the theme of suffering caused by evil. The conflict between Good and Evil is schematically developed. During the Second World War she became a significantly social, if not a political, poet, capturing in 'Still Falls the Rain' the anguish and the recurrence of anguish, man's suffering at man's hands, in a skilfully developed framework of religious imagery and in a Biblical cadence. The poem has a condensation rare in her later poetry. It is marred by one of her mannerisms. She adopts a line from Marlowe's *Doctor Faustus*. It intrudes, wrecking the rhythm. In 'Serenade: Any Man to Any Woman' she brings Raleigh's and Marlowe's most famous poems into play in a wryly and superficially developed Second World War setting: 'Then die with me and be my love: / The grave shall be our shady grove.' Literary influences show clearly in the later poems. 'The Swans' and 'A Bird's Song' reflect in organization – unfortunately, as it happens – the ending of Yeats's 'Among School Children'; 'The Poet Laments the Coming of Age' echoes Yeats's 'Byzantium'. She attains none of his formal subtlety.

The dropping of the first Atomic Bomb turned Edith Sitwell into an apocalyptic poet *par excellence*. With 'Three Poems of the Atomic Bomb' the evil myth of human apocalypse unites with her religious vision. She becomes prophetic, but a prophecy strangely lacking in particulars, chilly and inhuman. Dust, sun and wind, three elements in all her verse, come into triumphant sway. What is lacking from her later verse is the fine humour which tempered the experimental aestheticism of the early poems. In the *Façade* poems particularly, as Louis Untermeyer wrote, 'there has rarely been so brilliant an exhibition of verbal legerdemain'. But contempt and anger overtook nostalgia; rhetoric swamped the poetry, in the later work.

In *Façade* and poems written at the time, the particular eye and emotion give the quality to what they observe. Moreover the rhythms, based as they often are on dance tunes or rhythms, are novel and unexpected. In 'Some Notes on my Poetry' – more a defence than an essay – she tells us that she rebelled against the 'rhythmical flaccidity, the verbal deadness, the dead and expected patterns'. Rhythm was to her 'one of the principal translators between dream and reality'. The *Façade* poems are '*abstract* poems – that is, they are patterns of sound'. But as Jack Lindsay, her most eloquent critic, has demonstrated, each poem has a consistent 'plot' and organization. The apparent nonsense is illusory. Edith Sitwell, borrowing a phrase from Cocteau, best describes the *Façade* poems as 'the poetry of childhood overtaken by the technician'. Full of verbal innocence and novelty, they are also poems of scrupulous craft.

Sadly, she ceased experimenting and discarded her poetic sense of humour. Her effort to confront the 'discord and contradiction in our world – but not to stay at the point of frustration', as Lindsay puts it, resulted in a subjective idiom striking for its apparent vacuity. Her attempt to get at the common symbols of a pre-Industrial age is essentially romantic. She has some of the quirks of Blake in his visions. But when in *Gold Coast Customs* and afterwards she confronts social issues in her version of a naked language, we get strident rhetoric. We are perhaps justified in retreating again to *Façade*.

There we find Midas and Apollo, the physical world and the world of light, witches, natural phenomena expressed as animal motions: 'Grey as a guinea fowl is the rain / Squawking down from the boughs again.' The image is contrived, but witty. Other images work better: 'The trees were hissing like green geese' or 'The leaves that like asses' ears hung on the trees'. The tension in the early poems is between the glimpsed, romantic world where dreams come true, the nightmare world, and the workaday world where dream and nightmare go off into daylight. The poems occur in the shadow of the big house and are inhabited by chambermaids, governesses, princesses. There is always the air of an opulent nursery ventilating them. The buildings in the poems are often stately, and they have their marionettes and ghosts. 'The rooms are vast as sleep within.' There are black people wishing to be white or simply contrasting with white people. There are sailors. Intersecting the real world is the world of nymphs and satyrs.

Façade is a language made for music. It is hard to read the poems without hearing Walton's settings. Some of the poems are supple, with unsentimental tenderness – particularly

'Jodelling Song', with its wide range of reference. It is about the end of childhood, heroism, fantasy. The dance poems recall Hilaire Belloc's 'Tarantella' – but they are, as she indicates, abstract, thoroughly original, while his poem is innovative only in rhythm. The unity of the *Façade* poems is not logical but rhythmical. Sometimes the poems enter the world of irresistible nonsense:

Don Pasquito, the road is eloping
With your luggage, though heavy and large;
You must follow and leave your moping
Bride to my guidance and charge!

Circumstance, commitment, conscience overtook the early style. She rejected what she must have seen as the irresponsibility of the work. Yet it is not unmitigated humour. The poems have often a deeply disturbing burden, a message more durable than that of her later rhetorical style.

Elizabeth Daryush (1887–1977)

These grew,
these vines, I know not how, though upward ...

Elizabeth Daryush has been forcefully championed for her
originality as a poet, but little read in England. Yvor
Winters, the American poet and critic, referred to her as 'one
of the few distinguished poets of our century and a poet who
can take her place without apology in the company of
Campion and Herrick'. Roy Fuller described her as 'a
pioneer technical innovator, whose work demands study by
poets and readers on this account alone. Further ... she is a
poet of the highest dedication and seriousness.' The poems
'grapple with life's intensest issues'.

Elizabeth Daryush was born in 1887. Her father, Robert
Bridges, was later poet laureate and one of the outstanding
prosodists in the English tradition. Her first home was in
Yattenden, the Berkshire village, and most of her life
was spent in rural Berkshire. In 1907 her father built
Chilswell House, Boar's Hill, near Oxford, where she lived
until her marriage in 1923. Her relationship with her father
and mother was close – a continual dialogue about poetry
and poetics must have persisted from her earliest years. She
did not always agree with her father's prosodic theories, and
their disagreements may have extended his apprehension of
metre and syllabic verse, as well as her own. In 1923 she
married a Persian and moved to Persia where she lived from
1923 to 1927. She made a study there of Persian poetry and

produced a fine syllabic 'translation' or imitation of Jalāl ad
Din Rūmi:

I am your mother, your mother's mother,
I am your father, his father also;
look on me, see each living ancestor;
it is well you should understand your kin,
should learn who your body's bound to, should know
who they are whose house you are prisoned in.

After her return to England, she moved in 1929 to Stockwell,
Boar's Hill, near her father's house, where she lived until her
death in 1977. All of her collections of verse, apart from
three early volumes which she suppressed, were written at
Stockwell. The only early poem preserved was 'O Strong to
Bless', written around 1912.

Through her seven volumes of poetry, there is no stylistic
development – rather, a perfecting of technique. The poems
from each volume are subjected to later revision so that, in
her *Selected Poems, Verses I–VI* (1972), most of the poems
appear in carefully revised versions, and relate as a single
sequence, progressing thematically rather than chronologic-
ally.

Elizabeth Daryush wrote poetry on three different
rhythmic models. The first is accentual syllabic – that is,
every line has a predetermined number of syllables and
metrical feet, with minor variations. This is the tradition of
English lyric poetry, and Daryush accepts the tradition
and writes subtly. The second type of poetry she writes is
accentual. Every line has a predetermined number of
accented syllables and a variable number of unaccented
syllables. This is in effect Hopkins's 'sprung rhythm', and
she imitates Hopkins's form from 'The Wreck of the
Deutschland' in her most ambitious poem, 'Air and
Variations'. In it she uses only Hopkins's metre, not his
diction nor his assonance. The poem is essentially in her own
idiom, full of her characteristic precise mystery. Nor does
the rhapsodic form deceive her into rhapsody. There is the
same phrased quality as in her taut lyric poems. The poem

is carefully constructed on a mathematical and logical progression, but one stanza from it illustrates the technique,
especially in the dramatic line endings which in their
movement accent the intellectual and image content:

> I said: I have seen
>> The wall of a mountainous wave
> Foam into spheres, then sink through green
>> Of fields to a human grave;
>> I have followed a sky-filled river, whose flickering throe
>> Leapt from its actual nodes, to a moon-tide gave
> Its might . . . nor forward urged nor backward formed that flow,
>> Each was the older twin . . .

The logic of line indentations is simple. In accentual poems,
those lines with most accents are ranged farthest left; in
syllabic poems, those with most syllables are ranged farthest
left. The shorter lines are indented correspondingly.

Her third rhythmic model is syllabic. In syllabic verse,
each line has a predetermined number of syllables, and
there is considerable variety in the distribution of stresses. In
1934 she published the classic definition of syllabic writing:
'Metres governed only by the number of syllables to the line,
and in which the number and position of the stresses may be
varied at will'. They are printed without capital letters at
the beginning of the lines 'as a reminder to the reader to
follow strictly the natural speech-rhythm, and not to look
for stresses where none are intended'. She adds, 'I have long
thought that on some such system as this for a base, it
should be possible to build up subtler and more freely-
followed accentual patterns than can be obtained either by
stress-verse proper, or by the traditional so-called syllabic
metres. The bulk of English "syllabic" verse is, of course, not
really syllabic in the strict sense but more truly accentual.'

In a note to her *Collected Poems* (1975) she qualified her
earlier description. Syllable count is 'merely the lifeless
shell' of 'more vital requirements'. In accentual verse, the
constant is 'time' or stress, the variable is 'number' or
syllable. In syllabic poems this is reversed – the constant is

number, the variable is stress. Unexpectedness, a dramatic variety of rhythm can be achieved, but a far closer artistry must be observed.

A syllabic poem which closely approaches speech rhythm and avoids the easier tension of metrical verse without forfeiting the discipline of rhyme is an unusual 'war poem':

Plant no poppy (he said)
no frail lily sublime,
for in war's famine time
thou'lt need but corn for bread.

Hoard no jewel (he cried)
no dazzling laboured gem:
thou'lt be forced to sell them
for steel, so now decide.

Set no flower in thy word
(he besought, but none heard)
cut no flash to thy wit,
if thou must disown it
when see'st thou sorrow's sword.

Archaisms of diction were removed from many of the later poems.

Elizabeth Daryush is in no sense a romantic poet. Her work owes much of its authority to seventeenth-century models. Her use of the first person, even in the elegies, is not encumbered by autobiography. The dominant image in the work is weaving and unweaving, the 'past's assembling thread'. The image of roads, intersecting and leading, is part of the weaving image. The principal light is sunlight, not moonlight. The dominant theme is time, its passing, the capacity of memory to preserve. Most of the poems take a point in time ('Persian Dawn', for example) and draw to it its past and its future, setting it in a context. The body is 'present', the soul 'past' or 'memoried', and the imagination 'future', the enchantress.

Many of the poems are dramatic without a literal plot, tending towards allegory. One begins, 'Anger lay by me all night long, / His breath was hot upon my brow.' She dramatizes ideas. The poems are phrased, never rhapsodic. By rhythmic stress and line-ending she causes us to pause. The art is in the control she exercises over our progress through the poem. The poem's source is chancy, dark, incomprehensible. Its execution, its unexpected growth, takes place in the light, and she is fully in control.

In casting out many of her early poems, she rebelled against her earlier idiom. 'I have come to dislike what is an essential part of many of them – their style, with its archaisms and inversions. This style is now, for me, incompatible with sincerity and directness, although at the time I found it a natural mode of expression.' Her critics have rebelled strongly against the archaisms, but they are not prevalent in her work.

Other poets have used syllabic verse as a sort of sausage-slicer, replacing the discipline of metre with an arbitrary discipline of counting on fingers and toes. Elizabeth Daryush has made of syllabics a more exacting and precise art than that of traditional metrics. Syllabics lead not towards a greater freedom but a different freedom, where the rhythm obeys speech rhythms and the form and content are more completely integrated.

One of her poems in accentual syllabic metres reveals the pared intensity she achieves. In one long sentence the poem progresses through the four seasons. The line endings are perfectly measured:

I will hold out my arms
   To Spring who clothes me
     (Says the beech),
To kind Summer who warms
   My room and soothes me;
     I will reach
For rich Autumn's robe, red
   With pride and grieving;
     I will hold
Out my worn dress for dread
   Winter's unweaving
     In the cold.

As in an imagist poem, the woman and the tree are merged.
The bitterness and tenderness of her vision are expressed
best in 'Old Hunter for Youth's Head'. If, as many of the
poems suggest, only the unfulfilled dream does not end, the
unfulfilment can have its tragic consequences:

Old hunter for youth's head,
    These are your old decoys—
A matron diamonded,
    A man with golden toys;

And these, too, long ago
    Were children that you charmed—
This lad that failed to grow,
    This girl still empty-armed.

T.S. Eliot (1888–1965)

And I must borrow every changing shape
To find expression...

T. S. Eliot is a poet renowned for his impersonality. Marianne Moore referred to him as 'a master of the anonymous', and the most distinguished study of his poems is *The Invisible Poet* by Hugh Kenner. Yet Eliot's poems, criticism, and the better among his plays, are immediately recognizable as his. It would be difficult to confuse even the least known of his poems with the work of any other poet. Even so, Eliot himself was at pains to stress the 'impersonality' of his work. Though his description of the creative process is lucid, it does not relate altogether convincingly to his own work. He writes that 'the emotion of art is impersonal'. The writer experiences 'a continual surrender of himself as he is at the moment to something which is more valuable. The progress of an artist is a continual self-sacrifice, a continual extinction of personality.' What in fact occurs in Eliot's work is an extinction of biographical referents, but the personality is powerful and present in every line. His poems are the more profoundly personal for carrying the weight of particular traditions he has assimilated.

To Eliot, tradition is a matter of accretion and alteration. Each new work of literature relates to, and subtly alters, every work that has come before. The writer acquires tradition by labour: he must develop an historical sense to appreciate both the pastness and the presence of tradition. All literature is finally contemporary, no writer can be judged outside the context of this living tradition.

He developed his style at a time when some poets were seeking a modern colloquial idiom and attempting to renew poetic forms and accommodate new material. Eliot learned some lessons from the 1890s poet John Davidson, particularly about subject matter; and the essays of another 1890s poet, Arthur Symons, directed his attention to the French poet Jules Laforgue and to the French Symbolists. The poet's task was to discover analogy and unity in disparate experience and to communicate them. To Eliot this meant discovering a stable, independent 'objective correlative', a 'set of objects, a situation, a chain of events which shall be a formula of that *particular* emotion; such that when the external facts, which must terminate in sensory experience, are given, the emotion is immediately evoked.' Eliot saw it in terms of imagery, suggested plot, and sound organization. Only by organizing the sound qualities of words could the poet elicit meanings from areas of consciousness where language does not normally penetrate, but where meanings are latent: it is the 'auditory imagination' which performs the 'raids on the inarticulate', by placing words in a context, using them in full consciousness of their semantic nature, their literary associations, and then maximizing their rhythmic and aural power, bringing about a fusion of several levels of speech and thought. Though he mastered traditional metre, Eliot developed stress rhythms as distinctive as they are inimitable.

Thomas Stearns Eliot was born in St Louis, Missouri, in the United States, in 1888, the seventh child of Henry Ware Eliot. His father was secretary and ultimately chairman of the Hydraulic Press Brick Company. He provided his children with a prosperous home and a good education. In religion, the family was Unitarian, devoted to good works, trusting in human perfectibility, distrusting ritual. Piety without sacrament, a certain moral severity, surrounded the young Eliot, who seems to have enjoyed a happy, if formal, relationship with his parents. He studied at Smith Academy in St Louis, where he wrote a number of poems, some of which survive. At sixteen he wrote 'A Fable for Feasters' which reveals an affection for Byron and considerable panache and skill. His mother, Charlotte, was herself ambitious to be a poet, and she encouraged her son.

Eliot attended Harvard College between 1906 and 1910 and wrote the 'Ode' for the Class Day in 1910. He edited the Harvard *Advocate* and contributed poems to it. Boston and Cambridge, Massachusetts, left a strong impression on his early poems. He studied Greek and Latin, attended a course on Dante (about whom he wrote one of his outstanding critical essays), read French and German and some philosophy. The French poets attracted him – Laforgue particularly. His imitation of Laforgue, 'Humoresque', was published in the *Advocate*, and another poem called 'Spleen', in which alleys and cats get their first look in on his verse, along with signs of balding and excessive fastidiousness which came to typify Prufrock. In 'The Death of St Narcissus', another early poem, the presence of *The Waste Land* sensibility is felt. The poem has a strong element of mystical eroticism, combining the myth of Narcissus with the legend of St Sebastian, mingling them with material from Arthurian romance. In 1909 and 1910, when Eliot began his graduate work, he wrote 'Portrait of a Lady', 'Preludes I and II', and began work on 'The Love Song of J. Alfred Prufrock'.

Eliot responded to Laforgue's tonal suppleness, the precise imprecision, the clarity which eludes paraphrase. The earlier Symbolists had tended – as Donald Davie describes it – to set images at a certain distance from each other, letting the unspoken significance rise from the spaces between. It was a poetry where individual images had power of suggestion beyond the physical sense they were addressed to, where sounds became visible and smells palatable. Individual symbols were points where disparate meanings fused. The later Symbolists tended to regard the poem *itself* as symbol. It might have a plot, all the elements of which worked towards a more complex symbolic meaning. Laforgue in particular achieved great suggestiveness by developing plots which gave the poem lucid continuity without limiting it to particular significance – drawing, as it were, a map which related differently to different land masses. Organization became symbolic.

Eliot travelled to France in 1910. He returned to Harvard to work on his doctorate – on European and Indian philosophy – in 1911. In 1914 he travelled to Marburg to pursue his studies, but with the First World War he went to England, where he gravitated towards Oxford, became a student at Merton College, and continued work on his doctoral thesis on the philosophy of F. H. Bradley. With characteristic self-awareness, he came to realize that he was no philosopher. In 1915 he left Oxford and married for the first time. He taught at a junior school in London and then worked in Lloyds Bank. London at that time housed various coteries – Bloomsbury was at work, and so were the Sitwells. Eliot reviewed books and wrote articles. He came into contact with Ezra Pound and with Imagism.

Though never an Imagist himself, Eliot understood the Imagist programme and profited from it. He wrote later that Imagism was the *point de repère* for any study of modern English poetry. His association with Pound was a fruitful one. He learned with Pound to pare down his language, to economize for impact. He learned, most importantly, that juxtaposition was a valuable organizing principle, that the setting side by side of images or vignettes not obviously related could be used to dramatic and precise effect, without moralizing.

In 1917 Eliot took over the editorship of the *Egoist* from Richard Aldington. In 1922 he founded the *Criterion* which, with the short-lived *Calendar of Modern Letters* edited by Edgell Rickword, established high standards of critical and creative writing. Eliot's years as editor coincided with his early successes as a poet. In 1917 *Prufrock and Other Poems* appeared, and *Poems* (1920) widened his readership. In 1922 *The Waste Land* was published and Eliot became the most respected *avant garde* writer of his day. *The Hollow Men* (1925) did little to extend his reputation since, despite their excellence, some of the poems seemed a pastiche of what had come before. *Ash Wednesday* (1930) was received without general enthusiasm. The dramatic fragments *Sweeney Agonistes* (published in book form in 1932) have only in the last few years attracted the attention they merit. In 1944

Eliot's last major poetic work, *Four Quartets*, was published (*Burnt Norton*, 1935, *East Coker* 1940, *The Dry Salvages* 1941, *Little Gidding* 1942). Thereafter most of his creative energies were directed into dramatic writing.

Eliot's later career took him into the thick of editing and publishing. He won various awards, including the Nobel Prize and the Order of Merit, he was canonized as the poet of the century – all rewards for the major poet of *The Waste Land* and the critic of *The Sacred Wood, Tradition and the Individual Talent*, and the other major books and essays, not the editor nor the minor dramatist of the verse plays. Eliot's lucidity as a critic helped clarify a possible course for English literature this century; but his gradual recantation, evident in his plays, later poems, and criticism – where he changed his ground subtly on Milton and Goethe, two poets he had earlier criticized with severity – do little to diminish the impact of his early writing.

But Eliot must bear much of the responsibility for deflecting 'modernism', for lessening its impact on English poetry. The apparent climax of his poetry, *Four Quartets*, rejects the implicit intensity of *The Waste Land* and his earlier modernist work. The later poem is discursive and in places prolix – indeed, a strange dishonesty sometimes mars it. Though intellectually engaging and rhythmically rich, the poem has as much in common with late Auden as with early Eliot. He is expatiating before an audience, exploring his meanings, no longer communicating them vividly as experience. He becomes an explicit moralist. The subtle erotic undertones of his best writing have disappeared. The lax discursiveness makes too many concessions – particularly in *The Dry Salvages* – to the 'poetic', and the organization is prosy. Explorer has become missionary. When a poet of Eliot's stature seems in his later writings to reject the exacting practices of his youth, his followers can more readily participate in the rejection, sitting at the feet of the comfortable elder and avoiding tough debate with the serious young man.

Yet Eliot's situation as an expatriate, his psychological constitution, and his social and religious concerns, made these developments inevitable. E. M. Forster wrote of Eliot's religion, 'What he seeks is not revelation but stability.' The epigraph to 'Burbank with a Baedeker, Bleistein with a Cigar' reads, *'nil nisi divinum stabile est; caetera fumus'* (absolutely nothing divine endures; all else is smoke). Later, there would have been no irony in the choice of epigraph. In *Ash Wednesday* he 'Constructs something upon which to rejoice', accepting the forms of faith in the hope that faith itself would follow. The quest for stability is central to Eliot's work. The social and personal agony of *The Waste Land* and the individual agony of 'Prufrock' are responses to the instability of everything. The power of the religious poems is not in their faith but in the tormenting desire to believe – in the forms and dogmas as much as in the Deity. When stability is unattainable, the tone becomes elegiac, as in 'Prufrock', or satirical, as in the Sweeney poems. Desire for stability resulted in his lucid conservatism and his technical radicalism as a poet. A writer who craves stability based on the old order has to develop a form which will accommodate old values in the present. The desire to perpetuate old values is often sensed to be futile, and the great innovations occur in the elegiac mode and spread out from there.

Eliot saw the poles of dramatic writing as liturgy and realism. His own poems are enacted between these extremes, tending first towards one, then towards the other. They are often dramatic or dramatically self-conscious. Dramatic monologues are among his best work. Many of the poems' epigraphs are taken from plays, classical as well as English.

In *Ash Wednesday* Eliot began to dramatize not the voice but the content. The speaker here becomes morally implicated, expressing not generality but a very particular experience. The questions arise: is he posturing, is the internal combat real *in the way he suggests*, is he gesturing at religious meanings? More strongly the same questions arise with *Four Quartets*. When he speaks of 'the intolerable wrestle with words and meanings', the 'wrestle' is not felt in the lucid statements he treats us to. He seems to be constructing something with which to wrestle. The poet becomes visible, the personae dwindle. For Eliot, when he pauses to reason or puzzle out an idea, lets the poem go. He is far from his best as a philosopher, mingling ratiocinative with allusive poetry – except when he shatters the former with a decisive intrusion of the latter, or when he reports speech and is not himself speaking. So long as the impersonal experienc*ing* is maintained, the poet is safe. This 'impersonality' disappears not when we read the actual autobiographical data (Eliot is reporting a nervous disorder), 'On Margate Sands. / I can connect / Nothing with nothing', but rather when we read, 'After such knowledge, what forgiveness?' in 'Gerontion' and feel the images being moralized and left lifeless. Because Eliot reaches a point of experiential intensity unparalleled in modern poetry, it is natural – though regrettable – that he had to retreat into cogitation.

As Eliot tells us, illness, fever, nervous disorientation – like half-sleep – allow a freedom of association within the poet's mind. The images, long incubated, flow free under the releasing tension of mental and physical disability. This may have been what occurred in the rapid composition of *The Waste Land* and *Sweeney Agonistes*. Eliot says this is not inspiration but something negative, 'the breaking down of strong habitual barriers' that 're-form very quickly'. Some would say this *is* inspiration, clearly defined.

'The Love Song of J. Alfred Prufrock', completed when Eliot was twenty-three and published in a book six years later, is his most striking early achievement. The poem is discontinuous, fragmentary in plot, continuous only in rhythm and tone. Eliot generates a strong sense of place without locating the poem. Though ostensibly a 'love song', the poem is more an elegy, particularly in its conclusion. It evokes a desire for and the impossibility and failure of love in a specific milieu. Juxtaposing fragments of conversation, observation, experience, Eliot creates a vivid mosaic, a characterization which does not stop at character but gives a lucid impression of a particular social class and experience which Eliot knew well. It is at the same time an inner and an outer landscape, a state of mind and an evanescent narrative. The poem functions as a complex cultural symbol, as does the more overtly symbolic and less successful 'Gerontion'.

'Portrait of a Lady' is the companion piece to 'Prufrock' though written earlier and, because more specific in plot and in the relationships it evokes, less resonant. Eliot takes his epigraph from *The Jew of Malta*:

Thou hast committed—
Fornication: but that was in another country,
And besides, the wench is dead.

The epigraph contrasts sharply with the tone of the poem. The quiet, proper lady serving tea, the equally proper Prufrockian visitor, are illuminated by the epigraph which suggests the possibility of lust, of action, and the fact of oblivion. Nothing happens: manners have desiccated the protagonists, who gradually brim with disgust. As in 'Prufrock', manners and attitudes make communication of any importance virtually impossible. 'That is not what I meant at all . . .' complains one of the characters in 'Prufrock'. Failure of communication is a theme which dominates even Eliot's most assured and least successful later work.

In 'Preludes' Eliot was exploring the same thing obliquely, with reference to other social classes:

I am moved by fancies that are curled
Around these images, and cling:
The notion of some infinitely gentle
Infinitely suffering thing.

The poem turns on the word 'thing'. Against the anguish of almost-recognition, the poet savagely counsels:

Wipe your hand across your mouth, and laugh;
The worlds revolve like ancient women
Gathering fuel in vacant lots.

Throughout Eliot's poetry the image of music plays an

important part. In titles of poems we read 'Love Song', 'Rhapsody', 'Preludes', 'Five Finger Exercises', and 'Quartets'. The image of music has special significance for him, suggesting at once a certain type of organization and a certain attitude to language. In *The Waste Land* it is tragic music, while later it becomes the painful redeeming Shakespearean music. Images relating to the other arts – architecture, painting, and of course various literary allusions – inform the poetry. A recurrent figure is that of the old sexless man – sometimes Teiresias – who has achieved a numb, knowing stability.

Eliot and Pound rebelled together against what they saw as the misuse of free verse, and a new acerbity enters Eliot's blackly humorous and suggestive 'Sweeney' poems and the other poems in rhymed quatrains. Though style and themes change, the organization remains the same. The 'Sweeney' poems have the same precise imprecision, the same sudden juxtapositions and transitions of imagery. They depend on the English Metaphysical poets as much as on the late Symbolists, and are dense with literary allusion. Where they are less supple than the poems that precede them is in tone. The chosen quatrain form, used with the verbal intensity Eliot requires of it, is incapable of the sudden shifts of tone and mood that characterized the earlier work. It is only in these poems that Eliot achieved a thoroughgoing impersonality.

Sweeney Agonistes, fragments of a verse play, was published no doubt with some trepidation by the author. It seems to have been written without premeditation and at great speed. The rhythmical compulsion of the near-nonsense verse is impressive. Despite the brevity of the fragments, characters and strangely unanchored situations are suggested. These fragments reveal what originality Eliot might have achieved as a dramatist had he premeditated verse drama less and let his imagination write the plays. The telephone conversations, the unexpected arrivals and departures, the card readings, the intrusion of characters from other poems – including Mrs Porter and Sweeney – and the undisguised eroticism and cruelty, make it not only unique in Eliot's work but central to it: in it we see the fascinating 'might have been' of Eliot's dramatic talents. His later plays have little of the compelling vitality of *Sweeney*. In them Eliot tried, especially after *Murder in the Cathedral*, to make the verse unobtrusive and to communicate subtle, esoteric meanings with a didactic purpose. The effect is flatness, not conversational but prosaic writing, relieved by occasional memorable scenes, where the poetry is resonant, the action stylized.

In *The Waste Land* Eliot demands that we read him differently from the way we read most verse. He alters our way of reading, if we read him properly. The poem does not respond to analysis of its meanings – meanings cannot be detached from the texture of the poetry itself. The idiom is synthetic, fusing various experiences in a sequence of images. The complex of suggested 'plots' and myths, the shifting tones of voice, generate a sense of a cultural and individual stage of development, as well as suggesting a process. The critic Craig Raine advanced a convincing interpretation of the processes of *The Waste Land*. He suggested that the central process was 'reincarnation' in the metamorphoses of imagery; but where reincarnation is ideally towards higher forms and perfection, Eliot takes it in the other direction, degeneratively. Thus in 'A Game of Chess', three Shakespearean tragic heroines – Cleopatra, Desdemona and Ophelia – are alluded to. The allusions suggest not only potential, but its betrayal, a falling away towards a present sterility.

Eliot's literary allusions in the poem are apt – lines from Spenser, Dante, Baudelaire, allusions to Wagner, and so on. The alteration to the original lines that takes place when they are set in the new context of Eliot's poem redefines their meanings in terms of *The Waste Land*. Past culture is implicated, the poem is enhanced by our recollection of the significance of the quotes in their original context.

In the opening lines of 'The Burial of the Dead', the first section of the poem, Eliot uses five present participles: 'breeding', 'mixing', 'stirring', 'covering', and 'feeding'.

Each occurs at the end of a line with the emphasis of enjambment and suggests an ongoing process, organic and
natural. In the first eight lines of the poem Spring, Summer
and Winter are suggested. Memory and desire (past and
future) are latent in the cruel rebirth of the year.

The natural progression is juxtaposed with the nattering
recollections of Marie. Her voice is replaced by the dark
tones of, perhaps, Teiresias, 'for you know only / A heap of
broken images' . . . 'I will show you fear in a handful of dust'.
The longing strains of *Tristan und Isolde* are silenced by the
hopeless passage, 'Oed und leer das Meer'. The cruelty of
false starts – Marie curtailed by Teiresias, memory by the
present – lead to the sham hope that spiritualism will
answer, and we visit Madame Sosostris, the clairvoyant. Her
turning up the cards – a sequence of images – is in emblematic form what the poet is doing. The relationship between
card and card, the meaning of the sequence of images, must
be inferred. The cards are an ideal correlative for the discontinuous technique of the poem. They offer no revelation.
The future cannot be predicted, the present is without
direction.

'A Game of Chess' takes the process of degeneration into
the intimacies of relationship. The opening passage, compelling us to recall Shakespeare's Cleopatra, Virgil's Dido,
and the heroine of Pope's *The Rape of the Lock*, repeats the
central process. The verse breaks off suddenly in a jazz-tune,
the cheapness and accuracy of which recalls the verve of the
songs in *Sweeney Agonistes*. In 'The Fire Sermon', the third
section of the poem, Marvell's work 'To his Coy Mistress'
degenerates into an insalubrious ballad, and Sweeney himself puts in a brief appearance. The Buddha's 'Fire Sermon'
was preached against the fires of lust, envy and anger, and
other destructive passions. It, too, is put to work in an
altered context. A suggestive eroticism dominates. There are
hints at perversion in Mr Eugenides's advances, of impotence in Teiresias, of loveless sex. No satisfactory relationships are suggested. But the section is not in the end
satirical – more, painfully elegiac. It is verse containing the

process of decay, most aptly when it introduces the theme through allusions to great art and artists, historical personages, and the history of a particular river – the Thames – in the heart of a particular urban society, post-First World War England.

'Death by Water', the fourth section, evolved out of Eliot's own French poem, 'Dans le Restaurant'. The passage intensifies and alters the recurrent image of water, with its normally curative and baptismal powers. This particular image of drowning is an emblem of futility: the futility of worries over profit and loss, youth and age, the elements, all forgotten in the transforming death, without suggestion of rebirth.

The last section is the most difficult and perhaps least successful: 'What the Thunder Said'. As the drought gradually breaks and the thunder speaks, we have various elusive suggestions of hope – the fleeting image of Christ at Emmaus, for example. But despite the Thunder's advice to 'give, sympathize, and control', the speaker emerges as the mad prince, without inheritance and without posterity, snared in the present. The poem is inexhaustibly rich because it vividly evokes a particular social, moral, historical and aesthetic sterility but fails, even as it tries, to suggest a coherent solution. The poem is incomplete because the poet has not managed to 'construct something upon which to rejoice'. It does not compromise its truths.

In *Ash Wednesday* the subjective element, however, dominates more than in any of the other poems. It is neither wholly discursive nor committedly allusive and spare. The liturgical allusions, used in the same spirit with which he uses literary quotes, cheapen the over-all effect. Something of the subjectivity is to be felt in 'The desert in the garden, the garden in the desert' – the internal and external landscapes are interchangeable, the 'I' is growing more powerful than its correlatives. A hauntingly psalmodic cadence is at work, as though the poet has chosen a liturgical rhetoric to convince himself. 'Journey of the Magi' and 'Marina' celebrate and suggest answers more tentatively and more wholly effectively than *Ash Wednesday*. 'Marina' is Eliot's finest short poem, intense and sensuous, a poem of desire based on memory, not working against it.

Four Quartets are more readily comprehensible than most of Eliot's earlier poems. They include a number of subtle thoughts and much fine verse but, considered as poems, we cannot help wonder at their laboured, discursive, and finally monotonous progression between vivid passages of poetry. The meanings are detachable, Eliot's thoughts change course, not for dramatic effect or to suggest fragmentation, as in the earlier poems, but simply because he can go no further with them. They are played out. Though he learned early that he was no philosopher, he returned to philosophical verse. There is a frequent flatness of diction and rhythm, a prosaic plumpness and roundness of phrase, but there is no 'intolerable wrestle / With words and meanings'. The battle was over long before that phrase was neatly turned round its enjambment. 'Burnt Norton' is the outstanding of the four, including some of Eliot's most memorable lines. And yet the *poem* is not memorable. Eliot has simplified his technique, if not his discipline, to appeal to a wider audience, not in order to clarify his meanings.

If we criticize *Four Quartets*, it is by the standard Eliot set himself in his earlier poems – the achievement of the *Quartets* is great, but disappointing in the light of what had come before. They lack the variety of tone, the intensity, and the eloquence of unspoken meanings suggested by juxtapositions of images, by allusion, by characterization. And they are not *quite* true, they seem to have been worked up. They are too reasonable, the product rather than the process of thought.

There can, however, be little doubt that Eliot's poetry will be seen in time as of crucial importance to our tradition, in the way that Dryden's and Wordsworth's poetry was. Writers who effect a partial renewal in poetic language are few; and those who achieve so thoroughgoing a renewal of our poetic language, our critical approach, and our sensibility, as Eliot did, are so rare that they can be numbered on the fingers of one hand.

Isaac Rosenberg (1890–1918)

The troubled throng
Of words breaks out like smothered fire through dense
And smouldering wrong.

'Let the public ask itself,' wrote T. S. Eliot in 1920, 'why it
has never heard of the poems of T. E. Hulme or Isaac
Rosenberg, and why it has heard of the poems of Lady
Precocia Pondoeuf and has seen a photograph of the nursery
in which she wrote them.' The unavailability of Hulme's and
Rosenberg's work is a partial explanation. More pertinent in
Rosenberg's case, for all his promise, he was killed in action
before that promise matured. He has none of the authority of
form and diction we find in Owen and Sassoon. He was feeling
his way towards another kind of poetry, a poetry he did not
attain, and he left his uneven attempts. But he was the only
poet involved in the First World War who consciously set out
to develop a language to engage the experience without
compromise, veering neither into Owen's public rhetoric nor
Sassoon's ironizing. His uniqueness is the product not only of
a rich literary mind but also of an unusual social background.

He was born in Bristol in 1890 into a family of Russian
Jewish *émigrés*. At the age of seven, he went with his family to
London, moving from relative poverty into far worse poverty.
Isaac was sent to elementary school in Stepney. When he was
fourteen he was apprenticed as an engraver to a firm of 'art
publishers' and attended evening classes at the Art School of
Birkbeck College. He was ambitious to be a painter.

In 1911, after his apprenticeship, three ladies provided the means to send him to the Slade. His graphic work has many of the startling elements of the verse – careful heightenings and subtle distortions, a boldness which at times recalls the work of the young Wyndham Lewis. But his painting career was curtailed before he achieved a style adequate to his vision.

He began writing poems when very young and circulated them, attracting some attention. In 1912 he published privately the first of three pamphlets, *Night and Day*, including principally poems of his adolescence. *Youth* (1915) and *Moses: A Play* (1916) followed. The total page count of his pamphlets, including preliminary matter, is sixty-eight pages. His reputation rests not on these works so much as on his war poems which were not fully collected until nineteen years after his death, in 1937, by Gordon Bottomley and Denys Harding. Siegfried Sassoon provided an introduction. A *Selected Poems* had appeared in 1922.

In 1914 Rosenberg went to South Africa for his health, but returned the next year, having been unable to make a living by teaching or by his graphic work. He delayed enlisting as long as he could, for he was physically and temperamentally ill-suited for military service. Nonetheless, driven by poverty, he enlisted and in 1916 was sent to France, where he fell in action in 1918.

Siegfried Sassoon's introduction to the *Collected Poems* raises several important points. 'I have recognized in Rosenberg,' he writes, 'a fruitful fusion between English and Hebrew culture.' He speaks of a 'racial quality, biblical and prophetic'. With a few exceptions, notably 'The Jew', the poems are not about *being* Jewish. The biblical imagery and the strange accent – for many of the poems seem to be spoken by a voice with a foreign accent – enrich the poems and do not make them ethnically exclusive.

Sassoon speaks of him as 'scriptural and sculptural' – he '*modelled* words with fierce energy and aspiration'. Rosenberg did not readily accept words as they came to him. He questioned them, meditated on them, and combined them in startling new ways. What are received language and diction to Owen become to Rosenberg dynamic language and diction, struggling to accommodate extreme experience. He paid little attention to punctuation. He did not shy away from mixed metaphors or from questionable usages. Most important, when he had a war image to convey, he conveyed it with brutal objectivity, neither making it rhetorical nor distancing it by irony. In 'Dead Man's Dump' we read, 'A man's brains spattered on / A stretcher-bearer's face.' But he does not dwell for effect on the image. He sets it in a wider context. He is not a photographer or a journalist. When he uses in the same poem the image, 'a lid over each eye' in describing the dead, he suggests decomposition, the isolation of the twinned organs of sight in death. Though they decompose, the dead are united as well:

The grass and coloured clay
More motion have than they,
Joined in the great sunk silences.

The sparse concrete images are brought alive by the verbs: bones 'crunch' under wheels. But his best effects depend on a psalmodic quality, on words which without specifying meaning carry a burden of suggestion and are integrated in a rich cadence. Freed from mere description, freed too from prescriptive meanings and associations, they find new areas of significance. In 'Dead Man's Dump' one stanza wavers between image and symbol, between experience and response:

None saw their spirits' shadow shake the grass,
Or stood aside for the half-used life to pass
Out of those doomed nostrils or doomed mouth,
When the swift iron burning bee
Drained the wild honey of their youth.

There is none of Owen's sugar in that honey. He presents time in war not as a chronology but as a terrible, unrelenting present: 'The shells go crying over them / From night till night and now.'

In the war poems Rosenberg came close to achieving the

kind of poetry he wanted, though there is a haunting incompleteness about them. Though they are more accomplished than his early work, there is a close continuity between the apprentice pieces in *Night and Day* and his last poems. In the early pamphlet, the poet muses – is he a god-finder or a sin-bearer for man? He wakes in the morning with 'a larger capacity to feel and enjoy things'; having 'communed with the stars, his soul has exalted itself, and become wiser in intellectual experience'. The burden of the early poems is that, 'By thinking of higher things we exalt ourselves to what we think about'. Prophetic and didactic voices dominate. What is striking about the early poems is not what they achieve but the foreignness of the idiom:

Sing to me, for my soul's eyes
Anguish for these ecstasies
And voluptuous mysteries
That must somewhere be,
Or we could not know of them.

There are, too, the strange vivid images:

Sudden the night blazed open at my feet.
Like splintered crystal tangled with gold dust
Blared on my ear and eye the populous street.

The only stylistic affinities we sense are with Blake. The style is larded with archaisms: 'starven', ' 'gainst', the 'en-' prefix added to verbs to render them intensive. Language is under pressure, seeking everywhere for sustaining resources. He is the least ironic of English poets. He writes poems because he has something necessary to communicate, and only poetry will serve.

In the early poems he rejects a benevolent god. Gradually he comes to realize that compassion and endurance are insufficient. The struggle against a bad god, against evil generally, is worthwhile only if it effects 'realignments' in individual modes of perception and in social attitudes. Rosenberg's critics have often commented on the radical tendencies in his verse, seeing in his revolutionary approach to poetic diction, his openness to experience, a political correlative. But there is more in his verse of the seeds of 'vorticism', more affinity with the imagists, than with the more directly social writers.

His principal theme is power, whether of god, of evil, or of man. Biblical allusions charge the poems. He casts himself in the role of Absalom and God in the role of David, and in 'Chagrin' describes the inexplicable, unexpected, and apparently malevolent power at work, snaring him:

From the imagined weight
Of spaces in a sky
Of mute chagrin, my thoughts
Hang like branch-clung hair . . .

The formal imagination, peopling the void air with forms, concretizing thoughts but avoiding poetical apostrophe, is 'sculptural' in Sassoon's sense, aware of space and its potentialities:

We ride, we ride, before the morning
The secret roots of the sun we tread,
And suddenly
We are lifted of all we know
And hang from implacable boughs.

Power has, as its contingent, responsibility – to past and future, as well as the present. In 'The Dead Heroes' he writes, 'Strong as our hurt is strong / Our children are.' In his often potentially sensational subject matter, there is no sensationalism. His power to define through indefinition – as Poe does, or Milton in Hell – and his refusal to make pretty or ugly what is neither pretty nor ugly, reflects his integrity. He is always a thinker in his poems, especially in his attitude to language. 'Snow is a strange white word', one of the poems begins. Elsewhere, he would 'bruise the air' with words. They have magical power, are enigmatic shadows of the things and qualities they denote.

There is in his work, too, humour – sometimes black humour. In 'Break of Day in the Trenches' he addresses a rat: 'Droll rat, they would shoot you if they knew / Your cosmopolitan sympathies.' It has brushed the hands of men in opposing trenches. Later he plucks a poppy and places it behind his ear:

Poppies, whose roots are in men's veins
Drop, and are ever dropping;
But mine in my ear is safe,
Just a little white with the dust.

The rhythm of the last two lines is entirely his own. Edwin Muir characterizes Rosenberg's achievement best: 'He gives above all a feeling of power which is not yet certain of itself, which is sometimes tripped up by its own force.'

Hugh MacDiarmid (1892–1978)

For ilka thing a man can be or think or dae
Aye leaves a million mair unbeen, unthocht, undune,
Till his puir warped performance is,
To a' that micht ha' been, a thistle to the mune.

Hugh MacDiarmid is uncontestably the greatest Scottish poet since Burns. Because his most powerful poems are in Scots, he seems at first glance linguistically difficult, even foreign, to some readers. But his language is as rich and supple as it is easy to master. He merits outside Scotland a far wider audience than he has yet been able to command.

Perhaps his unwillingness to compromise with English literary and political establishments, scathingly evoked in *In Memoriam James Joyce*, and his adherence to certain political orthodoxies contributed to a reluctance among many critics to take his work seriously, until recently. He characterized the English literary scene in *Lucky Poet* as a 'whole gang of high mucky-mucks, famous fatheads, old wives of both sexes, stuffed shirts, hollow men with head-pieces stuffed with straw, bird-wits, lookers under beds, trained seals, creeping Jesuses, Scots Wha Ha'evers . . . commercial Calvinists, makers of "noises like a turnip", and all the touts and toadies and lickspittles of the English Ascendancy.'

Christopher Murray Grieve – Hugh MacDiarmid – was born in 1892 and raised in Langholm, Dumfriesshire. Among his early teachers was the Scottish composer F. G. Scott, an important influence on his development. From

Langholm he went to Edinburgh and began teacher's training, but changed his mind and took up a career in journalism
instead. He worked for the Fabian Research Department and
contributed to A. R. Orage's *The New Age*. He served in the
Royal Artillery Medical Corps (1915–19) and returned to
journalism after the war, working in Montrose, Liverpool
and London. In 1922 he adopted the name Hugh Mac-
Diarmid, a 'nom de plume (et de guerre)'. He was a Scottish
Nationalist and a Communist, expelled by the Nationalists
for his membership of the Communist Party, and expelled by
the Communists for his Nationalism.

Poverty and a breakdown in health followed his second
marriage and he withdrew (1933–41) to a croft on Whalsay
in the Shetlands. During the Second World War he worked as
an engineer on the Clyde and eventually settled in Biggar,
Lanarkshire, where he lived until his death. He was awarded
a Civil List Pension in 1950. The experiences he accumulated
in his alternately active and retiring life, and the breadth of
his reading, make him one of those rare, encyclopaedically
informed writers like Ezra Pound and James Joyce.

MacDiarmid was distressed in the early part of the century
by Scottish attitudes of subservience towards England, Scots'
ignorance of their own rich heritage, and willingness to forget
those common traditions which could make them again a
nation with a culture distinct from the English. To revitalize
Scottish culture he worked out a programme which included
reanimating the Scots literary language, basing the new
idiom on the spoken dialect of his area and infusing it with
words from the language of the great Scottish Chaucerians,
particularly Henryson, Dunbar and Gavin Douglas, and
some elements of English. He adapted, too, modernist techniques. Relentlessly he attacked the Scottish culture heroes
of the day, in order to replace them with authentic models.
Despite his love of Robert Burns's poetry, he saw in him the
worst conceivable model for a modern Scottish literature.

Unlike earlier Scottish writers, MacDiarmid's imagery is
drawn from the industrial, not the rural world. Accommodating this new content in Scots rendered that language more

supple. An early influence on his language was Jamieson's *Etymological Dictionary of the Scottish Language* (1808), from which he borrowed words to plant in the context of the current dialect. Gregory Smith's *Scottish Literature: Character and Influence* (1919) clarified for him a particular Scottish quality: establishing and then resolving contrasts or antitheses between the real and the fantastic.

MacDiarmid constantly stresses thematic antinomies and apparent contradictions which are in fact complementary and necessary to each other. The sublime and the ridiculous are next-door neighbours. As Alexander Scott has written, Coleridge is behind MacDiarmid in his belief in Imagination as 'the balance or reconciliation of opposite or discordant qualities'.

John Davidson, too, showed MacDiarmid the way. Davidson, a poet of the Rhymers' Club, advanced a Darwinian and wholly materialist explanation of reality. His social concerns were transmuted through a relentless egotism into a form of 'representative' autobiography. He had an almost sentimental regard for the unity of nature through the elements. His was a poetry of fact, of the tangible, and so is MacDiarmid's, accurate and full in detail. Poetry should grow out of fact, it is detected in things and experiences, not imposed upon them. This is, in essence, the modernist element in MacDiarmid's work, a wariness of the metaphysical, a reliance on the concrete.

Though MacDiarmid's poetry in Scots was his major achievement, he was a considerable poet in English as well. His long poems are cumulative, though voice and motivating passion are often deadened by weight of detail, disrupted by obscurities, and vitiated by propagandist aphorisms. But the *Second Hymn to Lenin* (1935) and *In Memoriam James Joyce* (1955) are full of good as well as over-burdened verse. His great poem – for each poem he has written is part of a total 'work in progress' – much now to remain open-ended, like Pound's *Cantos*.

The poems devour trivial matter and important ideas, facts, images, feelings, thoughts, memories. Though Mac-

Diarmid had not the selectivity that makes Pound's and Eliot's erudition compelling, he had a monolithic comprehensiveness we will not find in any other writer. Prolixity and lack of concentration in his English verse are undeniable weaknesses. But he made a verse plain and strong enough to deal with any subject. In a jumbled way he was the most learned poet of the century – text-bookish though much of his learning was. His book, his poem, was not an end in itself: it was intended to serve a newer age.

The early poems in Scots are fascinating in conception as well as execution. 'The Innumerable Christ', for example, was suggested by Professor J. Y. Simpson's comment, 'Other stars may have their Bethlehem, and their Calvary too.' In his poem, MacDiarmid concludes:

An' when the earth's as cauld's the mune
An' a' its folk are lang syne deid,
On coontless stars the Babe maun cry
    An' the Crucified maun bleed.

Earth is continually cast into cosmic perspective, where it achieves due insignificance and a clearer significance. In another poem, he writes:

The moonbeams kelter* i' the lift†
An' Earth, the bare auld stane,
Glitters beneath the seas o' Space,
White as a mammoth bane.

MacDiarmid's greatest poem – indeed one of the great poems of the century – is *A Drunk Man Looks at the Thistle* (1925). The speaker is resolutely Scots, highly literate, and drunk. As he tumbles into the half-dream beside the thistle in the moonlight, a flood of thoughts pours through him, jostling one another for precedence. The suppleness of his language, its power to change tone and mood suddenly, its ability to fuse the real and the fantastic worlds naturally, are fully confirmed. Scots, as Edwin Morgan has suggested in the introduction to his translations of Mayakovsky into Scots, has an implicit rhetoric lacking in modern English, an ability to

* undulate.   † sky.

harness opposing impulses in a balanced single statement.

In parts, the poem is mordantly satirical, particularly about the pseudo-Scots, the sentimental expatriates, the desecrators of Burns, and the small-minded bourgeoisie who ' 'ca their obstinacy "Hame" '. The satire on intellectuals and factions is also telling. From it he moves into a credo which is pertinent to all his work:

I'll ha'e nae hauf-way hoose, but aye be whaur
Extremes meet – it's the only way I ken
To dodge the curst conceit o' bein' richt
That damns the vast majority o' men.

For I've nae faith in ocht I can explain,
And stert whaur the philosophers leave aff...

He stands at the point of synthesis between extremes, articulating that synthesis.

The poem is written in quatrains, sestets, triplets, couplets and verse paragraphs, varying verse form with great virtuosity to suit the content. MacDiarmid incorporates his translations and imitations of other poets, including Alexander Blok, Zinaida Hippius, and so on. It is sad that he did not devote more time to translation into the Scots language.

Platonic and physical love (the latter graphically evoked) are another double theme. But the dominant theme, here and elsewhere, is the limits imposed by choice. In a later poem, 'Light and Shadow', he writes, 'On every thought I have the countless shadows fall / Of other thoughts as valid that I cannot have.' To choose one thing is to exclude another, to be a Nationalist one cannot be a Communist, and vice versa. MacDiarmid does not accept this willingly. He would contain the opposites. This in part explains his refusal to be selective in his long English poems, his attempt to push everything into the foreground, to make an *all*-encompassing poem.

The thistle changes in its implications throughout the poem, altered by the speaker's half-dream. At one moment, moonlight turns it to a skeleton – his skeleton. Then it stands for Scotland, and later sprouts a great red rose, the General

Strike, which suddenly deflates like a balloon and the thistle stalk is left literal and poor. As the symbols change, he ruminates:

The vices that defeat the dream
Are in the plant itsel',
And till they're purged its virtues maun
In pain and misery dwell.

This poem, more than any of MacDiarmid's other writings, gives a comprehensive image of the antinomies of life – political, emotional and religious. The poem, centred on the physical fact of the thistle and the drunk man, illuminated by the moon, is a dramatic monologue, working by accretion of suggestions and association, lamenting the high price and low quality of Scotch, meditating on sex, the possibility of Revolution, the future of the Scottish language and nation, and other themes. He manages to 'Exteriorize things in a thistle', 'The grisly form in which I'm caught'. He calls up various ghosts, principally Dostoyevsky's, but more appositely Herman Melville's, for only Melville in recent English language literature has achieved the scope MacDiarmid tried for without forfeiting detailed accuracy. The thistle is – like the white whale – 'A symbol o' the puzzle o' man's soul'. The vivid accuracy of detail in MacDiarmid's poem is unforgettable; for example, we hear, 'God passin' wi' a bobby's feet / Ootby in the lang coffin o' the street'.

After *A Drunk Man* MacDiarmid wrote other poems in Scots, some highly successful, though none to equal this early *tour de force*. He begins to lament poverty and drudgery, his Scots comes closer and closer to English, until he begins to write principally in English. One of his best Scots poems from the transition is 'North of the Tweed'. Another is his elegy for his father:

We look upon each ither noo like hills
Across a valley, I'm nae mair your son.
It is my mind, nae son o' yours, that looks,
And the great darkness o' your death comes up
And equals it across the way.

In 'The Seamless Garment' he speaks, using the image of the weavers of the local textile industry, of Rilke's 'seamless garment o' music and thought'. This describes, in effect, the kind of poetry MacDiarmid tried to write – a poetry of wholeness which is inclusive, a poetry not whole in itself so much as in its capacity. 'On a Raised Beach' is a good example of his achievement, a major celebration, an examination of the relevance of geology, the expressiveness of accurately presented facts, with a rhetoric as powerful as Neruda's. In the *Second Hymn to Lenin*, MacDiarmid agrees with Joyce:

> the principal question
> Aboot a work o' art is frae hoo deep
> A life it springs—

and how high, from that depth, it can rise, and how much it can raise up with it. He sought after a poetry 'full of erudition, expertise, and ecstasy', as he says in 'The Kind of Poetry I Want'. He tried to achieve the multifaceted 'fly-like vision'. His was an inclusive talent like Lawrence's or Whitman's, only more austere and particular, less subjective–intellectual, profoundly satirical, and at once prophetic. In one poem he writes:

> So I am delivered from the microcosmic human chaos
> And given the perspective of a writer who can draw
> The wild disorder of a ship in a gale
> Against the vaster natural order of sea and sky.

Perspective, distance, are essential to his inclusive vision.

'Crystals like Blood' is MacDiarmid's best elegy, perhaps his best short English poem, beginning with the matter-of-fact but arresting lines: 'I remember how, long ago, I found / Crystals like blood in a broken stone.' The poem examines the memory minutely; the elegiac note is sounded as a celebration.

MacDiarmid's self-knowledge is impressive. He knew his arrogance, and the romantic and mystical impulses which tug against his materialist vision, his achievements and his shortcomings, all of which he exposed candidly in *In Memoriam James Joyce*, particularly in the section which in extract is called 'The Task'. MacDiarmid's paradoxes are evident everywhere in his work, even in his choice of the Scots language, an act at once reactionary and revolutionary, trying to cast a living literature in the mould of a minority dialect.

T. S. Eliot wrote, 'It will eventually be admitted that he has done . . . more for English poetry by committing some of his finest verse to Scots, than if he had elected to write exclusively in the Southern dialect.' In serving Scotland best, he served English literature best as well.

Wilfred Owen (1893–1918)

Escape? There is one unwatched way: your eyes,
O Beauty! Keep me good that secret gate.

Wilfred Owen admired Yeats, using lines from the older poet
as epigraphs to some of his poems. Yeats did not reciprocate
the admiration. He excluded Owen from his Oxford anthology of modern poetry, later describing him as 'all blood,
dirt, and sucked sugar-stick ... he calls poets "Bards", a girl a
"maid", and talks about "Titanic wars". There is every
excuse for him, but none for those who like him.'

Owen's poetry is so closely linked with his death, his sentiments, and the heroic cloak that posterity has draped around
his ghost, that a balanced assessment of his actual achievement and contribution as a poet has been delayed. His poems
answer certain readers' preconceptions about poetry and
war; they *seem* true, even if they do not expand but merely
endorse or clarify what men already believe or feel. Owen's
work may have helped to shape these feelings and beliefs; but
do the poems *now* evoke experiences, or report journalistically,
or merely feed our preconceptions? The naïve reader is
drawn to the appealing naïvety of Owen's passion. But he has
attracted serious artists too, notably Benjamin Britten, whose
settings of some of the poems in his *War Requiem* further
expanded Owen's audience.

Wilfred Owen was born in 1893 in Oswestry, Shropshire,
where he led a pleasantly pampered childhood. At the age of
ten he visited Broxton by the Hill and – in good Words-

worthian fashion – his vocation as a poet was affirmed. There 'first I felt my boyhood fill / With uncontainable movements; there was born / My poethood.' Owen wrote copiously in his early years. His education was conducted at the Birkenhead Institute, Liverpool, the Technical College, Shrewsbury, and at London University. Edmund Blunden recalls how Owen chose his friends for what he could get from them – intellectual stimulus, principally. His early poetic apprenticeship was to Keats, whom he celebrated and to whose shrines he made pilgrimage. His devotion to the Beautiful often partakes of Keatsian particularity. Shelley, Gray, Arnold, Tennyson, and Yeats affected him as well. His sensibility was steeped in romanticism.

In 1913 Owen wrote half seriously of his plan to publish 'Minor Poems – in Minor Keys – By a Minor'. The early writings are little more. They have moments of Keatsian sensuousness and some vivid passages set in a relentless tide of assonances and alliterations. The 'music' of poetry attracted Owen. Sounds generally, but especially the sounds of instruments, are imitated or evoked:

I have been gay with trivial fifes that laugh;
And songs more sweet than possible things are sweet;
And gongs, and oboes.

Ineffable 'sweetness' and 'music' made him overfond of adjectives which clot the verse and steal the limelight from perfectly adequate nouns. The adjectives often define qualities implicit in the verbs. 'Pale flakes with *fingering* stealth come *feeling down* our faces' is close to tautology. Sound rather than sense dictates unhappy epithets: 'dull rumour' and 'the poignant misery of the dawn' in 'Exposure', for example. This quality mars some of the best poems, where agony becomes mellifluous, aestheticized. In the first eight lines of the sonnet 'The Seed', another fault becomes apparent. The same syntactical construction, 'the — of the —', occurs seven times. It was a fault Dylan Thomas imitated.

He may have learned some of his poetic 'music' from the French poet Verlaine. He spent two years teaching English in

France (1913–15) and made some literary friendships. Verlaine cast a salutary gloom over his early optimism, though the tone is hardly native to him.

Owen enlisted in the Artists' Rifles in 1915. Under intolerable stress, he was invalided out in 1917 and convalesced for a time near Edinburgh. There he became friendly with the poet Siegfried Sassoon, with whom he discussed poetry, and for whom his admiration knew no bounds. Owen's letters were always rhetorical, but those he wrote to Sassoon achieved an unprecedented adolescent verve. He calls Sassoon his 'Keats + Christ + Elijah + my Colonel + my father-confessor + Amenophus IV, in profile'. No doubt Sassoon's enthusiasm for the promising work of an attractive young man helped bolster Owen's confidence. In 1917 he was able to write to his mother, 'I am held peer by the Georgians'.

Sassoon discussed war with Owen – and pacifism, the Christian duty of passivity before violence, and other problems of conscience. Owen agreed – his letters, even from the Front, echo Sassoon's sentiments. His mission as a war poet became didactic: to tell those at home what the trenches were like, how fear of death and the presence of suffering numbed the sensitive or drove them mad. He wanted to make the civilian population sensible of its responsibilities for the war. He carried about photographs of the war injured, while on leave, to illustrate his points.

As biographical material has accumulated and the psychologists have got to work, it has become clear that Owen was what Martin Seymour-Smith has characterized as an 'injustice collector'. A sense of duty and a gnawing masochism sent him back to the Front, and after writing more poems and enduring the worst of the last campaign, he was awarded the MC and killed the week before the armistice, in 1918. Edith Sitwell and Siegfried Sassoon published the first collection of his poems in 1920.

In some ways Owen resembles the equally idolized Rupert Brooke. Unlike Brooke, however, he was not known by his trench comrades as a poet, and he thus preserved a receptive anonymity. His poetic approach was rhetorical, like Brooke's; his aim, to accommodate the new subject matter in the old forms. Though his work ostensibly reverses Brooke's 'noble heroics', his attempts at realism are parallel to Brooke's. Brooke had the journalistic audacity to describe sea-sickness in a poem – an experience not celebrated in English poetry since Byron. And Owen, rather more penetratingly, describes the effect of gas on soldiers. Whereas Brooke's poems were useful politically to advance the war cause, Owen's more journalistic, though no less emotive, poems were from the other side. Each poet was putting new wine in rather different old bottles.

'The new material, if it could be presented at all, needed a profound linguistic invention,' C. H. Sisson has written. Owen lacked this quality. Owen *did* experiment effectively with what Edmund Blunden called 'para-rhyme' – off-rhymes such as head / lad – and Blunden praises the effect: 'remoteness, darkness, emptiness, shock, echo, the last word'. Less successfully he experimented with internal rhyme, strong assonance and alliteration. But the experiments were developments of common poetic technique. Owen's approach was neither verbally nor formally radical. His blending of irony and pity is not new – we have it in Hardy and Housman and Kipling. It is only the subject matter which is wholly new, and his fascination with the details of physical suffering which reveals a strangely adolescent mind.

Owen was not a realist but an idealist, attracted to the ugly and sordid *because* he was attracted to the beautiful. His passion for poetry was not, and never could have been, overwhelmed by pity. Others among the Georgians faced the same problem – masked as realists they followed beauty down urban alleyways or into the trenches. They adapted the rhetoric attached to 'the beautiful' in poetry to 'the ugly'. Rosenberg and Edward Thomas were the exceptions, discerning in extreme experience the new, unique language of extremity.

When Owen discovered that the hideous could be poignantly conveyed in the terminology of beauty, he did so to dramatic effect. However, traditional poetic diction, particularly Keatsian, carries a certain neutralizing moral effect: it depends on balance, proportion, and perspective, qualities which, since they were absent from the war experience, the poet had to fabricate, resorting at times to irony. In his poems pain does not cry out and break the form open, poise is not violated. The resonance must be in the understatement. This is why Owen's poems are so adaptable to musical setting: the expression can be left to the music, since the unspoken anguish in the vivid reportage *remains* unspoken. In Rosenberg's work language and form answer content, content is not neutralized or sentimentalized – it is realized. But Owen expresses intense love and intense physical agony in the same forms. The deformed man and the pastoral landscape are given in the same rhythms. Suffering is aestheticized. Owen sensed the unfortunate neutrality and, to overcome it, resorted to moralizing. In 'Disabled', he displays his war photographs, and with grotesque sexual overtones dwells in fascinated detail on wounds. This is sensationalism.

What makes Owen a war poet exclusively, while Edward Thomas and Isaac Rosenberg – both victims of the war – are not 'war poets' in the same sense, is the biographical accident that Owen was a very young and inexperienced man when he went into the trenches. Thomas and Rosenberg had endured a life of hardship before – the war was for them an extreme experience in a life of experiences. The war was Owen's only vital experience, his dominant theme. It did not for him come in the context of a varied life: it supplied its own absolute context.

In his famous 'Preface' to the poems – in fact rough notes, not a finished gnomic essay – he is completely dominated by his immediate experience. He promises a rhetorical and moralistic collection. The arrogance of, 'This book is not about heroes. English poetry is not yet fit to speak of them', shows the degree of his literary and political naïvety. 'Above all,' he writes, 'I am not concerned with Poetry.' In fact – in contrast with Rosenberg – he is so concerned with 'poetry' that half the experience of war necessarily eluded him.

Poets of the Second World War turned to models other than Owen. Keith Douglas turned to Rosenberg, Alun Lewis to Edward Thomas. The reason is clear. Douglas and Rosenberg are concerned with power, with the issues – moral and psychological – that motivate men in war and the lasting transformations that war brings about in them. Owen is more concerned with phenomena, the vivid externals, and his poetry is finally journalistic and didactic rather than psychological or penetratingly moral. His models are in the nineteenth century, his grotesques are romantic grotesques, his beauty a late romantic beauty.

But Owen's actual achievement is considerable. A few of the poems are not specifically war poems, though the violence is in them. 'Shadwell Stair' is a fanciful, disturbing 'spirit of the place' poem:

I am the ghost of Shadwell Stair.
   Along the wharves by the water-house,
   And through the dripping slaughter-house,
I am the shadow that walks there.

Other poems are less felicitous. In 'Fragment: "Cramped in the Funnelled Hole" ', he overwrites. In nine lines, the possessive form is used over-often: 'yawn *of* death', 'middle *of* his throat *of* phlegm', 'one *of* many mouths *of* Hell', 'teeth *of* traps', 'odour *of* the shell', and so on. In 'Arms and the Boy' the over-writing is evident in the insistent alliteration and the bathetic sentiment:

Lend him to stroke these blind, blunt bullet-heads
Which long to nuzzle in the hearts of lads.

We can contrast this with the entirely successful word choice in 'Conscious': 'The blind cord *drawls* across the window-sill'.

The authority with which Owen uses traditional forms ensures that many of his poems have powerfully dramatic endings. 'The Parable of the Old Man and the Young' re-tells, with a final twist, the story of Abraham and Isaac. The poet censures religion, tradition, 'responsible' men. 'Greater

Love' and 'Dulce et Decorum' are driven by a powerful rhetoric. They are humane political speeches about the conditions of war, and as such they could not be surpassed. They are like verse epistles or speeches to 'My friend' and 'you' up civvy street. But the rhetoric sometimes gets out of hand. In 'The Dead-Beat' a doctor is made to laugh at the death of an apparent malingerer, 'That scum you sent last night soon died. Hooray.' In 'The Next War' a similarly disastrous tonal error occurs.

Owen's diction is most lucidly developed in certain spare, carefully executed passages where the movement from line to line is heart-rending and inevitable. In 'Asleep' some of the best lines occur:

After the many days of work and waking,
Sleep took him by the brow and laid him back.
And in the happy no-time of his sleeping
Death took him by the heart.

The few adjectives are simple and well-chosen. Sadly, in the lines that follow, the poet forfeited this effect.

Few of Owen's poems were conclusively finished. They existed in several drafts, and the invidious task has fallen to his editors to piece together 'definitive' versions. Thus we may imagine that Owen himself would have pared down his overwritings, have perfected his forms, and have further developed the best of his longer poems, 'Strange Meeting'. The perfection of 'Futility' – which does not once specifically mention the war – shows what finality he could achieve. And 'Anthem for a Doomed Youth' mixes pastoral and war imagery to strong rhetorical effect.

'Hospital Barge at Cérisy' – a poem not much anthologized – achieves an effect as rare in Owen's work as it is in modern English poetry: a sudden fusion, in a moment of broken quietness, of allusions from various areas of experience, a poetic rather than a rhetorical resonance. Though the poem is not wholly successful, it includes some of Owen's most mature writing. 'Her' in the second line quoted refers to the barge:

One reading by that sunset raised his eyes
To watch her lessening westward quietly;
Till, as she neared the bend, her funnel screamed,
And that long lamentation made him wise
How unto Avalon in agony
Kings passed in the dark barge which Merlin dreamed.

The echo of Yeats's version of Ronsard, 'When you are old', is heard in the first two lines. But Owen moves on to a momentary transformation here well beyond the scope of Yeats's early style.

David Jones (1895–1974)

> ... it is easy to miss Him
> at the turn of a civilization.

David Jones, a convert to Roman Catholicism, celebrates immanence in his poetry, the presence of Christ in a world that is revived by the Incarnation and the Mass. Gerard Manley Hopkins, whose influence is felt throughout Jones's work, described how the Christian faith transforms the way one sees the world. He expressed it in contrasting images. Imagine the world reflected in a drop of water – the reflection retains the colours and shapes, it is merely a reduced image. But imagine the world reflected in a drop of Christ's blood: the processes of sacrifice and regeneration come to mind. A world suffused with the sacrifice of Christ is a world wholly meaningful and purposed. Jones looks no further than that: to the Incarnation and its momentous consequences, not to Heaven but to the redeemed earth. 'The Mass *makes sense* of everything,' he wrote.

David Jones was born in Brockley, Kent, in 1895. His father was Welsh – and a Welsh speaker – who worked as a printer's overseer. Jones early in life came to understand typography, platemaking, and the processes of printing. He also learned from his father an affection for Wales. His mother came of Cockney stock. Her father was a mast and block maker, and Jones learned about the river, the subtleties of ships and sailing, and the language of the docks.

He studied art at the Camberwell School of Art and at the Westminster School of Art, where his principal enthusiasms were for Blake and the English watercolourists and, one imagines, the work of El Greco. Drawing and painting occupied most of his time. His first book, *In Parenthesis* (1937), was not published until he was forty-two, already a mature graphic artist.

Four principal events shaped Jones's life. The first and most devastating was the Great War. He enlisted in the Royal Welch Fusiliers and was involved in active service for three years. The image of war, its devastation and at once the camaraderie it engendered between men, is dominant in his prose and verse. War is a central and recurrent fact of history, much as the Incarnation, re-created in the Mass, is the central, recurrent fact of faith.

The second event of moment was Jones's conversion to Roman Catholicism in 1921. This choice of a faith which had at its centre a vital sign – the host – rather than a formal symbol is significant. Jones does not deal with symbols. The signs, the 'anathemata' he retrieves and displays, do not stand for something other: they contain in themselves the nature of the larger thing they signify.

The third important event was Jones's relationship with Eric Gill, the great illustrator, typographer and visionary, at Ditchling and later in Wales. At Ditchling Gill had founded 'The Guild of St Joseph and St Dominic' – a secular community of artists and craftsmen, with ideals of service and dedication which made it almost a secular order. Discussions with Gill clarified Jones's thought. His artistic maturity dates from this period.

Though it seemed of little importance at the time, the fourth formative event was Jones's visit to the Holy Land in 1934. Suffering from a nervous disorder, he went to Palestine in a state of passivity, without energy or enthusiasm. He stayed there some months, and was intrigued by the historical remains, especially the inscribed stones from the time of the Passion. When he remembered the experience years later, his response came powerfully, after the event. Many of his poems are set in Palestine and much of his imagery relates to his stay there. His delayed responses to experience were a result of the war. The intense hardship of the trenches made it necessary for him to cultivate a surface insensibility to suffering, in order to hold experience at a distance, to survive. *In Parenthesis* was the last great account, by a combatant, of the War – published almost twenty years after it.

Jones's poetry is frequently difficult and obscure. The recurrent image of the Roman border guard, pacing the remote battlements that delimit civilization, gazing into the dark marches around empire and faith, is an image of the poet as well. The violence at the heart of the sacrament – the Crucifixion – and the violence implicit in the extension of Roman civilization, become the dominant facts of the poetry. Almost always in the poems there is a tension between the functional prose of Rome and the evocative poetry of the signs. Verse and prose are mixed in the poems: different experiences and qualities demand different modes of language to express them. There is, as well, a tension between the various registers of English he uses: a strange rustic colloquial (like Kipling's Cockney dialect), a Middle English thread, an Elizabethan thread, and a more standard prose and verse language, intense and formal. There are also echoes of folk songs, ballads, old saws, allusions to the work of other writers, echoes of Pound, Eliot, Hopkins, Smart, Joyce. Further, he introduces Latin quotes from the Church Fathers, from the Roman Mass and the Latin Bible. He introduces Welsh and other words into the texture of the verse, and lards some passages with place names and references which he glosses at great length in entertaining, but unfortunately distracting, footnotes. Coleridge wrote, 'Nothing can permanently please which does not contain in itself the reason why it is so, and not otherwise.' The truth of this observation can be tested in many passages of Jones's poetry, where poetic effect is suddenly dissipated by a sequence of footnoted obscurities. It is a language of disorientation, but despite its obscurities conveys a range of effects beyond the scope of a more traditional style. Because the language draws on so many social and historical registers, and because the rhythms are of a subtle and expressive nature, Jones's poetry is meant, as he tells us, to be read aloud 'with deliberation'.

The Welsh elements in his writings have a special significance for him. Wales is the source of British Christianity, and he evokes Christ and the Passion in a Welsh setting more than once. It is one of the places the Irish saints chose for the 'white martyrdom' of exile. It is a place Rome never subdued. Its language still miraculously lives, its landscape has a ruggedness and beauty that possess the quality of a sign.

Jones is a contemplative rather than a meditative writer. He does not analyse the mysteries but accepts and embodies them. He quotes Picasso, 'I do not seek, I find.' To understand his work, which is not descriptive or expository but evocative, a poetry *of* experience, not *after* experience, the fact of his faith and his purpose as a specifically religious writer must be borne in mind.

The control with which he deployed his poetry was that of a man who expresses his vision naturally – though he was not a spontaneous writer, and subjected his poems to interminable revision. His intention was to provide a possible way, a bridge, should we wish to cross it, to what he considered our cultural and communal roots – in history and a shared faith whose signs are still vital and operative.

Art is, by nature, 'gratuitous', Jones tells us. In his provocative book of essays, *Epoch and Artist* (1973), he says that if a beaver placed one gratuitous twig on its dam, the dam would become a font, the creature would enter the 'sign world': 'a culture is nothing but a sign, and the *anathemata* of a culture, "the things set up", can be set up only to the gods.'

Jones sees himself as a contemplative craftsman, a 'joiner' of song. He is scrupulous in his craftsmanship, relating everything directly or indirectly to the object of his contemplation, the sacrament. As René Hague noted, Jones's preference for the past participle form (whit*ed*, dark*ed*, etc) implies that an actor has been involved in imparting the quality to the object. If a wave is 'whited' it has been *made* white.

His craftsmanship is evident too in the accuracy of his description. He gets the details of the crafts he describes correct – whether shipbuilding, soldiery, or armoury. When he tampers with historical fact, it is to emphasize an historical point – and he draws our attention to his anachronisms in footnotes. By putting Greek, Roman and Celtic soldiers anachronistically together in one legion, for example, he expresses the universal nature of the empire.

He is engaged in remembering – as he writes, 'Our making is dependent on a remembering of some sort.' Poetry is the 'song of deeds', and to Jones the two great deeds are War and the Incarnation. He sets himself the task of 'making the signs available for today' – to provide a text which re-presents the deeds as they continue to signify in this world, 'at the turn of a civilization'. Remembering and revalidating the signs is the meaning of 'sacrament', seeing the universal in the nature of the particular – or, as Coleridge wrote (translating Bacon), seeing 'the latency of all in each'. This is why Jones's precise materialism and his meticulously localized images have a self-transcending or mystical quality. 'Art is the sole intransitive activity of man', he wrote – the poem is there, available. It does not impose itself on the reader.

Among Jones's allusions are many to prehistory, the ice age. 'Deposits' and 'stratifications' recur. The geological time scale intensifies the historical time scale, the layers of alluvial time overlaying one another much as the layers of history, the new cities built on the old, overlay one another. Time preserves, and there is a close analogy between the processes of nature and of history.

Kenneth Clark, in describing one of Jones's still-life paintings, evokes the qualities of the poetry as well. 'Although no exclusively Christian symbol is visible, we at once have the feeling that this is an altar, and that the flowers in some way represent parts of the eucharist. There are wine-coloured carnations and ears of corn, thorny stems of roses and blood-red petals, which drop on to the small white table cloth. Yet none of this is insisted on, and we are far from the closed world of symbolism. Every flower is there for a dozen reasons, visual, iconographical, or even on account of its name.' There is a two-dimensional quality about many of Jones's paintings. The signs and images are granted equal importance in a sort of perpetual foreground (an effect he achieves in writing by changing registers of language continually, allowing none to gain dominance). The paintings give emphasis by size of figures, not by prominence: the larger figures often dissolve into intricate detail.

Jones regarded the *Anathemata* (1952) as his most important work, and many poets have agreed with him. Eliot found it rewarding – though he felt it demanded three readings before it came clear. David Wright called it one of the 'major poetic efforts of our era', and Auden described it as, 'probably the finest long poem written in English this century'.

In his 'Preface', Jones writes, 'The action of the Mass was meant to be the central theme', with the implications of sacrament and re-presenting the signs. He intends that 'the workman must be dead to himself' while engaged upon the work, otherwise we have the sort of "self-expression" which is as undesirable in the painter or writer as in the carpenter, the cantor, the half-back, the cook.' His admirers have taken him at his word. And yet it is difficult to imagine a writer *less* 'dead to himself', less constantly aware of the extremely personal nature of his quest, the material of his poem (which is often based on particulars of his own biography), and the recurrent poetic process which determines his work. As Jones revises his poems, making them over the years denser and more allusive, he makes them always more personal and intricately difficult. When he lets them go it is only on the understanding that they are subject to revision, incomplete. The *Anathemata* is subtitled, 'fragments of an attempted writing'.

The poem, in eight sections, begins and ends with the 'action of the Mass'. There is no centre of interest or plot to the poem – rather a repeated process of re-presenting the signs with various material. In a sense, to read one section of Jones's poetry with understanding is to have read the whole work, for it is a matter of variation rather than extension. Salvaging material from oblivion, he is also 'trying to make a shape out of the very things of which one is oneself made', he writes. The artist is hardly 'dead to himself', then; as the poem says, '(For men can but proceed from what they know, nor is it for / the mind of this flesh to practise poiesis, *ex nihilo*.)'. 'What I have written has no plan,' he wrote later, 'or at least is not planned. If it has a shape it is chiefly that it returns to its beginning. It has themes and a theme even if it wanders far. If it has a unity it is that, what goes before conditions what comes after and *vice versa*.' This definition of the unity of the poem – subjective as it is – defines the unity of Jones's vision – the total interpenetration and relatedness of past, present and future.

Early in the first section of the *Anathemata* there is an example of Jones at his most intense. He describes the making of a table. It becomes a description of the making of an altar, a ship, and a cross, all at once. The act of carpentry and the thing made become a sign for the Mass, the Pilgrimage, and the Sacrifice, three central themes of the poem. This confluence of meanings is the key to Jones's style. He also uses rapidly shifting perspectives, almost oxymoronic until we realize the perspective is Christ's – 'the high room' is 'the high cave', and the haunting phrase 'down / among the altitudes' suggests almost a divine cinematography.

He celebrates presence, does not lament transience. Under the moraines of the ice age, the temporal *point de repère* of the first section, he finds vital traces. The ice had been like the covering on a dead body – 'the sea-borne sheet'. Its melting made possible the miracle of new life. The natural process is analogous to the historical process: the Incarnation released the frozen inner landscape. While insisting on distance, repeating 'long, long, long before', Jones also insists on presence. The ice age is vividly evoked:

As though the sea itself were sea-born
and under weigh
    as if the whole Ivernian *mare*
directed from hyperboreal control-points by strategi of the
axis were one complex of formations in depth, moving on a
frontage widening with each lesser degree of latitude.

The second section, opening with Troy and Hector's death,

moves to the first journey to England, alluding to the myth that Trojan Brutus was the colonizer of these islands. There are powerful inner-rhymes and assonances, strong alliterations. Jones makes verbs out of nouns and adjectives to strange effect: we read 'diaphanes' and 'saliva'd', for instance. In the third section, when the ship arrives, Jones presents the arrival in a series of questions which are not answered. But the vividness of the questions, without committing the poet to a description, gives a detailed picture of the ship's arrival:

Did he shelter in the Small Downs?
Keeping close in, did he feel his way
Between the Flats and the Brake...

And so the series evocatively progresses, suggesting all the possible perils that might have prevented the arrival and our history from beginning. He suggests there was some design (and designer) in the almost miraculous survival.

The fourth and fifth sections are based specifically on his grandparents' experiences: 'Redriff' is said to be an evocation of some of the characteristics of his maternal grandfather, speaking in a strange, slow Cockney slang. He insists on his own slow perfection as a craftsman, refuses to cheapen his craft or change his schedule for a reward. The poem takes the form of an oblique dialogue. The fifth section, indebted as Jones tells us to the 'Anna Livia Plurabelle' passage in *Finnegans Wake*, begins and ends with the cry of the lavender sellers in London streets. It is spoken largely by a woman to a sea captain – the same captain who asked in the fourth part for a speedy repair job on his ship and was rebuffed. The woman who speaks does not trace her biography but is, rather, part of the process of naming – an ignorant but receptive transmitter of the signs. She has belief without understanding.

She recalls, in an amusing passage, her lover, a man overburdened with signs, continually distracted from the business of love making:

   And then, as if he perceive a body – coming
as if he hails a personage
                    where was but insentience
and baulk of stone
                         he sings out clear
REDDITOR LUCIS ÆTERNÆ
These, captain, were his precise words – what sentiments I
can't construe – but at which, captain, I cried: Enough!
                    Let's to terrestrial flesh, or
bid goodnight, I thought.

We can't but wonder that her patience had lasted so long, for
he has been patting the wall and speaking sibylline phrases
for several pages.

   The woman's character seems to combine elements of
Ophelia, Molly Bloom, Mary Magdalen, Woman, and
Matriarch. A long tale of shipwreck, drawing on Coleridge's
'The Ancient Mariner', becomes a sign of the Passion; and
as in the first section the ship (as it were in reverse) becomes a
cross, an altar and a table. Finally the woman becomes Mary,
and one is tempted to conjecture that, in the original scheme,
this was to be the last part of the poem, since the shape is so
lucidly complete. One of the poetic climaxes of the book is
here. It combines allusions to Chaucer and Eliot, nursery
rhyme and Anglo-Saxon customs, among other things:

                    On the ste'lyard on the Hill
weighed against our man-geld
                    between March and April
when bough begins to yield
                    and west wood springs new.
Such was his counting house
                    whose queen was in her silent parlour
on that same hill of dolour
                    about the virid month of Averil
that the poet will call cruel.
                    Such was her bread and honey
when with his darling body (of her body)
                    he won Tartary.

After the *Anathemata*, Jones published another important volume, *The Sleeping Lord* (1974), the best book for the new reader of Jones's poetry to approach. It is ordered in such a way as to give access most readily to his idiom and style – a sort of primer for the *Anathemata*. In the first poem in the book, 'A, a, a, Domine Deus', he clarifies his mission as a poet. Open-minded, without prejudice, he seeks signs of Him in 'his manifold lurking places'. In the poems that follow – the best are 'The Wall', 'The Dream of Private Clitus', 'The Fatigue' and 'The Tribune's Visitation' – he finds the signs in a sort of short story form, largely in the ancient world, for the modern, mechanized world seems almost devoid of signs.

Jones, despite his craftsmanship and the seriousness of his dedication, belongs essentially to the romantic tradition. His poetry is rigorously circumscribed by his adherence to a single theme and a similar poetic process practised on a wide range of subject matter. Part of the limitation is his reticence, erecting a palisade of allusion and obscurity that only the most stalwart and well-armed reader can hope to breach. He is embattled – a strange stance for a giver – as though he would like to give but at the same time is eager to retain his gift.

Robert Graves (born 1895)

Every choice is always the wrong choice,
Every vote cast is always cast away—
How can truth hover between alternatives?

Robert Graves, when he called on Thomas Hardy, was
startled to learn that the older poet revised his poems very
little, subjecting them at most to three or four drafts. Graves,
even at that time, was reviser *par excellence*, endlessly adjusting
and altering, often years after a poem's first emergence into
language. His acumen for revision extended to other works
of literature. In 1933 he prepared a 'condensation' of *David
Copperfield*; in 1934 he wrote the novel *I, Claudius* – an
historical distillation. He is also a free translator from
Classical, Celtic and Oriental texts, and even in his criticism
he attempts to impose, if not detect, new orders. His
insistence on forming and re-forming, on revision rather than
vision, is central to his work. It reflects his desire always to
move closer to an elusive final statement.

Graves's craftsmanship makes the poems classically impersonal. Their effect depends entirely on the power of
words and rhythm to evoke experience, not on stimuli to the
senses – visual or otherwise; not on qualities inherent in
images, but on qualities inherent in the language.

The poems and the poet exist in a sort of exile, set apart
speaking from the borders. The experience of the First World
War strengthened his strangely alienated voice. War is a
persistent ghost in many of the poems. Graves suffered from
an acute sense of the chanciness, loneliness, even the un-
worthiness of his survival. The memory of war is heavy with

personal consequence. It does not, however, as in Blunden's case, seem to relate and bind him to the community of the dead. More negatively, it serves to set him apart from the living: it comes to seem that his is a charmed or chosen life. This sense liberated him into exile. His poem 'The Survivor' expresses the problem that confronted him, how survival altered everything for him.

Exile in the physical sense is expressed in two fine poems, 'The Cloak' and 'A Country Mansion'. In 'The Cloak' Graves presents the self-exiled peer. Graves traced his pedigree with a perseverance and pride reminiscent of Rilke's, or a royal corgi's, back to Henry VII. The peer of 'The Cloak' has various affinities with Graves's view of himself: 'This nobleman is at home anywhere, / His castle being, the valet says, his title.' Graves, too, has the title – poet, survivor, lover.

Has he no friend at court to intercede?
He wants none: exile's but another name
For an old habit of non-residence
In all but the recesses of his cloak.

Graves's 'old habit of non-residence' is prompted as much by a love of the Mediterranean as by rejection of dehumanizing industrialism, the desecration of landscape, the contemporary devaluation of relationships and standards. He expresses this, sometimes with contempt, more often with nostalgic concern, in poems such as 'On Dwelling'. Rather than stay at home and endure – or resist as Betjeman has done – the general impoverishment, he retires, sending us messages of his and our progress. He is a retrospective radical, not a reactionary, longing for an unregainable world. It has become a private battle, lost long ago, though he continues fighting. In 'The Cuirassiers of the Frontier' it is the guards at the outposts of empire who embody the empire's values and soul, while Rome, the heart of empire, has decayed. The Cuirassiers serve the ideal and not the fact of empire. The empire is in them, though they are not in it.

Robert Ranke Graves was born in London in 1895, son of the Irish poet and song writer Alfred Percival Graves. He grew up in a highly literate and privileged household. He was admired in his pram by Swinburne. He went to Charterhouse School and then to Oxford. The war interrupted his education. He joined the British Expeditionary Force and served in France, where he was wounded and suffered from shell-shock. He was reported dead; indeed, he read his own obituary in *The Times* before his twenty-first birthday.

Graves was provident enough to realize that – if he wanted independence to get on with his serious creative work – he would have to write some popular books. His first major success was *Good-bye to All That* (1929), a candid autobiographical account of his early years, the war, and the breakdown of his first marriage. The book recounts his various attempts to earn a living between the end of the War and his withdrawal to Majorca, an opportunity which the book itself facilitated.

Collections of his poems began appearing in 1916 – *Over the Brazier* and *Goliath and David* contained war poems of considerable accomplishment, though not as naked and alarming as Sassoon's. In 1917 *Fairies and Fusiliers* appeared. As the title suggests, he set out to find the common ground in extreme contrasts: truth hovers between alternatives. There is an almost blithe wit and irony about the war poems. *Country Sentiments* (1919) retired into more pastoral themes and modes. The early work developed largely out of ballad and nursery rhyme rhythms and forms. 'Allie, call the birds in, / The birds from the sky!' They possessed an engaging and often disturbing playfulness. Or they presented images of war in a particularly distinct and simplified form. He depended on the traditional poetic idiom of the Georgians. Many of the poems were larded with adjectives. Later revision tempered and tightened them.

Graves saw the limits of his chosen, traditional modes even as he recognized the restriction of his life in England, the various limiting choices with which he was hedging himself in. He engaged in serious academic work and more fanciful researches into the creative process, the importance of the unconscious in creative activity. For a period he considered poetry as therapeutic, but he moved beyond this phase. He explored what he called 'Poetic Unreason', he investigated modernism and reacted harshly against the work of HD and the Imagists. The tension in his poetry changed. From the craftsman-poet tending towards aestheticism, he gradually became a metaphysician, psychologist, and whimsical philosopher. He moved from innocence to knowledge. Later, he returned to innocence – the passionate, aroused old age of innocence, intensified but not betrayed by experience.

Certainly the early poet would have objected to the poet Graves was becoming in 1926. In a youthful poem he called on sudden justice to overtake:

Blasphemers trusting to hold caught
    In far-flung webs of ink
The utmost ends of human thought
    Till nothing's left to think.

For a time he became such a blasphemer. He also became a novelist, critic, mythographer and translator.

In 1926 Graves's life changed abruptly. He met Laura Riding and 'the strong pulling of her bladed mind'. Their names were closely associated between 1926 and 1939, and Laura Riding, a woman of powerful character and intellect, influenced the course of Graves's thought about poetry, bringing him to a clearer understanding of his technique and voice. She saw the poet's task as that of truth-teller. She contended that the poem could not be manufactured: it had to be discovered in the language. Michael Roberts summarizes her beliefs in these terms: 'Poetry is the final residue of significance in language, freed from extrinsic decoration, superficial contemporaneity, and didactic bias.' Certainly she had much to put right in Graves, for his early style is decorated; it often depends on a hackneyed or poetical vocabulary. And nor is it free from those tendencies almost inevitable in war poetry, 'superficial contemporaneity and didactic bias'.

Riding, like Graves and Roberts, believed – again in Roberts's words – that 'the poetic use of language can cause discord as easily as it can cure it. A bad poem, a psychologically disordered poem, if it is technically effective may arouse uneasiness or nausea or anger in the reader.' The poet has actual verbal power, the ability to affect other men. He must work with extreme care.

With Laura Riding, Graves prepared *A Survey of Modernist Poetry* (1927). One idea in particular is relevant to Graves's work. He writes that, 'the reader should enter the life of the poem and submit himself to its conditions to know it as it really is.' Adopting the same impersonality – indeed neutrality – as the poet has adopted, the reader must accept before he can know.

The relationship with Laura Riding came to an end in 1939. With the Second World War, Graves had to leave Majorca where he had spent ten years. He returned in 1956 to establish permanent residence there. The most provocative prose book of the post-Riding years was *The White Goddess* (1946, extended and amended in 1952 and 1961). His thesis is that true poetry is written in thrall to the Muse, the White Goddess. She is a figure defined in some of the poems, notably 'To Juan at the Winter Solstice' which celebrates her omnipresence, persistence, and her ineffable quality, and in 'The White Goddess'. She is reviled by saints and sober men, the goddess of extremes, vitality, imbalance; creative and destructive, she lives inside and outside the individual. She has no constant rules, she is 'Sister of the mirage and the echo'. Primitive, matriarchal, she is Nature as well, inspiring love and fear. Through her, Graves externalizes and mythologizes his own tensions, as Yeats did in *A Vision*. The myth expresses his intensely personal experience and universalizes it. The goddess has developed in his later work. She has now acquired a dark-skinned sister. Although Graves makes so much of her, he never finally trusts himself to her.

The power of sexual love brought the Goddess into being. In 1965 Graves wrote, 'My theme was always the practical impossibility, transcended only by miracle, of absolute love continuing between man and woman.' The alternative between 'practical impossibility' and 'miracle' led to the goddess, with whom he could will a relationship. One of Graves's most beautiful love poems, 'Love without Hope', resolves in celebration. Most of the poems relate to the theme.

The formal experiments in Graves's work usually occur well within the bounds of tradition. There is no startling innovation in his verse – indeed, what startles is the authority with which he deploys subject matter and imagery of romantic love poetry in the present age and with entirely contemporary authority. This is 'Love Respelt'. His secret is in the pared quality of the language, the weighing and placing of words rich in meaning in the right context, and the management of strongly colloquial rhythms built on a traditional prosodic base. 'Love is the echoing mind, as in the mirror / We stare on our dazed trunks at the block kneeling.'

Especially in the recent poems, he has developed a classical precision reminiscent of poems in the Greek Anthology. It is a poetry which distrusts facility. 'In Broken Images' expresses the distinction between the true and the facile poet, the poet who knows what he has to say before he writes and the one who discovers as he writes: 'He becomes dull, trusting his clear images: / I become sharp, mistrusting my broken images.' The poet trusts not facts but his senses: 'He in a new confusion of his understanding; / I in a new understanding of my confusion.' The theme is further lucidly developed in 'The Cool Web', perhaps Graves's best poem.

The formal deftness of his poems seems to contradict his critical cavils – and yet formal certainty is the only certainty he has. It overlies, or draws together, uncertainties, clarifying areas in the confusion. From the confusion and the paradoxes he wrests the occasional poem of fitful but compelling celebration of love. 'Counting the Beats', in a compact, repetitive form with a vocabulary pared down to the minimum and a tentativeness and experiential directness, must be numbered among his outstanding love lyrics.

Craft is always exercised on the uncooperative, the mysterious content of passion, and against the erosions of time. The poems illuminate small areas in chaos, clarify or resolve certain contradictions, reconcile one set of alternatives. Beyond each poem, the darkness forms again, or the poet comes up against a mirror and discovers he has been travelling in the wrong direction, into the self. 'Loving True, Flying Blind' describes his continuing career:

> no soft 'if', no 'either-or',
> Can keep my obdurate male mind
> From loving true and flying blind.

Austin Clarke (1896–1974)

In your decline, when truth is bare,
The thorn is seen without its crown.

When Robert Frost asked him what sort of poetry he wrote, Austin Clarke replied, 'I load myself with chains and then try to get out of them.' The 'chains' are as much formal as thematic, for even in his most apparently simple poems, Clarke is a genuine *poeta doctus*, and a close look at the exacting forms he devises, some of them based on Irish models, with *rime riche*, internal rhyme, complex assonantal and alliterative patterns, and difficult stanza forms, shows how his poems achieve complex resonance without calling attention to their formal complexities.

The poet John Montague described Clarke as 'the first completely Irish poet to write in English'. In *Twice Round the Black Church* (1962), Clarke's autobiography, he evokes his particular Irishness – Irish subject matter, versification, way of speech, and so on. Charles Tomlinson compares Clarke with MacDiarmid, commenting 'how a sense of nationality can deepen a comparatively narrow talent'. Clarke's talent is narrow in comparison with Yeats's, but he gains from being thoroughly rooted in an historical Ireland in a way Yeats was temperamentally unable to be. Clarke's nationalism is not, Tomlinson says, 'the inertia of chauvinism, but a labour of recovery'. He revitalized and adapted elements from a tradition essentially alien to the English, working as it were towards a separate Irish poetry in English.

Austin Clarke was born in Dublin in 1896. He was

educated at the Jesuit Belvedere College and the University of Dublin, where he later lectured in English. He travelled to England and worked as a journalist for a time, returning to Ireland in 1937, where he founded the Dublin Verse Speaking Society and the Lyric Theatre Company for his own and others' plays. Clarke's verse dramas are, with Padraic Fallon's, the most important after Yeats's. He was a founder member of the Irish Academy of Letters and acted as its President (1952–3). In his later years he travelled widely, reading and lecturing, and after a long period of eclipse, due largely to neglect of his work in Ireland, he re-emerged in the 1960s as an important voice in English poetry. The publication of his *Collected Poems*, edited by Liam Miller (1974) shortly before the poet's death, was a literary event – though widely neglected. He wrote three novels, criticism, memoirs, over twenty-eight verse plays, and some eighteen books of poetry.

Clarke's sense of time is insistently historical, unlike Yeats's. The early poems attempt to realize legend – the story of Finn, of the struggles between Ulster and the South, of Cuchulan, and a cast of characters made familiar by Yeats. But Clarke's approach in the early poems, albeit romantic and rhetorical, is psychological on the one hand – his characters are flimsy but more real than Yeats's; and historical, for Clarke sees in the early struggles analogies to the struggles of his day.

After the seventeen-year poetic silence (1938–55) in which Clarke was active with the Lyric Theatre Company, he returned to verse. His approach then was more direct, his concern with the quotidian affairs of Ireland, and he had developed a strong sense of the power of satire. Later still, the poems took a step into autobiography, became confessional in a particularly Irish way. Clarke wrote that 'The Confession poem was a recognized literary form in Gaelic and lasted until the eighteenth century.' He attempted to revitalize the form.

His first published poem was 'The Vengeance of Fionn' (1917). He describes the poem's process: 'The poem begins in the middle age of Diarmid and Grainne, and changes rapidly, visionally, to their youth and love – so that the reader has an awareness of the past – ideal in itself, yet further idealized by memory – in the present.' The quality of 'vision' is sometimes vivid in particular images, and the poem is governed by a subtle continuity of rhythm, not emphatic in a Yeatsian manner, but supple and always controlled by the subject. Basically iambic, in pentameters rhymed *ababcdcd*, it varies mimetically to contain dialogue, action, straight narrative, and evocative description. The poem is often mannered, at times stilted, and nouns carry an exhausting burden of adjectives. It is nonetheless compelling reading. From the dialogue in the poem Clarke learned lessons which were useful in his verse plays.

'The Fires of Baal' and the later narrative poems, on Celtic or Biblical themes, take plots that are largely familiar to most readers. They provide Clarke with a dramatic shape which he develops, lavishing most of his attention on the telling, on establishing varied time perspectives, placing the incidents within a temporal and spatial context. The poems are written with rigorous bardic impersonality. He could write such poems, he later commented, because at the time 'the future of our new State seemed so hopeful . . . Irish writers could delay for a while in the past.' The hope was ill-founded. The State soon demanded Clarke's satirical attention.

In *The Cattledrive in Connaught* (1925) Clarke began to work with short interrelated poems, exchanging the epic panorama for something more condensed and immediate. Though he retained his impersonal voice, the poems were no longer bardic. They referred less to an idealized past, though they were based on Irish models. 'A Curse' exemplifies both the indignation Clarke could express outside satire and – more important – the development of the exacting chains of rhythm, cross-rhyme, assonance and alliteration with which he loaded himself. 'Assonance,' Clarke wrote, 'takes the clapper from the bell of rhyme. In simple patterns the tonic word at the end of the line is supported by a vowel rhyme in the middle of the next line.' Donald Davie sees this, rightly, as a manifestation of the same impulse to intricate patterning we see in Celtic carving and graphic art.

Pilgrimage and Other Poems (1929) is Clarke's first major collection. In it he begins to develop one of his favourite roles, that of erring priest. In 'Celibacy', the image of ribs, with Biblical associations, is vividly developed: the 'self' climbs upon itself. The cross-rhymes 'briar/fire', 'nettle/fell', 'hunger/rung' are used with characteristic subtlety:

Bedraggled in the briar
And grey fire of the nettle,
Three nights, I fell, I groaned
On the flagstone of help
To pluck her from my body;
For servant ribbed with hunger
May climb his rungs to God.

A number of the poems consider the ephemerality of beauty. The incidents the poems arise from are rendered with frightening drama in 'The Cardplayer' or – at their most intense – in 'The Young Woman of Beare', which like many of the other poems has a strong erotic current, even in the chaste diction and sparse imagery. 'Although the clergy pray, / I triumph in a dream.' This is the triumph:

See! See, as from a lathe
My polished body turning!
He bares me at the waist
And now blue clothes uncurl
Upon white haunch. I let
The last bright stitch fall down
For him as I lean back,
Straining with longer arms
Above my head to snap
The silver knots of sleep.

The Irish models have served him well, astonishingly so in the short-lined stanzas.

In *Night and Morning* (1938) Clarke's transition to poems

set in the present and his achievement of a personal and particular voice are complete. Public themes – in the Irish context this includes religious themes – are developed, and with a hankering after eighteenth-century qualities of mind, clarity and purpose, Clarke begins to work towards satire. The echo of Yeats is faint when heard at all. Clarke's hallmark at this period is the unstressed line ending, with its modulation of rhythm and therefore of tone.

'Martha Blake' evokes the human impoverishment that religious inhibitions impose, with strong erotic resonance: the Mass provides her with almost sexual fulfilment, but final human emptiness. If Martha Blake's life is cheapened, we need look no further back than 'The Young Woman of Beare' to witness intense human fulfilment beyond the morality of the Church. Clarke revisits Martha Blake in a later collection, *Flight to Africa* (1963), in a poem entitled 'Martha Blake at Fifty-One'. Her unfulfilment is tragically complete, 'Her last breath, disappointed'.

Images of the Church's power abound. Every Irish coin has probably at some stage passed through the collection. The orgy, the antithesis to grim repressiveness, itself grim, fills dreams and is whispered in the confessional. As Clarke progresses, his anger accelerates, against the Church particularly, and its patterns of alienation. In 'The Straying Student', he characterizes Ireland:

> this land, where every woman's son
> Must carry his own coffin and believe
> In dread, all that the clergy teach the young.

Yet his anger is ambivalent. If, in 'The Jewels', he says, 'The misery of common faith / Was ours before the age of reason', he cannot help feeling nostalgia:

> O to think, when I was younger
> And could not tell the difference
> God lay upon this tongue.

The eucharist has left him hungry; reason lacks the solving nourishment of faith.

Seventeen years elapsed before *Ancient Lights: Poems and*

Satires, First Series (1955) was published. Most of the poems are satirical. Ireland, with its religious consensus and the immediacy of political issues, is a land where popular satire still has a role. The Church's attitude to birth control is one of his butts. In 'Three Poems About Children' Clarke's satire is most scathing, recounting a fire in an ill-equipped orphanage and a Bishop's consolatory platitudes.

The poem 'Ancient Lights' itself is one of Clarke's 'confessional' poems, about childhood and the anguish of religious confession. Other poems are suggested by incidents, newspaper articles, conversation, observation – small recollections taking shape in a changed present, becoming clear in and clarifying it, often humorously. Clarke's characters, though necessarily simplified, are rounded, not archetypal or emblematic characters of imagination nor clauses in a private myth, as in Yeats.

A second and third series of *Poems and Satires, Too Great a Vine* (1957) and *The Horse Eaters* (1960), appeared. In the first of these, 'The Loss of Strength' carries autobiography further. The rhythm, progressing in irregular, condensed phrases, and using the enjambment dramatically, catches with directness the movement of speaking under pressure. The poet finds a stream which, unlike the others, 'had never come to town' – is pure, unfished. The rhythm follows the eddying progression of the stream. It is a 'lost water'. The word 'monk-like' is especially apposite:

> Now engineering
> Machinery destroys the weirs,
> Directs, monk-like, our natural flow:
> Yet it is pleasant at Castleconnell
> To watch the salmon brighten their raincoats.
> The reeds wade out for what is gone . . .

Clarke draws an analogy between the dogmatic restraints the Church imposes on human nature and the harnesses which the Machine imposes on landscape and nature at large. Thus he can satirize at once the values embodied in the Church as currently constituted and the cash values embodied in industrialization; he can in effect reject what he sees as extreme expressions of analogous forces, both motivated by profit, both preying on and impoverishing human life. The 'ill-fare state' is a recurrent expression in the later poems.

'Hippophagi' in *The Horse Eaters* is a long poem on Ireland – a satire on its evils as they are summed up in its eagerness to export horse-flesh to the Continent for human consumption. Exporting the flesh of the old friend and servant to man typifies for Clarke the degradation of values in modern Ireland. 'Horse-eating helps this ill-fare state.' He returns to the theme in *Forget Me Not* (1962), his next major poem, in which he evokes through autobiographical detail the part the horse played in Irish life. The poem is a celebration and an elegy, as well as a satire, more varied, vivid and convincing than the romantic epics, though in scope as vast as his early poems. Epic gesture has resolved itself here in vivid particularity:

> Too much historied
> Land, wrong in policies, armings, hope in prelates
> At courts abroad! Rags were your retribution,
> Hedge schools, a visionary knowledge in verse
> That hid itself.

Clarke's most original poem is arguably 'Mnemosyne Lay in Dust' (1966), which non-Irish critics hailed as a masterpiece of the 'confessional' mode. It recounts a nervous breakdown, hospitalization, and return to the world. The central character, Maurice, is obsessed with various vivid memories of places, past pleasures, past fulfilments. Debilitated in his breakdown, the associations flow freely into his mind, until 'Terror repeals the mind'. Through the eyes of debilitation and madness, he evokes the other inmates and their particular delusions and agonies. His loss of memory is personal, but serves emblematically for a cultural loss of memory, a loss of connections with the past and therefore with the future. Finally Maurice emerges 'rememorized', 'his future in every vein'.

Old Fashioned Pilgrimage and Other Poems (1967) includes incidental poems about Clarke's tour of America, where he sees the country through the eyes of its writers – Poe, Whitman, Longfellow, Emerson, and others – and through the eyes of Dickens. Other poems are about Frost, Pound, Lorca and Neruda. Though the core of the collection consists of these tributes, the best poems are the laments of the ageing man suffering the indignity of failed sensuality.

Three further collections and a few late poems complete the *Collected Poems*. Some of the later poems are technically mechanical – 'The Labours of Idleness' and 'A Centenary Tribute', for example, have none of the subtle sound organization of the earlier work. The *rime riche* arrests the progression of the verse. The sound techniques have, in a sense, come to the surface. There are amusing poems, particularly 'In the Saville Club', in which he satirizes himself and Yeats. His last major poem, 'A Sermon on Swift', is anecdotal, amusing, and cutting, with much of the quality of his best satire.

Clarke's work suggests a distinctly *Irish* tradition, drawing from Celtic models and modes those 'chains' he described to Frost. His sense of what Rickword called the 'negative emotions', the uncompromising nature of his best satires and the vividness of his love lyrics and more visionary poems, and his powerful civic conscience, contribute to his large and generous poetic achievement.

Edmund Blunden (1896–1974)

We went, returned,
But came with that far country learned;
Strange stars, and dream-like sounds,
changed speech and law are ours.

Edmund Blunden's 'War's People' describes how war alters
the individual's speech, values, and nature, though it does not
alter a country. In Blunden's case, the war experience
changed him from a 'celebrant' to an elegist, lamenting the
loss of optimism, the betrayal of promise. Only the natural
landscape seems untouched by the betrayal of the war. When
Blunden became a celebrant again in some of his poems set in
Japan and the Far East, there is a manufactured quality about
the celebration. In one of his best poems he writes, 'I spoke of
peace, I made a solitude.' Blunden's solitude is a peculiar
mixture of Hardy's and Rosenberg's. He is isolated because he
survived a war in which so many perished. The fortuitous
nature of his survival is best expressed in *Undertones of War*
(1929), an outstanding prose account of service in the First
World War. So, too, in the poem 'November, 1931' he expresses loneliness and incomprehension at his survival – 'We
talked of ghosts; and I was still alive.' Though he wrote poetry
during the war, the best of his war poems came later.

Born in Yalding, Kent, in 1896, Edmund Charles Blunden
spent his early years in the Kentish countryside. He studied at
Christ's Hospital in Sussex. His youth was entirely rural, and
his pastoralism is authentic. At Christ's Hospital he distinguished himself in Latin and Greek and earned a scholarship

to Oxford. Christ's Hospital determined his literary tastes to a degree. He wrote critical studies of Leigh Hunt and Charles Lamb, and showed a deep interest in Coleridge, three old boys of the school. He prepared a study of Shelley, whose English countryside he knew from his school years. No doubt the rural background sharpened his taste for Hardy, whose work he wrote about. He edited the works of John Clare, and – as a tutor at Oxford, a Professor in Japan and Hong Kong, and Professor of Poetry at Oxford – he showed himself wholeheartedly dedicated to English romanticism.

During the First World War he was a lieutenant in the Royal Sussex Regiment and saw extensive action. In 1916, three small volumes of his pastoral poems were published privately and in 1920 published together in his first book, *The Wagoner and Other Poems*. Returning to Oxford after the war, he found it incongruous with his war experience and soon went down, moving to London where in 1920 he became assistant editor of the *Athenaeum*. In 1924 he went to Tokyo as Professor of English Literature, and thus began his academic vocation which ended in 1968 when, on grounds of ill health, he resigned the Chair of Poetry at Oxford. He died in 1974.

Blunden adheres to the pastoral mode even in his war poems, which do not confront the details of war in the way that Owen's do, or attempt to plumb the personal consequences of the experience as Rosenberg's do. Instead, the poet fixes his attention on a point of stillness in the tumult. Though most of the poems are marred by a hackneyed diction, a preponderance of stock epithets and often stock attitudes, what is original is the tone – reticence, humility and perplexity at the experience and the fact of his survival. The war poems focus on what survives war, even if only momentarily, for instance an old house where the panes of glass are yet unbroken and the farmer has not moved out. The house is eventually destroyed. Or Blunden recalls flowers, or a ruined church which somehow survives despite the shelling. In presenting these precarious monuments he evokes the intense calm moments between the periods of hell.

His refusal to dwell on the unpleasant, or artificially to

prolong the pleasant – in other words, his sense of experience in the context of time and change – guarantees his honesty as a poet. He loved Japan because he found a temperamental affinity with elements in Japanese character, and his oriental verse is full of the gently persistent 'soul which knows no wild extremes'. This also circumscribes his accomplishment, for excessive balance, a reticence too great to perpetrate an over-statement, makes for the sameness and repetitiveness of his verse and an evasiveness which fails fully to confront extreme experience. Thus in his best poem, 'Report on Experience', which opens powerfully, he moralizes, forces a balance on his material. He is the academic romantic, the English poet at the end of a long and, in his terms, as in the terms of many Georgian poets, no longer fully viable tradition. Unwilling to adopt fashionable cynicism, to devalue the poetic act by de-bunking it with irony, and unwilling too to learn from modernist practice, he kept to a poetic process that became a necessary formula, but a solipsistic one too, remaining in touch with *his* roots. In his own words, he wrote poems 'to avoid estrangement from a way of life beloved since child-hood'.

Despite formal affinities with the work of de la Mare, Blunden's poems are the product of an entirely different tem-perament. 'The Barn' evokes a place of age, valued because it is *old*, not because it is haunted: 'The barn is old, not strange.' His writing has a greater particularity than de la Mare's, too. 'The Poor Man's Pig' humorously describes a scene where 'apple boughs as knarred as old toads' backs / Wear their small roses ere a rose is seen'. For Blunden, there is no mystique about this world of particulars: they express loss, but it is death rather than dream that makes them significant. 'The Midnight Skaters' describes the relationship of man to death. Men skate perilously over waiting death – 'let him hate you through the glass'. 'The Almswomen', one of his most anthologized poems, tells of two old women who, loving one another and life with passionate intensity, labour to make as much as they can grow, and sit at evening worrying about death.

The natural world is eloquent. In 'The Recovery' he writes:

> here dwell
> Twilight societies, twig, fungus, root,
>   Soundless, and speaking well.

Animals, too, have meanings – many of the poems examine the beauty and cruelty of their world. The precise observation, rendered with an acute sense of the power of line endings, improves many otherwise weak poems. In 'The Quick and the Dead' there is a point of clarity typical of Blunden, which inspired Keith Douglas: 'Pools where carp doze through their green / Eternities.'

Trusting clarity, he will not place confidence in the deceptive mist which seems to alter landscape. Mist – like the dream – is an enemy in the poems:

> I am too old a realist
> To make sea dreams
> From you,

he says, addressing the mist, but nonetheless deriving some powerful images from it before he dismisses it. He refuses to place too much trust in subjective response: it alters with circumstance. He appreciates the relativism of subjective impressions, but will not bow to them, shirking their extremes. In 'Values' he writes:

> It is my chance to know that force and size
> Are nothing but by answered undertone.
> No beauty even of absolute perfection
> Dominates here – the glance, the pause, the guess
> Must be the amulets of resurrection;
> Raindrops may murder, lightnings may caress.

War is felt in some of his quietest poems, even in details like 'volleys' of bird song. In his verse romances, his dramatic monologues and tales, violence and disruption are always near at hand. 'A Shadow by the Barn' describes his best effects:

> though glorious noon delights me, still
> Something of sadness pleases more; the skill
> Of imminence, of omen is the best.
> I hear this moment my beloved unrest.

Yet most of the poems are too finished, too literary in ambition and effect, to admit of this unrest. They are the work of a keen intelligence, a fine translator from the Greek, with skill as a humorous versifier – as in 'An Ominous Victorian' and the subtle long poem, 'The Geographer's Glory'. But in striving for balance he generally achieves neutrality.

The excellence and limitation of Blunden's style are best revealed in 'The Blind Lead the Blind' and the less typical 'Report on Experience'. Though the second of these is sadly neutralized by the last stanza, the opening lines, adapted from a passage in Dickens's *Martin Chuzzlewit* which itself contains Biblical references, are unsurpassed in the rest of Blunden's work:

> I have been young, and now am not too old;
> And I have seen the righteous forsaken,
> His health, his honour and his quality taken.
>   This is not what we were formerly told.
> I have seen a green country, useful to the race,
> Knocked silly with guns and mines, its villages vanished,
> Even the last rat and the last kestrel banished—
>   God bless us all, this is peculiar grace.

The directness of statement, even through abstractions, the tone of quiet public address, and the theme of the betrayal of innocence and expectation, are powerfully conveyed.

Edgell Rickword (born 1898)

And we, too, with as little fuss
might thus ignore the world's dark edge,
but those dead rays of coatless us
augur the thin end of time's wedge.

Edgell Rickword abandoned writing poetry – except for one
outstanding satire – in 1930. His poetic career spans fourteen
years, between the end of the First World War and the depths
of the Great Depression. His work as a poet was almost
finished in 1930; he had expressed as much as he wished,
without repetitions, in that medium. His integrity prevented
him from developing facility, from turning out self-imitations.
He moved on to political activism. His poetry included not
only some of the best satires of our time but also individual
and powerful war poems, Symbolist poems, haunting lyrics,
and metaphysical poems after the manner of Donne.

He was born in Colchester, Essex, in 1898. His household
was 'moderate Tory' – mildly literary, attending to the Victorian novelists and poets. He left this rural, bourgeois childhood in 1916, enlisting in the Artists' Rifles. Already he was
writing poems in the Swinburnian mode. He became an
officer in the Royal Berkshire Regiment, and after the
Armistice was invalided out, having been awarded the
Military Cross.

He wrote his war poems after the war, unlike some of his
contemporaries who composed in the trenches. Having
taught himself French while in France, he went up to Oxford
on his return to England to read French. The Oxford course

only went as far as Victor Hugo – but his interests were in Verlaine and Baudelaire. He came down after four terms, married and penniless, and began reviewing for the *Times Literary Supplement* and the *New Statesman*.

Rickword's critical work is still a touchstone for serious literary criticism. F. R. Leavis's first published book was a selection from Rickword's *Calendar of Modern Letters* which he subtitled 'Towards Standards of Criticism'. David Holbrook called it 'the first critical prose in English written this century, apart from the greater essays of T. S. Eliot'. All his critical work was 'directed towards the possibilities of creation'. Rickword's first critical book was *Rimbaud: the Boy and the Poet* (1924), a seminal study of the French poet. He edited the *Calendar of Modern Letters* (1925–7) and edited two volumes of *Scrutinies* (1928, 1931), reassessments of inflated reputations and revaluations of underrated talents. After he ceased writing poetry, Rickword continued to review and write essays. He edited the *Left Review* (1934–8) and *Our Time* (1944–7). From a primary concern with literature and its place in society, he moved to more exclusively social commitments. His Marxism matured and he assumed the only activist role available to him in England at the time – editing magazines aimed at a wide readership. Some of his critics believe that Marxism was responsible for his giving up poetry. And yet, without the development of his social conscience, his poetry would hardly have attained the commitment, range, and power that it did, before he moved beyond it.

Early in his writing, Rickword sensed the difference between the critical and the creative intelligence – the one analytical and objective, the other intuitive and in its associations subjective. Marxism intensified the critical intelligence. In a recorded conversation Rickword described his brand of Marxism: 'I am a Marxist in the sense that I try to relate public happenings to the tissue of cause and effect which Marx divined in the interplay of material and economic forces.'

In the poems, Rickword writes intuitively *with* the 'common man', not didactically *for* him, and in this respect differs from the 1930s Marxists who condescended to preach and instruct. Rickword writes poems as a man acquainted intimately with the sordidness of poverty. His antipathy for cliques, for elitism of the sort Eliot and Wyndham Lewis came to stand for, is intense (though he was among the first critics to appreciate Eliot's achievement). 'One condemned modern civilization,' he said, 'for its uniformity and mass-mediocrity. Eliot and Wyndham Lewis had a wrong sort of elitism, believing themselves cut off from common humanity.' Rickword, on the other hand, despite his childhood, felt himself alienated from the middle classes. In 'Ode to a Train-deluxe', subtitled 'Written on a railway embankment near London and inscribed to our public idealists', his aversion is clear:

Far from the city, grossly real,
through Nature's absolute they stroll,
and nimbly chase the untamed Ideal
through palm-courts at the Metropole.

Rapt in familiar unison
with God, whose face must now appear,
they show their wife and eldest son
the fat-cheeked moon rise, from the Pier.

The 'fat-cheeked' moon, an epithet for the sentimental outlook of the comfortably off, bites deep. They ignore 'the world's dark edge'. This satire is gentle compared with 'Twittingpan' or 'To the Wife of a non-Interventionist Statesman'. In the latter poem, his last major work in verse, written in 1938, the prophecy proved all too accurate. He imposes himself on the Statesman's wife and urges her to deny her husband sexual satisfaction, indeed to berate him, for his non-interventionist stand towards Franco's Spain. He warns:

Euzkadi's mines supply the ore
to feed the Nazi dogs of war:
Guernika's thermite rain transpires
in doom on Oxford's dreaming spires:
in Hitler's frantic mental haze
already Hull and Cardiff blaze

and Paul's grey dome rocks to the blast
of air-torpedoes screaming past.
From small beginnings mighty ends
from calling rebel generals friends,
from being taught at public schools
to think the common people fools,
Spain bleeds, and England wildly gambles
to bribe the butcher in the shambles.

The satire, specifically political, still retains its resonance. The intensity of his anger and the urgency of his message are reflected in a certain technical roughness.

Rickword's programme was to remake poetry by a use of 'negative emotions'. 'The poetry of my contemporaries was kind and nice and sweet, [but] there was no need to confine poetry to the expression of such feelings.' Instead, the effect striven for was 'something like the cubists, perhaps, who wanted to paint all sides of an object, to show an object in full . . . to synthesize the various facets of an emotional experience.' Rickword concedes that modern poetry, since his time, has learned perhaps too much about 'negative emotions' and senses a new vein of negative sentimentality, a sentimentality of violence, just as vacuous as the facile optimism of greetings-card Georgians and imperial apologists.

Rickword's attempt to 'paint all sides of an object' leads to a close study of the 'negative emotions' as revealed in literature, psychology, history, myth and science. The best examples Rickword found were Rimbaud, Baudelaire, the English metaphysical poets (particularly Donne), Charles Churchill, and Swift. With these poets he had a temperamental as well as a programmatic affinity. He called Swift 'the most vigorous hater we've ever had in our literature'. Rickword's early poems, especially the love poems, reveal a sense of reciprocity in sexual relations rare in English love poetry. They were composed under the spell of Donne:

Since I have seen you do those intimate things
that other men but dream of; lull asleep
the sinister dark forest of your hair

and tie the bows that stir on your calm breast
faintly as leaves that shudder in their sleep;
since I have seen your stocking swallow up,
a swift black wind, the flame of your pale foot,
and deemed your slender limbs so meshed in silk
sweet mermaid sisters drowned in their dark hair;
I have not troubled overmuch with food,
and wine has seemed like water from a well;
pavements are built of fire, grass of thin flames;
all other girls grow dull as painted flowers,
or flutter harmlessly like coloured flies
whose wings are tangled in the net of leaves
spread by frail trees that grow behind your eyes.

This poem is carefully integrated: a single sentence. It is full of the wit of language and hyperbole – the wit of celebration. The imagery of fire is evolved, and more subtly the image of the forest, of leaves, which suggests a vital permanence through which ephemeral birds fly. Extrovert wit, not introvert irony, makes the poem powerful.

The satires and the love poems are opposite poles of Rickword's poetry. When he began writing his model was Donne, when he fell silent it was after he had achieved something of the power of Swift. The early poems celebrate physical passion, but gradually revulsion overcomes the lover, he moves from pure celebration to the sense of ephemerality of pleasure, the uncertainty of relationship, the uncertainty of even the most natural recurrences. In 'To the Sun and Another Dancer' he writes:

Weak as a girl deserted when she loves,
my fancy roamed its dim and hopeless groves
and climbed in turn the five thin towers of sense
out of those dank, autumnal airs of absence
by the whole being realized as pain,
forgotten only to be proved again.

Later in the poem come the lines, 'Dawn is a miracle each night debates, / which faith may prophesy but luck dictates.' The poet, unable to ignore 'the world's dark edge', cannot avoid the negative emotions which leave experience raw, uncertain.

'Terminology' explores how language, like time, engages and disengages reality. The poem is about the limits of fancy and of language. The poet's power is to use language to break the bounds of language, to imply and contain meanings in an ordering of connotations. In poetry the language begins its work only after the denotative meanings have been assimilated. In Rickword's best poems, the thought is so complete, and so completely contained within the images, that quotation out of context falsifies the statement. For the thought, throughout the poem, functions consistently on various levels.

In 'Birthday Ruminations' Rickword confronts the problem of death and ephemerality most intrepidly. 'Time has no pity for this world of graves,' one of the poems says. The almost savage beauty of the vision in 'Birthday Ruminations' culminates in a stanza where, beside the integrating world of the sea, man's disintegration is cast into relief:

The crepitation of the restless grains
and the soft integration of fresh worlds
and the vermiculation of the flesh,
is the procession of the pastoral soul;
a piscine epic, mammal tragedy.

The moon is a frequenter of Rickword's poems, but not the usual poet's moon. She comes sometimes as a courtesan wooing over the corpse-littered battlefield, or as fat-cheeked, or she is neutral, or sometimes the emblem of change and fickleness. So, too, the sea, and its unknown world of fishes, often counterpoints with power and delicacy the world of upper air and its inhabitants. Images of suburbia are contrasted with rural images, images of order and fecundity qualify those of chaos and sterility, and all are held in a subtle tension by Rickword's skill in expressing a complex of ideas through one structure of images.

Desire, Time, Pity, Shame, Solicitude, and other Augustan abstractions gain new significance in the poems. Rickword foreshadows in many ways – not merely politically – the generation of Auden and his colleagues. In 'Divagations (ii)', for example, he experiments with Anglo-Saxon forms and finds them as sterile as Auden, at greater length, was to find them. In 'Incompatible Worlds', a poem dedicated to Swift, he uses a metre and indeed a diction so closely reminiscent of Auden's famous elegy to Yeats that we cannot help but wonder if there was direct influence. In his attempt to fuse the world of Freud and Marx, Rickword prefigures the 1930s poets, though where they sensed a choice, he confronts the paradox and refuses to sidestep the issues it raises. It would be hard to find a poet in the succeeding generation to match him for integrity and consistency, and his skills, too, are on a par with those of the best 1930s poets, though the bulk and range of his verse is smaller.

'Trench Poets' and 'The Soldier Addresses his Body' are the best-known of his war poems. In 'Trench Poets' the speaker watches his dead friend's body decompose. There is anguished wit in the incomprehension with which he attempts to revive the body – reading Donne to it, and finally in desperation quoting from *Maud*. But:

His grin got worse and I could see
he sneered at passion's purity.
He stank so badly, though we were great chums
I had to leave him; then rats ate his thumbs.

The impotence of art and love before the central fact of death is expressed without pity – and hence without condescension – in this poem. There is, too, anger at the powerlessness of love, which is a central theme in Rickword's work.

Basil Bunting (born 1900)

I hear Aneurin number the dead, his nipped voice.

Basil Bunting, after almost total neglect for several decades, was abruptly 'discovered' in the 1960s, championed and promoted with such enthusiasm by some, and so disparaged by others, that a balanced assessment of his achievement has been difficult. He suffers – as Pound and David Jones do – from his admirers. Their advocacy – pedantic or adulatory as it sometimes is – antagonizes those readers who, hostile to modernism, see in Bunting a further manifestation of dubious rhythms, sterile severity, distracting mannerisms, and imprecise forms. He can plead 'not guilty' on all counts.

Basil Bunting was born in Northumbria in 1900. Northumbria provided him with a particular accent and vocabulary which he did not suppress, despite his long exile from England. He was educated locally, and chose eventually to become a journalist. He spent some time in prison as a conscientious objector to National Service after the First World War, and when released he went to London. In 1927–8 he was music critic for *The Outlook*. He reports that his own first experience of poetry as a possibility for himself came with the recognition that the order and movement of *sound* in a poem might itself create a cohesion of the emotions underlying – a recognition he came to through music. He was sub-editor in Paris of Ford Madox Ford's *Transatlantic Review*. He moved to Italy to be near his mentor, Ezra Pound, in Rapallo, and there met Yeats, who characterized him as 'one of Ezra's more savage disciples'. Through Pound he met Louis Zukofsky, who became a close friend, and with whom he shares a concern with music and its analogies with verse.

Pound dedicàted his *Guide to Kulchur* jointly to Zukofsky and Bunting, 'strugglers in the desert' as he christened them. And Pound included Bunting's work in his *Activist Anthology*. In 1931 Zukofsky included him in the 'Objectivist' issue of *Poetry* (Chicago), and later in the *Objectivist Anthology*. Objectivism was a shortlived movement. William Carlos Williams described it thus: 'The poem, like every other form of art, is an object, an object that in itself formally presents its case and its meaning by the very form it assumes. Therefore, being an object, it should be so treated and controlled – but not as in the past. For past objects have about them past necessities – like the sonnet – which have conditioned them and from which, as a form itself, they cannot be freed.' Objectivism was, in effect, an attempt to rationalize an instinctive approach to form, form that rose out of diction, was not imposed on it. Bunting, because he never developed the sort of diction from which form *could* follow (as Zukofsky, Pound and Williams did), hardly belongs in the group. But he assumed their attitudes to form.

During the Second World War Bunting was sent to Persia. He stayed on after the war as a member of the British Diplomatic Service and later as a journalist, but was expelled by Mossadeq. Persian language and literature had long been interests of his, and his sojourn there intensified his commitment. He returned to England and to Newcastle upon Tyne, where he worked on a local newspaper. He was taken up by the young Newcastle poets associated with the Mordern Tower.

Bunting's early work owes various debts. Tudor and Elizabethan models, early Eliot, Pound, Yeats, the French Symbolists in different ways show through. He adds to the list others 'whose names are obvious': Wordsworth, Dante, Horace, Manuchehri, Ferdosi, Villon, Whitman, and Zukofsky. His *Collected Poems* (1968) constitute a small *oeuvre*. He tells us that he wrote when he 'could do nothing else'. The first collection, *Redimiculum Matellarum*, was followed by *Poems 1950*. Fifteen years later *The Spoils* appeared at last in England, followed by *Loquitur* (a revision of *Poems 1950*) in the same year. Bunting's best-known poem, *Briggflatts*, came out in 1966, and then the *Collected Poems*. There is a sense of continuity and unity in the small body of work. The themes are not novel – poverty, particular loves, departure, return, regret, being misunderstood, being alone, social disgust, and so on. Innovation is rightly, with Bunting, a matter of making the familiar fresh, renewing vision by renewing the way we speak and see in poetry, not finding new subjects. The bias is anti-scientific and anti-positivist from the outset in 'Villon' (1925) through to *Briggflatts*. Antagonisms define Bunting as much as positive passions, for he is *par excellence* a self-embattled poet.

For Bunting, poetry 'lies dead on the page, until some voice brings it to life, just as music on the stave is no more than instruction to the player'. In drawing the analogy with music, which he often does in his prose writing, he says, 'To me it seems that history points to an origin that poetry and music share, in the dance that seems to be part of the make up of *homo sapiens*, and needs no more justification or conscious control than breathing. The further poetry and music get from the dance and from each other, the less satisfactory they seem.' In *Briggflatts* he says:

It is time to consider how Domenico Scarlatti
condensed so much music into so few bars
with never a crabbed turn or congested cadence,
never a boast or a see-here . . .

In his preface to the *Collected Poems* Bunting wryly says, 'Unabashed boys and girls may enjoy them. This book is theirs.' The first poem is 'Villon'. It has some of the austerity of Nashe in its presentation of the death theme, and more than a small echo of Yeats. Bunting often uses the series – of proper names, verbs, or nouns – to create a rhetorical effect. In 'Villon' he writes:

Abelard and Eloïse,
Henry the Fowler, Charlemagne,
Genée, Lopokova, all these
die, die in pain.

The resonance of the passage comes from associations already attached to the names and from the Yeatsian rhythm. But Bunting uses rhyme and a variation on the eight-syllable line with a more individual cunning elsewhere:

The Emperor with the Golden Hands
is still a word, a tint, a tone,
insubstantial-glorious,
when we ourselves are dead and gone
and the green grass growing over us.

In passages such as this, with controlled development of back vowels, Bunting achieves some of his best effects.

'Villon' is a satire, an elegy of sorts, a love poem, an 'autobiography', and a dramatic monologue. In other words, it is a poem without a fixed mode, and its power is in its range. 'Attis: Or Something Missing', lacks this scope, satirizing T. S. Eliot who appears as an eunuch (Attis's self-emasculation in service of Cybele is the legend at the back of the poem). Bunting claims his target was Lucretius and Cino de Pistoia – in fact, it is an ageing Prufrock.

The Spoils, written in 1951, is one of Bunting's best poems. It is in three sections. In the first, the four sons of Shem, son of Noah and father of the Semites, speak from exile in Babylon where they lead a profitable, usurious life. They are rootless within an alien society, rich without contentment. In the second section Bunting describes with nice historical sense an ancient social stability, darkly threatened:

Have you seen a falcon stoop
accurate, unforeseen
and absolute, between
wind-ripples over harvest? Dread
of what's to be, is and has been—
were we not better dead?

In the third section, against the antiquity and durability of the historical setting, the modern European war is enacted in Africa and elsewhere. The juxtaposition of the three sections reveals cultural incompatibilities: the war occurs against a backdrop of cultural permanence, but parallel to the first section of unsettled and predatory exile. The first and third sections are about 'we who would share the spoils', while the central section describes the values and things that are to be despoiled. Commerce and war are at the heart of the destructive cycle.

Briggflatts is subtitled 'An Autobiography'. We are warned not to read it as literal autobiography. In the first section Bunting peoples a Northumbrian landscape with images and then skilfully coordinates them. We meet the lively bull, Rawthey, and the less lively tombstone maker, reading his new inscription with his fingertips. Life, passion and 'music' are embodied in Rawthey, while death is embodied in the mason. Against the backdrop of these images, two lovers come, watch 'the mason meditate / on name and date', and generally appreciate what they see. They go home and make love before the fire, in a passage where Bunting's rhetoric gets the better of him and he produces banal effects. The lover unties 'tape / of her striped flannel drawers' and at last 'on the pricked rag mat / his fingers comb / thatch of his manhood's home'. The unfortunate rhyme and conceit, the academic poise, are totally out of keeping with the poem.

After the event, the lovers fall into mutual blame, regret – but, Bunting tells us in near doggerel verses, the deed can't be undone. The altered lovers return to the altered landscape. The bull is no longer 'sweet' but 'truculent, dingy'. The carved stone is the headstone of dead love.

In the second section the poet becomes embattled, accusing, out to show up the bogus world that despises him. But he succumbs to insincerity and degradation. He goes to sea. He is forgotten. 'Love is a vapour, we're soon through it,' he says. He goes to Italy. Again we have tombstones and bulls – this time the bull turns out to be the minotaur, approached in the transition of images between the music of

birds and the complications of 'Schoenberg's maze'. The
image of the labyrinth – Muir's image for the mind – comes
into play. The third section is documentary, descriptive, and
tautly written. What the poet sees is charged with a sense of
vulnerability to exploitation and destruction.

The passage about Scarlatti comes from the fourth section.
Beginning with long lines, Bunting lets the cadence gradually
dwindle. After a battle, after a flood, 'I hear Aneurin number the dead, his nipped voice.' The progression to the
nipped statements of personal moment casts strong emphasis
on the lines: 'Where rats go go I, / accustomed to penury, /
filth, disgust and fury.' The fifth section delivers the most
personal message Bunting has achieved in verse. He describes
the new year, the change of seasons, men with their dogs.
The past rushes on him, 'silence by silence sits / and Then is
diffused in Now'. Fixing his attention on a star whose light
has travelled fifty years to reach earth, he ponders on the
amorous incident from the first section: the light of the star
is, poetically, from the same date, from the past:

Fifty years a letter unanswered;
A visit postponed for fifty years.

She has been with me fifty years.

Starlight quivers. I had day enough.
For love uninterrupted night.

The poem obliquely enacts a kind of autobiographical
exorcism. The early incident remained a gnawing presence.
Spoken at last, in age which is 'starlight', the speaker has
come to terms with it. The poem ends with a 'Coda', with a
portentous analogy between the dying poet and the executed
kings.

Throughout his career, he has written what he calls
'Odes', in fact satires, love poems, meditations. He has also
prepared 'Overdrafts', translations from Latin, Persian, and
Italian into English, or from Zukofsky into Latin. He has
adapted Machiavelli in 'How Duke Valentine Contrived' –

taking Machiavelli's text, he retells it in concentrated verse.

For me, Bunting's outstanding poem is 'Chomei at Toyama' written in 1932 in much the same manner as 'How Duke Valentine Contrived'. In the earlier poem he condensed, he tells us, a prose book by Kamo-no-Chomei, a twelfth-century Japanese figure. In condensing it, he chose the ideal original for his purposes and worked it into a unique English poem, an individual mode. Rigorous though he normally is about his diction, he is not notably successful in developing a convincing over-all structure for his poems. Here the structure was supplied by the original – the shape of the Japanese autobiography, the public and private content. The descriptive passages are lucid, hard, evocative. The natural ravages of Kyoto, the impermanence of habitation, the dispassionate enmity of the elements, the insecurity inherent in the human condition – these themes are embodied in detail. 'This is an unstable world and / we in it unstable in our houses.' Aged sixty, Chomei settles in withdrawn Toyama, in a shack on a mountain, leading a contemplative life, almost a hedonist among the sparse pleasures of the hillside. After the ravages of his early life, the only *stable* habitation is a bamboo hut and a contented existence. He knows himself and 'the others':

I am out of place in the capital,
people take me for a beggar,
as you would be out of place in this sort of life,
you are so – I regret it – so welded to your vulgarity.

Bunting and Chomei share a number of predispositions, to be sure.

Stevie Smith (1903–1971)

Oh I know we must put away the beautiful fairy stories
And learn to be good in a dull way without enchantment ...

Towards the end of her life, Stevie Smith achieved wide popularity on the reading circuit. Few poets could rival her persuasive and charming recitals. But she has been treated cautiously by the critics; they portray her often as a naïve writer whose expression was spontaneous and whose skills were fortuitous. This reveals the success with which she projected the mock-innocence of her public image. When asked at a poetry reading, 'Whose poetry do you read, Miss Smith?' she replied, 'Why, *nobody's* but my own.' She concealed not only the breadth of her reading but, more important, her dependence on traditional or literary rhythmic models. She is an artist whose originality and authority of style are firmly rooted in English and American literature.

Born in Hull in 1903, Florence Margaret Smith's childhood is best described in the poem 'A House of Mercy':

It was a house of female habitation,
Two ladies fair inhabited the house,
And they were brave. For all though Fear knocked loud
Upon the door, and said he must come in,
They did not let him in.

The house also included 'two feeble babes', the younger of them being the author. The father had gone to sea and came home only to get money 'from Mrs S. / Who gave it him at once, she thought she should'. Also living in the house was the 'babes' great-aunt, Mrs Martha Hearn Clode'. Mother died, great-aunt died, and sister went away, leaving the 'younger of the feeble babes' to look after mother's sister, 'The noble aunt who so long tended us, / Faithful and true her name is. Tranquil. / Also sardonic'. The poem concludes with the authority of rhythm Stevie Smith's best poems possess:

It is a house of female habitation
A house expecting strength as it is strong
A house of aristocratic mold that looks apart
When tears fall; counts despair
Derisory. Yet it has kept us well. For all its faults,
If they are faults, of sternness and reserve,
It is a Being of warmth I think; at heart
A house of mercy.

The undemonstrative reserve of this Edwardian childhood did not end with childhood. Indeed, childhood never ended, its patterns persisted, enforced by the ethic of Duty and the dedication of gratitude and love, until the aunt died and Stevie Smith was left alone. She followed shortly after.

During her childhood, she and her relations looked after wounded soldiers from the First World War, and a late poem, 'A Soldier Dear to Us', recounts the love she felt for the soldiers, one in particular. The soldiers haunt many of her poems, and the image of war is a frequent one.

Stevie Smith wrote three novels, the most notable being *Novel on Yellow Paper* (1969), which has the same fluency and poise as her poems. She also published eight collections of poems before her death in 1971. The titles tell much about her style, her skill at re-animating platitudes and trite phrases, her sense of wonder, and her sly use of sentimental material to undercut sentimentality. Her first collection, *A Good Time Was Had By All*, was published in 1937, and the next year *Tender Only to One* followed. Four years later came *Mother, What is Man*, and eight years after that, *Harold's*

Leap. Her last three collections, *Some More Human than Others* (1958), *The Frog Prince and Other Poems* (1966), and the posthumous book *Scorpion* (1972), are full of valedictions. A *Selected Poems* appeared in 1962. Most of the books were illustrated with her own childish line drawings. She earned her living working as a secretary in the City.

Many of her poems, concerned with Good and Evil, carry on a direct debate with God over the mysteries of the Trinity, the nature of Christ, the cruelty implicit in the Crucifixion, the doctrine of damnation, and the imperfection of God as seen in the imperfections of creation. Her direct approach to God, like a woman attacking a greengrocer for selling bad cabbages, is humorous, but she also confronts without sidestepping the paradoxes of faith – a faith towards which her ambivalent feelings were never convincingly resolved. The poem 'How Do You See?' in her last collection is a closely argued and penetrating examination of the Mysteries. Like the other religious poems, it reveals more than a casual acquaintance with academic theology. It is not the wilful passion of whimsy but of learned mystification. She adopts an anarchic Christianity, accepting the central ethical distinctions but dispensing with the cruelty of the story and the dogma. She would aim at being good without enchantment – but instead she devises alternative enchantments.

Anarchy describes several aspects of her approach. Her attitude to language and to tradition (as to religion) is gently anarchistic. In 'The Donkey', a late poem, she evokes the ageing animal. She looks forward with it not to paradise but to a dissolution of consciousness:

But the sweet prairies of anarchy
And the thought that keeps my heart up
That at last, in Death's odder anarchy,
Our pattern will be broken up.
Though precious we are momentarily, donkey,
I aspire to be broken up.

Anarchy is present in her attitudes, which change as situations do. One moment she celebrates God, the next she berates him, the next she prays. In 'To Carry the Child' she writes:

But oh the poor child, the poor child, what can he do
Trapped in a grown-up carapace,
But peer outside of his prison room
With the eye of an anarchist?

The most striking characteristic of her work is the rhythm, a speech rhythm slipping naturally into metre and out again, a rhythm so strong that it overrides considerations of syntax and punctuation and – in releasing language from its formal structures – finds new forms, new tones. Language thus released from traditional bonds and held tenuously in new bonds of rhythm, doggerel rhyme, assonance, and tone of voice, becomes capable of a range of expression unusual in more traditional usage – though she forfeits certain formal effects, of course.

As she treats language, so she treats our common reality. Her fanciful vision illuminates our world and elements of our common experience. It disengages emotions and situations from their actual contexts and presents them distilled in a fanciful context. Her world of fancy is not escapist. It is like a mask through which she trains her eyes on actual experience; her transmutations of actual experience clarify it with knowing innocence and seldom sentimentalize it. The fanciful world is a cruel one – of fairy tales, legends and myths peopled by princes, princesses, ogres and ghouls, neurotic animals and good spirits whose emotions and frustrations are ours. It is a world where guilt is out of place. In effect, she creates a modern pastoral. The short story poems about aristocrats or legendary people are another aspect of the same fanciful pastoralism. Her themes grow powerful through 'enchantment' – rhythms and the voice persuade us emotionally. Human self-deception is an evil enchantment; against it Stevie Smith marshals the beneficent enchantment of poetry, which throws the self-deception into relief. Her aim is ethical and didactic as well as to entertain.

With her anarchy she approaches literature – whether the written literature of the poets and theologians or the spoken literature of nursery rhymes. This is the essence of her art – why the poems are, in their simplicity and apparent stylistic clumsiness, powerfully resonant. Her attitude to her models – for many of the poems have specific models, particularly nineteenth-century British and American poems, hymns and popular tunes, and plainsong conventions – is ambivalent. Some she approaches in the spirit of parody, writing a poem about a swinging ape to the tune of 'Greensleeves'. At other times she depends on our recollection of the strong rhythms of an earlier poem to lend resonance to her own poem. Her individual voice speaks above the rhythm of another poet, defying and then confirming our expectation. Her models do *not* include Emily Dickinson, a poet with whom she has often been compared. Where Emily Dickinson took rhythm as her constant and concentrated on the effective combination of carefully chosen words, Stevie Smith takes her vocabulary – which is generally simple and similar throughout her work – for granted and expends most of her energy on the rhythm.

Edgar Allan Poe echoes through much of her verse. 'The Stroke', 'The True Tyrant', and 'November' contain specific echoes of Poe and each poem develops his rhythms. Stevie Smith seems to have been haunted by 'Ulalume' and 'Annabel Lee' and the underwater kingdom of some of Poe's poems. Many of her characters drown, and several watery gods preserve the victims as relics, deep and dead, but seeming asleep and pricelessly beautiful. She must have sensed a justice and ghostly permanence in rivers and the sea, as Poe did. Poe also suggested some of the odd and macabre names she uses. And though she builds on him with a mixture of dependence and parody, her power often derives from his rhythms, though the speaking voice is her own.

'One of Many' has verbal and thematic roots in Hardy's *Jude the Obscure*. So, too, her most famous poem, 'Not Waving but Drowning', begins (again with specific verbal echoes) in the first volume of the poet George Buchanan's autobiography, *Green Seacoasts*. She picks up a rhythm or a strong image and works a variation on it, driving it to one possible extreme. Thus we are aware often of the presence of Struelpeter, Mother Goose, Alice in Wonderland, Edward Lear, or traditional children's songs. Sometimes the poems derive their content from other sources: 'Mother, among the Dustbins' is a direct comment on a passage from St Teresa of Avila.

The poems, then, sending down taproots into some text or musical tune, have an authority not entirely their own and yet not plagiarized either. In 'The Grange' we hear Kipling, in 'Our Bog is Dood' we hear the Blake of the 'Book of Thel' and in 'A Fairy Story' and a number of short-lined poems we hear the Blake of the 'Songs of Innocence and Experience'. Cowper and Browning are there too, and Tennyson of the *Idylls* and 'The Lady of Shalott'. Coleridge with the cadences of 'Christabel' and 'Kubla Khan' announces himself from behind several poems. Hymn tunes and rhythms, prayer book and Biblical echoes can be heard. Hence the poems that reveal the passing of love, or of life, or of social orders, are nostalgic not in diction or specific content, but in the echoes the rhythms suggest, hinting at other sources and analogues.

Given the preponderance of Victorian models, her use of often antiquated diction littered with 'Oh' and 'Alas', her quaintness, her painful mock-Victorian doggerel rhymes, how is it that she evades banality? How does she manage to revitalize an outworn poetic language by means of the language itself? The answer lies in her humour – not irony but wit which refreshes the language and makes it meaningful again. If one says 'alas' glumly, one is being banal. If one says 'alas' slyly, the humour and the lament coexist, if the context is correct. Her humour redeems the outworn language. The unexpected intrusion into her poems of arch malapropisms and modern colloquialisms is often effective. The humour does not wear thin on re-reading. The lines on

'Mr Over' are a small example of this skill:

Mr Over is dead
He died fighting and true
And on his tombstone they wrote
Over to You.

As compelling as the humour is the innocent artistry with which she speaks in simple words and strong rhythms in her more serious poems:

Into the dark night
Resignedly I go,
I am not so afraid of the dark night
As the friends I do not know,
I do not fear the night above
As I fear the friends below.

Patrick Kavanagh (1905–1967)

But the wren, the wren got caught in the furze
And the eagle turned turkey on my farm.

Among the outstanding Irish poets of this century, Patrick
Kavanagh occupies a curious place. The rich measured
achievement of his early poems is betrayed by the prolixity,
clumsiness, and self-conscious anger of his later satires.
Beginning with pastoral poems about real peasants, he left
the countryside for Dublin, where he came to reject much
of his early prose and verse and turned his attention to
satire, expressing self-pity as much as genuine indignation,
the feelings of the outsider denied admittance to a thinly
glamorous society which fascinates even as it repels him.
Ambitious, competitive, he begrudged other writers their
success. He was a heavy drinker, a habit which – as he
points out – affected his later career.

He was born in 1905 in County Monaghan, the son of a
local cobbler. Largely self-educated, as a young man he
became a small farmer and for a time a shoemaker. His first
collection, *Ploughman and Other Poems*, appeared in 1936, and
in 1938 he published *The Green Fool*, an autobiography he
later dismissed as 'stage-Irish rubbish'.

The relative success of his early literary efforts tempted
him to Dublin in 1939, where he worked as a freelance
journalist, gossip-columnist, and film reviewer. But his
living in Dublin remained precarious until in 1955 he joined
the Board of Extra-Mural studies at University College, and
enjoyed some financial security. In the 'Author's Note' to

his *Collected Poems* (1964), he comments, 'Looking back, I see that the big tragedy for the poet is poverty.' He recalls that during the Depression his hardship was intense – penniless, unskilled in any trade except that of 'small farmer'.

In 1942, three years after he went to Dublin, his most famous poem, *The Great Hunger*, was published in book form. It was followed five years later by *A Soul for Sale*, and the next year by a novel, *Tarry Flynn*. The poems in *Come Dance with Kitty Stobbling* appeared in 1960. After the *Collected Poems* he wrote a number of other poems. He died in 1967.

Kavanagh's talent is for the lively rhythm, not the striking phrase. Like Edwin Muir, he uses an ordinary vocabulary. Unlike Muir's, the intellectual content of his poems is often trite, but the rhythms bring many of the poems alive. The early poems develop variable, generally short lines, with a resolute ruggedness of matter but a sparse and supple manner. In 'Dark Ireland' he writes:

We are a dark people,
Our eyes are ever turned
Inward
Watching the liar who twists
The hill-paths awry.

The Yeatsian rhythm suggested in the first two lines is quenched by the third, and the poem becomes pure Kavanagh. His rhetoric is careful, intensely quiet, confidential, not public.

Yeats became something of a *bête noir* to Kavanagh. Jealousy played a part, but honest indignation and the need to come out from under the Yeatsian shadow complicated Kavanagh's development. He detested Yeats's rumbustiousness and his early twilight. He wanted a world 'otherwise than through ideas', and his bitter, clumsy 'Lines to Yeats' attack all that the man represented:

Yes Yeats it was damn easy for you protected
By the middle classes and the Big Houses
To talk about the sixty year old protected
Man sheltered by the dim Victorian Muses.

There is nothing Victorian about Kavanagh's ragged Muse. In Dublin, he tried to rid himself of the specifically Irish Peasant identity that had adhered to him after the publication of his first two books, but the urban Muse he turned to has little common ground with Yeats's. Her anger rises out of actual incident, not Yeatsian attitude. Kavanagh's quest seems to be for 'truth' and 'wisdom'. He writes often about the quest, without any very clear sense of what its processes are. When he writes in the 'Author's Note', 'I have a belief in poetry as a mystical thing, and a dangerous thing', he has fallen for the Yeatsian vatic role. He is not a mystic, and nor is his poetry dangerous in the way he would have us believe. His social and spiritual conscience rebelled strongly against what he, like Austin Clarke, saw as the betrayal of the ideals of Irish Nationalism into *petit bourgeois* values; against the impoverished peasant life which he saw luridly magnified in the cities. His own social failure was an aspect of his spiritual success, perhaps, but his poetry – particularly the satire – does not achieve sufficient power to endanger anything. Austin Clarke satirizes Irish institutions far more effectively because his is an Augustan skill, and he can write with impersonality, something beyond the ability of Kavanagh.

In the early poems, Kavanagh works with surprising images. In 'Tinker's Wife' he says, 'Her face had streaks of care / Like wires across it.' He is drawn, too, to invented words ('spirit-fires', 'winter-kindled'), and – less subtly than Clarke – to assonance and inner rhyme. The poetry is more immediately rewarding than Clarke's because the surface is less subtly worked and the rhythms are not contrived to surprise us but to reassure us, to carry us along.

'To the Man after the Harrow' and 'Plough Horses' are characteristic of his early style. He sees pastoral activity, and the animals in particular, as archetypal, rather as Muir does, but not in a tragic pattern of re-enactment. They express moments of vivid connection, suggesting the possibility of vision rather than illustrating a preconceived idea. He is 'Seeing with eyes of Spirit unsealed / Plough-horses in a

quiet field'. His poems evoke a pattern in nature. The
pattern is not imposed but seems to be inherent in his
subject. Naming of places and things is of almost magical
significance, especially in poems such as 'Shancoduff',
where he suggests the importance – and the hardships – of
ownership. The cattle-drovers say:

> 'Who owns them hungry hills
> That the water-hen and snipe must have forsaken?
> A poet? Then by heavens he must be poor.'
> I hear, and is my heart not badly shaken?

His poverty is double: not only does he own the barren hills,
but he is a poet, too.

Though Kavanagh came to dislike *The Great Hunger*, it
remains his most impressive poem. It develops through
fourteen sections, and the rhythmic variety is impressive.
Some of the lines are twenty syllables, others three, and a
free-playing rhyme provides connections. This varied technique helped him escape entirely from Yeats. Patrick Maguire
is the protagonist, a farmer who lives with his cruelly
possessive invalid mother and his sister on a farm. He
presents a stable, industrious front to the world. But he
becomes in himself the hollower, as he becomes in the public
eye more admirable and prosperous.

The hunger Maguire feels is produced by his mother's
power over him and by his religion. It is hardly surprising
that the poem roused animosity in Ireland when it first
appeared. In the first section, Maguire watches the potato
gatherers:

> His dream changes again like the cloud-swung wind
> And he is not so sure now if his mother was right
> When she praised the man who made a field his bride.

He longs to be married. The poem recounts his life, the
hunger for sexual fulfilment, for a stable relationship with
a woman. Each time the possibility presents itself, Maguire
is torn between impulse and inhibition. In his life, religion
seems to replace sex. In the third section, Kavanagh writes:

Yet sometimes when the sun comes through a gap
These men know God the Father in a tree:
The Holy Spirit is the rising sap,
And Christ will be the green leaves that will come
At Easter from the sealed and guarded tomb.

The poem is 'the story of a life'. Caged in his biography, social milieu and religion, he seems a good and happy man. His sister is the same. The tourists who come romanticize him for all the things he is not and cannot be. They, too, are hungry; their hunger makes him into an idyllic rustic. Few poems conjure so vividly and sombrely a particular saga of human unfulfilment, and subtly generalize the experience until it implicates a wide range of subject matter.

After *The Great Hunger* Kavanagh lost what he called his 'messianic compulsion'. Weary of writing of the 'woes of the poor', he reports that, 'My purpose in life was to have no purpose.' With this decision he moved into what is, perhaps, his most distinctive period. He writes of childhood, particularly in 'A Christmas Childhood', and draws details out of his own past for many poems. Memory and dream, the dream of innocence, become important themes. In 'The Long Garden' he revives the experience of innocence:

It was the garden of the golden apples,
A long garden between a railway and a road,
In the sow's rooting where the hen scratches
We dipped our fingers in the pockets of God.

The immanent God is always perceived by him in the most earthy places. The perception is not theological but visionary, the innocence of which is uninhibited by dogmatic interdicts.

The Dublin satires do not live up to the earlier verse. In 'The Paddiad', an attack on mediocrity in literary taste and in society, his formal skill is unequal to his subject matter and his ambitions. The roughness is not of art but of carelessness. In poems such as 'Bank Holiday' satire veers into self-pity. Kavanagh is too much an engaged romantic at heart to be a satirist. As he grew older, he demanded attention for himself, as speaker, rather than for his poems and their subject matter. 'Adventures in a Bohemian Jungle' and 'The Christmas Mummers' – like 'The Paddiad' – shoot at rather easy satirical targets.

Kavanagh sensed the falling off. He tried to return to earlier sources of inspiration – especially in poems such as 'On Looking into E. V. Rieu's Homer', 'Kerr's Ass' and 'On Reading a Book on Common Wild Flowers'. Sudden illuminations from the past 'purify a corner of my mind'. But the poet's quest has become self-conscious. He speculates on his role, on 'being a poet'. The real achievement of the late poems is in their colloquial rhythms, a spirited facility which, when it is not careless, is beguiling.

William Empson (born 1906)

Imagine, then, by miracle, with me,
(Ambiguous gifts, as what gods give must be)
  What could not possibly be there,
  And learn a style from a despair.

Eleven years after John Donne's death, Baltasar Gracián, a
neglected Spanish cleric, satirist and critic, wrote his
Agudeza y arte de ingenio, a remarkable treatise on the baroque
element in literature. Ambiguity, unconscious or calculated
verbal duplicity, the felicity of pun and double meaning are
at the heart of the poetry he examines. Gracián pursues with
more acumen if less clarity than William Empson some sixty
types of ambiguity in Classical and what was to him modern
poetry. There is more than a casual analogy between his and
Empson's work. For Empson better than any other modern
poet has understood and adapted the baroque and what
have come to be called Metaphysical poetic techniques to
modern usage. His poetry and criticism have, in a unique
way, affected the development and scope of some modern
poets' work, particularly those associated with The Movement. Empson's style evolved away from Donne towards a
more Augustan balance. He looked later to Rochester,
Dryden and Pope, and his work reached its climax in what
can best be described as the verse epistle.

William Empson was born in Yorkshire in 1906 into a
squire's family. He took his tone of voice from his privileged
background, and though sympathetic to the political Left,
he retains – especially in the way he presents the speaker and

the 'you' he often addresses – the poised civility and banter one associates with his class and his education. He studied at Winchester School and went on to Cambridge, where he read Mathematics and Literature and had the advantage of the supervision of I. A. Richards, whose influence was formative. From Richards he learned that we have a right to ask what a poem means, and therefore how it means. Though he came down from Cambridge suddenly and rather mysteriously, his time there was not wasted, for his dissertation work was turned into his seminal critical study, *Seven Types of Ambiguity* (1930). His scholarship then and later was not careful, and the book contains misquotations and small inaccuracies. But the little vices are amply compensated for by the methods and insights he provides.

Five years later his first collection, *Poems*, was published. His exploitation of ambiguity in this book is relentless. Donne may be his master, but even Donne does not require the sometimes extensive notes Empson provides. He followed *Poems* in 1940 with *The Gathering Storm*, a politically sophisticated book with less of the earlier obscurity. The book is sometimes prophetic, alive to the threats of fascism and the impending war. His *Collected Poems* was published in 1955, but he stopped writing poetry – except for a few minor pieces – around 1941.

Empson's experience as a teacher in Japan and China in the 1930s, his interest in mathematics and science, and his constant attention to English literature, contributed to the richness of his work. In 1953 he became Professor of English at Sheffield University, a post from which he retired in 1971.

His outstanding critical book is *Some Versions of Pastoral* (1935), in which he takes the theme of ambiguity in literature and examines it in formal rather than stylistic terms. He explores double plots and structures. No doubt this study contributed to the development of his poetic style away from puzzling local ambiguity towards formal ambiguity, which reaches its climax in the 'double poem' 'China'.

In 1951 he published *The Structure of Complex Words*, studying the changing values of words in social currency, and in 1961 *Milton's God* appeared – a full-scale assault on that unfortunate deity. The influence of Empson's critical writing has been extensive and is likely to prove more durable than the effect of his poems.

There is some disagreement about the extreme intellectuality of his verse. Is it the product of emotional intensity – personal and political; or is it a more literary passion, is his the impulse of the puzzle-maker? There is, to be sure, a certain monotony in his poetry, even within so brief a body of work. Always awake to every possible suggestion in his words, what he looks for, how he looks, and how he presents what he finds are peculiarly similar. He celebrates language in his poems, particularly the language of poetry. But there is a sense in which the language is more important to him than the poetry.

Only in his erudition is Empson an academic poet. 'Academic poetry' is now used as a term of abuse, normally implying that the poet takes an image or idea and worries it until it disgorges every possible hint of meaning it might have. Empson includes many meanings in a poem by carefully gauged suggestion. But his poem thrives on implication, not explication. Each of his words acquires or re-acquires full valency in his contexts. Words come richly and fully comprehended into association with other words equally well-chosen. The language is totally conscious of itself, with the burden of etymology, colloquial and literary usage. For this reason the poems are both obscure and inexhaustibly rewarding as language.

One can, without injustice to Empson, raise the linguistician's objection to his approach: that poetry is not a matter of one word suggesting many meanings but of many meanings choosing one word or word complex. It is the reverse side of Empson's coin, perhaps the more important one – though the point might not have been made without Empson's work.

The illuminations in his poetry are local, of detail. He does not bring about any profound readjustment in the reader's mind, though he clarifies and extends what are often the reader's preconceptions. He is fascinated, especially at the outset, with minuteness, with insect life, with ants, maggots and the like. They become emblematic or correlative. But Empson's scientific and mathematical facts are wilfully introduced into his poems, where we feel in Donne's work that there is an almost involuntary necessity in the scientific allusions, which take their place naturally in a wider context.

Empson once remarked that his poems 'turned out to be love poems about boy being too afraid of girl to tell her anything'. Any girl receiving one of his coded messages would certainly have been perplexed. But there is a facetious understatement in his remark. His poems, though often love poems, always take in more than merely the local experience of frustrated desire. Christopher Ricks sees the 'enabling tension' of the poems as that between desire to beget life and a sense that 'life is too dark and bleak a gift'. Hence misgiving is thematically central to his love poems: uncertainty, ambiguity. Recurrent images and themes in the poems relate to evolution, development, sequence, building, increasing, and the perils to all these. Darwin is evoked more than once. Sometimes he enters subtly guised, as in 'Sea Voyage', where a note tells us, 'The banquet (soup, fish, meat) follows the order of the evolution of the species.' Empson ceased to write poetry after his marriage in 1941 and the birth of a child.

He explains why he fell silent in another way. His experiences multiplied, and the very wealth of experience dissipated the poetic impulse. In 'Let It Go' he writes: 'The more things happen to you the more you can't / Tell or remember even what they were.' The explanation is only barely plausible, for the imagination which could control so much allusion in a poem would hardly have been expected to lose its power as his seems to have done.

Fear and endurance are recurrent themes in the poems. His apparent casualness of tone, his polite evasiveness and understatement, are parts of his defences. For he protects himself – by wit as well. The poems are well-fortified. The seriousness of his commitment is best experienced by the reader in the poems of self-defence against the strictures of critics such as F. R. Leavis – in 'Your Teeth are Ivory Towers' and 'Autumn in Nan-Yueh'.

The early technique is reflected in a note to 'Plenum and Vacuum'. He explains: '*Weal*: the scar of a burn, made as the glass was, the ground still under the control of their commonwealth, the circle of the glass rim, and the gain of death.' Not only 'weal' is intended to carry such a weight of significance, but other words about it as well. There are 'key' words that carry an extra burden of ambiguity in the early poems, coordinates between which the lines of the poem are drawn.

In 'Rolling the Lawn', one of his most famous sonnets, he writes, 'You can't beat English lawns. Our final hope / Is flat despair.' Into the poem he draws a wide variety of references. Milton, contemporary advertisements, natural history, classical allusion (to Troy), 'true' and 'false' religions, and a subliminal eroticism, coexist. The poem explores, too, the various implications of the word 'roll'. It appears with seven different meanings.

The style is capable of precise tenderness and gentleness, as in 'To an Old Lady'. By its very nature it renders the expression of sentimentality impossible. Small emotions appear intensified. Often he evokes singleness, integrity, individuality, isolation. In 'Letter I' he writes: 'I approve, myself, dark spaces between stars; / All privacy's their gift.' This is the function of his style: to single out the complex of ideas, to isolate the poet.

The same tendency can be detected in his rhythms. Most of his lines are syntactically or rhythmically end-stopped, or when longer cadences occur they are forcefully arrested at the end. The poems are not compelled by a strong driving rhythm. They are built of finished rhythmic units. The choice of forms often reflects his desire for the effectively end-stopped line. 'Villanelle' ('It is the pain, it is the pain, endures'), 'Reflections from Anita Loos' and 'Missing Dates' (also villanelles), and 'Success' (a modified villanelle) exhibit this rhythmic propensity. Each line is thus singled out; and when a line is repeated in the villanelles it comes, like a good refrain, with different implications. The forced rhythmic hesitations make us dwell on the sense. Because of this rhythmical device, lines exist side by side, in apposition as it were, rather than solely consecutively. Syntax is supplemented by this new rhythmic parallelism.

Images interest Empson for what they attract to themselves, like magnets. He chooses particularly those images which he can transform unexpectedly. The subject matter of 'Camping Out' would suggest satire – a woman brushing her teeth in a lake at dawn, the suds floating off like stars. Empson makes of it an exquisite love poem, much in the way Donne harnesses a flea to his passion. The note to the poem tells us, 'A great enough ecstasy makes the common world unreal.'

Ezra Pound talked of 'making it new'. Empson uses the word 'rebegetting' in much the same sense in 'Letter II':

Searching the cave gallery of your face
My torch meets fresco after fresco ravishes
Rebegets me . . .

The world, language and passion are full of fossil perceptions and expressions which the poet sets out to re-animate. He fills them with as much life as he can – so much, at times, that they sink down dead again in a new context.

The wealth of Empson's poems is their range of reference. In most of them, Biblical allusion (particularly to the Flood and God's promise confirmed by the rainbow), scientific matter, and love exist in tension. The effect is sometimes doomed to failure, as in 'Letter IV'. But 'Doctrinal Point' evolves a lucid proposition: 'The duality of choice becomes the singularity of existence; / The effort of virtue and unconsciousness is foreknowledge.' The language is spare here, but around it flower the magnolias, walk the saints, and puzzle the scientists.

Empson's best poems have the quality of verse epistles – and these are not exclusively the scattered 'Letter' sequence.

'Autumn in Nan-Yueh', for example, is intimate and public at the same time, there is a tone of voice and the poet seems to address us specifically. This quality can be sensed in many of the poems that speak quietly, yet specifically, always conscious of a listener. The love poems do not assault the beloved but rather attempt by subtleties to implicate her – and us. It is civilized, but civility never precluded passion.

John Betjeman (born 1906)

I SIT DOWN
In St Botolph Bishopsgate Churchyard
And wait for the spirit of my grandfather
Toddling along from the Barbican.

Why are John Betjeman's poems almost always recognizable as *his*? He writes in traditional forms, the 'I' that sometimes speaks is discreet and elusive. There is impersonality of treatment – and yet a unique tone of voice. Is it merely the recurrent allusions to North Oxford, churches, suburbia, gym-slips? Or is it the fact that in most of the poems landscape is evoked in terms of comfort, with a nice sense of class and propriety? In 'Love in a Valley', for example, there is no Lawrentian nakedness. The word 'homestead' appears twice, there is a 'lieutenant', a 'woodland', the statutory 'tennis-court', a 'gas fire'; the rhododendrons are 'cushioned', there is a 'summer-house', a 'carpet', 'welcome'; we hear 'the tiny patter, sandalled footstep', and so on. The poem breathes an atmosphere of static well-being – a characteristic effect. And yet, the satires are less accommodating, but they too have his hallmark.

More than content, what defines Betjeman's uniqueness is his rhythm. It is lightly controlled; and the poems have a smoothness – whether in rhymed quatrains, couplets, or blank verse – a well-gauged efficiency and decorum. Rhythm collaborates with sense, traditional values are celebrated, vulgarities chastised. The lightness and humour are complemented by undertones which make the poems delicately resonant and briefly disturbing.

John Betjeman was born in 1906 into a merchant family of Dutch extraction. He was educated at Marlborough School and at Oxford, where he wrote humorous verses for public declamation. Thus even at an early age he was an entertainer. Preferring a life of letters to a life in the family business, he gave himself to teaching, writing, and later broadcasting. His Oxford years confirmed an early passion for architecture – particularly Victorian – and for over three decades he has been a champion of Victorian churches, pubs and railway stations.

His early poems treated even serious themes with apparent levity. *Mount Zion* (1933), his first book, achieved little success. His mild parodies and imitations of minor Victorian poets, his eye for oddities of character and beauties of landscape, and his insights into English society, however, were pursued in later volumes, including *Continual Dew* (1937) and *Old Bats in New Belfries* (1940) and subsequent collections. Though Betjeman has not evolved in style, he has become more skilful. His long, mainly blank verse autobiography, *Summoned by Bells* (1960), more ambitious than his earlier poems, does not advance his art, though it broadens his scope as a poet. He suffers to a degree from facility, finding blank verse easier to write than prose. And facility is his worst enemy.

In 1958 his *Collected Poems* were published, and he achieved the rare distinction of becoming a runaway bestseller. Over a hundred thousand copies of the original editions are reported to have been sold. His poems attract an audience because they are entertaining. They are written for an audience, setting out to make certain social situations, certain perceptions, more vivid, to evoke nostalgic moods, to celebrate the past and warn the present, often through anecdote, that it impoverishes itself by losing contact with the past. But Betjeman is not always didactic. His real achievement is in presenting the data of the modern world in the old forms, and from within the system of values that animated the old forms.

There is a diverse sense of locale in the poems, for he has

lived in and observed many parts of the British Isles. During the Second World War he served as United Kingdom Press Attaché in Dublin, and some of his poems treat Irish themes. Much of his youth was spent in Cornwall, and he evokes the tin mines with no less charm and passion than he uses in evoking suburbia.

A man of close friendships, Betjeman is said not to be gregarious; and despite his public levity and bonhomie, he is reported to suffer from bouts of depression and to dread death. His elegies – for all their irony – are often disturbing, and one of his most powerful poems, 'Before the Anaesthetic', is a dramatic monologue that worries about death and is informed with his profound and precise love for the physical world. Despite his faith, his religious themes, his church-going, he suggests in his verse no cogent metaphysic, apparently content with the given world and afraid to leave it.

A pervasive and amusing sense of physical inferiority animates some of the 'love poems', in which Amazonian tennis girls attract his passion and lead him to wish masochistically to be crushed in their arms, to be their rackets pressed against their breasts. In 'Pot Pourri from a Surrey Garden' he declares, 'Pam, I adore you, you great big mountainous sports girl.' In 'The Licorice Fields of Pontefract' he writes:

Red hair she had and golden skin,
Her sulky lips were shaped for sin,
Her sturdy legs were flannel-slack'd,
The strongest legs in Pontefract.

The poet is 'held in brown arms strong and bare / And wound with flaming ropes of hair'. Rossetti's muscular Graces have nothing on Betjeman's girls. Though erotic desires are sometimes fulfilled in the poems, most memorably in 'A Subaltern's Love Song', full of healthy middle-class happiness, Betjeman often fails. In 'The Olympic Girl' he laments, 'Little, alas, to you I mean, / For I am bald, and old, and green.' In 'Senex' the old man is vividly pursued by spaniels (note the breed of dog) representing lust. Briefly the legend of Actaeon is suggested, but the poet chases that idea from our minds:

Your teeth are stuffed with underwear,
Suspenders torn asunder there
    And buttocks in your paws.

And in one of his weirdest poems, 'Late Flowering Lust', there is a communion of skeletons that calls Beddoes to mind: 'The mouth that opens for a kiss / Has got no tongue inside.' Abhorrence for death in this and other poems goes with his abhorrence for the destruction of beautiful things – the Downs, old buildings, old customs of courtesy, habits of discipline. Thus satire is as much his duty as elegy and celebration.

Betjeman harbours a hostile view of the – to his mind – less enlightened individuals in society, including the urban vandal and the insensitive bourgeois. But in a satire such as 'Slough' he suggests that the lesser minions of the destructive profit and loss machine are redeemable – at least not themselves responsible. It is the confirmed profit-at-all-costs boss and the city planner that bear the responsibility: the bombs should seek them out:

Come friendly bombs, and fall on Slough
It isn't fit for humans now,
There isn't grass to graze a cow
            Swarm over, death!

A more powerfully instructive satire is 'In Westminster Abbey', a 'war poem' in which a prosperous lady prays for the troops and more especially for herself, observing the religion of class and privilege. 'So Lord, reserve for me a crown, / and do not let my shares go down.' And the persuasive sonnet, 'The Planster's Vision', suggests the future if we do not take action:

'I have a vision of The Future, chum,
    The workers' flats in fields of soya beans
        Tower up like silver pencils, score on score:

And surging millions hear the challenge come
　From microphones in communal canteens
　　"No right! No wrong! All's perfect, evermore." '

Betjeman's principal skill is in evoking, with great economy, whole scenes, suggesting connection, relationship. His imagery creates settings, the details build always towards a real world – even in the mysterious 'A Shropshire Lad' – and interweave with something like pictorial accuracy: 'Up the ash tree climbs the ivy, / Up the ivy climbs the sun.' The narrative 'romance' of 'Sir John Piers' shifts precisely from scene to scene, while in the mature, later social narratives, with their arresting yet seemingly casual transitions from character to character and plot to plot, revealing great psychological insight (as in 'Beside the Seaside'), a panoramic effect is achieved.

Despite – or perhaps because of – his traditional formal accomplishment, Betjeman's scope is limited. Ironically evasive, he seldom shows *his* hand. He is present as a tone of voice, and those of his commitments that communicate themselves are strictly social. He is the entertainer *par excellence*, and this describes the scope of his success. He has performed the rare service of keeping certain traditional forms alive and holding a wide audience receptive to verse. His accession to the Poet Laureateship in 1973 was as merited as it was inevitable. And yet he does not, in Michael Roberts's words, 'add to the resources of poetry', nor is he 'likely to influence the future development of poetry and language'. 'New poetry,' C. H. Sisson wrote, 'is never popular unless it accepts the prejudices of the immediate past.' And yet the form Betjeman's acceptance takes sets him somehow beyond the debate between opposing critical camps, outside the main course of modern English poetry, in a territory distinctly his own.

Louis MacNeice (1907–1963)

A life can be haunted by what it never was
If that were merely glimpsed. Lost in the maze
That means yourself and never out of the wood
These days, though lost, will be all your days;
Life, if you leave it, must be left for good.

Since Louis MacNeice's death in 1963, some critics have decided that his poetry 'describes much . . . but illuminates nothing. His work abounds in the tired sophisticated clichés of the audience at which it is aimed.' MacNeice used clichés for a specific purpose. In 'Homage to Clichés' he employed them in such a way as to imbue them with new life. He did not set out to forge a new poetic language but to revitalize the spoken language – in poems and verse plays.

The American critic Conrad Aiken approached him from another angle. 'For sheer readability,' he wrote, 'for speed, lightness, and easy intellectual range, Mr MacNeice's verse is in a class by itself.' But, he adds, the poetry doesn't stick, 'it is *too* topical, *too* transitory, *too* reportorial' and 'it has very little *residual* magic'. The residual magic of poetry is not, however, subject matter but rhythm, and few readers would find the rhythms of 'Happy Families', 'The Hebrides', 'Troll's Courtship', 'Neutrality', 'The Accident', and the more obvious of MacNeice's rhythmic *tours de force* forgettable. His poems are topical, but as G. S. Fraser has pointed out, the issues are still with us, and even when the subject matter dates, the best poems will retain the authority of their rhythms to recommend them.

Louis MacNeice was born in Belfast in 1907. His father
was a Church of Ireland clergyman who later became a
bishop. MacNeice saw his creative work as partly conditioned by his Northern Irish background. Only Ireland
could rouse him to satire. No other theme could induce in
him the same nostalgia on the one hand and passion on the
other. His father's vocation, too, coloured his youth, and his
mother's early death. He speaks of 'repression from the age
of six to nine', of his inferiority complex as a child because
of his social class and his physique, his lack of social life and
his late puberty, his ignorance of music ('which could have
been a substitute for poetry'), his inability to ride or do
rhythmic sports. He also recalls an 'adolescent liking for the
role of *enfant terrible*', shyness with women until he was
twenty, an early liking for metaphysics, his first marriage
and divorce, his spell of teaching in Birmingham, and his
adolescent pleasure in gardens and wild landscapes. A few
facts may be added to this succinct autobiography. He was
educated at Marlborough School and at Oxford, where he
read Greats. Unlike Auden and Spender, he was an exact
scholar, and his translations from the Greek and German
have the same distinction as those of C. Day Lewis from the
Latin, a heightened competence. He lectured in Classics at
Birmingham (1930–36), in Greek at Bedford College, University of London (1936–40), and thereafter until his death
he was a feature writer and producer for the BBC. He
travelled widely for the British Council, spending a year in
Athens at the British Institute (1949–50).

Though MacNeice is grouped with the 1930s poets,
Auden, Spender and Day Lewis, he differs from them in one
essential. He was never drawn to Communism. His commitment was less naïve, more perplexed and hence in the poems
more potent than the early political rhetoric of his friends.
His dominant tone is gently elegiac. He could not in conscience adopt a solving orthodoxy of any sort; he was temperamentally involved with facts rather than programmes.
He never resolved the paradox of his uncommitment. While
Auden moved across the political spectrum, he stayed poli-

tically 'between'. 'Between' is a favourite word and stance in the early poems: 'In a between world, a world of amber', one of the poems begins. He does not have even the conviction of the liberal humanist. In 'Epitaph for Liberal Poets' he laments something foredoomed, he does not assail the enemy. He acknowledges the coming 'tight-lipped technocratic Conquistadores' but adopts the stance of Mark Antony, accepting even as he laments the inevitable triumph of Caesar, hoping the poems will survive to thaw out a later age.

MacNeice was early drawn to word-magic – riddles and nursery rhymes – and to hymns. Later, the saga, the allegory, and the Horatian Ode attracted him. His best poems are written in two different styles: one vivid, documentary, engagingly particular and linguistically inventive; the other argumentative and analytical. MacNeice sees the poet – in a sense like the broadcaster and journalist – as an extension of the common man, speaking and renewing his language and engaging and clarifying his problems, even if not offering answers. In part, this justifies MacNeice's reticence. Though we can recognize his voice, we are often uncertain whether he is speaking of his own experience, and the degree to which he is committed to his statement. He generalized his indecision into a poetic dogma: the poet must remain open, able to accept and express conflicting truths. He is the only poet who, affected deeply by journalism, accepts the challenge of creating a journalistic poetry that *is* poetry, not verse *reportage*.

MacNeice is often autobiographical, but never directly confessional. Presenting his particular past in various forms – in the extended *Autumn Journal*, less effectively in *Autumn Sequel*, in 'Carickfergus' and many late poems – he uses it to re-create and generalize, not to analyse himself. A dominant theme is the Hardyesque isolation of the individual. Images of glass barriers, shells, crusts, the journey of separation, recur. Like early Eliot, he had no faith in the continuity of the individual personality. His philosophical sympathies lay with those mentors who asserted the discontinuity of the 'I'.

He wedded himself at an early age to the 'I' of the moment, and later in life, in 'The Cromlech', he reasserted his dominant intellectual conviction: the fact of the moment (being in love, for instance) is in its immediate time and space context as true and durable a fact, even if it changes later, as 'The cromlech in the clover field'. MacNeice's aesthetic is rooted in this conviction, expressed concisely in 'The Cromlech':

> essence is not merely core
> And each event implies the world,
> A centre needs periphery.

Attention to the periphery may help to locate the centre.

He was a self-conscious writer. In the middle of his writing life he tried to clarify where he had been and to forecast where he was going. The dedicatory sestina to his 1948 *Collected Poems* is a retrospect and a programme:

> At one time I was content if things would image
> Themselves in their own dazzle, if the answers
> Came quick and smooth . . .

He concedes the facile element in his early fluency. Consciously he plans a change of direction:

> But now I am not content, the leaves are turning
> And the gilt flaking from each private image
> And all the poets that I know, both younger and older,
> Condemned to silence unless they divine the answers
> Which our grim past has cached throughout our present
> And which are no more than groped for in this volume.

Temperamentally unsuited to the task, MacNeice intended to set out after answers, following the example of his contemporaries. Even this decision is not necessarily right:

> Which was the right turning?
> Rhythm and image and still at best half-answers
> And at half-volume . . .

In the work that followed he found his half-answers, sadly at 'half-volume'.

The earliest poems were collected in *Blind Fireworks* (1929), published while he was still at Oxford. They are full of pleasant undergraduate affectation, less earnest, more joyful, than the committed verse of his contemporaries. The experimentation was prodigious. Not metrical so much as stress experiments occupied him: he remained true to the stress rhythms throughout his writing life. The early poems echo now Edith Sitwell, now Alfred Noyes, now Tennyson and Owen. The surface reveals a riotous discipline, while the content, such as it is, partakes of intellectual indiscipline.

The most effective image for the almost cinematic progression of his imagery is the train journey, to which he returns frequently, and to great effect in 'Train to Dublin':

All over the world people are toasting the king,
Red lozenges of light as each one lifts his glass,
But I will not give you any idol or idea, creed or king,
I give you the incidental things which pass
Outward through space exactly as each was.

The second line recalls the more famous image, 'The moment cradled like a brandy glass'. It is 'the moment' and its impressions, the experience of things but not the pattern between things. In the train he cannot touch – he is *being taken* at speed. His power is to record. It is not surprising that in 'Intimations of Mortality' nightmare seems to be a near neighbour of the unpatterned common world of face values.

Six years after his first book, *Poems 1935* appeared, followed by *Out of the Picture* (1937), *Letters from Iceland* (with W. H. Auden, 1937), and *The Earth Compels* (1938). The descriptive suburban poems, the elegies and odes, were written with speed and authority. It was around 1933 that the eclogues and verse dialogues began in earnest. MacNeice's personal indecision was parcelled out to several speakers, argued or more subtly developed. But MacNeice's indecision is most powerful when one voice speaks.

A number of MacNeice's best poems date from this period. 'Snow', his most analysed poem, was written in 1935. 'The Hebrides' was written then as well. He deploys the refrain

'On those islands' with dramatic emphasis, working an ambiguous syntactical line so that sentences modulate and unfold unexpectedly:

On those islands
Where no train runs on rails and the tyrant time
Has no clock-towers to signal people to doom
With semaphor ultimatums tick by tick,
There is still peace but not for me and not
Perhaps for long – still peace on the bevel hills
For those who still can live as their fathers lived
On those islands.

Apart from the refrain, the words 'still' and 'peace' recur, natural repetitions contrasted to the relentless on-going mechanical imagery.

From Icelandic and other ancient poetry MacNeice learned lessons in rhetoric. 'Les neiges d'antan' exploits the 'ubi sunt' motif, while 'Bagpipe Music' develops another form of popular rhetoric. It is more powerful than Auden's 'Danse Macabre' which it in some ways resembles. The poem is not didactic but experiential, moving from music-hall humour to a sudden change of tone. The theme is choicelessness, the tragic inviolability of individual isolation.

With the ambitious *Autumn Journal* (1939) MacNeice's style began to change. He apologized for overstatements in the poem: 'In a journal or a personal letter a man writes what he feels at the moment' – it would betray the form to revise retrospectively. He added, 'I refuse to be "objective" or clear-cut at the cost of honesty.' The poem begins in August and ends at the New Year. Public pressures – Spain, Hitler, the impending war – seem correlative for disruptions in the poet's life. Written under pressure, the poem possesses an interest and power at once particular and documentary. MacNeice chose a form that made minimal demands and in it achieved varied tonal effects. His propensity for combining the concrete and the abstract – 'With years behind her and the waves behind her' ('The Closing Album') – is widely developed. The abstraction is anchored in a serviceable concrete image and carries the weight of the image.

Three further collections, *Plants and Phantoms* (1941), *Springboard* (1944) and *Holes in the Sky* (1948) were included in the first *Collected Poems*. These books contained powerful poems of the civilian war – 'Bar-room Matins' and 'Flight of the Heart', for instance, where the public nightmare is firmly contained in particulars; and 'Troll's Courtship' and 'Neutrality', both dramatic, one allegorical and the other tending towards the metaphysical. 'Autobiography' itself, written in 1940, is a haunting evocation of childhood terrors.

'Prayer before Birth' was written in 1944, a political poem, but without a partisan or rhetorical burden. The cadences are dramatic, argumentative, lengthening from break to break until bitten off in an uncompromising five-syllable line. The irregular word order and the preponderance of monosyllables distributes the stresses, and the whole poem gives a spondaic effect, as though each word is equally weighted, producing a new hesitant and emphatic rhythm.

After 1948, MacNeice went in search of answers. The intellectual and emotional dislocations of the war needed interpreting, but not in the way he first attempted. He could no more give form to the past – the past which he had so lucidly expressed when it was present as experience – than he could project the future. So in *Ten Burnt Offerings* (1952) and *Autumn Sequel* (1954) he became the victim of his own contrivance. The poems are deliberately literary, an effect he had not succumbed to before. They abound with puns. They set out discursively to find answers, but they are as inconclusive as the early poems, without the early directness. Were they more conclusive they would be pompous. Instead, they are dull reading. A birthday poem, 'Day of Renewal', expresses his sense of predicament:

Do I prefer to forget it? This middle stretch
Of life is bad for poets; a sombre view
Where neither works nor days look innocent
And both seem now too many, now too few.

The failure of *Autumn Sequel* is complete. Writing in terza rima, MacNeice chose a rhetoric machine. The form impelled the poem forward, even when the creative impulse was spent. There are flashes of humour, but the self-conscious and heavy-handed literary wit quenches the poem. Statements that even Drinkwater would have blushed to read occur: 'But in a game, as in life, we are under Starter's Orders.'

MacNeice sensed his failure and turned again in his last books to his earlier manner. Three collections appeared before the definitive *Collected Poems* (1966): *Visitations* (1957), *Solstices* (1961) and *The Burning Perch* (1963). Poems such as 'The Here and Never' possess his earlier heart-breaking whimsy, but intensified. He plays his game more sombrely, the elegiac tone is more natural. In 'House on a Cliff' he uses juxtapositions, moving out from the 'between' world, giving himself to the paradox. The drama is enacted within the images:

Indoors the tang of a tiny oil lamp. Outdoors
The winking signal on the waste of sea.
Indoors the sound of the wind. Outdoors the wind,
Indoors the locked heart and the lost key.

His recovery was complete. The poems about London parks, the 'Dark Age Glosses', 'Vistas', 'The Wiper', and 'Selva Oscura' are direct, with more sense of a speaking voice. And that cluster of poems which includes 'After the Crash', 'Charm', 'The Introduction', and others shows the direction in which MacNeice's development might have gone – towards the evanescent mystery that perplexed and eluded him. The experiences of these later poems carry, like some of the early imagery, their own unparaphrasable answers, and a strong 'residual magic'.

W.H. Auden (1907–1974)

I suspect that without some undertones of the comic,
  genuine serious verse cannot be written today.

In 1937 Dylan Thomas contributed a dubious tribute to a
special double issue of *New Verse*, celebrating Auden's
thirtieth birthday. 'I think of Mr Auden's poetry as a
hygiene, a knowledge and practice, based on a brilliantly
prejudiced analysis of contemporary disorders, relating to
the preservation and promotion of health, a sanitary science
and a flusher of melancholia. I sometimes think of his poetry
as a great war, admire intensely the mature, religious, and
logical fighter, and deprecate the boy bushranger.' In the
same issue, Allen Tate comments on Auden's and his friends'
'juvenile' and 'provincial' vantage points, and the con-
spiratorial nature of Auden's ascent, on very real virtues, to
so early a canonization. The passions his verse aroused in
his readers changed as he outgrew his early concerns. Like
Eliot, Auden came to confuse truth with stability. So he
affronts his youth, the more engaging man, with his age, the
better poet. But there is a continuity between the two: each
is an aspect of Auden's complex but decisive integrity.

Wystan Hugh Auden was born in York in 1907. His father
was a doctor, and Auden enjoyed a warm relationship with
him. Auden's recurrent images of disease, healing, and the
bodily functions owe something to his father who, in 'The
Art of Healing', tells his son, 'Healing . . . / is not a science /
but the intuitive art / of wooing nature.' When Auden was
one year old his family removed to Birmingham. In the

landscape of the industrial Midlands the poet spent his early years, until he was sent off to Gresham School in Norfolk. The Midland landscape left a deep impression on him. His fascination with geology and mining provided much of his early imaginative energy. Between the ages of six and twelve he spent many hours fabricating 'a private secondary world' composed of inhuman limestone landscapes, lead mines, and the like. 'In Praise of Limestone' relates directly to these childhood images. In retrospect Auden saw his creation of 'secondary worlds' as formative for his poetry, he learned from it 'certain principles' that 'applied to all artistic fabrication'. Every work of art was a secondary world derived from and answerable to the primary world. Each work of art must therefore have meanings. He sensed the necessity for rules in the 'game' of creation. They could be invented but they had to be consistent. The substance of the poems, though ordered in new relationships, had to exist and be true to the primary world. The poet had to respect truth, he 'must never make a statement simply because it sounds poetically exciting; he must also believe it to be true'. There is a crippling element of premeditation in this axiom, a restricting subjectivity. The poet must believe what he says in a very literal way. Auden tells us the poet is not expressing himself but conveying 'a view of reality common to all, seen from a unique perspective'. Yet that 'perspective' becomes in Auden's later work so unique as to transform the common reality into a very exclusive Auden world.

The 'secondary world' is often expressed in imagery of the State and City. A poem is 'an attempt to present an analogy to the paradisal state in which Freedom and Law, System and Order are united'. A good poem is 'very nearly a Utopia'. Other images of order include maps, networks, telegraphs, trains, streets, buildings, geological strata, veins, mails – emblems of connection and pattern. We cannot help noting the ubiquity of the words 'between' and 'among' and prepositions denoting the relationship between objects in space. The modern hero is 'The builder, who renews the ruined walls of the city'. He adds, 'It is not madness we need to flee, but prostitution.' A new dogma is called for, a set of rules to live by.

Auden studied biology at his public school. At the age of fifteen, he discovered his poetic vocation. The stable childhood determined many of his prejudices and preoccupations as a poet; his class origins helped to determine his tone. In 'Profile', a careful if not flattering self-portrait, he asks:

A childhood full of love
and good things to eat:
why should he not hate change?

The gastronomical image, obsessive in the later Auden, in this context is amusing. Love and food were a sufficient stability. Aware of his class origins, and rather proud of them at the end, he writes in one of his fragmentary verses:

The class whose vices
he pilloried was his own,
now extinct, except
for lone survivors like him
who remember its virtues.

Wise in retrospect, with what Roy Fuller has called 'his honesty of self-characterization' – the poet atones for his early radicalism. But the key to his political reversal is clear in the late poem 'The Garrison': 'Whoever rules, our duty to the City / is loyal opposition.' Where, in the thirties, opposition – to the real threats of fascism – seemed to demand a Marxist stance, in the fifties and sixties it came to imply conservatism.

In 1925 Auden went to Oxford to read English. Old English poetry attracted him, and his early technical experiments included effective stress and alliterative metres. He twice edited *Oxford Poetry* and his first collection of poems was printed by a fellow-undergraduate, Stephen Spender, on a hand press. The 1930s group was gathering. The composer Sir Lennox Berkeley set some of Auden's poems and they were presented in recital sung by C. Day Lewis, another member of the group which included Louis MacNeice as well. Auden's love for music led to the composition of opera libretti (notably for Stravinsky's *The Rake's Progress*) and an unfortunate 'hymn' for the United Nations.

Poems and *Paid on Both Sides: A Charade* (1930), Auden's first important work, was enthusiastically received. The novelty of the alliterative metres, the spareness of the verse, and the authority of the descriptions, immediately established him. When he left Oxford, he earned his living briefly as a schoolmaster, but the poetic vocation was strong and he continued writing verse prolifically: *The Orators* (1932), *The Dance of Death* (1933), and *Look Stranger* (1936). He collaborated with Christopher Isherwood in writing Brechtian topical plays with songs and choruses, including *The Dog Beneath the Skin* (1935), *The Ascent of F6* (1936) and *On the Frontier* (1938). In 1937 *Spain* appeared, along with *Letters from Iceland*, composed with Louis MacNeice. Extensive travel and varied experiences – including a brief spell as an ambulance driver in the Spanish Civil War – extended Auden's range of experience. He travelled to Japan and China with Isherwood and they collaborated on *Journey to a War* (1939). In 1939 he and Isherwood emigrated to the United States. *Another Time* (1940) gathered the last of Auden's English poems. In 1946 he became an American citizen.

The unity of his early work – its concern with technique, its political commitment, its didactic strains, its openness to science and psychology – implies that the poems were aspects of a single complex statement of personal and social consequence. The Oxford Marxism he practised was giving way to an interest in Freud, and psychology – attention to the individual mind rather than the social organism – came to fascinate him. He did not find in Marx and Freud two aspects of a single paradox. They were alternatives, and he finally plumped for Freud. His Freudian poems – including the famous 'Elegy' to Freud and fine essay-poems such as 'Herman Melville' – use psychological terminology naturally and effectively.

A prosperous childhood, the experience of prep-school, public school and Oxford, the limited social range of his formative relationships, meant that he was denied the very social experience in which his sometimes naïve theoretical politics might have matured. The industrial landscape never gave up its claims on his imagination, but the men and women who inhabit that landscape play no prominent role in his secondary worlds. Auden, as he grew older, became a cosier poet. His magic, unlike Yeats's Blavatsky or Eliot's Jessie Weston, is of the here and now. His characteristic time scale is geological rather than historical: the pre-human helps to elucidate the strata of the human mind. His mystery is psychology.

It was the expatriate Auden, for whom images of travel, quest and exile had – for a time – replaced the imagery of place and rootedness, who wrote, 'Poetry is not concerned with telling people what to do, but with extending our knowledge of good and evil, perhaps making the necessity for action more urgent and its nature more clear, but only leading us to the point where it is possible for us to make a rational and moral choice.' This schoolmasterly tendency dominates the tone of his penultimate collection of serious verse, *Epistle to a Godson* (1972), in which he sets out to 'bother' the young with a message about taste, respect, manners and language.

After his removal to America, he developed a less public tone. He began to experiment with American forms, with syllabics and the very long line. The 'I' became clearly defined, and from exile Auden became more resolutely a British poet; his class roots became plainer as his antipathies subsided. In 1941 *New Year Letter* appeared, marking the beginning of the transition. Other notable collections followed, including *The Shield of Achilles* (1955) and *Homage to Clio* (1960). He was Professor of Poetry at Oxford (1956–60) and began to gravitate back towards Europe. *About the House* (1967) celebrates Auden's tenth year as the owner of a house in Kirchstetten, Austria – proud with a householder's pride, he celebrates too his own customs and habits. Later he wrote candidly, 'It is genuine in age to be / happily selfish.' There is no doubt about this 'genuine' quality in the later poems.

Many of them speak from and for a particular life-style, with such frankness that some readers find it difficult not to admire the craftsmanship while deploring the craftsman. In *About the House* and later books the poet reverses his public role, talks exclusively for himself, setting out a domestic landscape, inviting guests, gathering his possessions and his ghosts about him with a sort of celebratory confessionalism. 'Prologue at Sixty' is among the best of the later poems, extremely subtle in sound organization, depending on alliteration and assonantal inner rhymes. With this supple rhetoric, Auden takes stock of his progress and suggests a new beginning. He traces his development from a poet of landscape to a poet of social commitment, and then to a poet celebrating the representative individual (not the representative man). Autobiography plays an important part. Auden says elsewhere that each poem involves his entire past. This is certainly the case with 'Prologue at Sixty'.

In many of the poems the ideas are decorated, not contained, by the imagery. Argument, even when supported by persuasive rhythms, replaces passion. *Self* control is the chief discipline. Truth and Beauty, the poet notes, are not identical. His task is, he feels, to pursue them both at once and try to snare them in the same net. This disjunction between idea and decoration or expression is central to Auden. He frequently conceives form and content as distinct problems, and many of the poems seem to have been worked up, constructed. Form precedes content and does not emanate from it.

This is symptomatic of another element in Auden's work. The journalistic eye sees issues, particularly social issues, as themselves final. There is a reluctance to probe causes, to understand contexts, and an eagerness to generalize on immediate evidence. The naïve responsibility of the early poems and the sophisticated irresponsibility of the later ones ('It's heartless to forget about / the underdeveloped countries, / but . . .') are two aspects of the same approach. Though Auden admired Hardy's 'hawk's-eye view', his omniscient perspective, only in a few poems does he achieve a universality similar to Hardy's. He accepts the half-truth too readily. His ethic of 'honesty' is finally subjective.

A cause of his frequent failure to achieve a full perspective is his propensity for side-stepping paradox by irony. While Hardy's universe is ironic, confronting the poet with its paradoxes, Auden's universe is neutral, his irony is stylistic. He counsels the poet against using high-flown rhetoric if it is dishonest; yet it is often as hard to credit the throw-away irony as the rhetorical flurry. There is not necessarily more truth in self-effacement, in satirical deflation, than there is in open rhetoric.

But Auden would argue that there is. There is the matter of taste. He declares in the famous 'Foreword' to his *Collected Shorter Poems 1927–57* that he has discarded some of his early work because it was 'dishonest, or bad-mannered, or boring'. In this category he included his poem 'Spain'. He explains, 'A dishonest poem is one which expresses, no matter how well, feelings or beliefs which its author never felt or entertained . . . one must be honest even about one's prejudices.' But, we are entitled to ask, must the poet not question his prejudices? Is honesty, then, so passive a thing, so self-satisfied in self-acceptance? Good manners are not always honest, as Auden had occasion to indicate in some of his early satires. The comic undertones he feels make serious verse possible are in his work normally ironic, even in the broader comedy of his outstanding ballads 'Miss Gee' and 'Victor', with their cruelty.

The mature Auden's cast of mind is nowhere more apparent than in his 'commonplace book' *A Certain World* (1971). He assembles a collection of favourite excerpts. The entries on 'Commitment' would make his early admirers despair. But imbalance is pervasive. He includes various entries for 'Hell' but none for 'Heaven' (only 'Earthly Paradise'); there are many pages on 'War' but none on 'Peace', several on 'Sin' but none on 'Virtue'. The devil has all the best tunes, the God is straight out of the Old Testament. Opposite the stern and often cruel moral world is the world of facts: mines, rugged landscapes, volcanoes – presented in their elementality, power, and inhumanity.

Auden wrote 'Shorts' almost from the beginning – verse

fragments meant to convey their messages pithily, unrhymed epigrams. The tendency of his early verse is often towards epigram, brevity. This is hardly surprising, since Auden sometimes assembled poems from lines salvaged out of other, unsuccessful pieces, a type of craftsmanship at which he excelled. In a number of the early poems the lines are decisively end-stopped, as though the poet could not develop an extended cadence. This may have been due to the fragmentary composition.

An elegiac tone dominates even the love poems in Auden's early work: a concern with things passing and changing, a sense of alterable decay and instability. Satires such as 'Musée des Beaux Arts' or 'The Unknown Citizen' (the latter a mock epitaph) have this quality. There are also the great elegies to Yeats and Freud. Later, Auden turned to celebrating the durable prejudices and virtues he perceived, to discovering stability or suggesting disciplines. The early themes of recurrence and imaginative and human impotence before certain necessities foreshadowed his eventual abdication. Natural processes thwart human endeavour. We read of 'silted harbours, derelict works / In strangled orchards'. The later elegies include satire and autobiography. The lament is contented and accepting. The candid selfishness of his elegy to Emma, his housekeeper, stresses the depletion of *his* world. His world has some claim to generality; and in Emma are embodied certain values Auden applauds. We are less at ease with his elegy to Louis MacNeice, however, which has a quality of sang-froid, even in its protestations of friendship, a wilfulness in its attitude to the living, to the self, and to the dead, which render it – in Edgell Rickword's phrase – 'apostate humanitarian'.

In Auden's early poems he makes a wide range of formal choices. In 'The Exiles', for instance, he selects a stanza apt for describing diminution, and he uses it with varied rhythms. The formal rigour is not matched by a rigorous particularity of images and facts, for the effect is not intended to end at image. We come away from the poems with ideas, a tone of voice, in mind, but imagery is secondary. The poems tend towards generality, even when they emerge from particular experiences – specific elegiac subjects, specific relationships. Each man may have a landscape, but – so as not to limit the poem – the poet does not specify too carefully:

Who is ever quite without his landscape,
The straggling village street, the house in trees,
All near a church?

Despite his self-counselling, there is nonetheless an element of portentousness related to his resolute generality of statement. The choices are not *only* 'Between the needless risk / And the endless safety'. The poem does not support so loaded a line. And yet constraint and security are at odds with freedom and doubt. Conscience, like time, interferes with pleasure. Later, the vision changes, but the tendency towards generality remains.

'The Witnesses' is a memorable poem, perhaps because of the nightmare drama with which he deploys the ideas and the clipped control of the diction. The word 'Unpleasant', standing alone as it does, an understatement of dramatic force, in its usage is characteristic of a particular class of speaker with particular predispositions:

When the green field comes off like a lid,
Revealing what was much better hid—
    Unpleasant:
And look, behind you without a sound
The woods have come up and are standing round
    In deadly crescent.

In this and others of the early poems, Auden achieves a tone of voice without himself obtruding as a speaker. In the later work which – while refusing to mythologize – nonetheless makes a sort of dogmatic ceremonial of life-style and prominently celebrates the 'I' – it is the personality, not the voice, that speaks.

Throughout his work Auden tended to allegorize or caricature social misfits and 'enemies'. This tendency – particularly in the didactic later poems – might call into question the

social integrity of his work. Much as Yeats did, he falsified
human data to make a point, he generalized on inaccuracies.
It is when the protagonists are accurately portrayed, or when
they remain shadowy, indefinite, as in 'Lullaby', and we
focus on the relationship rather than the individuals, that his
best poems are achieved. 'Lullaby' is memorable because not
specific: the recumbent lovers' posture is suggested, but no
faces are drawn. The image is morally, not visually organized.
So, too, in his elegy to Yeats and the best of the later elegies
he celebrates a personal or cultural debt or loss, not the
particulars of the person.

Auden continued his technical experiments into his last
book, *Thank You, Fog* (1974) – and some of the most successful
experiments are in the later work. His best alliterative poems
are in *City without Walls* (1969), and his greatest syllabic
failure is in 'The Horatians' where, misunderstanding the
medium, he used the syllabic measure to slice up the poem
into lines of a predetermined length, without any warranty
for this in the subject matter or rhythm. He wrote haiku and
tanka, using them to express ideas rather than images, and
never tired of experimenting in the old forms, including the
sestina and villanelle.

His early debts – to Hardy, Edward Thomas, Eliot, Empson, and Owen – and his later debts – to Marianne Moore,
Laura Riding and others – are no less important than those
he owed to Old English poetry and other ancient verse, to his
contemporaries, and perhaps too to the younger poets he
championed. The styles he shaped were not technically radical in the way Eliot's style was, not original in concepts of
structure and organization; but they did evolve a rhetoric for
political statement and, later, a strong personal voice. His
authority in the use of various forms and metres and his
openness to a wide range of thought, experience, and subject
matter showed the way for many later poets.

One of his poems in *Epistle to a Godson*, 'A New Year
Greeting', embodies the best qualities of the elder Auden,
fusing a number of serious themes with Swiftean humour. He
envisages the nations of bacteria living on his body, meditates

their calamities when he bathes, dresses and undresses, and foretells the apocalypse of their world when he dies. This creation of a secondary world is expert and resonant:

Then, sooner or later, will dawn
  a day of Apocalypse,
when my mantle suddenly turns
  too cold, too rancid for you,
appetizing to predators
  of a fiercer sort, and I
am stripped of excuse and nimbus,
  a Past, subject to Judgement.

Roy Fuller (born 1912)

All art foresees a future,
Save art which fails to weigh
The sadness of the creature,
The limit of its day,
Its losing war with nature.

Roy Fuller's *Collected Poems* (1962), for all their variety of
form and theme, do not yield a clear picture of the poet.
Certain tensions, certain possibilities, seem to have been
neglected, as if increasing facility had seduced him away
from the original path hinted at in his early work. Fuller
deploys a local intelligence. He can spot technical flaws and
put them right. But his imagination often does not proceed
to generalize with authority. Frequently he prefers to cut
the poem short with irony rather than risk gestures, fibs.
His is a technical passion – hence his attraction to syllabics,
his formal experiments, his praise of masters of technique.
Hence, too, the moral indecision which is dramatized but
not resolved in the poems. A man of pragmatically liberal
conscience, stiffening with advancing years towards conservatism, burdened not too unwillingly with the para-
phernalia of modernity, he is at the same time a man of
severe aesthetic standards and impressive verbal skills. A
master of his art, he has little to say: even out of this poetry
can be made.

Roy Broadbent Fuller was born in Lancashire in 1912. At
the age of sixteen he left school and was articled to a solicitor.
He remained a solicitor much of his life, ending his law

career with the Woolwich Equitable Building Society. During the 1930s he fell under the spell of Auden and Spender and contributed to left-wing literary magazines. His first collection, *Poems*, appeared in 1940. Between 1941 and 1945 he served in the Royal Navy.

The poems that came directly from his military experience are included principally in *The Middle of a War* (1942) and *A Lost Season* (1944). In the second volume – full of close observation and a certain marring prolixity – he witnessed to the 'realities of service life' and the landscape of Africa. Of the Second World War poets, Fuller possessed the most acute sense of history and historical analogy. He, too, is the most profoundly and consciously didactic. Art is moral, should instruct and civilize. Fuller can never quite accept himself as a poet. Conscious, especially in his later work, of 'being a poet', he sees the vocation as a role he must consciously recall: 'A spider in the bath. The image noted.'

In 1949 *Epitaphs and Occasions* appeared, including satirical poems on modern English society and a gnawing personal discontent with his ready acceptance of the status quo. *Counterparts* (1954), *Brutus's Orchard* (1957) and *Buff* (1965) include his most accomplished work, and *New Poems* (1968) and *Tiny Tears* (1973) suggest little falling off in the poet's skills, though there is a doubtful quality about the poems – they appear undermined by the very tensions that bring them into being. The most recent poems show Fuller following Auden's footsteps into a world of threatened forms and values, half-heartedly defending himself and his way of life against the incursions of the media, of low standards and uncertain beliefs. He speaks with a representative voice, and the development of his social attitudes is typical of the liberal intellectual of the 1930s and 1940s; he experiences first disenchantment with his early idealism, then fear of the very causes he had championed. There is no battle of conscience, rather a modulation in the tones of protest and disaffection.

Fuller is a novelist as well as a poet, and his fictional techniques have affected his poetic techniques. Many of the

poems are discursive, rising out of – or building on – an
implicit situation. His war poems are distinctive for their
sense of context and their perspective on events: the ennui,
the waiting, the unextraordinary nature of the experience of
a warrior on the sidelines of war. Travel sharpens his sense
of what Europe and European ambitions represent to other
people. In 'The Green Hills of Africa' he writes:

The poisoner proceeds by tiny doses,
The victim weaker and weaker but uncomplaining.
Soon they will only dance for money, will
Discover more and more things can be sold.

Disease, whether the ennui of waiting or the slow recognition
of the cultural rottenness manifest in the individual European, dominates much of the imagery of the early poems.
In 'What is Terrible' he begins, 'Life at last I know is
terrible':

The apprehension has come slowly to me,
Like symptoms and bulletins of sickness. I
Must first be moved across two oceans, then
Bored, systematically and sickeningly,
In a place where war is news.

Rebelling against power, organization, destruction, and
against choicelessness in his existence, he evokes what most
distresses him:

          there is the hand
Moving the empty glove; the bland
Aspect of nothing disguised as something . . .

His conversion from radical disaffection is expressed in the
poem 'Translation'. He does not immediately accept what
he has before rejected, but elects, in terms his own subsequent poems were fortunately unable to substantiate, to
abdicate individual responsibility. 'I will dissemble no
longer,' he declares. 'I will stop expressing my belief in the
rosy / Future of man.' The poem ends:

Anyone happy in this age and place
Is daft or corrupt. Better to abdicate
From a material and spiritual terrain
       Fit only for barbarians.

Can he in conscience abandon both the material and
spiritual terrains? Can he abandon either? Not credibly,
and not for long.

Something like Fuller's final moral stance becomes clear
in 'Florestan to Leonora', where he debunks ironically (not
satirically) all that he wishes he did not accept but, com-
placently, does accept:

                    Yes,
Our values must shrivel to the size of those
Held by a class content with happiness:

And warmed by our children, full of bread and wine,
I shall dream of the discipline of insomnia
And an art of symbols, starved and saturnine.

It may be argued that the poem is spoken by a persona, not
by the poet himself. But Fuller chooses his personae not as
Browning does, out of fascination with character, but rather
out of a desire for a mask that will add eloquence to what he
has to say himself, without being himself answerable. A pro-
tective device, the persona occupies an area between the
poet's 'I' and the fictional 'I'.

The poems come *after* experience, the thought is preconceived. This Augustan trait of pre-meditation is accompanied
by no Augustan finality, authority or range. In all but
Fuller's short lyrics, there is a provisional quality in the tone
of voice and the ideas the voice expresses. They are what he
meant, but lack the power of their meanings because the
poem itself is not convinced of them.

Fuller, aware of these faults, makes use of them. In a
lesser poet the tentativeness would seem inconsequential.
But Fuller's best poems have a necessary quality, for he is
trying to make connections. His honesty is expressed in his
uncertainty.

In the earliest poems, Fuller uses a range of symbolic detail but does not achieve an over-all sense of setting. The poems abound in isolated effects. Uncharacteristic poetical excesses ('Clouds covered like a scab the blenched, / Raw sky') recall his Apocalyptic contemporaries. Most obvious is the debt to early Auden – in, for example, 'End of a City'. Fuller as a young man is plagued by guilt – particularly at the gap between his ideals and his actions. 'To M. S., Killed in Spain' reveals the tension:

I fear the plucking hand
That from our equal season
Sent you to war with wrong
But left me suavely wound
In the cocoon of reason
That preluded your wings.

He turns to satire, too, but he is temperamentally sympathetic to the butts of his wit – the aristocracy, for instance, and the moribund romantic tradition – so the satire is self-critical as well.

Even at the outset, there is an intellectual ambivalence. In the two collections of war poems the ambivalence is less apparent than later. *The Middle of a War* owes certain debts – 'War Poets' suggests Rickword's 'Trench Poets', though without Rickword's stunned humanity; 'Soliloquy in an Air Raid' takes Tennyson's 'Tithonus' as a rhythmic and, to a degree, thematic model. Individual deaths and suffering begin to have a terrible imaginative reality for the poet: he feels 'a certain sense' of the poems' 'inadequacy'. In 'The Middle of a War' the poet looks at a photograph of himself in uniform and imagines himself dead. From the photograph, itself an emblem of his choicelessness, his musing moves on to implicate empire, life itself:

Ah, life has been abandoned by the boats—
Only the trodden island and the dead
Remain, and the once inestimable caskets.

In *A Lost Season* he concentrates on the poem as a whole, not merely on local felicities. Less allegorical, more descriptive, it portrays the African panorama. The approach may be journalistic, but it is evocative. The climate is moral. 'Today and Tomorrow' is a dramatic postponement of the ideal that, after the war, would be postponed for good. In 1949 Fuller bluntly declared how careless he had been about human suffering, how easy it had been to consider abstractly. Because he felt the sham in his earlier commitment, he did not try to realize it – he satirized it.

The image of division is frequent in his poems: between the extremes in war and army life, its deprivations and its comforts, where in a deep sense the poet is not affected; between intellectual and emotional desire, social commitment and individualism. In the post-war poems, *Epitaphs and Occasions*, the impulse is at once to come to terms with the 'knowledge' of what had happened and to condense and interpret the experience. A number of eight-line poems attempt but hardly achieve epigrammatic concentration. The book includes exercises – poems about places, specific writers, and poets. He tries to particularize the 'actual nature' of places, people, and types of people.

The later poems develop from *Epitaphs and Occasions*. In 'Obituary of R. Fuller' the poet feels the division in himself as a lack of psychological intensities – traumas and the like; and of experiences of social extremity – poverty or wealth – which define a man. He reports, 'His life was split / And half was lost bewailing it: / Part managerial, part poetic— / Hard to decide the more pathetic.' The situation is seen as archetypal. He satirizes himself:

If any part of him survives
It will be that verse which contrives
To speak in private symbols for
The peaceful caught in public war.
For there his wavering faith in man
Wavers around some sort of plan,
And though foreseeing years of trouble,
Denies a universal rubble . . .

The older poet understands better the nature of his 'wavering faith' and suggests no absolute answer. Revisiting his youth, he is unable to identify with the intellectual constants it demanded. His landscape is finally not Africa but suburbia where, as in the war poems, and sometimes with equal power, he celebrates arrivals, departures, the long ennui. He writes sonnet sequences, the 'Faustian Sketches', the sixteen-line 'Meredithian Sonnets', and worries at myth, his boredom, his ambivalence. In *Tiny Tears* he explores Auden's geological time scale, coming momentarily to terms with his insignificance. The masks are less insistent, connections are perceived more naturally. It is not the experimental prose poems, or the Baudelaire translations, but the poems that look towards death that are most memorable. In 'One September' he writes:

Dear life, I struggle awake to greet you again—
Fetching the honeyed hot milk, finding my father's
Cigarette case among the debris of yesterday's pockets,
Realizing that after all it's not you that frightens us.

George Barker (born 1913)

Track any poet to a beginning
 And in the dark room you discover
A little boy intent on sinning
 With an etymological lover.

George Granville Barker was born in Loughton, Essex, in
1913, into an Anglo-Irish family. Ireland is celebrated and
idealized in 'Poem on Ireland', a country he had not visited
when he wrote the poem, a land of imagination. He began
writing early – at nine or ten, he recalls, he wrote 'The
Tournament', a ten-page epic in Spenserian stanzas. He was
educated at the local county council school and later, briefly,
at the Regent Street Polytechnic. Like David Gascoyne and
Dylan Thomas, he avoided the University. Indeed, he soon
avoided the Polytechnic and began to take up a number of
odd jobs.

In 1933 he published *Thirty Preliminary Poems* and a novel,
Alanna Autumnal. These books were followed by *Poems* (1935)
and the long political poem *Calamiterror* (1937). Barker, like
Dylan Thomas, had been seduced emotionally if not intellectually by surrealism. The great Surrealist Exhibition (1936)
left its mark on him. He never understood it in the way
Gascoyne did, but he was drawn to the element of distortion
in surreal art, and in *Calamiterror* he tells us, 'I was a figure
of the Surrealist Exhibition / With a mass of roses face.' He
felt a duty, imposed perhaps by the example of Auden and
his contemporaries, to speak of political themes, despite his
temperament. *Calamiterror* is 'about' fascism and Spain. It
enhanced his reputation. In 1939 he was appointed Professor

of English at the Imperial Tohoku University of Japan, a post which occupied him only briefly. With the war, he went to America where he stayed – in Canada and the United States – for three years.

In 1940 *Lament and Triumph* appeared, followed by *Eros in Dogma* (1944). Back in England, he published regularly, and his style evolved towards its later plainness. *News of the World* and the first part of *The True Confessions of George Barker* appeared in 1950. *A Vision of Beasts and Gods* (1954) followed, and in 1957 the *Collected Poems*, which excluded *The True Confessions* at his publisher's request. A number of books have followed, including *The View from a Blind I* (1962), *Dreams of a Summer Night* (1966) and *The Golden Chains* (1968). Barker is as unpredictable now as he was in the 1930s, when he haunted Soho and was a habitué of David Archer's bookshop. His celebration of Archer, *In Memoriam David Archer* (1973), includes some of his most candid and direct poems.

In all of Barker's work there are strong tensions between a natural naïvety and a secondhand sophistication, lucid images and surreal gesturing, keen wit and execrable puns, a functional traditional formalism and an irrelevant tendency to archaize, syntactical clarity and syntactical convolution. Few of the poems are successful all through. The word intoxication does not mean that the poems emanate from deep within the man or the language.

Barker is not a radical poet. He flirts uncommittedly with traditional formalism, and at the other extreme toys with radical formal experimentation. His main experimentation is in diction. The various influences on his work are clearly legible: Spenser in the stanza forms of *Calamiterror*, Dylan Thomas in some of the flourishes, Eliot in occasional cadences. Michael Roberts and Edwin Muir helped him to clarify his own thoughts on poetry. Barker was fond, too, of Owen, but most passionately fond of Hopkins. Hopkins's influence gave way to Yeats's, and the music of the latter was closer to Barker's own.

His *Essays* (1970) confirm Martin Seymour-Smith's verdict

that Barker was never really a surrealist, that 'his confusion came naturally to him'. What emerges most strongly from his prose writing is his concern with the identity of 'the poet' – his personality – which should in some way guarantee his poetic currency. The poet's responsibility – his very presence – is 'to assert and affirm the human privilege of perversity'. He is a programmatic eccentric, an Anarchist – though by anarchist Barker seems to mean individualist. He needs a dictionary, alcohol, and love, and he is all set. Barker is what Donald Davie might call a chronic Antigone, always in opposition. For Barker anarchy 'affirms the triumph of the imagination over the will' – 'perversity asserts the triumph of the living over the dead'. He distinguishes between rational (willed, dead, external, statistical) information and imaginative information; the poem speaks to us out of 'the heart of things'. It works from the inside out. This point assumes some importance when we read *Calamiterror* and other early poems.

He tells us that the 'anarchic void' lurks just beyond all our systems of formalizing reality and exercises its powers through the veils we spread before it. His role is to make us aware of the power and systematic lawlessness of the 'void'. When he defines his subject as 'the necessity of Anarchy' he gets it the wrong way round – for his subject is the fact of anarchy beyond common forms.

His early poetic programme is one of distortion: the warping, elongation, fragmentation of the image or statement. The poet intensifies and exaggerates at the same time. What is unknown cannot be expressed in terms of the literal known. The known must be placed in a hall of mirrors or distorted violently by other means. For Barker the poetry exists in the tension between the intellectual perception of reality and the imagination working away from and yet on reality. 'The image cannot be a poem because a poem is what happens to an image,' he writes. 'The greatest images are the images of twisted reality – images in which the facts are tormented so as to make them surrender their knowledge, their secrets, their special sources of information.' Metamorphosis is a central process. But the failure of this theory in practice is that Barker often does not establish the reality which he is going to distort. Distortion begins on the already distorted. There must be a background of expectedness to all that is unexpected, if it is to have effect. Barker tends to give – in the early poems – a background of unexpectedness. The metamorphoses often imply no qualitative change, release no meanings, but play with meanings. The naïvely conceived polarities – between Good and Evil, Intellect and Imagination, Man and Woman – are not clarified but continually and evasively contrasted and mingled.

All poetry, Barker claims, is celebration of some sort. Even satire celebrates by implying in its terms of censure what is possible, potential, in actuality. Certainly there is a celebratory element in even the most depressing of his poems. What is most often celebrated is the 'I' of the poems, which can sensationalize itself with relish ('I sip at suicide in bedrooms or dare pessimistic stars'), or praise its virility, or examine its past. But the 'I' is also the great assimilator, nowhere more assertively than in *Calamiterror*.

In the early poems, 'Daedalus' for example, the distortion is not only of content but of syntax. The linguistic distortion points away from the spoken language, towards a new poetic rhetoric. Distortion leads to tautologies – occasioned also by a rhythmic insistence – such as 'Descending down' and 'Unseen invisible'; and mixed metaphors. The body's various organs and limbs exist independently – 'the unit army of the body' – and the words are intended, within the overpowering rhythm, to release their meanings separately and rapidly. Even in his early work Barker's principal poetic genres are the erotic elegy and autobiography. The eroticism is often cruel, the autobiography – first masked by myth, gesture and attitude – becomes more direct as he proceeds. The more particular he is, the more powerful the effects.

An engaging clumsiness characterizes the best of the early poems. 'The Laughing Leapers' works on rhythmic and assonantal principles which MacNeice mastered decisively in 'The Sunlight on the Garden'. But where in MacNeice there is a poetic logic in the internal rhymes, in Barker's poems there is an arbitrary quality which makes the diction seem contrived and humorous:

Many men mean
Well: but tall walls
Impede, their hands bleed and
They fall, their seed the
Seed of the fallen.

There is in fact no clear pattern in the sound progression – it is associative, not formal. The word-inebriation is essentially romantic: 'gold' is a frequent term, leader among a number of indefinite conjuring words. His strongest effects are in rhythm. Like Hopkins he strives for the best of both worlds: a following cadence or rhythm *and* a phrased effect. 'Summer Idyll' achieves this:

... under the breast
Space of a vacancy spreads like a foul
Ghost flower, want ...

Line endings assume key importance. What vitiates the early work is prolixity and a streak of whimsicality in which Barker grounds an easy resonance.

'Kew Gardens' embarks on political themes, contrasting the deceit and violence of power with the peaceful, lenitive effects of nature. In *Calamiterror* he attempts a particular statement. The 'Introductory Stanzas' are the most carefully wrought in the poem. He effectively withholds the main verb, creating a tense passivity. Then the verbal storm breaks. The poem is enacted entirely in space. Time past and future are consciously excluded: 'The fourth dimension of this space is fear.' He works with surreal rhetoric, but the surrealism is not absolute, and this more than anything contributes to the poem's failure. It does not honour its stylistic commitments. It falls back lamely on Miltonic rhetoric and easy, thoughtless writing: 'Down what escarpments can the man escape / Consigned to profounds of his mind's abysms?'

The best poetic effects in *Calamiterror* are the correspondences Barker draws between things: the hand that touches the rose is the hand that destroys; or, more subtly, he draws out a natural correspondence in celebration:

The eye-shaped leaf, the topmost of the tree,
Examines heaven, the leaf-shaped eye examines
The eye-shaped leaf, and each observes in each
Heaven and heaven.

Such lines reveal that Barker is no surrealist. He will, when it suits him, surrealize content, but not form. His form demands recurrences, forcing the would-be surreal into patterns of static recurrence, even if not into a signifying order. The surreal images do not accumulate meaning or resonance: the boiling blood, the embryo, the eyeballs, bones, sexual organs in various disguises (the male genitals are seen as gas masks), the images pile up, recur, always in a rhetorical context.

Everything in the poem – even landscape – exists physically within the poet. The lark sings in the spine. The beloved briefly stands outside him; but in her outer existence she yet inhabits the landscape he has assimilated, and soon all women are in his bowels along with the rocks and stones and trees. The only way he finds to control 'the chaos of experience' is to internalize it: 'I recall how the rosetree sprang out of my breast. / I recall the myriads of birds in the cage of my head.' This is the ego he celebrates: 'The centre of the heart like a red tree / Shoots forth a hand pointing towards mirrors.' In the last part of the poem the hand points to the 'common red rose' and, after long labour, the poem delivers its political message. At the end Barker universalizes the poem – not ineffectively – by multiplying himself into a myriad men, suggesting that the experience is common to all men in extremity. But the idiom, capable of carrying a personal meaning, cannot carry public meanings with ease. His most compelling setting for poems is the Embankment, watching the river. His mind is freed into more usual poetic channels: it is Narcissus's position. The reflection of the self stays put while the river flows.

Barker developed from the sometimes hysterical, tortured tones of the early work towards a quieter, less erratic voice – though there were relapses. Perhaps one explanation for the early extremities of expression is that Barker had to generate his own extreme experiences, without the actual war experience which tended to chasten and consolidate style. This is not to deny the intensity of his personal experiences, but it does cast some light on the limitations of his public utterances which are so equivocally subjective.

The 'Pacific Sonnets' – not really sonnets – show Barker moving away from the tutelage of Hopkins to that of Yeats. It is an important stage for Barker, a move towards a more rigorous rhetoric and a more personal voice. The 'Secular Elegies' with their pared language are ruminative in effect, an unprecedented tone, and Barker's most wholly successful sequence. The 'Sacred Elegies' answer them – but there is little difference in tone. The sacredness is principally that of human love. Only the fifth elegy is directed to God, more an open letter than an intimate statement.

However, even in the love poems Barker does not achieve a tone of intimacy. This is characteristic of the so-called 'Apocalyptic' poets. It is caused by a stiffness and monotony of diction. The same voice, with varying devices – though developing in subtlety – always speaks. The poems are for recitation, to be heard, not overheard. Yet they carry obscure public meanings. It was this failure of intimacy, quietness, variety, that the poets who came to prominence in the early 1950s reacted against. What they saw as a problem of style and subject matter was in fact a problem of tone.

There are four cycles of love poems by Barker, all in a rhetorical vein. There are also the 'Personal Sonnets', outstanding among them 'To My Mother', a poem which presents a Rabelaisian woman with a degree of realism and sympathy unanticipated in the early work. Barker became technically more adventurous as he advanced, leaving surrealism behind, using the sestina with authority, and in 'The Five Faces of Pity' mastering terza rima in an effective way.

In *News of the World* he subdued the surreal impulse and used distortion with reference to an actual world. He gauged his sensational effects more nicely, producing a disturbing vision:

> Outraged, you, outcast,
> Leading your one-eyed sister through the night,
> From door to door down the locked zodiac,
>   Never come home.

The eye is a recurrent image, and in *The True Confessions* we learn why.

Barker always trusts sensation and emotion rather than intellect. The death poems and elegies have the authenticity of a man who fears rather than contemplates death. In 'At Thurgarton Church', the elegies from *Poems of Places and People, In Memoriam David Archer* and the 'Sonnet of Fishes' with the Thomas-like lines, 'the immense imminence not understood, / Death, in a dark, in a deep, in a dream, for ever', death seems to be a more emotive subject for him than war or violence.

In his later work Barker has used the short line more frequently. *In Memoriam David Archer*, despite the often forced rhymes, is a more precise sequence full of images, few of them surreal. He has his dreams and nightmares, but he wakes from them; his celebration is more direct. If less word-play and sound intoxication are evident, the newer virtues outweigh the loss. The world is no longer inside him – only dreams and memories are. The realism of section twelve, in which he describes how poverty destroyed his father, and his account of the incident in which he wounded his brother, are unprecedented in their candour.

Barker has advanced without worrying his vocation with any demanding questions, without much close attention to his tools. He frequently quotes Blake's dictum – that sun and moon would go out if they succumbed to doubt. Ask no explanations of your art: that becomes a rule. His exploration of language, carried on particularly in *The True Confessions*, raises no questions about technique: it describes poetry in the pragmatic terms of practice. He believes that language is tending one way and truth another – language by its very forms makes truth-telling difficult. He writes:

The crisis of the word,
the defeat of simply rational speech is what
the poem takes off in flight from.

But he has never faced 'simply rational speech' and its consequences.

The True Confession is Barker's most original poem. The originality is not in form or treatment of imagery but in the candid public tone. It has some of the charm of the 'Wife of Bath's Tale' – its satire implicates even as it celebrates the self. Self-disgust balances the speaker's conceit. Barker would doubtless be a better poet if he attended more to his dictionary, if he were willing to serve rather than use language, if he were less concerned with 'being a poet', more concerned with the poetry. But then, he would be a different poet.

R.S. Thomas (born 1913)

One thing I have asked
Of the disposer of the issues
Of life: that truth should defer
To beauty. It was not granted.

'R. S. Thomas is not at all literary,' John Betjeman wrote.
Thomas takes his forms for granted, worries little about
poetic theory. The verse emanates from his experience. If in
each collection there are dozens of limp poetical phrases it is
because he has not, until his later work, questioned his
language: he has questioned his experience and adapted a
conventional diction.

Ronald Stuart Thomas was born in Cardiff in 1913. He
grew up in Wales, learned to speak Welsh when an adult,
and was ordained in 1936 as a clergyman of the Church of
Wales. His parishes in rural parts of Wales, his relationship
with his parishioners, and the effect of change on their lives
have supplied him with much of his poetic material. He has
been described as a 'Christian realist', a classification which
fails to take into account his poems on Welsh legend, his
personal lyrics, and the later prophetic pieces. But the bulk
of his verse is pastoral in both senses.

The book which earned him wide popularity was *Song at
the Year's Turning* (1955), which included poems from two
earlier collections, *The Stones of the Field* (1946) and *An Acre
of Land* (1952), a dramatic poem entitled 'The Minister'
composed for radio broadcast (1953) and some additional
work. This major collection was followed by *Poetry for Supper*
(1958), *Tares* (1964), and *The Bread of Truth* (1963). With

Pieta (1966), Thomas began to change his ground. His style, tone and perspective underwent a readjustment that continued in *Not that he Brought Flowers* (1968) and *H'm* (1972).

In *Poetry for Supper* Thomas wrote:

Verse should be as natural
As the small tuber that feeds on muck
And grows slowly from obtuse soil
To the white flower of immortal beauty.

The description fits his early poems, and the precision of vocabulary, where each word carries its full weight, is characteristic. The soil is 'obtuse' as the men we meet in other poems, those who till it. Verse is cultivated, though it grows from literal particulars.

He is poet-clergyman in the early verse. Later, poet and clergyman sometimes speak in different voices. The power of the early poems is the uncompromising fusion, with the paradoxes it implies, between poet and clergyman. The poems rapidly evoke background, then dwell on a particular incident or image in it, having established a context in which the image comes to signify. When he deals with his rustic parishioners, his response vacillates from annoyance at their unthinking stolidity and passivity to a grudging admiration for their simple, elemental lives. Iago Prytherch is an omnipresent character in Thomas's landscape, 'Just an ordinary man of the bald Welsh hills, / Who pens a few sheep in a gap of cloud'. When Thomas writes, 'There is something frightening in the vacancy of his mind', we understand the poet's attraction: there is something equally frightening in the visionary fulness of his own mind, drawn to its rugged opposite. His disgust and shock at the smell of the peasant are responses of 'the refined, / But affected, sense' confronting 'stark naturalness'. The poet attempts to write 'The terrible poetry of his kind'.

Early in the poems Thomas defines what he sees as 'the natural' – the unreflective, unclean, habit-governed servant of the land and of the years. The body is a 'lean acre of ground that the years master'. If this is nature, then reflection, cleanliness, indeed intelligence, are not natural. In any event, godly or ungodly, they are drawn to Prytherch, as a moth to a naked flame. But paradox runs at the heart of Thomas's work. In 'Valediction', as in 'A Priest to his People', he rejects the bovine, unreceptive, and here *unnatural* peasant:

> For this I leave you
> Alone in your harsh acres, herding pennies
> Into a sock to serve you for a pillow
> Through the long night that waits upon your span.

It would be wrong to look for a consistent vocabulary in Thomas – words assume different meanings in different contexts. Indeed, intellectual consistency from poem to poem is lacking. For all his acerbity, Thomas is a poet of feeling rather than thought. He conveys indignation, compassion, awe, sympathy (though seldom empathy), the love of beauty, all in much the same rhythms, imagery and vocabulary. Though he often says 'Farewell' to the peasants and their poor life, he returns directly. The poems are not of meditation but enactment. Their power and their memorability is in the skilful choice of metaphor; for they are neither in form, rhythm, nor vocabulary innovative.

Thomas increasingly sees moral in terms of political responsibility. His moral responsibility is an outgrowth of faith and of his love of beauty and natural correspondences, and a desire to find the same order and beauty in man. When he fails, a humane misanthropy enters in, a momentary rejection of the imperfectible. He returns because he does not understand the peasant. Or he turns to Welsh history to find there, in the patterns and heroisms of the past, some elucidation of the present. In 'Welsh History' he concludes:

> We were a people bred on legends,
> Warming our hands at the red past.

> We were a people, and are so yet.
> When we have finished quarrelling for crumbs
> Under the table, or gnawing the bones
> Of a dead culture, we will arise,
> Armed, but not in the old way.

Yet history seems inactive in the present, despite the vivid images it inspires, – as in 'The Rising of Glyndwr', 'the woman with the hair / That is the raven's and the rook's despair'. Consulting the landscape, he concludes that history, a past, is all Wales possesses. In 'Welsh Landscape' he writes:

There is no present in Wales,
And no future;
There is only the past,
Brittle with relics ...

He cannot successfully posit a future for the landscape and community evoked in 'The Village'. His parishioners may eventually prove susceptible to teaching, but community exists exclusively in terms of its past. The future implies de-population, not regeneration of the rural community. 'The cold brain of the machine' gradually encroaches, further impoverishing his people. It even destroys Prytherch. In *Tares*, Thomas included his tragic poem 'Here':

It is too late to start
For destinations not of the heart.
I must stay here with my hurt.

From book to book, Thomas has become more overtly didactic. He holds up Prytherch and the imbecile to us as human beings, as though we would be tempted to deny them their humanity. Some poems enact Biblical incidents and parables. In *Pieta* Thomas begins to take his Wales and his parishioners for granted, and from the uncompromising clarity of acceptance he looks away from his parish, general-izing on his experience, commenting directly on wider issues. Prytherch develops a compelling, almost emblematic clarity:

Yet in your acres,
With no medals to be won,
You are on the old side of life,
Helping it in through the dark door
Of earth and beast, quietly repairing
The rents of history with your hands.

In this poem, grandiloquent though it is, Thomas and Prytherch are in a sense one, Thomas registers his Welshness. In later poems he records his experience in terms analogous to those he used for his parishioners. The landscape and its history have worked their changes on his mind. In 'The Belfry' he concludes:

There are times
When a black frost is upon
One's whole being, and the heart
In its bone belfry hangs and is dumb.

Part of the power of the later poems is due to Thomas's recognition that he is growing older. In 'The Dance' he asks – or laments – 'Let me smell / My youth again in your hair.' Yeats, whose influence is present in the early work, is replaced by a more developed personal idiom. As Thomas accepts his relationship with his parishioners, he turns to question his God (in terms sometimes reminiscent of Ted Hughes's), he travels, his scope widens, his tone becomes more varied. The later Welsh poems are addressed to England, some with the touch of a didactic travelogue, prefaced with, 'In Wales . . .' Wales provides a pulpit. He attempts technical experiments, too. 'The Place', an unsuccessful poem, includes a sentence eked out over fourteen lines. It is too self-conscious a feat, too laboured, to have the naturalness Thomas called for in *Poetry for Supper*.

In each of Thomas's collections the fourteen-line poem recurs, occasionally rhymed into a sonnet. When unrhymed, the form nonetheless retains the organization of a sonnet. His formal variety is small, however – a wide range of experiences can be accommodated in a very few forms. Even in *H'm*, dissatisfied with his passive acceptance of form, Thomas's experiments with the enjambment, the broken rhythm, and so on, are seldom startlingly successful. When he becomes self-conscious about technique, he distracts us from the poem on to *how* the poem is saying what it says. Of the later poems, however, 'Pavane', with its varied rhythms, is an impressive achievement, and 'Making' evokes and clarifies a point of faith, rather in the manner of Herbert.

The machine becomes a pervasive threat; the Welsh landscape is replaced at times by an almost allegorical landscape, where Thomas's portentous vision of the future is briefly enacted, or which God looks over and ruminates on in the first person. There is, too, a new bitterness, in a poem such as 'He' for instance:

Nothing he does, nothing he
Says is accepted, and the thin dribble
Of his poetry dries on the rocks
Of a harsh landscape under an ailing sun.

The 'He' is as much the God of the later poems as the poet himself.

C.H. Sisson (born 1914)

> So speech is treasured, for the things it gives
> Which I cannot have, for I speak too plain
> Yet not so plain as to be understood

The earliest poem which C. H. Sisson has preserved was written on a troopship going to India in 1944:

> I, whose imperfection
> Is evident and admitted
> Needing further assurance
> Must year-long be pitted
> Against fool and trooper
> Practising my integrity
> In awkward places,
> Walking until I walk easy
> Among uncomprehended faces.

The humility of the lines is genuine, the faces are uncomprehend*ed*, not uncomprehend*ing*. He does not feel misunderstood but unable to understand. The poems attempt to understand. In describing his work he writes, 'My beginnings were altogether without facility, and when I was forced into verse it was through having something not altogether easy to say.'

As the skill increased, he struggled against facility. 'As the inevitable facility comes, the poet's task becomes the rejection of whatever appears with the face of familiarity. The writing of poetry is, in a sense, the opposite of writing what one wants to write.' There are few repetitions in his work.

Themes that reappear are developed to different ends. Each poem is new, unfamiliar.

'Is not every sincere life, in a sense, a journey to the first years?' Sisson asks in an essay on Péguy. Sisson's work – as a poet, translator, novelist and critic – follows a course of exploration whose end is to re-establish connections with the 'first years' of the culture and the individual in that culture. The 'first years', the common source, are also the common ground between men, or should be. He develops in his poetry a quality of mind which apprehends things in their source; and his scathing satire of ephemeral trends and the vacuity of modern urban society and capital-culture complements his retrospective vision.

Charles Hubert Sisson was born in Bristol in 1914. He went to the University of Bristol to read English and later continued his studies in Germany and France. In 1936 he began work in the Civil Service. The next year he married. In 1942 he enlisted and in 1943 was sent on active service to India for a two-and-a-half-year tour. In 1945 he returned to England and resumed his work in Whitehall. Thirty-six years in the Civil Service took him to Under Secretary and comparable positions in the Ministry of Labour. He was a severe critic of the Civil Service, provoking indignation by his satires and essays. He summed up the experience of London life in *The London Zoo* (1961), his first extensive collection of poems. It included the epitaph: 'Here lies a civil servant. He was civil / To everyone, and servant to the devil.'

And yet what distinguishes Sisson from other contemporary poets is his belief that the writer serves best as a man of action, an insider in the social machine, who guards the integrity of historical institutions even as he criticizes and perfects them. Sisson adheres to the English Church (he accepts an Anglicanism with seventeenth-century overtones), and has no doubt about the continuing importance of the monarchy. Dr Johnson's definition of 'Tory' suits Sisson, who is in no way a Tory of the modern kidney, but 'One who adheres to the ancient constitution of the state, and the apostolic hierarchy of the Church of England'. Johnson defines 'Whig' as 'The name of a faction'. That the faction rules – and has done for many years – makes Sisson's stance a radical and an unpopular one. His submission to accepted institutions is, however, as his conduct has shown, anything but passive. The institutions are corrupt and corrupting. The God he worships is as often absent from his office as present, more often silent than responsive. 'What does not reply is the answer to prayer.'

As a man of action himself, Sisson admires Marvell for his double vocation; and Barnes for his teaching and pastoral work; and Swift; and Maurras. All were men of principle and conviction whose writing matured in a world of wide social concerns, relationships, and actual responsibilities. Sisson's attack on Walter Bagehot, who raised compromise into an ethic, is eloquent. His milder assessment of the 1930s poets' Marxism is telling. Sisson is one of the rare literary Creons of our day, with something of Creon's scorn for the querulous and inconsistent Antigones who crowd the poetry shelves. Writing, for the man of action, is not an end in itself. Ideas in the abstract are impotent. Sisson writes of Maurras, 'He believed in the effect and force of ideas.' Maurras suffered – some would say caused suffering – for his beliefs, which were 'heavy with personal consequence'. He not only expressed them but took responsibility for them. The writer should be no mere watcher of changes, no powerless prophet; he should be a discoverer and rediscoverer of continuities.

In his poems, Sisson's journey to the 'first years' is not personal, except as it is conducted by a powerful speaking voice. His quest is not for 'the lost child' or Wordsworth's cloud-trailing infant. The romantic element in his spare Augustan writing is that, while it masks as reason or logic, like Marvell's poetic 'logic' it is a language of association, not analysis – even in the satires. In his best poems he does not anatomize experience but establishes connections on the other side of reason, working towards a whole vision communicated to the pulse through careful, firm rhythms. 'Reason may convince, but it is rhythm that persuades,' he quotes Maurras as saying. In the preface to his *Collected Poems* he writes, 'The proof of a poem – any poem – is in its rhythm and that is why critical determination has in the end to await the unarguable perception.' Rhythm is authority. In 'The Usk', which Donald Davie characterized as 'one of the great poems of our time', the rhythm is at its most persuasive:

Lies on my tongue. Get up and bolt the door
For I am coming not to be believed
The messenger of anything I say.
So I am come, stand in the cold tonight
The servant of the grain upon my tongue,
Beware, I am the man, and let me in.

Effective rhythm integrates diverse material, performs feats of lucid fusion. In what is perhaps his best poem, 'In Insula Avalonia', Sisson taxes rhythm to its utmost, fusing religious and patriotic themes in the legend of Arthur, dreaming the centuries away on the Isle of Avalon, near Glastonbury. Sisson has made this Somerset landscape his own much as Barnes and Hardy appropriated Dorset. Davie speaks of the interweaving of the themes 'in a verse which, as it were, goes nowhere and says nothing, which is Shakespearean and at times Eliotic to just the degree that it is Virgilian'. It defies paraphrase: it is quite unnecessary to ask the meaning of the verse because the verse is the meaning. The third section reads:

Dark wind, dark wind that makes the river black
—Two swans upon it are the serpent's eyes—
Wind through the meadows as you twist your heart.

Twisted are trees, especially this oak
Which stands with all its leaves throughout the year;
There is no Autumn for its golden boughs

But Winter always and the lowering sky
That hangs its blanket lower than the earth
Which we are under in this Advent-tide.

Not even ghosts. The banks are desolate
With shallow snow between the matted grass
Home of the dead but there is no one here.

What is a church-bell in this empty time?
The geese come honking in a careless skein
Sliding between the mort plain and the sky.

What augury? Or is there any such?
They pass over the oak and leave me there
Not even choosing, by the serpent's head.

There are other rhythms, but the same controlled voice speaks them.

Sisson developed as a poet in the apprentice shop of translation. First he did versions of Heine's political poems – exercises in plain speaking through deceptively simple forms. Later he rendered the poems of Catullus into English. He was intent on conveying the tone of voice and quality of thought of the original, and he refused to poeticize it. Catullus emerges as a somewhat tight-lipped hedonist, but he has not been traduced into a pseudo-Poundian. Sisson was busy in his translations establishing a connection between verse and spoken language – an attempt he perceives in those modern poets he most admires. Part of his task is the sloughing off of literary skins to get back to a speaking voice. The 'literary' must be avoided – as he says of Barnes, 'The avoidance of literature is indispensable for the man who wants to tell the truth.' Elsewhere he writes: 'To know when one has a truth to tell is in a way the whole tact of the poet.'

As well as translation work, Sisson has written prose studies and novels. *The Spirit of British Administration* (1959) is one of his best prose books, a manual bristling with irony and good sense. Essays, critical biographies, autobiographies and anthologies, and an extended study of *English Poetry 1900–1950* (1971) are among his prose books.

After *The London Zoo*, 'plain speaking' came to have a different meaning for Sisson. In his second book, *Numbers* (1965), his rhythms became more complex, the forms more demanding as the subject matter turned less tractable. The social and natural themes were complicated by religious themes; the texture of thought and imagery became richer. In *Metamorphoses* (1968) the complex style went further (around this time he was translating Catullus and beginning versions of Virgil and Horace), until it flowered in the major poems included in the opening pages of *In the Trojan Ditch: Collected Poems and Selected Translations* (1974): 'In Insula Avalonia', 'Martigues', 'At Arles', 'Dialogue', and 'Somerton Moor', for example. The plain style had proved inadequate. Experience made each thought and image many-layered; each idea related to personal, religious, natural, cultural and patriotic contexts. A style developed which Davie typified as Virgilian – capable in one prolonged statement of suggesting the various contexts in which a single thought exists and acts. The later style is still lucidly plain – plain speaking, even. However, dissatisfaction with poems in which meaning can be separated and paraphrased out has led him to a quality of accuracy where the thought and its expression (as, in his theology, soul and body) are one, and cannot be prised apart or glossed in any terms other than itself.

The most recent poems emanate from dream situations or states of mind, from the vivid activity of the mind near sleep or death, when thoughts work free of logic and merge in unexpected forms. The dream is both literal – the poet often dreams – and metaphorical, for given the evanescence of the 'self', life is a dream. Randall Jarrell, the American poet, expressed the double dream rather as Sisson does: 'All this I dreamed in my great ragged bed, / Or so I dreamed.' The romantic dream is undermined, becomes the double dream of the fallen man in Sisson's work.

In effect his quest is for the integrated vision of the 'first years' of our culture. He is clearing passages to the vital common past, building bridges. His 'I' should not deceive us into imagining the poems are merely personal. His tools in the quest are rhythm, a mind that apprehends the manifold nature of his ideas and subject matter, and courage in the dark realms he is compelled to traverse.

He builds his bridges with various material. Classical legend and Biblical history are fused. 'Metamorphoses' is a long sequence of classical transformations culminating in 'the metamorphosis of all' – the Incarnation, which is seen as an extension of classical heritage. Many of Sisson's religious poems juxtapose the classical and Biblical, the Arthurian and Biblical, in such a way as to reveal the shared meanings. He does not, like Arnold, conceive of the Hebraic and classical roots of our culture as distinct, one theological and ethical, the other philosophical and aesthetic. They are in our culture expressions of a similar impulse, only one is redeemed and the other is not. In his mind, as in Donne's, the relationship of man and the immanent God is that of wooer and wooed, though in Sisson it is often man who vainly woos, not God. In one poem the relation of the soul to Christ is analogous to the relation of Psyche to Cupid; fulfilment is with the lover who may not be observed.

Despite the social urgency of Sisson's quest, he senses its futility in a society oblivious of what it has lost or destroyed. Both the satirist and the plain-speaking poet attack the ethics of the competitive society, where relationships are based on possessions, in terms analogous to those Pound uses in unveiling Usura. Notions of 'self' and 'identity' in a society where relationships are in constant flux are vanity and self-deception. Our notions of 'self' still depend on a residuum of religious faith – we exist as selves only in relation to an absolute, not in relation to other equally indefinite selves. Without the absolute, the objective self dissolves in subjective consciousness, or else it casts a golden calf and endows it with the attributes of an absolute. Money is the golden calf of this age. But it is a sham deity, for we possess nothing; we cannot even be said to possess memory. We are possessed by existence, and if we will, by God; and whether we will or no, by history and our historical institutions which we do well to accept and explore. We *are* only in relation to them, in all their ramifications:

What is the person? Is it hope?
If so, there is no I in me.
    Is it a trope
Or paraphrase of deity?
    If so,
I may be what I do not know.

'The Rope' develops the theme further:

Now money is the first of things
And after that the human heart
Which beats the time it can afford . . .

Money is 'the rope'. In a sense, each material gain implies a
spiritual loss. The malaise infects the whole social organism.
Since the individual culture depends on the group culture,
the group culture on the society's culture, our spiritless world
is deeply afflicted. Our concerns are so much with the
dynamic surface of reality that we have lost touch with the
static constants from which whatever cultural values we
could have emanate.

Sisson sees his role as a man of letters in traditional terms:
he is conservative, but 'opening up a new area in consciousness, indicating a point to which you may go from a point you
now occupy'. He has faith that great works of literature have
an actual effect on the reader. He recalls his first reading of
Pound, which caused 'one of those real adjustments of mind
which even the most omnivorous reader can expect from only
a few writers'.

Writing is, then, making and finding, not 'self-expression'.
'There is probably something in the nature of poetry,' Sisson
writes, 'which makes it necessary to avoid conscious pre-
meditation.' An amusing poem, 'Daphne', reflects the mind
waiting to be possessed, gradually cornered into signifying –
the elusive girl becoming a tree at Apollo's touch. After the
first four lines, the frivolity gives way:

You cannot start a poem without a word.
    Speak none, for then the silence is absurd.
Even the fishes swim against the tide.
    And do you never want to be outside?
Great God, your prisoner weeps, and so do I.
    Miracles are arranged accordingly.

While keeping the imagery 'within the limits of the perceptible', his (and consequently our) perception is always
expanding. He uses words which 'are *understood*, by which is

meant they have certain practical effects'. His task is to discern their effects and coordinate the words to maximize the harmonies between them.

Often the poems are dramatic in tone. Ideas are enacted, as they are in Marvell's verse. 'The Discarnation', Sisson's longest poem, is an intellectual exercise of breadth cast in a rigid form. The form is, in a sense, 'the dead hand of number', suggesting artificial discipline with which the voice must struggle, submitting itself unwillingly. As a whole, the poem must be judged as a failure, though it reveals a formidable skill, and a chain of reasoning and allusion, a combination of satire, theology, and latent lyricism, for which there are no modern analogues.

The drama of more human situations possesses an altogether different force, as in the opening of 'Virgini Senescens':

Do you consider that I lied
Because I offered silent hands?

And are my lips no use at all
Unless they have a lie to tell?

Because my eyes look doubtfully
Must they not look on you at all?

And if my hands drop to my sides
Are they then empty of desire?

And are my legs unusable
Because the linked bones of my feet

Rest where they are upon the floor?
I could have used them otherwise

And brought my legs across the room,
Lifted my arms and caught you up

And housed my eyes under your brows
And fixed my lips upon your own.

Or would you then have said that I
Performed and did not speak the truth?

The wit in the accumulation of indignant challenges is

qualified by the tonal change in line twelve, briefly proposing a tenderness which the last couplet reverses. The image of silence, since speech cannot hope to tell the whole truth and tends towards frivolity, recurs in several poems. Silence, while it avoids truth, avoids untruth as well.

Throughout Sisson's poetry, even in the unrhymed verse, there is a sense that rhyme exists. This is due in part to the balanced phrases, which correspond to one another rhythmically and through assonance produce the impression of a couplet even when technically we are reading unrhymed tetrameters or free verse. In part, too, it is due to his instinctive, accurate parcelling out of content in correct contrast from phrase to phrase, and the controlled development of the patterns of thought and allusion, that contribute to the sense of inevitability we get in reading his poems.

It is not the poems in which he orchestrates ideas, but those where he harmonizes disparate areas of allusion, where wholeness is revealed through a juxtaposition of fragments, that are his best. Obsessed by the realization of the Fall—of modern poets he is certainly the most aware that *he* is fallen – and its consequences in the Incarnation and Crucifixion, the truths he has at his disposal, the juxtapositions he can make, are restricted. He has very few poems which celebrate love, but many which, with excessive relish, explore the sordid scatalogical details of sex or remark the ephemerality of love. Another dominant theme is the sordidness and impotence of age. Sisson began writing verse more frequently at the age of thirty-five, and at forty he was already lamenting the passing years; at fifty he was assuming the mask of the old man; and at sixty he began to reveal some of the attributes of Methuselah. One is reminded in his latest work of Tennyson's Tithonus, who married the Dawn and was given eternal life, but not eternal youth. As well as age, the poet dwells on death. In his use of negatives he is as deft as Edward Thomas.

In many of the poems the thought is so intense, the rhythm so supple, that punctuation is disrupted or suspended, releasing phrases into relationships which seem to change with each re-reading:

Such a fool as I am you had better ignore
Tongue twist, malevolent, fat mouthed
I have no language but that other one
His the Devil's, no mouse I, creeping out of the cheese
With a peaked cap scanning the distance
Looking for truth.

The fluidity of the syntax merges Devil, speaker, and God, in a composite and evanescent being. In the second line the reader, too, is implicated. The poetry avoids allegory, depending on the perceptible to attain the just-beyond-perception.

One principle of organization is central to Sisson's work: his reverse chronology, a tendency to go backwards in time. The old man near death is useful in such a pattern of organization – the Teiresias figure who has the longest memory to travel back through, seeking the 'first years'. In the satires, reverse logic is used, reducing argument and pretence to the absurd. Sisson's novel *Christopher Homm* begins with the death of the protagonist and follows him relentlessly back to his ill-starred birth. The *Collected Poems*, too, are arranged in reverse chronology, working back towards his first years as a writer. He often writes from the standpoint of Too Late, observing the delicacies – sex, security, love – he was too late for. The clearest expression of this retrospective process, the attempt to find the constant in the past from which the flux began, is the poem 'Homo Sapiens is of No Importance'. It reveals in its spareness several of his unique skills: his ability to evoke sudden images – from history, nature, legend or theology; his use of negatives; his subtle presentation of time; and his rhythm, plain and direct:

And it may be that we have no nature
That he could have taken upon him.
Plato of course discussed it.
Deborah sitting under a tree
In a time of matriarchy:
Blessed be thou among women,
Blessed be the hand, the hammer,

Blessed the tent-peg as it drove through Sisera,
Blessed the connection between two interiors,
Blessed the wire between the switch and the bulb.
Not for the mind of Jael but for her hand
Not for the hand but for the hammer
Not for the hammer but for the tent-peg
Not for the peg but for Sisera dead
Not for Sisera dead but for his army routed
Not for that but the momentary ease under the tree
Not for that but for the tree itself
Not for the tree but the sand blowing by it.
If there was any nature it was in that.

Dylan Thomas (1914–1953)

Dressed to die, the sensual strut begun,
With my red veins full of money,
In the final direction of the elementary town
I advance for as long as forever is.

Dylan Marlais Thomas was born in Swansea, Wales, in 1914.
His father was a schoolteacher and poet who spoke Shakespeare and other verse aloud to his son before the child could
read. His mother was placid, childish, and devoted to him.
Thomas remembers his early infatuation with the sound of
nursery rhymes, the 'colours' that words suggested to him,
and the rhythms which excited him. This apprenticeship to
Mother Goose predisposed him to poets with strong rhythmic
qualities – the balladeers, Poe, Hopkins, Yeats, and Marlowe,
but also Keats, Lawrence, and the Imagists. Later in life
Thomas denied categorically the influence of Joyce, the
Bible, Freud and surrealism on his verse, but the denial
carries little authority. The poems bear witness against it.

Asthmatic, pampered, naughty, the child entered Swansea
Grammar School where his father was senior English master.
His early success was limited to literary activities. Otherwise
he stayed bottom of the form. His physical slightness, the
biographer Constantine Fitzgibbon suggests, made him
competitive. He wished to be either best or worst at everything, and he practised a 'flamboyant idleness'.

In 1931 he left school and spent fifteen months as a newspaper reporter. The work did not agree with him. He
returned home, and between 1932 and 1934 composed well

over half the poems he published during his lifetime. He engaged in amateur theatricals – specializing in dissolute roles. Role playing became a habit. Robert Nye speaks of his 'almost tragic willingness to play whatever part his friends wanted of him', though there was a feeling, in the life as in the poems, that 'none of his masks quite fit'.

In 1934 *Eighteen Poems* appeared, followed two years later by *Twenty-Five Poems*; and in 1939 *The Map of Love*, including poems and prose writings, rounded off his early career. These three volumes are much of a piece and represent what many readers feel is best in Thomas. They possess a stronger individuality than the more vatic and less obscure poems in his most famous collection, *Deaths and Entrances* (1946). During the war he did work for the BBC, publishing in 1940 his autobiography, *Portrait of the Artist as a Young Dog*. Posthumously, in 1954, *Under Milk Wood*, a radio play, was published, and in 1955 *Adventures in the Skin Trade*, a prose book which lacked the distinction of the earlier volume. Thomas died in 1953, aged thirty-nine, during an American lecture tour.

Describing his technique to a young fan, he wrote, 'I make an image – though "make" is not the right word; I let, perhaps, an image be "made" emotionally in me and then apply to it what intellectual and critical forces I possess – let it breed another, let that image contradict the first, make, of the third image bred out of the other two together, a fourth contradictory image, and let them all, within my imposed formal limits, conflict.' From these conflicting impulses, which as he describes them seem as much the product of will as of imagination, he tries to generate 'that momentary peace which is a poem'. But earlier, during his fruitful creative period (1932–4), he had written to Pamela Hansford Johnson, lamenting the increasing obscurity of his work: 'When the words do come, I pick them so thoroughly of their *live* associations that only the *death* in the word remains.' He added, 'I am a freak user of words, not a poet.'

The struggle with words, not rhythms, is in a sense the primary struggle in all his poetry. One of his outstanding poems is 'Especially when the October Wind', in which, walking out, the wind 'punishing' his hair 'with frosty fingers', all that he experiences has a language. His busy heart 'talks' and 'sheds the syllabic blood and drains her words'. He hears the 'vowelled beeches', 'oaken voices', 'water's speeches', 'the hour's word' and reads 'the meadow's signs'. The world itself is language. The poem turns back upon itself – the wind 'punishes the land' too, 'with fists of turnips', just as it punished him. Poet and landscape are momentarily fused. Both are extensions of language. It is not merely that nature speaks: it is speech, and so too is he.

'He is shut,' Robert Nye writes, 'in the twisted tower of his own observation, a tower where only words are real and can bleed': words and their uncontrollable suggestions, seldom words as specific meanings with a semantic history; words as keys to a world of analogies, assembled one by one. He describes sight in terms of smell, hearing in terms of taste, in a symbolist manner. His early attraction to surrealism was to the freeing of the word and image into suggestion, not significance – the language of obscure evocation rather than denotation or description.

The first poem in his first collection, 'I See the Boys of Summer', illustrates the power and weakness of his early style. The words do not fit together naturally. They have been, to use his word, 'forced' within 'imposed formal limits'. The language appears to be used at high pressure, but as Nye comments, it is a 'simulated intensity, a confusion of depth with thickness'. Not only do the words, rich in themselves and interesting in their suggestions, have an arbitrary quality in their organization: the lines, too, seem to be fitted together, not to grow out of one another. The rhythm in each line gives the impression of being end-stopped.

As well as rhythmic repetitiveness, there are repetitions of the same syntactical construction. 'There in the heat', 'There in the sun', 'There in the deep', 'There from their hearts', 'There, in his night' – suddenly shifting at the end to 'Here'. 'I see' is used four times, at last modulating into 'I am'. These schematic features of the poem are evidence of conscious construction, and the poet has an effect in mind which at least partly justifies them. The shift from the external, 'There' and 'see', to assimilation, 'Here' and 'am', is rhetorically effective. The form of the poem is not the six-line stanzas, rhymed lazily if at all *aabcbc*, but the structures of repetitions which establish a background of expectedness – in rhythm and syntax – against which the poet can effect his variations. Occasionally the words, used primarily for sound and suggestion, evoke a lucid-seeming image: 'We are the dark desirers, let us summon / Death from a summer woman.' The erotic undertone, Thomas's themes of inherent death, waste, and isolation, are contained in the opaque language which produces impressions, moods, the sense of sense, but not meanings.

The elegiac eroticism of Thomas's early poetry is heady, adolescent stuff. Some of his critics argue that the poems are 'about' masturbation and its aftermath – a partial explanation. But does such a theme demand the rigid syntactical parallelism, the monotony of organization, the repetitions? In 'A Process in the Weather of the Heart', for example, the poem exists as slabs of similar rhythm and syntax. There are eight sentences of parallel construction; they follow one rhythmic pattern and reach no rhythmic or verbal climax. The language is, indeed, so 'pitched' that the words *seem* to be used at the climax of their meaning. And yet, as often in early Thomas, the intensive vocabulary is unsustained by intense rhythm.

Thomas's religious poems, 'Before I Knocked', for example, sometimes attain in language a resolute opacity. He has been claimed as a religious poet, but despite the extensive religious imagery it would be difficult to prove his final commitment one way or the other. 'Before I Knocked' is replete with puns and allusions to Christ's life and agony – and Thomas's. Lines such as, 'And time cast forth my mortal creature / To drift and drown upon the sea', mean 'I was born' – after five stanzas of lurid gestation – and 'I shall die' after one more stanza. Most of the early poems have one such point of access, where the complications are incomplete and we appreciate the basically simple meanings Thomas is building away from. In his later poems the meanings are less elaborately hedged, and one can readily see the poet's narrow thematic frontiers.

Death casts his shadow on almost every poem. 'The Force that through the Green Fuse Drives the Flower' is among his most entirely successful poems. Conceptually it is arresting: Thomas draws the parallel between poet's and flower's, poet's and nature's vitality and confronts them with the universal fact of death. The poem also glosses Robert Graves's poem 'The Cool Web', apparently echoing the earlier poem in the fourth line of each stanza. Snared in 'the cool web of language', Thomas tries – but only half-heartedly – to escape along the threads: half-heartedly, because beyond the word he is unsure that anything can be comprehended. Were he indeed intent on transcending language, he would disrupt the syntax of his poems, cast out the rigid phrasal parallelisms, the elaborate verbal structures, in favour of a thoroughgoing surrealism (his is always a surrealism of the surface); or he would strive for minute accuracy, securing language to things, transcending it into the natural world.

'From Love's First Fever to her Plague' carries the language theme further:

And from the first declension of the flesh
I learnt man's tongue, to twist the shapes of thoughts
Into the stony idiom of the brain,
To shade and knit anew the patch of words
Left by the dead who, in their moonless acre,
Need no word's warmth.

The third line may add little, but the fourth suggests something of his poetic creed, to which the early poems adhere. Language is a covering, a province, a bandage over a wound, and perhaps itself a kind of prefigurative burial, preparatory for the 'moonless acre', a phrase rich with Thomas's distinctive verbal magic.

Language, undistorted, Thomas implies, can impose rigid order. He would distort: 'The code of night tapped on my tongue.' By distortion he would break through to the experiences language contains even as it conceals, and that ultimate experience, death, which inhabits the creature even as he is conceived or – in 'Before I Knocked' – prior to conception. 'Cadaver' is a character strolling through some of the poems. Man is addressed as 'mortal', the mask or form Cadaver wears on his visits.

In 'Light Breaks where No Sun Shines' Thomas achieved a varied and supple rhythm for the first time, a rhythm answering to a degree the intensity of his vocabulary: erotic, tentative, the lines do not seem to be end-stopped. The poem flows from line to line, reaches a climax, and recedes. The rhythm is sufficiently varied so that the syntactical repetitions come with the emphasis of refrain, not reiteration – not the rhetorical 'fibs of vision'. In poems such as 'The Seed-at-Zero' he is, however, back to arbitrary forms. The stanzas are paired. Each pair shares the first and last word of every line respectively. Formal rigidity reaches an absurd climax in 'Vision and Prayer', where shape and syllable count govern a sequence of poems that appear to illustrate nothing so well as Yeats's gyres.

The implicit rhetoric of the mechanical repetitions, the contrived coordinates, serves well in the poems which make apparently social statements. 'The Hand that Signed the Paper' has a ruminative authority, the repetitions rise to a tone of anger. It is the rhetorician, writing for public delivery, who dominates the later poems: a spell-binder. In 'Death Shall Have No Dominion' – recalling Donne's 'Death, be not proud' – rigid form is like a dressmaker's dummy. Thomas displays his language on it. *Display* is the keynote.

His elegies, including 'After the Funeral', 'Ceremony after a Fire Raid', and 'Refusal to Mourn the Death, by Fire, of a Child in London', in the poet's self-indulgence over the objects he laments go well beyond Yeats's extreme: not only are the dead simplified and made emblematic, with little regard for the actual human creature lamented; they are sentimentalized as well, swept grandiosely into Thomas's death-centred cosmos.

The unique quality of Thomas's successful poems is the

immediacy of their highly wrought language – an immediacy where the sense of experience precedes the specific meanings of words, where the poetry is in the surprising combination of disparate words; the enigmatic mingling of senses, the presence of death, the hot-house sensuality. His skill is such that on first reading the poems impress, and those that reward re-reading do so largely because of their compelling vagueness. The abandoned pleasure with which we run through 'Fern Hill' is due in large part to the poem's vagueness, into which we can read all the heroic self-pity we will; and 'Do Not Go Gentle' appeals because of its rhetorical courage against Cadaver. But the incompleteness of the experience in the poems, the sense that they arise from sentiment (despite the vivid particulars of 'Fern Hill') and resolve themselves in sentiment, is responsible both for their popularity and their shortcomings as poems. Thomas weaves spells; he has not engaged experience but only language. When the spell releases us, it has clarified nothing. The word magic of the early poems, for all their obscurity, has authority. They rise out of the frustration of being caught in language and circumstance and generalize the experience, even if the particulars are camouflaged. If they have a secret, it is a secret we all share, part erotic, part elegiac. The later poems rise out of personality.

There are exceptions in the later work. 'Poem in October' is brilliant in its details, celebrating – with 'Refusal to Mourn' – against the tragic grain. What distinguishes the later poems – the primary reason for their wide popularity – is not their greater simplicity nor their sentimentality but the rhythmic drive. In 'A Winter's Tale' the mature poet's rhythmic achievement is most subtle. The later work is rhetoric of a high order.

David Gascoyne (born 1916)

Each stanza is a round, and every line
A blow aimed at the too elusive chin
Of that oblivion which cannot fail to win.

David Gascoyne published his first volume of poems, *Roman Balcony* (1932), when he was sixteen. The next year his novel *Opening Day* appeared, and *A Short Survey of Surrealism* (1935), one of the best English critical studies of that movement, came out before he was twenty. *Man's Life Is His Meat* (1936) was his first full-bloodedly surrealist collection of poems. He reacted against his English literary predecessors in 1932 much as the Imagists had in 1914, though without their polemical spirit and corporate energy. Surrealism was Gascoyne's apprenticeship. Because he has been labelled a 'surrealist' by the critics, his later work, which should have led to a reassessment of his achievement, has been generally disregarded.

David Emery Gascoyne was born in Salisbury in 1916. He studied at Salisbury Cathedral Choir School, where he developed a deep interest in music; and later at the Regent Street Polytechnic in London. At the age of sixteen he was frequenting a literary Soho. George Barker remembers him at the time but cannot say for sure if the young man spoke exclusively in French or not. It is true that Gascoyne was already well-acquainted with modern French literature, and that he was writing poems in French. French surrealism was for him not merely a stylistic affectation: it implied an approach to content and form, a mode of vision.

Predictably, he spent time in Paris as well as London, his work developing in solitude towards a less prescriptive surrealism – what one might call a psychological surrealism – in *Hölderlin's Madness* (1938), his third collection. Hölderlin haunted several writers of the 1930s and 1940s. From an intensely thoughtful and passionate formal style, with the gradual advent of madness, Hölderlin broke into the famous 'Scardinalli' poems, notable for their vivid expression of a disrupted personal vision. It was modish to respond to Hölderlin's biography – the madness of poets attracted many 1940s writers, and they celebrated Smart and Clare and the suffering late Hopkins as much for their lives as for their work. But Gascoyne went beyond biography to learn lessons from Hölderlin's art.

He was a regular contributor to *New Verse*. Michael Roberts, the editor, found his poems unlike those of other contemporary English surrealists – including Hugh Sykes Davies and Philip O'Connor – not exercises in surreal rhetoric but necessary statements. For Gascoyne writes only when he has something to say, and his message is as often political and religious as personal.

In 1943 he published *Poems 1937–42*, with Graham Sutherland's illustrations. The poems express the suffering and loneliness of modern man. The later volumes, *A Vagrant* (1950), *Night Thoughts* (1956) and *Collected Poems* (1965) show the continuing development of a poet under acute pressure from internal and external forces, recognizing himself as a 'demented wrestler' doomed to lose the bout with the blank page, but struggling nonetheless to express a vision he believes relevant.

No one would accuse him of writing perfect or even finished poems. Like D. H. Lawrence, he would say that this is not his purpose, for how can a true poem be finished? But he would suggest – and this is indicated in his careful ordering and reordering of poems in sequences and groups – that the poems exist to signify in their relatedness to one another, that there is unity, or a progression, in the work which is nonetheless open-ended. The unity is not imposed but seems to rise out of the poems. They cohere as aspects of a developing vision.

Gascoyne moved away from doctrinaire surrealism as he recognized that English literature, and the English language itself, contain a powerful irrational element. Hence surrealism was not wholly novel nor particularly relevant to the language, as it seemed to be to French. Symbolism, surrealism, and Imagism (as Pound pointed out) were inherent in the English tradition, but English poets had not felt a compulsion until the early part of this century to tease out one thread to the exclusion of the others.

Gascoyne, in his mature work, adapted elements of surrealist technique to an English tradition, tending towards the Lawrentian (he celebrates Lawrence in an elegy). His recurrent religious imagery is often reminiscent of Lawrence's. In the *Miserere* sequence, however, his vision is unrelated to Lawrence's: he evokes the terror of being without God. Where George Barker internalizes his material, swallows the landscape, Gascoyne is swallowed by Christ, becomes Him. He psychologizes, but not in a clinical way – psychology is one of several tools in his search for truth.

He also discovered in English, through the prose of Henry James and others, the subtle variety of English syntax. He developed skill in writing long, penetrating sentences, full of suspensions, hesitations, and dramatic involutions in his prose poems as well as his verse poems. Often the sentence leads him astray. Equally often it brings him nearer to the dark opponent from whom he tries to wrest some meaning. 'The Gravel-Pit Field' shows his syntactical subtlety at its best. What had marred the early surreal poems was the syntactical monotony – subject, verb, object – coming as regularly as heartbeats.

In the later poems the surreal elements serve to intensify a mental drama which is powerful for being rooted in the real. In 'An Elegy: R.R. 1916–41' he balances real and surreal evocatively. The tension is between what he can say and what a language, wrenched and disrupted, can only hope to imply:

Yet even in your obscure death I see
The secret candour of that lonely child
Who, lost in the storm-shaken castle-park,
Astride his cripple mastiff's back was borne
Slowly away into the utmost dark.

The main lesson he learned from surrealism was rhythmical.
Throughout his work, his sense of line and rhythm units is
subtle. In the surreal poems, it is rhythm alone that renders
the distorted imagery effective, that fuses disparate elements
into an apparent whole. Since the genuinely surreal pieces
lack punctuation, the rhythmic unit must be the line; the
lines work together to create certain rhythmic expectations,
while content remains unpredictable. The poem's form is a
function of its rhythmic arrangements. Rhythm conveys a
sense of meaning, sometimes of humour, to the conscious
mind while the images attempt their alchemy on the unconscious. 'Charity Week', a poem dedicated to Max Ernst,
reads:

Garments of the seminary
Worn by the nocturnal expeditions
By all the chimaeras
Climbing in at the window
With lice in their hair
Noughts in their crosses
Ice in their eyes

In the poems that are more intellectually organized, less
overtly surreal, the sense flows from line to line, but the
rhythmic unit remains the line. Stress falls on first and last
words; Gascoyne becomes a master of enjambment.

In 'Unspoken', he writes of 'Following certain routes to
uncertain lands'. The rhythm in all the poems, even the
organized chaos of 'Night Thoughts', is the reader's 'certain
route'. It is not a prosodic but a colloquial rhythm. In it,
with few exceptions, we hear Gascoyne's compelling gentleness. He is firmly persuasive but not cajoling. He is not
interested in personal power in any facile sense. His hallmark is the humanity of his tone.

His most original qualities reached their climax in the poems of *Hölderlin's Madness*. There is dramatic power in 'Figure in a Landscape':

Infinitely small among the infinitely huge
Drunk with the rising fluids of his breast, his boiling heart,
Exposed and naked as the skeleton – upon the knees
Like some tormented desert saint – he flung
The last curse of regret against Omnipotence
And the lightning struck his face.

Delaying the use of the possessive 'his' in the third, fourth, and fifth lines quoted, makes its appearance in the last line telling. Pain and revelation define the possessor.

Gascoyne fuses religion and politics in poems such as 'Ecce Homo', where he invokes the 'Christ of Revolution and of Poetry'; in 'De Profundis', one of his best poems; in 'The Vagrant', where by inaction he retains spiritual integrity within a social context; and in 'Night Thoughts', which Michael Hamburger described as 'the most Baudelairean exploration of an urban inferno written since the war'. Gascoyne, even at his most anguished, is celebrating what might be. A poem of vivid insight such as 'The Sacred Hearth' shows his power as a celebrant. He is interested, not in the image, but in what happens to it. This in particular is his postsurrealist originality. The surreal extends vision, renews words and objects. In his much anthologized elegy to Paul Eluard he speaks of: 'The youth who's rejected all words that could ever be spoken / To conceal and corrupt where they ought to reveal what they name.'

Desire and fear are the forces that pull at Gascoyne, one from the future, the other from the past. In their conflict in the early poems they produce frustration. The titles – 'The Cold Renunciatory Beauty', 'The Unattained', 'No Solution', 'The Last Head', and 'Unspoken', with a strongly sexual element in their anguish – provide a key. From this frustration Gascoyne moved gradually through religious half-belief to conviction and celebration. His religion is always social *and* personal. He is a poet of immanence, working through the given world, representing it in ways which, when he is successful, reveal its moral and aesthetic qualities lucidly. Gascoyne is a far more original and accomplished poet than he is normally given credit for being. Dedication and integrity such as his are rare qualities.

Charles Causley (born 1917)

O Clare! Your poetry clear, translucent
As your lovely name,
I salute you with tears.

The ploughman poet John Clare has a special significance
for Charles Causley. 'At the Grave of John Clare' and –
written twenty years later – 'Helpston' are poems that
celebrate the poet and the man, or the poet *as* the man for,
to Causley, Clare is as much an emblem as a model. He
writes of the work: 'The bad grammar, the spelling, the
invented words, / And the poetry bursting like a diamond
bomb.' He also imagines the dead poet's face staring at
him:

As clearly as it once stared through
The glass coffin-lid
In the church-side pub on his burial day . . .

Clare's energy (the poems 'beat' in his skull) attracts Causley,
but more than that, his rugged simplicity, his rootedness in
a particular landscape, his innocence and its betrayal.
Innocence is Causley's principal theme. It can be the innocence of Blake's infant or it can resemble madness, as in the
case of Clare. It is a quality of vision, trust, and receptivity
to experience.

Charles Causley was born in Launceston, Cornwall, in
1917, and he still lives and teaches there. Before the war he
worked for a builder and in the office of an electricity

corporation. He played the piano in a four-piece dance band during the 1930s, and the rhythms and lyrics of popular songs stayed with him. He started trying to write poetry in the Navy in 1940. In 1943 he completed what he regarded as his first poem.

It was eight years before a collection appeared: *Hands to Dance* (1951). A number of collections have followed: *Farewell, Aggie Weston* (1951), *Survivor's Leave* (1953), *Union Street* (1957), *Johnny Allelulia* (1961), *Underneath the Water* (1968) and *Figgie Hobbin* (1970). Causley has edited anthologies as well.

The earliest influences on his writing were Scott and Tennyson, but the first poet he consciously learned by heart was Siegfried Sassoon. He grew acquainted with the work of Eliot and Pound, but he retained close affinities with poets in the Georgian tradition, and most closely with Housman. Without Housman's classicism – Causley's lads always have real blood in their veins, and his pessimism is not unredeemed – he slips easily into Housman's metres and shares many of his themes. We sense, too, similarities between his work and de la Mare's, and the formal facility of Betjeman. There are occasional telling echoes of MacNeice. But Causley's voice is powerful enough to recall others' rhythms without succumbing to them.

Two complexes of imagery recur in his poems: the sea, which with its beauty and unpredictability has always fascinated him, and which he came to know intimately during his naval service; and War. There is also a matrix of religious imagery, connected principally with the Fall from innocence, the Nativity and the Crucifixion. Causley's religious ambivalence makes it possible for him to write such resonant poems as 'I am the Great Sun', redolent of firm faith, with an echo of MacNeice's 'Prayer Before Birth' in the final rhythms; poems of simple, even superstitious faith; allegories such as 'Three Masts'; and poems of intense doubt, almost surreal in their unexpectedness. 'I Saw a Shot-Down Angel' is in the last category:

I stretched my hand to hold him from the heat,
I fetched a cloth to bind him where he bled,
I brought a bowl to wash his golden feet,
I shone my shield to save him from the dead.

My angel spat my solace in my face
And fired my fingers with his burning shawl,
Crawling in blood and silver to a place
Where he could turn his torture to the wall.

The balladic stanza – which Causley deploys in many of his most popular poems – provides a plain, even primitive rhythm, but the poem develops with carefully worked parallelism and the words are chosen with a full sense of their weight. The 'I' is not particularized – the poet seldom speaks in his own person. The poem tends towards allegory, but will not submit to a final interpretation. It is about vulnerable innocence, for the 'I' is innocent in Blake's sense; about Satan; and about war. In the passage quoted, there are fleeting allusions to Medusa, to Hercules's fire-poisoned cloak, and elsewhere in the poem to Christian grave art. Mary Magdalen and the Last Supper are hinted. The poem draws in a range of conflicting experiences, exploring the central symbol of sacrifice. The conflict is not resolved:

Alone I wandered in the sneaking snow
The signature of murder on my day.
And from the gallows-tree, a careful crow
Hitched its appalling wings and flew away.

The Navy, where under strict authority he experienced choicelessness, compelled him to work out survival tactics. Poetry became a natural place to assert, without insubordination, a basic independence. The Navy took him to many ports, taught him a vivid naval dialect where each thing central to the sailor's life had its appropriate epithet. Fingers were 'grab-hooks', rum was 'stagger juice'. In the poem 'Immunity' he uses the naval jargon to good effect. It was a language rich in metaphor, like the language Federico Garcia Lorca learned from the Spanish peasants in his region and in which he wrote many of his ballads. Causley composed an elegy for Lorca, and his elegy for Louis MacNeice ('Death of a Poet') echoes Lorca's most famous elegy in its imagery. More than any English poet, his work resembles the popular poems of the Spanish poet. Causley seems to envisage an audience analogous to Lorca's and his ballads in particular attempt to speak *for* as well as *to* that wide audience. Much of the power of both poets' ballads is in their impersonality, their artful simplicity, the sense that the language, not a particular poet, made them.

The Navy provided some of his early subjects: 'separation, loss, death in alien places, extraordinary characters, a perpetual sense of unease about how things might end'. Change and loss of innocence, or the rare preservation of innocence in adult life ('extraordinary characters') are his main themes.

Many of the poems dramatize the betrayal of trust and innocence. The long ballad in *Survivor's Leave* called 'The Song of Samuel Sweet' is a compelling example. In 'By St Thomas Water', a more condensed poem, two children 'borrow' a jam jar from a grave and plan to catch tiddlers. They pause half-guiltily to read the gravestone. It says, 'He is not dead but sleeping'. In terror, they flee. Their fear and the humour of their credulity are rendered in simple language. The poem ends with the voice of experience:

Waiting in the cold grass
Under the crinkled bough,
Quiet stone, cautious stone,
What do you tell me now?

The rhythm tries to charm a meaning from the stone. Once terrifying, it is now 'cautious'. Its meaning has changed, or man has found a significance for it different from the child's. Similarly, in 'Reservoir Street', the innocent child is subjected to an alien world: the country cousin is confronted with the poverty and terror of the city. But he escapes back to his home.

'Grave by the Sea' more subtly develops the same theme. The choice of words is dramatic:

Once this calmed, crystal hand was free
And rang the changes of the heart:
Love, like his life, a world wherein
The white-worm sin wandered not in.
Death played no part.

The drowning of the man, whose life is recounted in elusively allegorical terms, occurs:

So he set from the shaken quay
His foot upon the ocean floor
And from the wanting water's teeth
The ice-faced gods above, beneath,
Spat him ashore.

But the poem continues:

Now, in the speaking of the sea,
He waits under this written stone,
And kneeling at his freezing frame
I scrub my eye to see his name

And read my own.

Causley relates everything to his central themes. In 'The Question' – a poem without a plot – the enigmatic riddle-style has the authority of folk rhymes. The rightness – the apparent inevitability – of the words in their particular order is intensified by the strong rhythms.

He calls his poems 'entertainments'. But they are not, in general, merely stories and anecdotes. He usually blurs the simple lines of the sketched plot, requires us to return to the poem to see how the well-placed more-than-descriptive words, the key words, work together, provide a moral or an allegorical dimension, often Biblical in character. In the poem 'Recruiting Drive' the 'butcher-bird' initially suggests allegory. We are compelled to ask why the wood is 'magic', the fair 'freezing', the sea 'scribbling'. The 'plot' of the poem too is susceptible to various readings.

Though his tools have become sharper with use and his range has broadened, Causley has not 'developed' as a poet. Like Betjeman, he knows his area of activity well. His experiments with surreal rhetoric he abandons, returning to his richly allusive idiom, to his own landscape. His subjects are sometimes historical, sometimes legendary or fantastic. The poems occur in specific settings. Each requires modulations of Causley's idiom. Often we sense the primitive character of his chosen form in tension with the sophistication and subtlety of content.

W.S. Graham (born 1918)

Images of night
And the sea changing
Should know me well enough.

W. S. Graham's reputation has suffered from what one critic called 'bad planning'. His second major collection, *The Nightfishing* (1955), appeared the same year as Larkin's *The Less Deceived*. It came when The Movement was in the ascendant, and despite the impressive novelty of Graham's book, the positive development from his earlier style, it excited little interest. Fifteen years passed before another collection appeared, years of hardship and general neglect. Even today, Graham's poetry is not treated with the seriousness it merits.

William Sydney Graham was born in a tenement in Greenock, Scotland, in 1918. It is not surprising that the sea is a dominant image in his poems, that it often assumes symbolic power. He was brought up on Clydeside, attending Greenock High School, and later spending a year at the Workers' Educational Association College near Edinburgh. His formal education went no further, though he later held an academic post as lecturer at New York University (1947–8). His present home in Madron, Cornwall, answers to the Greenock seascape, without the industrial clutter. Many of his recent poems are set in Madron, rooted there, as the early work at its best was rooted in Scottish particulars. He senses a 'Scots timbre' in his poetic voice, and the reader can sense other Scots qualities, particularly in the rhetoric which can change tone deftly from raucous to tender, from shouting to a whisper.

His first collection, *Cage Without Grievance* (1942), was published in Glasgow. He was twenty-four, a poet deep in the thrall of Dylan Thomas. His next two collections, *The Seven Journeys* (1944) and *Second Poems* (1945), continued this allegiance. It was with *The White Threshold* (1949) that Graham began to move towards an individual style, and in *The Nightfishing* the dimensions of his talent became clear.

The poems that imitated Dylan Thomas adopted from that erratic master his least successful qualities. They are word-drunk, crowded, cacophonous. Imprecision would be a mild word for the chaos of style where, purely for rhetorical effect, words occur without a full sense of their semantic value, without attention to syntax. The poems are spineless. We may after long meditation discern a meaning in the text, but when we do, the meaning is neither novel nor striking. 'O Gentle Queen of the Afternoon' and 'Many Without Elegy' are among the few early poems of any merit.

Graham records his debts as a poet to Samuel Beckett, James Joyce, Marianne Moore, Ezra Pound, and T. S. Eliot. But this list was compiled in the 1960s, and he scrupulously omitted to mention Thomas and Gerard Manley Hopkins. It is hard to detect the influences he suggests, except that of Beckett, who is most strongly felt in the characterization of Malcolm Mooney, and in two of the dominant themes, 'the difficulty of communication; the difficulty of speaking from a fluid identity'. Other themes Graham lists are, 'the lessons in physical phenomena; the mystery and adequacy of the aesthetic experience; the elation of being alive in the language'. What is significant about Graham's list of literary debts is his attempt to place his own work in the context of the modernist writers. There is some justification for this stance. Edwin Morgan has described Graham's 'obsessional preoccupation' as 'the endless dyings and metamorphoses of the self'. This is true of many of the poems written since

The White Threshold. It is a theme that Beckett and Eliot have explored.

Part of his reaction against his early excesses was a closer attention to complex syntax, an acceptance of the need for syntactical form if the verse was to be affective on any but a rhetorical level. The step was important, for when he mastered his new discipline, he was able to develop an individual voice. The egotism of the early effusive style became the isolation (with all that that implies of grandeur and humility) of the later. If the poems in *The White Threshold* are excessively purified and cold, they mark the transition between their molten predecessors and the ruminative passion of his later work. The poet of *The White Threshold* has accepted too much discipline, has become timid, unwilling to shape and renew, though he can surprise: 'The sun with long legs wades into the sea', one poem ends. Present in this first volume of Graham's maturity are the qualities that bear fruit later: a colloquial, rugged diction, a penchant for monosyllables which seem to have an isolated verbal integrity for him, and an erratic but authoritative use of rhyme and slant shyme. Most important, he begins to develop his own peculiar, evasive metres, whose presence we sense without being able to define. From an early attitude of complete trust in words, in their capacity to evoke by sound, he grew more cautious with them, introducing discipline and distance between them. He grew morbidly sensitive to their betraying power, their ability to mean differently to different people. His uneasiness is responsible for his late style, for his originality, and for the severe integrity of his work.

'The Nightfishing', title poem of the 1955 collection, is an ambitious long work in seven sections, centring on the third which recounts the 'nightfishing' for herring. The poem moves from uncertainty about the continuity of individual identity; through the momentary, apparent certainty the speaker gets at the heart of activity; and then returns to the evanescent 'I':

Lie down, my recent madman, hardly
Drawn into breath then shed to memory,
For there you'll labour less lonely.
The rigged ship in its walls of glass
Still further forms its perfect seas
Locked in its past transparences.

Graham's pun – he often puns – on the word 'rigged' is
effective. There is an unnatural dishonesty in the continuity
of the artefact, be it a ship in a bottle or a poem, taken out
of time, its patterns static and complete. The constancy is
cold and unreciprocating. But the bottled ship and the
written words do seem to endure. 'The Nightfishing' ends
on an elegiac *and* celebratory note:

So I spoke and died.
So within the dead
Of night and the dead
Of all my life those
Words died and awoke.

If a man's language is any guarantee – it isn't for the recent
Graham – then the continuity of his identity could hardly
be doubted from the continuity of his development.

The sea in 'The Nightfishing' – itself discontinuous, with
a wide range of appearances – assumes a special, almost
redeeming quality. Against its flux, briefly, the active man
becomes compact of himself. Momentarily defined, his self-
consciousness subsides, he registers sense impressions deftly:
'The moon keels and the harbour oil / Looks at the sky
through seven colours.' Autobiography is a strong thread in
the poem. When the poet is at sea, the language becomes
mimetic – perhaps excessively so – imitating the shifting sea
geography. Language and the sea are equated (as, later,
language becomes a place where the reader 'walks'). Briefly,
'My ghostly constant is articulated.' But the catch and the
coming light dispel this self-recognition.

In the shorter sections of 'The Nightfishing' and in the
seven 'Letters' in the collection, Graham often uses a three-

stress line. Without caesura, each line is a complete rhythmic unit, imposing a strong discipline on the language and thought. 'Letter VI', one of his best short poems, celebrates love, where silence is possible without fear, where for a moment he seems to be loving a whole landscape, not only a particular person. The poem ends with a sudden sense of fate, or guilt: a parrying off. Sea is language as well as sea:

The great verbs of the sea
Come down on us in a roar.
What shall I answer for?

'The Broad Close', obliquely autobiographical, evokes the poet speaking to his grandfather and his own past selves across 'the grey table of the grave'. Graham effectively deploys a ballad metre. A grim humour – as in many of the later poems – and a redeeming whimsy, reminiscent of Beckett, are at work. The poet makes a persona for himself and watches it, develops it – and *is* it only partly; there is too much positive irony for identity. Graham is not Malcolm Mooney, either, though Malcolm dramatizes Graham's predicament. The dramatic turn of the verse in 'The Broad Close' recalls Burns, perhaps:

'If I am you all over again
    By the joke and by the grief
Dodge if you can this very word,
    For it is the flensing knife.'
And I have put it in his breast
    And taken away his life.

It has the naïvety of the folk ballad, powerful because not over-stated. The poem ends with a disconcerting echo of 'The Ballad of Reading Gaol'.

In 'Malcolm Mooney's Land' Graham achieves a style at once more spare and more ruminative – 'riches with poverty' Calvin Bedient has called it. The themes are so bleak and 'poor' that much of the power of the poems is in the tension between the attempt to write and the implicit fruitlessness of the attempt. His eccentricity in this collection is cultivated. It must be, for the theme is language, how it creates barriers while at the same time parrying off silence, the chief threat.

Graham feels a strange hostility towards the reader, the 'you' he addresses; he watches us warily, at the same time watching himself, for the Graham who reads is presumably another Graham from the one who wrote and died. His wariness is reflected in his reluctance to state with finality. But the evasions are fraught with energy and humour. In this collection, the monosyllables function once again, stressing the isolation and distance *between* words. 'Between' comes in for frequent use. Graham tries to string his words out in space: places, particularly Madron, are correlatives for language. The background is taken for granted, and the poet fixes his poem to it with occasional deft allusions. If the background is an ice floe, as in 'Malcolm Mooney's Land', or a specific shared landscape, as in 'The Thermal Stair', Graham advances with the same locating technique, making his geography of words.

The later poems rigorously avoid the expected – rhythmically, syntactically, intellectually. The would-be magical language of the early poems has devolved into a tenuous, mistrustful dependence on the word. Words were bridges between the isolated, evanescent self and the world. But, 'I burn my words behind me' – the spoken word falls on silence. Each word takes him deeper into isolation. The only hope is to establish the poem as a geography where he *is*, and the reader walks. The language aspires to the permanence of an object in space.

'Malcolm Mooney's Land' itself is in five sections, following a sequence of five days in the frustrated life of Malcolm, caught in a great freeze. He seems to be at the Pole, and each image collaborates the cold. The poem opens with the snow burial of past selves and his departure from them. The early hunters, the past selves, are heard; but they pass by and cannot be addressed. He is left:

I have made myself alone now.
Outside the tent endless
Drifting hummock crests.
Words drifting on words.
The real unabstract snow.

'Yours Truly', a verse letter in reply to one of his earlier
'Letters' in *The Nightfishing*, addresses a dead 'I'. He cannot
make contact.

I know you well alas
From where I sit behind
The Art barrier of ice.

In 'The Constructed Space' the poem again aspires to exist
outside time. It contains the haunting line, 'Here in the
present tense disguise is mortal.' The present tense, denoting
time, becomes a habitation.

The limitations of Graham's work are readily apparent:
thematic narrowness, for each poem worries at the same
themes. Each poem, that is, but those few which are shaken
by a surprising experience – of love or death – out of the
isolating themes. 'I Leave This at Your Ear' is an outstanding, lonely love poem. 'The Thermal Stair' is Graham's
most powerful elegy, addressed to Peter Lanyon.

In it Graham refers to particulars of landscape, ties the
poem firmly down to the world of Madron and its environs.
Lanyon, Alfred Wallis (another painter whom Graham
addresses here and elsewhere), and the poet himself share a
knowing naïvety. Peter Lanyon was killed in a gliding
accident (hence the 'Thermal' of the title), and Graham
draws surprising analogies. The ascent of the glider is like
the ascent of the artist, implying important risks on different
levels.

In the first two stanzas, the poet calls on his friend,
searching familiar places. The places named are tin mines
in the Madron area. There is an imaginative reality about
the search, which takes the poet to 'Little Parc Owls' as
well, Lanyon's house. The landscape is to a degree a private
world shared by Lanyon and Graham.

Graham explores the function of art – 'to make / An object that will stand and will not move.' The natural, industrial and aesthetic landscapes and the seascape are drawn together to this end, seen as aspects of a single pattern. He draws analogies between the arts, between vocations, between periods of time. In the end, however, the poem celebrates a friend and laments a particular loss, a dislocation in the well-ordered world, the incursion of time and its depradations. The poem moves from morning to evening. Coming home, the poet calls: 'Uneasy, lovable man, give me your painting / Hand to steady me taking the word-road home.'

Keith Douglas (1920–1944)

So in conjecture stands
my starlit body; the mind
mobile as a fox sneaks round
the sleepers waiting for their wounds.

When Keith Douglas was killed in action in 1944, he was
twenty-four, a year younger than Owen at his death. But
Douglas was not a 'war poet' in the sense Owen was. His
poems have not dated: they share a quality with the work of
Edward Thomas and, to a larger extent, Isaac Rosenberg.
This has to do with the spoken tone of his verse, the non-
programmatic character of his vision, and his individual
attitude to form which he never uses prescriptively. More
than that, Douglas, though young, had a wide range of
interests and of non-military experience. War and soldiering
had attracted him from childhood, but so had music, the
dance, and literature. His earliest poems explore themes of
war and conflict, but always in a wider context.

Keith Castellain Douglas was born in Tunbridge Wells in
1920, an only child of an English father and a mother of
French extraction. When he was eight, his father went away,
and Douglas did not see him again. His childhood was often
solitary, and he spent his time drawing, beginning at the
age of two to cover scraps of paper, floors, walls, and any
flat surface with his illustrations. One of his favourite childhood books was the *History of the Boer War*.

From his youth onward the chief ingredients of his
character were a strong sense of 'the manly' and a love for

creative activity, which matured into a love for literature, music, the dance, costume, the theatre, and the graphic arts. There was an unusual variety in his activities: the rugger player, the enthusiastic OTC trainee, wrote fine poems at the age of fourteen. He attended Christ's Hospital School in Sussex where both aspects of his character were encouraged, and went up to Oxford in 1938. His tutor there was the poet Edmund Blunden, another Christ's Hospital veteran, whose poems influenced the younger man. At Oxford Douglas edited *Cherwell* and was active in amateur theatricals – usually backstage as designer. In his memoir of Douglas, Blunden describes the undergraduate's essays – 'Brevity – but nothing impecunious about it . . . he did not care about novelty when he was feeling his way.' The description fits his poems, for only seldom, as in 'I Experiment', does Douglas strive for novelty, and even there his ambition is to achieve a greater fluency of style. What is startling is the rightness with which, in the early poems, he deploys a received idiom.

When war was declared, Douglas enlisted. He served first in England, then in North Africa, where he courted action in the Desert Campaign. His prose book, *Alamein to Zem Zem* (1946), is an outstanding account of his experience. He was injured by a land mine and hospitalized briefly in Palestine, but soon returned to active service. He was killed. in France

Small successes came early. At the age of sixteen one of his poems was accepted for *New Verse*. Later his poems appeared in *Poetry London* and in minor anthologies. But he did little to advance his career, and he may have undervalued his talents. His *Collected Poems* (1951) appeared seven years after his death, but general recognition came only after Ted Hughes edited a *Selected Poems* (1964) and provided an introduction whose measured enthusiasm was well-gauged. In 1966 a revised *Collected Poems* appeared, and since then Douglas's audience has grown steadily. Ted Hughes's summary of his achievement is accurate: 'He has invented a style that seems to be able to deal poetically with whatever it comes up against . . . It is a language for the whole mind, at its most wakeful, and in all situations.'

The poets of the 1930s turned to Owen as a suitable model. Douglas, involved in a real war, adopted Rosenberg. His subjects are not so much the external documentary aspects – the immediate physical horror – of war. These facts take their place in a larger context of concern. Both poets share a sense of choicelessness within their situations which determined patterns of conduct, regardless of individual conscience. In Douglas's 'How to Kill' the sniper is reduced by the conscienceless process that involves him, under orders, under coercion.

Impending death, which Douglas sensed as soon as he enlisted, is felt everywhere, but always subtly, never rhetorically. Charles Tomlinson has written, 'Death may be the chief factor behind his verse, but it focuses rather than blurs the vision. Sensuous detail grows compact in its presence; life takes on an edge.' The power of Douglas's best poems is in the way they envisage death as a force *within* the object, an inherent quality. In 'The Prisoner', a love poem invaded not by melancholy but by the apprehension of implicit death, the syntax is ambiguous until the last moment, as if undecided; and the enjambments add to the drama. Touching the beloved's face, he says:

But alas, Cheng, I cannot tell why,
today I touched a mask stretched on the stone

person of death. There was the urge
to break the bright flesh and emerge
of the ambitious cruel bone.

In the last three lines, the syntax suggests the speaker's urge will be violent; but the violence is in the object itself. The poet, 'mothwise', would preserve her.

The poem 'Leokothea' bears a resemblance to Rosenberg too, the resemblance we find in Geoffrey Hill's work. 'So all these years I have lived securely,' Douglas writes of the fantasy of unperishing beauty. But the poem is decimated by the dream: 'Last night I dreamed and found my trust

betrayed / only the little bones and the great bones dis-
arrayed.' The same element of Rosenberg is felt in 'The
Creator', 'Search for a God'. In 'Desert Flowers' he
addresses Rosenberg directly.

A quality which distinguishes Douglas's poems from those
of other war poets is the absence of the elegiac tone. They
manage to accommodate their subject matter on its own
terms, not to blur it by sentiment or to force the extreme
experience into an alien framework or to temper it with a
poetic predisposition. And nor do they permit imbalance:
the violent experience in the foreground is placed in a time
context, where it occurs but is limited as experience *by* its
context. The violent is not exaggerated into facile nihilism;
love and beauty are not idealized out of the context of
relationship. An aspect of the novel balanced quality of the
poems (so unlike Blunden's balance) is that Douglas identi-
fies himself with all his characters and themes, with the poets
of the First World War, with the Jews, with the European
predicament, with his enemies and his comrades. His poetry
contains, without resolving, the paradoxes of commitment.

In a polemical letter to J. C. Hall, written in 1943,
Douglas declared: 'My rhythms . . . are carefully chosen to
enable the poems to be *read* as significant speech: I see no
reason to be either musical or sonorous about things at
present . . . I suppose I reflect the cynicism and the careful
absence of expectation (it is not quite the same as apathy)
with which I view the world.' The attitude is passive only
to a degree; for in Douglas, the state of mind he describes is
one of intense critical receptivity as well. He adds, 'To be
sentimental and emotional now is dangerous to oneself and
others.' An attitude of distrust, of no expectation of a better
world, yet a commitment to work for one, to work without
hope ('it doesn't mean working hopelessly') is the closest he
came to a programme.

He places his work and that of other war poets in the
context of the war poetry of the past. 'The soldiers have not
found anything new to say. Their experience they will not
forget easily, and it seems to me that the whole body of

English war poetry of this war, civil and military, will be created after the war is over.' This has not occurred – yet.

Douglas dismissed his early poems as 'long metrical similes and galleries of images'. The description is hardly fair. 'Mummers', written when he was fourteen, shows a remarkable sense, in the use of 'light', of the completed or circular image as practised by Keats and Clare, and – if not with much authority – a reliance on difficult forms, two-syllable rhymes, and a strong irregular rhythm. Even so early, the line endings are well-turned. The image of conflict is already present. Another early poem, 'Famous Men', introduces the underwater imagery and the image of bones which the later poems develop. In 'Caravan' we first encounter Douglas's desert. There is exoticism in his work even at the outset, an unwillingness to be confined to the given English landscape. At the age of fifteen he wrote '.303', about guns and soldiery. Though the poem relies on facile rhetorical effects, the last two lines foreshadow the power of 'How to Kill':

Through a machine-gun's sights
I saw men curse, weep, cough, sprawl in their entrails;
You did not know the gardner in the vales,
    Only efficiency delights you.

The early achievement was considerable.

His writing underwent no radical change when he reached Oxford, though it developed a greater sureness and variety of tone. 'Forgotten the Red Leaves' is one of his best poems, cataloguing things forgotten, with an echo of Hart Crane's 'I can remember much forgetfulness'. It would be hard to find another poet who, at the age of eighteen, could write with Douglas's unemphatic originality:

These and the hazy tropic where I lived
In tall seas where the bright fish go like footmen
Down the blue corridors about their business,
The jewelled skulls are down there.

The poem further develops the underwater geography where

'The Marvel' and later poems are enacted. 'Poor Mary' and
other fine lyrics followed in the next year, and 'Invaders', a
poem which seems to owe an obscure debt to MacNeice (as
does the later 'Villanelle of Sunlight'), though the idiom is
Douglas's own.

Intelligences like black birds
come on their dire wings from Europe. Sorrows
fall like the rooks' clatter on house and garden.
And who will drive them back before we harden?
You will find, after a few tomorrows
like this, nothing will matter but the black birds.

Douglas's black birds in this poem (written before he began
active service) foreshadow the *bête noire* of the later work. He
intended his first collection to be entitled *Bête Noire*, the
'beast on my back' about which he wrote an unfinished
poem in jazz rhythms. It was an obsessive presence he could
not identify, like Edward Thomas's 'The Other'. It shares
some of the characteristics of the inherent death in objects
he explores in 'The Prisoner'. He reports that he was always
setting out to write the *bête noire* poem, but that it eluded
him and another poem was written instead.

Many of the Oxford poems are about music, costumes,
dance, formal relationships, the deceit on the literal level
and the enactment on another level of truths through disguise. He is often the watcher, 'in the wings' of the stage at
Oxford, and later 'in the wings of Europe', when the drama
finds a wider sphere. The impending violence disrupts some
of the poised poems on themes of art. 'A Ballet' is invaded
by brutal reality: the maimed perform; just as later, in
'Landscape with Figures', the poet writhes on the backcloth
of a war drama.

In the Oxford poems, punctuation and syntax, often
unresolved, become ambiguous. Punctuation is used – as in
'Farewell Poem' – more as a pause notation than a prescriptive system. Douglas retreats from the conventional literary
language towards a clear speaking voice. His rhythms are
original in the way they advance speaking and are not

betrayed into easy singing cadences. Usually they achieve a spoken clarity, unparaphrasable and mordantly particular. He seldom generalizes, except in the early poems. The power is in the particulars. He infrequently moralizes. In the original version of 'Cairo Jag', a poem written in Egypt, he drew out the moral, not ineffectively. But in revision he cut the poem short, so that it resolved as unexplicated experience. Among the cancelled lines five stand out. They describe his particular mode of apprehension. Abruptly the experience of war – as in Blunden's poems – changes everything:

You do not gradually appreciate such qualities
but your mind will extend new hands. In a moment
will fall down like St Paul in a blinding light
the soul suffers a miraculous change
you become a true inheritor of this altered planet.

Army life, because Douglas had prepared himself well in advance, did not effect a sudden change in his poetry. The increasing complexity and lucidity of his style was coming anyway. 'Simplify Me When I'm Dead' subtly expresses his foreknowledge of death. 'The Marvel' is one of his most achieved poems. In it a swordfish is cut open, its eye prised out by a sailor who uses it as a lens to focus the sunlight and burn the name of his latest 'harlot' in the wood of the ship. The eye:

  is one most curious device
of many, kept by the interesting waves,
for I suppose the querulous soft voice

of mariners who rotted into ghosts
digested by the gluttonous tides
could recount many. Let them be your hosts

and take you where their forgotten ships lie
with fishes going over the tall masts—
all this emerges from the burning eye.

As the eye focuses the sun, the image of the swordfish focuses, with the dramatic syntax Douglas mastered, a range of experience and association.

The poems written during and after service in the Middle East are less polished, suggestive of what might have come. The variety of subject matter and the intensity of the poet's experience made him move further from literary models, though the influence of 'Report on Experience' and others of Blunden's poems can be felt in the organization of poems such as 'Negative Information'. The world of appearances and the real world, the betrayal inherent in experience, are expressed:

> the girls who met us at one place
> were not whores, but women old and young at once
> whom accidents had turned to pretty stones,
> to images slight with deceptive grace.

Here, too, the living perceive their own and one another's ghosts, hideous inherent presences. Eventually Douglas senses not merely the presence of death in living things, but the identity of the living and the dead. In 'The Sea Bird' the terrible conclusion comes in a rare generalization: 'all our successes and failures are similar.'

The love poems of this period, 'I Listen to the Desert Wind', 'The Knife', 'Song', and others are by turns strongly erotic and chilling. The influence of Rimbaud, three of whose sonnets Douglas translated, can be felt in 'Christo-doulos', 'Egypt', and others of the desert poems. In 'Egypt' there is a compelling dissonance, a seeming-marriage between themes from Blunden and Rimbaud. The beggar women – beggar girls, in fact – are evoked:

> And in fifteen years of living
> found nothing different from death
> but the difference of moving
> and the nuisance of breath.

This tragic vision informs the fatalistic poem, 'Behaviour of Fish in an Egyptian Tea Garden'. An attractive woman is like a white stone at the bottom of a pool drawing the fish down; but destined, herself, to be a chattel.

In 'Cairo Jag' the vision of two coexisting worlds, apparently dissimilar but profoundly similar beneath appearances, broadens out further. The sour, rank city with its violent but resolving pleasures is abruptly set beside the landscape of war: 'But by a day's travelling you reach a new world / The vegetation is of iron.' The world is new only in that it is recent. It expresses aspects of the same humanity as the city. It too has its resolving experiences. In 'Dead Men' the 'sanitary earth' cleans and neutralizes the rotting dead. The dogs dig them up, and 'All that is good of them, the dog consumes'. The pointedly materialistic use of 'good' intensifies the theme. The poem ends, 'The prudent mind resolves / on the lover's or the dog's attitude forever.' Douglas is not prudent. He perceives a possible choice, but cannot make it. It is characteristic that his irony is positive, serving to expand, not to limit, the themes. It is an aspect of his caution – he is not willing to overstate, but his irony, rather than reducing the theme, leaves it open.

One feels a relentlessness in the themes of the last poems – understandably. 'Mersa', for instance, advances the same argument as the other Egyptian poems. But Douglas's matter is diverse. 'Vergissmeinicht' is his set pieces about war, with 'How to Kill', undoubtedly the most searing of his poems. The neutrality of the tone makes it a far more potent indictment of war than a journalistic or rhetorical effort could be. Child's play becomes sniper's play. 'How easy it is to *make* a ghost,' Douglas writes, as though killing were playfully creative. The sang-froid of 'Aristocrats', too, and of the early 'satire', 'Russians', convince us that here the poetry is in the *pitilessness*, accurate and chilling.

Edwin Morgan (born 1920)

What time has barely kept
let that be the most dearly kept

Poetry, Edwin Morgan says, should 'acknowledge its
environment'. It can do this in the development of its
themes, in its imagery – drawing from particulars of place
and time – or in its approach to language, reproducing in
the word order or in the word itself specific processes of the
environment. In a sequence of poems called 'Interferences',
for instance, the failure of language in various extreme
circumstances is expressed in the deformation of certain
words at the climax of the experience; in the 'Glasgow
Sonnets' the references are drawn directly from the city, its
history and the present; and in the Science Fiction poems
the themes relate to actual human ambitions and actions,
with analogies to actual experience, but carried into other
spheres – 'imaginative poetry exploring time and space'.
Morgan writes, 'I have slowly developed my own brand of
free verse to enable me to build up effects over paragraphs
rather than within single lines.' The poems are memorable
as plots and occasionally as rhythms, but phrases and lines
seldom stay in the mind, except from the lyrics. Morgan is
drawn towards 'directness' and 'realism', though he recognizes the danger in over-directness.

Edwin George Morgan was born in Glasgow in 1920. He
attended Rutherglen Academy and Glasgow High School.
His early infatuation was with Keats and Tennyson, and he
was susceptible, too, to the popular songs of the day. His

early writings were 'huge fantastic narratives', for he was from the outset drawn to Science Fiction. At the age of seventeen he went to Glasgow University. There he read Eliot, Rimbaud (in French) and Mayakovsky (in Russian). They opened up for him the world of modern poetry. From 1940 to 1946 he was in the Royal Army Medical Corps, and he travelled widely, particularly in the Near East. He returned to Glasgow and in 1947 took his MA in English at the University, where he is now Professor of English.

In the 1950s, Morgan, always open to influences from abroad, read William Carlos Williams, the Beats, and the Black Mountain Poets. His own writing was affected by their different practices. Contact with the Brazilian Concrete Poets led to Morgan's experimental concrete poems. His essay on Concrete Poetry is the outstanding account in English of that short-lived movement. He also wrote 'sound poems', based entirely on the dramatic arrangement of vowels and consonants and the shape of the poem, created for public recital. 'The Loch Ness Monster's Song' is the best known of his exercises in this vein. His mentor seems to have been the Belgian poet Ernst Jandl.

Morgan has translated poetry from a surprising range of European languages. He has translated into Scots as well as English. Scots he finds an idiom more capable than English at effecting the quick transitions of mood and tone and capturing the rhetoric of the Russian poet Mayakovsky. His best original poems draw on the Scottish experience, but are not themselves in Scots.

He has come to prefer the poetry that emerges from newspaper stories, small incidents, 'what time barely kept', to poetry that built on earlier verse, and to poetry of subjective experience and observation. Hence he has written 'instamatic' poems and other incidental pieces to capture, and in captivity to explore, 'what actually happens'. The long series of *Instamatic Poems* (1972) attempt a photographic immediacy. They are unfortunately thin linguistically, neither particularly accurate nor evocative. The language, coldly used, aspires to be a lens. In the best of them –

'Mougins Provence September 1971', for instance – he achieves an almost surreal effect by suspending the real moment, without its cause or aftermath, in a perpetual present. It is the surrealism of photography. But few of these experiments are successful.

Morgan's concrete poems take the immediate 'happening' into language, or treat words as themselves images capable of surrendering multiple significance. This is best illustrated in 'Message Clear'. In a sense Morgan's work is all translation, translating 'the real' into language, not modulating it through language. His is not a poetry of metamorphosis or even process. He attempts to evoke what *is* in a real or an imagined world.

His first extended collection of poems was *The Second Life* (1968). On the contents page each poem carries the date of composition or of the incident to which it refers. Each witnesses to a particular experience in time, whether in the poet's life or the planet's history. He is wary lest the poems slip anchor from their specific temporal origins.

'The Old Man and the Sea' is a poem about Hemingway's death. A sea mist engulfs the landscape and the novelist takes his life:

Questions, not answers, chill the heart here,
a chained dog whining in the straw,
the gunsmoke marrying the sea-mist,
and silence of the inhuman valleys.

The images are vivid and, not moralized, acquire an elusive symbolic value through juxtaposition. The next poem in the book is 'The Death of Marilyn Monroe' which moves out rhythmically into Whitmanesque rhapsodizing. It is followed by 'Je ne regrette rien', a dramatic monologue spoken by Edith Piaf. The three elegies are at the same time celebrations, in entirely different forms. The first is precise, imagistic; the second rhapsodic; the third dramatic. Each subject demands a distinct approach and tone, a different form.

The range of reference throughout Morgan's work is

wide – to history, literature, travel. The variety of detailed
allusion characterizes the best of his work. Often, too, there
is an engaging whimsy, comedy, and wit. But in his first
collection the memorable poems are the sober ones, particularly the animal poems which stress man's inhumanity to the
animal world and introduce the theme of innocence that
dominates the later work. He cautions the beasts, 'O wild
things, wild things / take care, beware of him.'

His documentary technique is most successful in the love
sequence, opening with 'The Second Life': 'Is it true that
we come alive / not once, but many times?' These lyrics are
at times unabashedly sentimental. Their veracity, down to
the details, cannot be doubted. Nothing has been rearranged:
the poems bear witness. In other documentary poems
Morgan tends to moralize implicitly or explicitly. The
images become fixedly emblematic in rhythms altogether
too rhapsodic for the subject matter and the moral burden.
In 'Glasgow Green', for example, he goes a step too far:

This is not the delicate nightmare
you carry to the point of fear
and wake from, it is life, the sweat
is real ...

The portentousness, 'it is life', comes to mar a number of
poems. The images are – or should be – sufficiently eloquent.
But there is a sense that many of Morgan's poems are *about*
something, conscious attempts to accept a challenge of subject matter or form and, willy-nilly, to forge a poem out of it.
The challenge has replaced an inner poetic necessity; the
very variety of the work worries the reader. Morgan has an
enviable facility, with all the implicit dangers of facility.

In *From Glasgow to Saturn* (1973) the moralizing is more
contained. In the documentary 'Stobhill' he explores, in a
sequence of dramatic monologues, an incident: the disposal
of a living foetus in a hospital. No judgements are passed.
The sequence has the authority of his lyric poems, a number
of which are included in this second extended collection. In

'Columba's Song' the saint arrives in search of souls and, finding an uninhabited landscape, says:

Where's Brude? Where's man?
There's too much nature here,
eagles and deer,
but where's the mind and where's the soul?
Show me your kings, your women, the man of the plough.
And cry me to your cradles.
It wasn't for a fox or an eagle I set sail!

Other lyric poems develop the theme of self-deception in fantasy or dream. Returning to the real world:

We take in
the dream, a cloth from the line
the trains fling sparks on
in our city. We're better awake.

Most of the lyrics lament elegiacally the impossibility of fantasy, the thwarted romantic impulse. Temperamentally Morgan is a romantic, but unwilling to let himself be carried away. 'The Woman' is a haunting poem about frustration:

Nothing she was waiting for
came, unless what took her
in the coldest arms.

Even the love poems are elegiac, with little of the happy incredulity of the earlier sequence. The burning of the letters in 'For Bonfires' brings to an end the sequence begun in *The Second Life*.

Another of Morgan's forms is the free ballad – 'Blue Toboggans', 'Song of a Child', and 'Flakes', for example – which with innocent rhythms effect subtle tone changes. The freedom from punctuation produces a suggestive, fluid line-to-line syntax. Morgan calls many of his poems 'songs' and the effect – a lightness of language, a strong rhythmic emphasis – is in quality song-like. There is a thematic and formal analogy with Blake's 'Songs'. Frequently Morgan confronts human and natural innocence with experience, often technological. But the experienced men who use technology often become its victims, especially in the astronaut poems, and the innocents are more sensible and active than in Blake, often exacting – almost without meaning to – revenges on their oppressors, as in 'The Mill'. A moral warning, gentle but insistent, comes from Morgan's world, a caution to observe and experience the moment, as in 'London':

The season's spent, they've come towards us
as the air clears. They smile and hold out bowls
of water, fine linen cloths, fat oranges.
It looks like water, linen, oranges
but where is summer, winter? Where is the world?
When we've lost time we have lost everything.

Morgan's romanticism finds vent in social optimism, a belief – even in the debris of the Glasgow slums – in the possibility of a better world. The political message is cast in Biblical terms in 'The Fifth Gospel', where he rewrites the parables, reversing their moral burden. Christ becomes a Michael Foot figure, urging industry, cooperation and community. The 'Glasgow Sonnets' are less apparently optimistic, but they are documentary, evocative, and socially critical, implying his basic humane optimism in the terms of their criticism.

Some of Morgan's poems are simply entertainments, short stories with mysterious unresolved tensions, as in 'Christmas Eve'. There are, too, imaginary conversations – Morgan has a good ear for dialogue. This form is taken to great lengths in the sequence 'The Whittrick'.

If Morgan has never 'found his own voice', as some of his critics claim when confronted by his versatility and facility, he has created an extensive and varied body of poetry which, from various angles, explores certain central themes. For a poet so committed to the 'real' and the 'moment', it is strange that many of his poems exist finally only within the tensions of language, without analogy in the wider environment they should – in his belief – be witnessing to. Yet this is Morgan's achievement: exploring tensions in language, whether the single word, the verse paragraph, or pure sound, showing how language can be renewed from an understanding of its inherent qualities and how these qualities can at times engage intractable subject matter.

Donald Davie (born 1922)

There has to be a hero who is not
A predator...

Donald Davie began his career as a poet in the thick of 'The
Movement', and his critical book, *Purity of Diction in English
Verse* (1952) described the early aspiration of some of the
writers associated with it. It was in part a reaction against
the excesses of the Apocalyptic poets of the 1940s, a retrench-
ment; but also a reassertion of the validity of syntactical
clarity, traditional forms, and reason. Davie wrote, 'there is
no necessary connection between the poetic vocation on the
one hand, and on the other exhibitionism, egoism, and
licence.'

The Movement's 'rules' were, to begin with, restrictive,
curtailments of poetic ambition and scope. In the case of
poets such as Kingsley Amis and, to a degree, Philip Larkin,
the rules hardened into dogma and little Englandism. Other
poets – John Wain in particular – eventually discarded the
rules and drifted into the rhetorical waffle against which
The Movement had been directed. For Davie, however, the
rules were a discipline, not a dogma. Rigorously applied,
that discipline has stayed with him, though his themes and
forms have changed. He translated poetic ambitions into
terms that were at first, and have to a large degree remained,
Augustan. Taken as a whole, his work is ambitious but
always controlled; his achievements are poetic rather than
rhetorical. There is, too, a strong didactic impulse in most of
his verse.

Donald Alfred Davie was born in Barnsley, Yorkshire, in 1922. It was a landscape that he later called 'poisoned for the imagination' by generations of industrial exploitation. Educated there, he went on to Cambridge after military service and took his degree in English. He lectured in Dublin (1950–57), Cambridge (1958–64), and became Professor of English at Essex (1964). In 1968 he emigrated to the United States and became Professor of English at Stanford University and in 1978 at Vanderbilt.

His second major critical book, *Articulate Energy*, extending the arguments of his first volume further into poetic syntax, appeared in the same year as his first collection of poems, *Brides of Reason* (1955). These early books reflect a desire for the discipline of a rigid language, where words – in Johnson's sense – are clearly and finally defined. The poet's task is to use such a language to its full potential; his study is syntax and form, the organization of specific words with specific meanings. *A Winter Talent and Other Poems* (1957), *The Forests of Lithuania* (1959), and *New and Selected Poems* (1961) extended Davie's discipline to its limits.

The Augustanism to which he was drawn began to seem doubtful to him. In an unpublished interview, he said, 'It seems to me now that the eighteenth-century enthusiasms in which I started and the eighteenth-century effects that I tried to reproduce in my early poems, are in fact motivated very romantically; that is to say, for a twentieth-century person to yearn towards the rigidity of the couplet and the rigidity of the Johnsonian vocabulary and the rigidity of those steady civilizations which they held in mind, is very different from an eighteenth-century man wanting it.' He 'came to suspect' this romantic element, and in suspecting it qualified it, so that without surrendering his disciplines he shrugged off the specifically Augustan affectations, becoming – instead of a romantic Augustan – an essentially modern Augustan, with all that this implies of reason and receptivity, optimism and tempering scepticism.

His translations of Pasternak had a marked effect on his development. A further stage in the transformation of his style was his close reading of Ezra Pound which resulted in his study *Ezra Pound: Poet as Sculptor* (1964). His poems began to choose other than traditional forms, and yet, in his new forms, he tried to retain the sharpness of definition and meaning he had achieved in his early work.

With *A Sequence for Francis Parkman* (1961) the transition definitively comes. The poem is 'made up almost entirely of phrases and expressions and locutions lifted direct out of Parkman'. He describes it as an Alexandrian type of poem, a 'cento', 'made up entirely of fragments of other writings, juxtaposed in a new way and given a new context'. Juxtaposition was a lesson he had learned from Pound. In the poem he explores various colonial figures, their dramas played out against the background of a new continent and a recollected Europe. The sequence performs a special function for Davie. He needs to fill the 'void centuries' not with facts but with motives, to find the human root in numb facts and dates.

If it was romantic and politically unmodish for Davie to hark after a pre-Darwinian social and cultural stability – rejecting the modern judgement that institutions and cultures are best considered in the light of their adaptability, their formal fluidity – it was equally romantic for him to emigrate to the western United States, a landscape which he felt – and perhaps still feels – is not 'poisoned' in the way Barnsley is. He saw America as still possessing a frontier and a wilderness, it was a land where the imagination could be a gentle expropriator. He advances the figure of tourist as hero: 'The only eye that you *can* trust is the tourist's eye; the eye . . . of the man who is moving, and moving quite fast, and moving quite light.' Rootlessness – or uprootedness – must be the modern poet's – at least Davie's – condition.

Several collections have followed on the Parkman sequence: *Events and Wisdoms* (1964), *The Poems of Dr Zhivago* (1965), *Essex Poems* (1969), *Six Epistles to Eva Hesse* (1970), *Collected Poems* (1972), and *The Shires* (1974). Each has extended Davie's range and confirmed the rightness of his chosen discipline. He has gone further, and achieved considerably more, than any other poet associated with The Movement. His critical openness and catholicity of taste, aspects of his essential integrity of purpose, have made him the outstanding poet of his generation.

Davie's early poems are part of an implicit programme. They are much concerned with poetry, the intellectual challenges of form and the range an accurate formal poetry can aspire to. They presuppose a poetic consensus and address themselves to it. The more disillusioned he grows with this mode, perhaps accepting too the absence of a valid literary consensus, the better the poems become. In later poems, particularly *Six Epistles to Eva Hesse*, he has imagined a new consensus and addressed it, wittily persuading and admonishing it, with the knowledge that it does not yet exist, but that imagining it may hurry it into being.

As irony, common sense, and traditional forms came to seem inadequate, Davie – in the poems published in 1961 and 1964 – senses the 'metaphysicality' possible in and necessary to poetry, something which runs counter to his earlier analytic impulse.

Early in the *Essex Poems* he says:

The practice of an art
is to convert all terms
into the terms of art.
By the end of the third stanza
death is a smell no longer;
it is a problem of style.

He defines the distance between the experience of the poem and its expression: to express the experience, a *formal* perspective is necessary, a distance which guarantees a degree of objectivity and impersonality, so that the reader engages the experience and not the poet experiencing. Implicit in this is a preference for what Davie loosely terms 'closed structures', closed in the sense that they are self-contained. A number of his poems do not strive for this, continually refer to areas of fact and allusion not contained within, nor finally necessary to, the poem. They force us to adjust regularly to our jarring ignorance, to distracting surprises (Thom Gunn rides into the midst of one poem on a motor-bike), to a mild sense of betrayal. Davie supplies footnotes to the more demanding of these poems; and yet rhyme, complex syntax, and the well-controlled rhythms are sometimes not enough to provide the elaborate switch-back system which validates the parts of the poem even as it is read, which arrests it, gives it edge, even as it moves in time.

If the early poems are confident in tone, the later poems ape confidence; the poet assumes the guise of explorer among uncertain certainties, a tourist, an observer of heroes. He moves from a poetry of minimum risks to one of maximum risks; he is willing to court failure. A complex change occurred in his attitude to his work and himself. Writing of the poem 'With the Grain' in 1957, he took himself to task for not having a naturally poetic mind, for his principally analytical, intellectual preoccupations. 'I have not the poet's need of concreteness,' he said, adding that the thought in many of the poems from before 1957 'could have been expressed . . . in a non-poetic way'. He resolves in future to write only poems which are 'if not *naturally*, at all events *truly* poems throughout'. He will write 'against the grain', striving for a 'concrete fantasy' of the abstractions crucial to him.

Few poets could have had the skill and acumen consciously to redirect their efforts in this way. 'Winning to the concrete through the abstract' is a common process in the poems after 1957. The images no longer merely decorate a line of thought: they contain the thought in their development and relationship. This is perhaps the best way Davie has found to penetrate hard intellectual surfaces. Images of permanence, particularly place, assume special importance.

His experiments with form include many notable successes and failures. His rhymed syllabic verse is, with Elizabeth Daryush's, the most distinguished yet written by an English poet, while a poem such as 'Pieta', with its short lines, reads like Davie run through a meat slicer. Form and content are not in tension but seem to relate arbitrarily. If one of his most ambitious experiments, 'England', is unsuccessful, it presages important developments to come.

The poem evokes a plane journey to England from America. The poet peoples from history the lands beneath him; from a literal bird's-eye view he scrutinizes customs, tastes, and changes. The present at its worst seems to him to be revealed in some of the poetry. Of Ted Hughes he writes:

Brutal manners, brutal
simplifications as
we drag it all down.

The sentimentalism of violence he senses in the new art, a sentimentalism which is irresponsible, simplifying complex conflicts, seems to him incapable of the precision necessary for clarification, incapable of providing contexts in which the violence takes place. To him – as we might expect from his Augustan disposition – the sin against language is a mortal sin. Blurred and broken, language becomes harmful. The debasement of language leads to the debasement of the individual. 'England' moves into whipping satire, and a number of Davie's *bêtes noires* are left wounded by the road-side. He laments, too, the cheapening of values within his native society, the cheapening of relationships, the essentially shallow quality of the new 'English experience'. In cadence, some of the lines recall Maud's rant against 'idiot gabble':

And what's there left to be seen
by Tom the butler now
we couple like dogs in the yard?
Display! Display! Display!

The *Six Epistles to Eva Hesse*, Pound's German translator, are an extension and qualification of 'England', an attempt to vindicate the valid elements in English tradition. 'The main objective,' Davie writes, 'was to show that . . . as much variety of time, space and action can be encompassed in one of the traditional forms of English verse as in the much vaunted "free forms" of the American tradition originating in Pound's *Cantos*.' It is as though the proof of Davie's case is not in what is said but in how it is said, for this is Davie's *tour de force* in traditional form. The alternatives to the values he champions are unsettlingly called up:

Here making a distinction is
Nearly the worst of felonies,
Only exceeded, it appears,
By entertaining clear ideas . . .
Here the surreal is the true
And hashish may be good for you.

He describes the moral role of the poet and the ill-effects of his moral abdication. He argues for literary consensus. He defends rhyme, contending that the systematically broken norm – in syntax, rhythm, and so forth – is in the long run less elastic than the apparently silly conventions of traditional form and syntax which compel accuracy of language.

Davie has largely restricted himself to the short-line poem; though one cannot resist the longer cadences of 'Time Passing, Beloved', it is atypical. Sometimes the early poems include painful rhymes, and the later poems are marred by a verbal self-consciousness which demands attention for nice effects, for example:

A neutral
tone was (note the passive
voice) preferred . . .

This sort of cuteness is no part of Davie's art. And yet it points again to what is a main concern of the poems: language. The rightness of form, word choice, syntactical turn, often naturally arrest us.

'Pentecost' is a poem about the gift of tongues in the half-articulate pop-culture Davie despises. The perceptual and moral implications of a depleted language are clarified:

Our sons and our daughters shall
Prophesy? The gift of tongues
To the Beat and post-Beat poets,
The illiterate apostles,

Is what, if I should cherish
Much or mourn the lack of
Or ape their stammerings,
I must betray myself.

It is a theme which runs through the critical writings as
well. The poem 'Epistle. To Enrique Caracciolo Trejo'
could in part be a verse paraphrase of a passage from one of
Davie's critical books:

The English that I feel in
Fears the inauthentic
Which invades it on all sides
Mortally. The style may die of it,
Die of the fear of it,
Confounding authenticity with essence.

Most of the time Davie realizes that he is reasoning with the
unreasonable and the morally deaf. In 'To Helen Keller' he
writes – with an echo of MacNeice:

The Gutenberg era, the era of rhyme, is over.
It's an end to the word-smith now, an end to the skald,
an end to the erudite, elated rover
threading a fjord of words. Four-letter expletives
are all of that ocean's plankton that still lives.

The manner in this passage contradicts the matter. The
word-smith lives to lament the desecration of his forge. He
returns to clean the tools and relight the fire. Rebuffed,
Davie comes back again and again.

The return is another of his dominant themes. He returns
to Barnsley, to England, to the wilderness of America,
bringing to bear on each landscape the experiences he has
accumulated elsewhere. The return reveals the enduring
elements in the poet and in the place without sentimentality.
'Rodez' is his most powerful poem on this theme; and yet
the whole of *The Shires* can be read as a return to England;
the poet looks with the eye of a tourist, but brings to bear a
collection of particular memories as well. The place and the
poet recognize and reveal one another.

Davie is a craftsman. Many of his poems are 'worked up', and he has been called a 'cold' poet because his heart is seldom sported on his sleeve. He has other ends in mind when he writes. He knows that there is a difference between the expression of anguish and the experience of anguish. From the early 'pasticheur of late Augustan styles' he has come many leagues, his ambitions have become larger, his vision more humane. His compulsion to write and the breadth of what he has written attest to a passion for and a commitment to the art of poetry, the language, and the tribe. His own quest is clear: 'Needing to know is always how to learn; / Needing to see brings sightings.' He proceeds through this necessity:

In all but what seems inchoate
We quiz the past. To see it straight
Requires a form just out of reach.

Philip Larkin (born 1922)

The heart in its own endless silence kneeling.

Philip Larkin was born in Coventry in 1922. In so far as any of his poems is specifically autobiographical, we can assume from 'I Remember, I Remember' that he had an unremarkable childhood:

'Was that,' my friend smiled, 'where you "have your roots"?'
No, only where my childhood was unspent,
I wanted to retort, just where I started . . .

The unspent childhood included education at King Henry VIII School in Coventry. As a child he wrote prose – 'a thousand words at night after homework' – and poetry which he bound up in little books. His first published poem, 'Ultimatum', appeared in the *Listener* when he was eighteen.

Then he went to Oxford in the early 1940s, where he read English and made the acquaintance of John Wain, Kingsley Amis, and others. At Oxford he was only *in ovo* the Larkin we have come to know. He was actually a *young* man, with a young man's ambitions and affectations. He wrote letters, according to Michael Hamburger, on 'reddish-mauve note-paper', which he described as one of his 'indulgences'. He was composing his early poems, and he wrote to Hamburger that, to him, the 'tradition of poetry' is 'emotion and honesty of emotion, and it doesn't matter who it is written by or how, if this is conveyed'. Only one adjustment of this point of view has been made since, but it is all-important: 'how' has become crucial. Honesty is only possible if one's own voice speaks.

Larkin the undergraduate wrote poems in the shadows of Yeats, Auden, and Dylan Thomas, relieved a bit it seems by the benign shadow of Betjeman. In 1945 *The North Ship* was published – poems spoken by several 'abandoned selves'. The young poet was not imitating his mentors: he was echoing them:

Let the wheel spin out,
Till all created things
With shout and answering shout
Cast off rememberings

he writes, and a Yeatsian 'muffled drum' sounds. In another poem man becomes 'a sack of meal upon two sticks'. He confesses that, with the early poems, written in a large green manuscript book, he would warm up his talents by thumbing through his collection of Yeats. It included only poems up to *Words for Music Perhaps* – hence none of Yeats's later asperity rubbed off on Larkin. This is fortunate, for Larkin has learned his own asperity which owes nothing to Yeats.

In 1946 Larkin's novel *Jill* appeared, followed in 1947 by another, *A Girl in Winter*. But his was not the novelist's vocation, though the discipline of novel writing contributed to his development as a poet. His poems often have dramatic or narrative plots, and details are enlisted not decoratively, but to clarify aspects of plot and character.

From Oxford, Larkin entered the lists of University Librarians and served at Belfast, then at Leicester, and finally at the Brynmore Jones Library in Hull. It is important to note his distance from the London literary 'power centre'. He takes the trip down in his poems, but he does not tell us what happens when he arrives. He has not, apparently, coveted the praise that has been lavished on him – praise he neither fully merits nor, perhaps, relishes. And nor has he been prolific. His entire *oeuvre* to date, if we take into account *The North Ship*, consists in collected form of 117 poems, thirty-two of which he has republished on sufferance.

The mature Larkin reacted against the naïve idealism of

the 1930s poets, and also against the garbled romanticism of Dylan Thomas and the Apocalyptics. He was a contributor to *New Lines* (1956) and came to be seen as the centrepiece of The Movement. His was passive acceptance of the various frustrations and defeats of life – active only in apprehending and describing, and not until the later poems counselling action, albeit obliquely in specifically social poems. If Larkin's technique has not developed since *The Less Deceived*, his perspective nonetheless has broadened, and his conservatism has tended cautiously towards satire.

Frequently he presents himself in the poems as an outsider, a man without a past to be nostalgic for and without much faith in the future, a man on the fringe of the academy and literary life, an isolated bachelor, a provincial, rejecting all that is not English, refusing to travel beyond the British Isles. Denial and self-deprecation are recurrent themes. However, this stance must be increasingly difficult to sustain in view of the fact that he is, willy nilly, the darling of the London literary establishment, has been crowned by journalists and honoured by the Queen, and has edited the *Oxford Book of Twentieth Century English Verse* (1973). This has placed strains on the poet. He no longer speaks with confidence as outsider and provincial. He has been spirited inside. The best poems in his fourth book, *High Windows* (1974), abandon the old stance altogether. 'The Explosion', 'How Distant', and 'The Old Fools' – poems of observation – take their tone from the experience. If Larkin is to avoid self-parody in future (something he fails to do in several poems in *High Windows*) he will have either to assume impersonality *de rigueur*, or find himself a new stance.

In the poems, people are illuminated by the objects they collect about them – their possessions reveal their ambitions, self-deceptions, unfulfilments. The industrial and the pastoral landscapes tell us about the minds of the urban and rural communities that made or sustain them, just as the particular vase or the lack of bookshelves in a room describes the inhabitant. Objects thus lend a reality to the person, not the person to the objects. This inverted romanticism is one of Larkin's characteristic and compelling effects.

Though the poems are subtly made, they are self-contained – we can grasp the allusions without footnotes, without consulting any document beyond the daily paper. The poems are replete with the small tragedies, losses and frustrations which add up to the large gradual tragedy of lives in a thousand furnished rooms, in a particular country at a particular time.

His first book of poems, *The North Ship*, is generally dismissed as juvenilia. But he was twenty-three when it appeared, and the next year his novel *Jill* was published. If the majority of the poems are juvenilia, a sudden maturing must have occurred in the space of eighteen months. *The North Ship* is a thin, unsatisfactory collection, full of fabricated attitudes, atmospheres, symbols, yet it suggests some of the thematic and technical virtues of the mature Larkin. Implicit in it, too, are the roads not taken – the possibility that he might have adopted a more hermetic style, or a more rhetorical style, or that he might have become a song writer, infatuated as he was by the 'music' of Yeats. But he didn't. The 'abandoned selves' were abandoned resolutely.

The apprentice poet was not hard-working. He was impressionable, but in his college rooms, confronted with Yeats's passion, he was himself passionless. Later, with technical development and growing self-awareness, he came to write the poetry of the passionless, and in so doing achieved an accurate warmth, and those occasional lines which penetrate to loss of passion and its consequences. In 'Dawn' – a very early poem – he writes: 'How strange it is / For the heart to be loveless.' Another early poem tells us, 'the deft / Heart was impotent.' We are in the presence of the later themes, if not the mature voice.

The year after the first collection was published, he began reading Hardy. Hardy taught him to look outside, to fix the eye on detail, and to leave the impulsive, private, impressionable world of *The North Ship* behind, to disembark on the *terra firma* of landscape, of the time that is now and the world that is the Welfare State. Hardy showed him how to write as a person who stands just on the edge of the crowd, wishing to share in its mass oblivion but prevented – by a habit of mind which asks questions and is uncomfortable.

There were, thereafter, only *poems*, no concept of poetry or even a desire to interrelate poems into a single 'statement'. In 1972 he wrote, 'I never think of poetry or the poetry scene, only separate poems written by individuals.' This wariness of theories amounts to a programme. Though he learned only little from Hardy's technical practice, except perhaps his formal experimentation within traditional limits, he learned from him about time. Hardy juxtaposes the impoverished present and the unrealized past, where Larkin juxtaposes the impoverished present and the blighted future – and death. The blues are his music – indeed, he is a jazz critic.

His ostensible aesthetic motivation is 'to preserve things I have seen / thought / felt'. His poems are 'verbal devices' to reproduce in the reader the experience – 'verbal pickling' as he calls it. The poems generally are cumulative – the scene is set, details assembled, until there is a point of lift-off, a modulation of tone or a deepening of seriousness. From the evocation of externals, the poet proceeds to release their composite meanings. When the 'lift-off' fails the poems are sometimes vivid verse catalogues only, as in 'To the Sea' and 'Show Saturday'.

Time does not destroy his illusions – it intensifies his disillusion. For him – in contrast to Hardy – things somehow could not have been different. We did not look away, or make a specific wrong choice in the past – for all choices are partly wrong. Choice implies the forfeit of what is not chosen. There is a terrible inevitability – which is pessimism – in the poems. Time is an Indian giver.

His use of negatives is a central part of his technique. But usually, except in a few poems such as 'I Remember, I Remember', his negatives do not suggest what could have been. They simply draw a black circle around what is, the tight frontiers of being. His apparently negative words do not always carry a negative meaning, however: 'unfakeable', 'unpriceable' and 'unignorable' are obliquely positive. He tries to extend language by making hybrid words or hyphenated kennings. The effective phrase 'solemn-sinister' recalls Edward Thomas's 'tender-gorgeous', and Larkin has learned some lessons from Thomas – lessons of diction and enjambment and, in a few instances, rhythm.

The North Ship sometimes specifically prefigures what is to follow. The young man writes:

To wake, and hear a cock
Out of the distance crying,—
To pull the curtain back
And see the clouds flying ...

while the older poet, swaddled in middle age and numbed by sleep, says in *High Windows*:

Groping back to bed after a piss
I part thick curtains, and am startled by
The rapid clouds ...

The first poem laments lovelessness; the second sadly half-celebrates youth from the safe distance of middle age.

The themes in *The North Ship* – unwilling capitulation to the system of things, love's unsuccess, frustration, boredom, loneliness, and especially Time, 'the echo of an axe / Within a wood' – inform the later books. All that is lacking is the Larkin scenario to make the emotions or lack of emotions come alive memorably, through particulars. The early problem may have been that the 'I' was not a voice but a fabricated poetical persona, much as the 'I' in *High Windows* is sometimes an outdated 'I' who no longer sounds true.

The adjustment of style between *The North Ship* and his second book, *The Less Deceived* (1955), is complete. The first poem in the second collection, 'Lines on a Young Lady's Photograph Album', is Betjemanesque, though more sinewy than Betjeman, with an Edwardian archness. The poet's attraction to the young lady is strongly sexual. The images are not symbolic – they are evocative particulars. 'Next Please', in the same book, is perhaps Larkin's most haunting 'time' poem, formally varied. 'Wants' has something of the power of MacNeice, though it is more condensed in expression.

The most interesting poems in *The Less Deceived* are 'Church Going' and 'At Grass'. 'Church Going' expresses finally the speaker's respect for what he cannot commit himself to, the hallowedness of a dead faith. He is an ironic cyclist, removing his clips as one might remove one's hat, 'in awkward reverence'. Religion is for him a matter of aesthetics. The details he notices illuminate the faith that has had its being there and the visitor, his attitudes, and his unparaphrasable response, tinged with superstition and wishfulness, rationalized as respect, though it goes much deeper: 'someone will always be surprising / A hunger in himself to be more serious' is strangely pious; the speaker stands at the tomb of something he has not known, except through its history, ceremonial and rich language. Faith cannot get inside him; he feels no grief, but a sort of hunger.

Another change came in *The Whitsun Weddings* (1964). The perspective widens, the images derive from broader experience, and the vision becomes social. In a world heavy with late capitalism, a world of transactions and relationships which time renders senseless, the tragedy of ephemerality and unfulfilment moves out from the 'I'. The first poem in the book, 'Here', progresses panoramically through the details of landscape that reveal a community, its history and ambitions, much as the details in 'Church Going' revealed a faith. The panorama is urban, with the teeming 'cut-price crowd'; and rural, 'where removed lives / loneliness clarifies'. The juxtaposition of two isolations – individuals isolated in the crowd and the individual isolated in the landscape – is heightened by the speaker's isolation from both, a middleman undertaking a verbal transaction. In 'Wants', a particularly powerful poem, the world divides between those who find despair incomprehensible and those who find it unspeakable. Other poems in the collection revisit earlier themes from the position of advanced maturity.

'Ambulances' may be Larkin's most entirely successful

poem. It fuses various themes allusively. The ambulances are 'closed like confessionals', an image which sets going a thread of religious suggestion, implying absolution. Later in the poem Larkin writes, 'All streets in time are visited' – implying Visitation and redemption from life, as much as the congenial arrival of friends. In seeing the ambulances people sense 'the solving emptiness / That lies just under all we do'.

In *High Windows* there seem to be more Larkins at work than at any time since *The North Ship*. The Larkin of 'Here' reappears – without his earlier power – in 'To the Sea' and 'Show Saturday'. His attempt to celebrate certain social customs and rites is hampered by his native temperament. He knows the rites, too, have their date. The voice of Browning can be heard in 'Livings (iii)': perhaps Larkin will embark on dramatic monologues. There are, too, some notable successes in essentially new tones. 'High Windows' itself has, in all but the first stanza, assurance, candour, and an unresolved suggestiveness only seldom found in the earlier work. The same quality, but a different tone, informs 'The Explosion', about a pit disaster. 'The Old Fools' has a brutality and asperity which are tempered into tenderness. Age is treated with more sense of immediacy.

A disturbing aspect of *High Windows* is that six of the poems are cheap in some of their effects. The poet hankers to be one of the chaps, to speak their sort of language. This ambition was anticipated in *The Whitsun Weddings* in such poems as 'A Study of Reading Habits' and 'Send no Money'. But the faults run deeper in *High Windows*, the fake bonhomie results in an entirely gratuitous vulgarity. Is Larkin trying to embody the process of degeneration he sees in society within the very language of the poem? His power in the past derived from an unwillingness to compromise form and voice with subject matter: *they* at least remained clear and powerful. Here language begins to ape experience, to unfortunate effect. In chastising certain types of shallowness and self-deception, he uses the language of the shallow and self-deceived.

If *The Whitsun Weddings* opened into a wider social and topographical perspective, *High Windows* looks to the future of society and the polluted landscape. It is Larkin's most civic-minded display. There is fatalistic prophecy, even as he celebrates recurrences, however trivial. The loss or the wastage – of empire, landscape, values, rites, and so on – are a dominant concern in *High Windows* and may be further developed in its sequel.

Michael Hamburger (born 1924)

What had he seen, ushered behind the gate?
The dress and furniture of his own terrors,
A glittering medal pinned on his own wound,
And, at the heart, an empty hall of mirrors.

The distance between Michael Hamburger the young poet and Michael Hamburger the mature poet, translator and critic, is so great that we can readily sympathize when the later poet speaks of his difficulty in 'relating myself to work done by a writer altogether different from the one I now feel myself to be'. From the chilly craftsmanship of the early poems he first multiplied his formal resources and then began experimenting with free verse and stress patterns as well as metre. The young and the older man share little but the seriousness of their vocation and certain themes. While the young man's poetry was devoutly literary, its models visible in phrasing and rhythm, its concerns primarily aesthetic, the older man feels that perfection, neatness, and formal demands which reduce, simplify or blur experience are invalid, that poetry is not a literary activity so much as a quest. Though he is one of the most erudite of modern poets, he is also among the least 'literary' in his recent work.

Born in Berlin in 1924, Michael Leopold Hamburger's early childhood was characterized by the starched propriety of the prosperous pre-war bourgeoisie. His father was a distinguished physician and amateur musician, and his son inherited his interest in music. As tension mounted in Germany, the Hamburger family emigrated (1933), first to

Edinburgh and then to London, exchanging the comforts of their German life for the hardship of readjustment. In London Hamburger attended St Paul's School and, later, Oxford, where his term of study, interrupted by military service, was completed. At Oxford his interest in Hölderlin matured and he prepared translations of the German poet whose work – in England – became closely associated with his name. His first collection, *Flowering Cactus*, appeared in 1950.

He had two totally different traditions to draw on and his work has always drawn on both. His eyes have been resolutely open to European and, more recently, American poetry in both traditional and experimental veins. As Joyce Crick has written, 'He can place himself in that line of linguistic scepticism and eclecticism of tradition that characterizes the modern movement.' His major critical book, *The Truth of Poetry* (1969), reveals a breadth of reference and sympathy unusual particularly in British literary criticism.

Recognizing the multiplicity of choices open to him, he has not, like Christopher Middleton, been drawn to experimental writing. Perhaps this is because Hamburger learned – among many lessons – one in particular from Edwin Muir, whose 'utter lack of pretension' Hamburger has commented on in his perceptive essay on Muir. Hamburger works towards an intellectual clarity; and while he is always conscious of surface effects, he is primarily interested in what he has to say and form.

Yet his style integrates material from other writers – from Hölderlin, from Beethoven's letters (in 'At Fifty-five'), and from a variety of other sources. His poems are rooted in a consciousness of Western literature. There are curious verbal and thematic cross-references, too, from poem to poem. In a way he has developed in the opposite direction from Middleton: from an early, hermetic, literary and sometimes obscure style he has tended towards lucidity, complexity of thought rather than artificial complexity of expression. He has outgrown the Yeatsian manner (G. S. Fraser spoke of him 'ghosting for the ghost of Yeats' in his early poems), and his Metaphysical manner (though this sometimes afflicts him still in the would-be satires of recent years).

Hamburger's principal collections since *Flowering Cactus* include *Poems 1950–51* (1952), *The Dual Site* (1958), *Weather and Season* (1963), *Feeding the Chickadees* (1968), *Travelling* (1969) and *Ownerless Earth: New and Selected Poems* (1973), in which he prunes severely from the *oeuvre* and rightly discards many of his most artificial poems in favour of less perfect literary objects, but more vital poems.

The earliest work is dominated by the image of the double: reflections, exact analogies, twins. These are the two lives, as well, German and English, as yet unresolved. The young poet saw – in 'A Poet's Progress' – the final artistic achievement as aesthetic sterility, 'the cold intensity of art' – poet and poem to be endured by others. This ascetic, devotional approach, reliant as it was on French Symbolist models, led to obscurities of style, a lack of social commitment, indeed an almost total devotion to the forms. Few of the early poems are generous in what they give the reader.

An exception is the poem 'Hölderlin', the most gnomic, clipped, and irregular of the early poems, spoken by Hölderlin in his madness. It has a passion and veracity lacking from other early poems. The speaker's madness makes it possible for Hamburger to short-circuit images, transform them, and juxtapose the intensely emotional with objective description, integrating, too, lines from Hölderlin's poems. Yet there is an element of calculation even here. The speaking voice sounds stilted, the persona is too well-rehearsed.

In 'The Tempest', an early poem, the speaker is Prospero, the arranger. His magic has failed, he is enslaved by Caliban, while Miranda bears little Calibans to people the isle. The poem reflects the young poet's sense of being miscast, finding himself at once aloof and humiliated, having power and yet being a victim – of that power. The poem stylizes the tensions from which Hamburger's later poems develop. He is undecided, neither insider nor outsider. He is attracted to the madman, the outlaw, the damned, the bohemian, but he cannot join them. They are the dark side of his chilly adolescence and early manhood: Judas, Hölderlin, the traduced Prospero, Icarus, and the frog, ugly and longing, suffering in the lake 'his tortured multiplicity', consumed by a desire to be other. Some of the poems are humorous and perhaps for this reason more powerful than the glumly earnest ones. Hamburger is drawn to the Christians lionized at the Roman circus, to Philoctetes and – unfortunately and at some length – to Narcissus. Consumed by internal passions, these characters are all aspects of a basic inharmony.

In 'The Dual Site' – an epistolary ballad – Hamburger achieved his first outstanding poem. Though his craft is barely up to the chosen form, he uses the form freely, pares down his over-adjectival early style, and defines the basic tensions of his early work: 'To my twin who lives in a cruel country / I wrote a letter at last,' he begins. The reluctant decision to write to that twin was perhaps poetically the crucial act in Hamburger's development. We may feel that the model of this poem has stayed fresh in his mind, that its doric simplicity of diction has restrained his later rhetoric, while its dramatic directness has helped to perfect his tone. Of the twins, one is an accountant, earnest, dedicated, conventionally stable but not content. The other fuses aspects of those types which had drawn Hamburger earlier. He is:

... one who forgets what I remember,
  Who knows what I do not,
Who has learnt the ways of otter and raven
  While I've grown polyglot.

Careless, brutal, he seems to possess a vital truth his twin craves and fears. The political and psychological overtones are disturbing. There is some hope of an eventual, if brief, reconciliation – in the act of building a house on 'the dual site'. Only in that creative act can the time-bound and the time-taunting come together, the man of mind and the man of energy.

It was some time before Hamburger ceased hankering

---

after a complex style. His early poems lacked a sense of the physical world, the art was stronger than the experience, though he has since 'learnt the ways of otter and raven' and used the knowledge in his poems. There was, too, a tendency to expatiate and moralize on inadequate particulars. There were, however, a number of successes: 'Weather and Season', 'Arctic Explorer', 'Horseman, Pedestrian, Dog', and 'Epitaph for a Horseman' among them. As the poems began to convey experience rather than thought after experience, Hamburger came to understand the possibility of an imperfect, responsible, open manner.

Satire stirs in his middle poems, and he vividly expresses his own self-discovery in 'Conformist', perhaps the best of his shorter poems. From being a conformist he moves through an initiation ceremony and out again 'to breathe the ownerless air':

His own place found at last; his own self found—
Outside, outside – his heritage regained
By grace of exile, of expropriation.

He became an outsider, and has remained so ever since, 'Healed now, of health, unmasked, of honesty', he has seen through the sham of conformity. The new freedom has implicit terrors for the newcomer, 'Come late into the freedom his from birth, / To breathe the air and walk the ownerless earth'. He is now one of those outsiders he had long admired.

Language, Hamburger realizes, can falsify through sophistry, irresponsible word choice, imprecision, and through the schemes it articulates, excluding whole areas of experience. In 'Words' he admits how 'curious' the poet's trade is, 'Turning a thing into words so that words will render the thing'. The debasing of words through journalism is one danger. Matters of great moment are neutralized, defused, made statistical, until 'nothing hurts – Nothing'. The line contains the paradox: nothing is able to pain us, and yet that very nothing pains us. This is Davie's theme, too, but he takes it in a different direction. To him the debasement of language implies a loss of history and values, not merely of responsiveness; and the deprivation of posterity. Hamburger sees it as destructive of community, Davie sees it as destructive of the individual, a necessary step in our descent into inarticulate mass culture.

Hamburger is not often a successful satirist. 'The Soul of Man Under Capitalism', 'Little Cosmology', 'Orpheus Street, SE5', and other social poems have a facility in their ironies. The attitudes and some of the allusions are too easy. Hamburger requires the agreement of his audience. His satires are to a degree elegiac, for he is involved in the losses he laments or evokes.

In his dream poems Hamburger began the course that would lead to 'Travelling'. He passes through imaginary landscapes, the transition from dream image to image is deft, and there is a fluidity which characterizes his later style. The stylistic model for 'Travelling' may be the poem 'Gone', an elegiac dramatic monologue interspersed with Hamburger's commentary, dedicated to and in part spoken by the poet Thomas Good. Hamburger transforms him into an archetypal, rootless, travelling man; a man who failed, but seems to transcend failure in his decision to up and go. One further step preceded 'Travelling' – the development of poems sufficiently direct to carry obliquely, not confessionally, details of autobiography of some importance and pain to the poet. Two such poems are 'Dust' and 'Mad Lover, Dead Lady', the latter effectively allegorized by drawing on the Hölderlin analogy.

'Travelling' grew from one poem with four sections to five poems (as it appears in *Ownerless Earth*) and, later, a sixth poem was added. The 'traveller' stops, observes, and then moves on. Desolated by a personal loss, his experience does not fit in with the world he moves through. Images of his own past recur, and historical images are suggested by marks on the landscape, ruins in particular. Ruined buildings in the context of natural continuity are evocative images for Hamburger. In observation the traveller seeks self-forgetfulness, but memory keeps breaking in. Gradually through the poems he comes to terms with the loss of his beloved – a resignation made possible by the poet's giving himself over to observation. He finds his bearings in a painfully physical world, and he eventually asserts the fact that love continues even when relationship ends. As 'Travelling' has grown, it has drawn in more and more experiences. The poems are interrelated by cross-reference, recurrent imagery, and the evolution of the theme – travelling without a necessary destination. It is Hamburger's most original poem.

In his later poems Hamburger has resolved the dual tension of his early work. He chose finally to be an outsider. Purging himself of his moral rigidity, loosening too his forms, he has none the less not ceased to be something of an ascetic, and the true economy of his later style shows the virtue of his asceticism, much as the severely well-wrought and adjective-larded early style reflected an ascetic's over-application to the labour of writing. Hamburger remains in doubt about the continuity of his personality, in view of the distance he has travelled from the young man he was. But in the poems we read an evolution.

Elizabeth Jennings (born 1926)

Haven't you often been caught out in dreams
And changed your terms of reference, escaped
From the long rummaging with words, with things
Then found the very purpose that you mapped
Has moved?

'Poets work upon and through each other,' Elizabeth
Jennings wrote in *Every Changing Shape* (1961) – a critical
study of mystical and poetic expression. She adds that 'the
real meaning of tradition and influence' is the natural, indeed
inevitable, relationship and interdependence between poets.
She shares Eliot's notion of the contemporaneity of all literature. Her own poetry – that of a devout Roman Catholic
whose faith colours even her secular poems – does not surprise
us when it suggests analogies to Traherne, Herbert, Vaughan;
or to Hopkins, Eliot and Muir. Her verse, however, is not
derivative. Distinctive in tone, with at times telltale mannerisms and an individual appreciation of traditional form, an
unassertive rigour and candour characterize her best poems.

Elizabeth Jennings was born in Boston, Lincolnshire, in
1926, the daughter of a physician. When still a child her
family moved to Oxford. Roman Catholic by birth, her
religion was of crucial importance to her even as a child. The
severity of English Catholicism, a certain formality in her
parental relationship, made her reticent and acutely sensitive.

She went to school in Oxford, and later to the University,
where she read English. After going down, she worked in the
Oxford Public Library. She encouraged various near-

contemporary poets, undergraduates at the time. The influence of her early poems can be felt in the apprentice work of Alan Brownjohn, and of Anthony Thwaite who in reviewing her *Collected Poems* called her 'one of the two best living English poets under forty-five'. The other was Larkin.

She began writing poetry as an adolescent, turning out mock-Eliot free verse. But her contact with Metaphysical verse and the work of Graves and Auden at University chastened her style. In 1953 her first collection, *Poems,* appeared in the Fantasy Press list. It drew attention to her talents and *A Way of Looking* (1955) won her the Somerset Maugham Award, on the proceeds of which she travelled to Italy for the first time. Italy held a strong attraction for her, and so did Italian literature. She translated *The Sonnets of Michelangelo* (1961).

Her early successes – which later came to haunt her as 'The stance of prowess and the famous days' – included various awards, and her collections followed on one another with regularity. *A Sense of the World* (1958) and *Song for a Birth or a Death* (1961) were followed by the collections in which the intellectual tensions of the early verse began to be intensified into the particular emotional tensions of her nervous illness. *Recoveries* (1964) and *The Mind Has Mountains* (1966) were the culmination of her early style, the latter concentrating on her experiences of hospitalization with other mental patients. Her *Collected Poems* (1967), published when she was forty-one, reflect in their chronological progression her development from an essentially thinking poet to a feeling and suffering poet.

Though Robert Conquest adopted her for The Movement, she shared only superficial similarities with the hard-line Movementeers, Kingsley Amis, Conquest himself, Larkin, John Wain, and early Davie. She – and they – employed traditional metrics, strove for a plain diction and a lucid line of exposition. But where Empson seemed a viable model to the young John Wain, and where other Movementeers depended on the pseudo-honesty of understatement or ironic deflation, Elizabeth Jennings showed no traces of ironic wit, nor was she capable of satire. A lyrical poet, her main attitude is of trust, quite out of keeping with the Movement's programmatic distrust. Nor did she react against the Apocalyptic poets of the forties. She has written sympathetically and at length on the work of David Gascoyne and other *bêtes noires* of The Movement.

Before her illness, she worked in publishing in London, and her editorial projects have included anthologies, critical writing, and children's books. Since her recovery, she has been a freelance critic, anthologist and poet, making occasional lecture and reading tours.

Poetry is essential to her. There is more than vocation in her need to write. A solitary person, through poetry she can make connections between her often insecure world and the apparently stable world about her, between her doubt and the objects of her faith. She has compared the making of poems to the practice of prayer. Each is an attempt to reconcile the individual with what is outside it, a momentary 'loss of self' or breach of isolation. Her many poems on art and artists explore not the works themselves but their applicability to life, or the nature of the artist's own commitment to his work. In 'Rembrandt's Late Self-Portraits' she writes: 'To paint's to breathe / And all the darknesses are dared.' The idea that to express the personal darkness will alleviate it – confession as well as prayer – is inherent in her vision of art: sacramental in the sense of *binding*. The Christian element goes deeper; it affects technique. She often writes with implicit allegory. In 'Visit to an Artist' she best embodies the sacramental function of art. There the host and wine – the sacrifice – which the experience underlies, validates and sanctifies, are most real and impart an ultimate validity to the poetic act.

She began as a love poet and a poet examining relationships – between objects and between individuals. There was also a concern with self-definition, and her reiteration of the theme of individual isolation is as obsessive (though more subjective) as Hardy's. 'The Island', an early allegorical poem, addresses Donne and the Arnold of 'To Marguerite':

Each brings an island in his heart to square
With what he finds, and all is something strange
And most expected.

The 'mind', a word she uses frequently, has its own unpredictable patterns, is a place where the betrayals of self deeper
into self occur. Time rather than space obsesses her, despite
the images of travel, exploration and discovery; and in this
she resembles Muir. The elegiac note dominates even the
poems of celebration. Love seems to exist in tension with the
mind, that unbreachable isolation; time in tension both with
the ephemeral that it sweeps away and with the recurrences
it brings round. Dreams, silence and solitude recur as well. A
further image is that of habitation – whether bed-sitter or
house – with its always vulnerable stability. Recent poems
have explored the disruption of uprooting from one dwelling
to another, the sudden confrontation with the objects a lifetime has accumulated for a particular world, as that world
crumbles.

What her early poems allegorized and imagined became
real: the nightmare of mental illness where 'the mind' became a labyrinth. Out of that experience came a different
poet whose human insights are more penetrating and whose
formal style has moved closer to individual voice. The disrupted style of her expressionist poems, gathered near the end
of the *Collected Poems*, where she abandoned metre, rhyme,
and punctuation in favour of free association, are notable
failures. She is not temperamentally a formal innovator. She
needs traditional form to discover order *or* disorder – the
sense of form in a way precedes the experience of the poem.
The experience of loss, uncertainty of continuous identity,
frustration, the ephemerality of time marks and land marks,
her rootlessness, all contributed to her disorder. They were
themes carefully explored in the early poems. 'It was by
negatives I learned my place', one poem says, and another,
'It is acceptance she arranges', having understood the
desolation and survived it.

An outstanding poem of her early period is 'Song for a

Birth or a Death'. Love and fear, sharing and isolation, become painfully real:

Last night I saw the savage world
And heard the blood beat up the stair;
The fox's bark, the owl's shrewd pounce,
The crying creatures – all were there,
And men in bed with love and fear.

The slit moon only emphasised
How blood must flow and teeth must grip.
What does the calm night understand,
The light which draws the tide and ship
And drags the owl upon its prey
And human creatures lip to lip?

'And cries of love are cries of fear', the poem ends. The extreme experiences which followed distorted her early style. From within the regimented, more or less secure world of the hospital, poems in the old forms, using the new content, were possible. Back in the 'savage world', the poet's adjustment was difficult. Her early style seemed too oblique, 'a clearer style' became her object. Still within the confines of her early forms, she began to write more directly, and the evolution was gradual. As she says in a poem to her father, 'I had all my emotions to rearrange.' The confessional note dominates in *The Animals' Arrival* (1969), *Lucidities* (1970), and *Relationships* (1972). Fearing the loss of her poetic skills, she came to rely on an unalloyed directness sometimes betrayed by her forms, causing her to force rhymes, to oversimplify. These faults were inherent in the transition to a new style. The reciprocity she had managed to establish in her early poems, discovering meanings in objects so that with authority she could write, 'Now deep in my bed / I turn and the world turns on the other side', was temporarily beyond her power.

In the best poems in *Growing Points* (1975) she achieved her new voice and a new authority. Here the old symbols, images and themes recur, but with different significance, in more personal rhythms, and often in the context of celebra-

Elizabeth Jennings 351

tion. The sonnet sequence that opens the book includes poems of love observed and received, not of the lover; sonnets, in other words, from a peculiar standpoint of gratitude and sympathy, not passion. To be loved is an intense experience, just as, in her earlier writing, the experience of thought could be as intense as physical experience.

The collection includes experimental long-lined poems, owing a debt to Hopkins, and tending towards a rhapsodic style which is new ground for her. To rhapsodize ideas is difficult, and a certain prolixity mars the attempts. But the poems which contain an element of fantasy, 'The Princess', for example, suggest a possible further development in this direction. She has always written prose poems, and the long-lined poems grow out of that practice, attempting a less restricted idiom.

Without confessional detail, the intense lyrics in *Growing Points* avoid the pitfalls of the three previous collections. 'I Feel' develops with a self-absorbed repetitiveness, a tension near hysteria. The control intensifies the experience and the poem resolves in an ambiguous death-wish – it is also a wish to give life:

But better to be turned to earth
Where other things at least can grow.
I would be then a part of birth,
Passive, not knowing how to know.

Her inability to be passive to suffering, to construct adequate defences, is the source of some of the best poetry, particularly the religious poems. In 'Towards a Religious Poem' the first stanza describes the degradation of faith and the corruption of its language. The poem ends:

In my stanzas I'll only allow
The silence of a tripped tongue,
The concerns and cries of creation
To hold you, as always, but more now.
The prophets and all their books prosper,

But here as a Christmas comes closer,
Awe will be speechless, and magic
Be dropped like an acrobat's pitfall
The absence, the emptiness echo,
A girl with a cradle to borrow.

Doubt does not arise now, but there is the recrimination of the believer against an all too often distant deity: 'When we most need a tongue we only find / Christ at his silentest.'

What seems to have disappeared from the later poems, a quality too prevalent in the poems of transition, is the 'I' incapable of generalizing a particular experience of disorientation. In *Growing Points* trust has returned, the poet has 'changed her points of reference' – naturally, for the style and the thematic experience has evolved, has not been forced forwards, and the fretful self-concern is transformed into a poetry of wider reference and greater particularity than before – with, too, the added resonance of new rhythms.

Christopher Middleton
(born 1926)

as I climb forever
out of myself

Christopher Middleton's style developed more rapidly than the taste of his readers, and at the height of his early success he chose to emigrate. His work has, as a result, been neglected in England. An acute critic, his thought about poetry and poetics is still ahead of his poetic achievement. But it is probable that the lessons of modernism embodied in his later poetic and critical work will be the lessons most accessible to young poets in the next ten years. Though Middleton has not settled finally on a style, in all his explorations he suggests new choices, breaks new ground.

He was born in Truro, Cornwall, in 1926. His family removed to Ely and later to Cambridge where his father, a distinguished organist, became a Senior Lecturer in Music. Middleton attended school at Lowestoft and Felsted, spent three and a half years in the Air Force, and returned to read German and French at Oxford (1948–51). He lectured in English at Zurich, in German at King's College, London, and in 1965 emigrated and became Professor of Germanic Languages and Literature at the University of Texas.

His poems have always explored the *idea* of poetry as well as their subjects. The first collection he acknowledges, *Torse 3: Poems 1949–61* (1962) owes a debt to Wallace Stevens, but already his eyes are opening on experimental fields. Translation, fiction and criticism supplemented his poetic activity.

In 1963 he was awarded the first Geoffrey Faber Memorial

Prize. In 1965 *Nonsequences/Selfpoems* appeared, and his direction was clear. None of his readers could have been surprised by the multiplicity of possibilities suggested in his third collection, *Our Flowers and Nice Bones* (1969), and the refinement of those tendencies in *The Lonely Suppers of W. V. Balloon* (1975) and *Pataxanadu* (1976). In the latter books he has settled more or less on a single process, if not a consistent style, having learned lessons from his experiments with concrete and sound poetry, surrealism, expressionism, and so on.

'Torse 3' marks the opening of Middleton's experimental career. He takes the definition of 'torse' from the dictionary and makes a 'found poem' of it:

Torse 3
[f. med. L. torsus, —um,
for L. *tortus* twisted.]
Geom. A developable surface;
a surface generated
by a moving straight line
which at every instant is turning,
in some plane or other through it,
about some point or other
in its length.

The 'torse' is the poem. Sculptural, musical and graphic analogies are implicit in it. There is a constant from and about which the poem develops.

So abstract a statement is perhaps too open. It can accommodate any form of experimentation. Middleton meant it to do so. He has followed every experimental development – in the United States, on the continent, and elsewhere. He has written poems for the sound poet Ernst Jandl, translated the German expressionists, the Russian Acmeists, learned from Jarry and from Browning, late Hölderlin, Brecht, and Edward Lear, from the Dadaists and Spanish poets. The eclecticism of his work is startling.

Perhaps the guiding influence is Robert Walser. Middleton learned from him lessons of disruption: the effect of broken syntax, abrupted rhythms, free association. Words seemed more weighty if scattered in visual patterns, and Middleton has at times practised 'field theory'. He has written skeletal poems which the reader fleshes out. In effect, de-formation of language must precede significant formation.

He quotes Jarry – 'a painter who does what *is* and not what is conventional'. De-formation avoids the prescriptive, the forms must always be new, unique. There is at the same time an attraction for the abstract, which is pure form. This provides a corrective for the poet. The tension is between regenerative tendencies – attention to things – and decadent, post-symbolist tendencies. There is no primitivism in his work, though Middleton calls himself a 'Byzantine primitive' – only a sophistication which sometimes attempts a pseudo-naïvety. 'Truth' lies in the contradictions: there is no formula but a committed noncommittedness; not ideas but the processes of thought and association. 'The work of contradiction entails constant attacks on the cliché,' he wrote. It also entails a resolute impersonality – which, as in Eliot's case, becomes a strong *sense* of personality.

He shares something of the Scottish poet Ian Hamilton Finlay's eccentricity. Finlay writes – in a prose that mimes the difficult and tenuous process of his thought – of 'the poem, of an order which is different from the sort of order known to those who feel society stretching to the *edge* of the world, as it were – who are safe in that *family*, and who don't know in their *body* that question about *form*, and who therefore feel language as a *home*-thing, which I don't and never have. (But by *form* it is made familiar.)' The poet does not take language as given. He questions its function, not merely its meanings, even as he writes. The poem is self-conscious, self-involved. The dangers of such an approach are all too evident in some of Middleton's poems.

He has said that, in his case, 'the act of writing is often prepared by a distinctive moment in experience . . . at which everything, including . . . language, seems to be decomposed. This (Dada) moment is announced by the birth of a phrase, which has a distinct rhythm and resonance.' The phrase may

become the 'point' in the 'Torse 3' poem, serving sometimes
as 'a rhythmic and harmonic model for the evolving poem'.
Poems are 're-visions' of 'the code' of language, of vision. His
rhythms often reverse common notions of rhythm as 'integrating flow, a continuity factor', stressing instead discontinuity. What occurs in his poems sometimes occurs *only* in
the language – the poet is so busy gazing at his vehicle that it
fails to get him anywhere. But the impulse of many of the
poems is strong enough to render the problem secondary.

There is, logically if not always poetically, a radical truth
in Middleton's approach. 'I seek to interdict the code, so that
a true message may be generated.' 'Poems have become
experiences which did not exist before the poem.' Poems
which 'interdict the code' do it often on a basic level, breaking
syntax, introducing pauses. These gaps, pauses, silences,
become functional and eloquent, the visual disposition of the
poem on the page assumes importance. He calls his structures,
rhythms, and visual patterns 'enactive'.

'Seven Hunters' shows Middleton's early technique and its
dramatic directness. The line endings and quiet rhythms
release the energy of the image with clarity:

Now in our town the streets
and houses have gone.
Here, underground, we
who were seven are one.

Obscurity, even in the early poems, is not in the vocabulary
but in the difficult allusiveness. Furthermore, the rhythms
suggest logical progression, while in fact the poem is frequently discontinuous in syntax and works by association.
He can develop a complex perceptual or intellectual insight
that defies paraphrase, in which the *sense* of meaning precedes the meaning. 'Climbing a Pebble', like 'At Portcothan',
carries its meanings in the relationship between the images.
The fortuitous, the unexpected, is always near at hand. He
rejects the Augustanism of his contemporaries in The Movement: 'The owls / have built a stinking nest in the Eighteenth
Century.' Yet he is after order, too: if not a total order, then

points of order in an apparent chaos. He is also concerned with antecedents – individual poets, and earlier genres which he tries to extend: the aubade, the psalm, the ballad, and forms adopted by analogy from other arts. The impulse behind his creative work is fear of chaos. In 'Five Psalms of Common Man' he writes: 'The orders resolve in improvisations against fear, / changed images of chaos. Without fear, nothing.'

'Itinerary for the Apparent Double' is a thematic key to Middleton's transition in *Nonsequences/Selfpoems*. It describes the stable road and the fears and threats lurking beside it. Dominant images are travel, pilgrimage; tensions between what the mind remembers and what it senses it has forgotten; the disturbing duplicity of experience, betraying us out of what might have been. With quiet rhetoric he achieves some powerful political poems, especially 'January 1919'; and the love poems are strongly lyrical, 'For a Future' among the best. Middleton carries the political analogy into the heart of his technique, and in 'Difficulties of a Revisionist' – with a nice pun in the title – he writes:

All day fighting for a poem. Fighting against what?
And for what? What? being its own danger, wants
to get rescued, but from its rescuer?

In *Our Flowers and Nice Bones* (1969) the quest for the new leads Middleton to formal dissipation, a poetry which exists largely to worry at itself. The broken code releases few new meanings: it is too busy looking at its scars and bruises. He tells us, 'I have been trying to write poems which are structures, not declarations.' But the best poems in the collection *are* declarations of perception or experience: witnessings. He talks about the various voices, the one that speaks, the one that examines the act of speaking, and so on. There is a vitiating cuteness, a belief that poetry can exist in disjunction only. He looks to surrealism, but refuses to commit himself to it. The comic element vindicates a few of the experiments, in particular 'Armadillo Cello Solo'; and there are some fine poems of a serious nature, notably 'Avebury: The Temple',

'The Armadillos', and 'Bonard', and a number of prose poems prefiguring the rich development of that mode in *Pataxanadu*.

The Lonely Suppers of W. V. Balloon shows that Middleton learned valuable skills from his experimental work, that he is coming closer to his own voice and that he has identified his own processes as a poet. He has in places achieved a wholeness of expression unprecedented in his earlier work. The poems resist quotation. An example of this wholeness is 'Snake Rock' in which three images are seen interchangeably in terms of one another. The confluence (not fusion) is of linguistic as well as sense associations – the tension is not merely in the language. In 'Mandelstam to Gumilev 1920' he freely translates a passage from Mandelstam, integrating it into his poem. It expresses the process of his own poems:

So take this gift, for the joy of it, this
Necklace, unassuming, made of dead bees:
They wove the honey, wove it back to sunlight.

To *de*-form, to *re*-form, to get behind the surfaces of language and of things, to renew by breaking and reassembling: this is Middleton's task.

And his achievement is considerable. 'Opoponax' ('all-healing juice') contains vivid effects in an unpunctuated passage where each line is a rhythmic and sense unit bearing similar weight, and great emphasis is cast on specific words:

A blue field for summer
Rib curve the dotted line of lavender
Discontinuous flesh beating a signal out
And a man
Lifts a heart on his knife
High

Violence and fear – like humour – hover at the edge of every experience.

In 'The Monk of Montandon' – an imitation of a dramatic monologue in the tradition of Browning's 'Soliloquy in a Spanish Cloister' – Middleton chooses a traditionally regular form. The monk manages to have his cake and eat it – he gets both Sanchicha *and* Dolores. The character sketches – whether of people or of animals – are Middleton's most immediately accessible poems.

Not bound to any prescriptive formula, *The Lonely Suppers* has the usual abundance. The 'micropoems' of 'The Fossil Fish' sequence, fleeting but at times vivid impressions, present not the static 'instamatic' effects which Edwin Morgan tries for, but something more deft and direct. The fifteenth 'micropoem' reads:

> the fossil fish
> hides in time
> for now it is the season
>
> & all the hunters come
> with long clean rifles

Variety of forms and subject matter are essential to Middleton. The same – even similar – forms cannot accommodate different experiences. Each poem must start from scratch.

Charles Tomlinson (born 1927)

Having mislaid it, and then
  Found again in a changed mind
The image . . .

Charles Tomlinson is a fastidious poet in his regard for
natural detail, technical effect, rhythmic nuance. Ascetic as
his work appears, it apprehends the realities he chooses to
write about far more elementally than the work of wilfully
primitive poets whose natural world is merely an extension of
the 'I'. Tomlinson fixes his attention on what *is*, opposing the
romantic impulse in himself. He does not personalize the
world he writes of, as Ted Hughes does. He respects the integrity of his subject matter which he once described in these
terms: 'The hardness of crystals, the facets of cut glass; but
also the shifting of light, the energizing weather which is the
result of the combination of sun and frost – these are the
images for a certain mental climate, components for the
moral landscape of my poetry in general.'

Charles Tomlinson was born in Stoke-on-Trent in 1927 into
a working-class family. He was educated locally and then
went to Cambridge, where he was tutored by – among others
– Donald Davie. Despite radical differences between their
poetries, they share certain qualities. Davie's chaste Augustanism and Tomlinson's imagism, and both poets' reluctant
optimism, stem from a similar temperament. They share
certain models. Each has learned important lessons from the
other.

Tomlinson's first collection, *The Necklace* (1955), showed

influences not then fashionable in England – particularly of Wallace Stevens, whose collection *Harmonium* was crucial to him. His reading had ranged widely in French as well. He has since translated from Spanish, French and Russian and been drawn towards surrealism of both the French and the Latin American schools, but only seldom has he attempted surreal writing. The main formal models for his early work, after Stevens, were William Carlos Williams, other American modernists, and the French Symbolists. It is not surprising that his verse found its early audience in the United States. He travelled and taught in that country and visited Mexico as well.

American critics have, however, been uneasy about him. One reviewer spoke of him half-scornfully as a well-mannered houseguest. Davie replied pertinently that an ill-mannered houseguest would have been more to the critic's taste. Tomlinson's poetry is, certainly, well-mannered. It consciously eschews the modish extremes – whether apocalyptic, confessional, ironist, or the analytical tendencies of experimental verse. In 'Against Extremity' he attacks imbalance and asserts the necessary reciprocity between poet and subject matter. It is a theme he returns to later in 'Ars Poetica', a poem dedicated to Al Alvarez.

His second collection, *Seeing is Believing*, was published first in the United States (1958) and later in England (1960). It was followed by *A Peopled Landscape* (1963), *American Scenes* (1966), *The Way of a World* (1969), *Written on Water* (1972) and *The Way In* (1974). Editorially and critically he has performed several valuable services for English readers, helping to popularize the poetry of Stevens, Williams, and other American writers, introducing in translation the work of Fyodor Tyuchev, Octavio Paz, Antonio Machado, and others, and he was among the first critics to recognize the stature of Rosenberg and Douglas. He is now Reader in English at the University of Bristol. He lives in an isolated part of Gloucestershire.

He is a graphic artist as well as a poet. The paintings, collages and sketches in some ways resemble the poems. The artist intrudes primarily as editor. The early drawings are bleak perspective renditions of images: skulls and cork-screws, for example. He moved on to collages, to 'landscapes' which were chance brushstrokes or smears that happened as landscapes – or faces. There is a sense of the paintings *occurring*. The creative act comes after, is the scissors that snip out the formed bit and discard the rest. So, too, the poet finds, does not impose. The clarity of the graphic work is however sometimes surreal, sometimes abstract, occasionally allegorical, while the poems rest firmly in a real world, however much they move out from it.

'According objects their own existence,' Tomlinson describes as his purpose in his first book. This means their existence in *time*, not arrested – as the Imagists urge – in a timeless way. The objects change or develop as the light alters. Recently, he has summarized his themes as 'place' and 'the return'. In poems evoking the western American landscape, he returns to the fantastic rocks in different lights. Their configurations change.

In a recent essay Tomlinson quotes D. H. Lawrence's dictum, 'All creative art must rise out of a specific soil and flicker with the spirit of place.' He adds, 'Since we live in a time when place is threatened by the violence of change, the thought of a specific soil carries tragic implications.' He suggests the difference between time-hallowed ruins and our contemporary experience of seeing ruin*ed* by development all that we know and love. There is a difference between the heaped-up history of Rome, where past and present coexist, and the erasures of modern Bristol, destroyed by 'avarice and callous utopianism'. Modern Bristol is being robbed of historical identity.

Earlier in his career, he was not so alive to the changes as to the things. In the first poems the theme of return was synonymous with contemplation, an attempt to translate objects and experiences truthfully and objectively in language. His first poems owe to the French Symbolists certain aspects of technique. In registering the impression of sight, he engages all his senses: colour has a taste and sound, sound has a texture. Analogies are drawn, too, between the arts. The early poems develop with a lightness of touch, but complex perceptions are communicated. Objects seem to acquire for him a symbolic quality.

Seeing is Believing is more Tomlinson's own book. Still impersonal in the best sense, he presents a world of objects not aspiring to symbolic value, objects which gain 'content' or meaning from their context in a natural setting. In *A Peopled Landscape* he takes a further step, rebelling against the popular critical view of his work as coldly aesthetic.

Among the best poems in *A Peopled Landscape* is 'Return to Hinton' – modelled on the technique of Williams. Tomlinson breaks the lines: they progress as phrases, rhythmic units. The rhythm is tentative – he will not let a metrical regularity take hold for fear of blurring the experience: a continuous rhythm might impose a tone of response untrue to the subject. This poem, like others in the book, moves with compelling unexpectedness. Syntax tends one way at the end of a phrase, but when we read on, it goes in another direction; or the rhythm points one way, is arrested, and goes off in another direction. The technique compels a slow, phrased reading. The rhythmic subtlety can be appreciated in a formally less inventive poem, 'Winter-Piece':

Gates snap like gunshot
as you handle them. Five-barred fragility
sets flying fifteen rooks who go together
silently ravenous above this winter-piece
that will not feed them.

The third line is iambic, a pentameter with an extra unstressed syllable, smooth and flowing. It is the line of action, the flight of the birds. The metrically irregular lines before and after build up to and down from the action, set the scene and then resolve it. The subtle manipulation of the rhythms eases the image into action, and then into significance.

If there is more energy in his third volume, it may in part be due to his reading of Keith Douglas, whose direct influence can be felt in the poem 'The Chestnut Avenue', especially in the phrasing of lines six and seven. There is, too, from book to book, a broadening of scope and a refusal to cover the same ground twice. Once a poem is written, it has made some area of experience intelligible. That area of experience need not be approached again by the imagination. The imagination, Tomlinson suggests in 'The Impalpabilities', can only act upon material that is not yet intelligible, where connections are perceived solely by imagination:

It is the sense
    of things that we must include
        because we do not understand them
the impalpabilities
    in marine dark
        the chords
that will not resolve themselves

American Scenes includes experiments with a 'witty' language. In 'The Snow Fences' he describes 'the breathtaking rareness of winter air'. Alliteration and inner rhyme arrest us, and then the double meanings in 'breathtaking' and 'rare'. There is, too, in this collection, a tendency towards the abstract. The poet brings the poem back to the images, but the impulse is away from them. Detail and image are, however, no longer ends in themselves. They anchor the poem in a perceived world, but the poem's ambitions are elsewhere: in the metamorphosis of images and what this implies. From perceiving a stable world of things, Tomlinson turns to the processes that implicate those things and change them. The word 'process' comes to have special significance for him.

One of his best short poems, 'The Fox', illustrates his technical processes. The image is of a dead fox. The poet focuses attention on it so intensely that it comes to fill the whole frame; the fox's skull becomes the winter landscape, through which the poet stumbles. Both fox and landscape are points of departure. The poet's real concern is with death, the permanent 'ambitious, cruel bone' (Douglas's phrase) underlying externals, the recurrent winter underlying the processes of the other seasons, and the moods of winter. Another poem,

'Bone', attempts the same effect more directly. But in comparing the poems we see how much better Tomlinson is at obliquity, indirection, implicit statement, than at direct meditation on the image.

The Way of a World is Tomlinson's first major collection. It opens with what many readers consider his best poem, 'Swimming Chenango Lake'. In it, the whole body engages the image of Chenango Lake in North America. The image is registered as sensation and – on another level – as an extension of the body. Yet there is reciprocity. The body (not itself described) is an extension of the image, the point at which the image becomes articulate.

To begin with, visual detail dominates. The speaker's eye observes the scene, before the body dives. It perceives the surface reflections as:

> a geometry and not
> A fantasia of distorting forms, but each
> Liquid variation answerable to the theme
> It makes away from, plays before:
> It is a consistency, the grain of the pulsating flow.

The word 'grain' is important, signifying a constant texture. When the eye has seen, 'Body must recall the eye to its dependence'. The body dives and itself becomes dependent on water, is for a time part of what it swims in, yet distinct:

> to swim is also to take hold
> On water's meaning, to move in its embrace
> And to be, between grasp and grasping, free.

The swimmer begins to 'construe' a 'lost language' in which the name 'Chenango' existed, a past language in which he is nameless. He swims in an alien history with which he briefly and instinctively participates. What Tomlinson expresses is the relationship and interplay between integrities: man, and the particular lake with its history.

'Prometheus', another poem in the collection, based on Scriabin's tone poem and his 'hope of transforming the world by music and rite', explores the nature and limits of artistic vision. It summons the spectres of the great artists of the early Russian revolution:

Scriabin, Blok, men of extremes,
    History treads out the music of your dreams
Through blood, and cannot close like this*
    In the perfection of anabasis. It stops. The trees
Continue raining though the rain has ceased
    In a cooled world of incessant codas.

The idealism produces great art – but Tomlinson notes the tragedy of such ambitions, referring to 'The daily prose such poetry prepares for'.

He uses frequently a form in which alternate long lines are indented. The indented lines take a secondary stress, and even where the lines are not end-rhymed, the form produces the effect of a couplet.

Perceiving as he does the integrity of different images, different worlds – in 'The Fox Gallery', contrasting the human and animal worlds, he comments, 'how utterly the two worlds were / disparate' – he shows them relating, modulating into one another but returning to themselves. 'Processes' are prose poems, a form he chooses for argument and abstract thought. In them he writes, 'One accords the process its reality, one does not deify it; inserted among it, one distinguishes and even transfigures, so that the quality of vision is never a prisoner of the thing seen.'

In his next book, *Written on Water*, he develops his aesthetic fully in the poem 'Movements'. He contemplates not only the process through which images reveal *their* nature, but the process of contemplation itself. In the fourth section of the poem he evokes the paradoxes of the process and how imagination reconciles them. The passage is subtly bound together by internal rhyme, assonance and alliteration:

How soon, in the going down, will he
    Outdistance himself, lose touch to gain
The confidence of what would use him? Where
    Does he stand – beyond the customary ritual,

* art

The habitual prayer? We live
    In an invisible church, a dirisible hurt,
A look-out tower, point of powerlessness:
    The kingdom he has entered is a place
Of sources, not of silences; memory does not rule it,
    But memory knows her own there
In finding names for them; reading
    By the flames the found words kindle
Their unburnable identities: the going down
    Is to a city of shapes, not a pit of shades
(For all ways begin, either from the eyes out
    Or the eyes in): to a Piazza del Campo
For spirits blessed by a consequence of days:
    For all that would speak itself aloud, a season
Of just regard, a light of sweetened reason.

Justice, praise, reconciliation, balance, receptivity – it is a rich aesthetic which does not end in aestheticism; an Augustan sense of balance, humane and optimistic. Tomlinson can believe in language, push it to its limits, use it to engage varied experience, by learning its rules, not by changing them.

The Way In is his seventh collection, a 'peopled landscape' indeed, with what is for him a new civic vision, a humane concern with the destruction of place. In the title poem and later in the book he often uses the car as his vehicle: it imposes a dynamic vision – he sees in glimpses, unable to focus for long on images, and unable to effect change. From his car, powerless, he witnesses the demolition of Bristol and expresses the communal impoverishment. The book also returns to his birth place, Stoke, and reconsiders his first landscape, 'a land / Too handled to be primary – all the same, / The first in feeling'. The directly social poetry, with something of the quality of a film documentary, treating the geriatric wards, the ravaged landscapes, the working-class childhood, the felt, ineradicable origins, adds a new dimension to his achievement. This is as close as he will come to 'confessional poetry': it is a far richer achievement than directly confessional verse.

If, apart from the first two sections of *The Way In*, there is a sense of uncertainty and tenuousness, even occasionally of slightness, it is a sign that Tomlinson is attempting to cope more directly, less obliquely, with the 'I' of the poems, trying a further range of experience, exploring memory (his own and our common memory) which before coloured his images, but seldom seemed to supply them, for the poems in the earlier volumes usually emerge from what is presented as immediate perception. The word 'vague' occurs more than once in *The Way In*. The poet is going beyond the sharply defined, exploring 'the mist'. Language is not always in this collection water reflecting the world: it is the mist that contains, and touches what it contains. As in 'Swimming Chenango Lake' he is fully engaged – but in the new book memory, not body, is immersed. This is true especially of those poems which seem to be indicating a new direction.

Burns Singer (1928–1964)

Like the two limbs of a cross
Your words, my answers lie
Together in the place
Where all our meanings die.

Burns Singer achieved only a limited popularity in his lifetime, and since his death in 1964 – at the age of thirty-six – he
has found few champions. An incomplete *Collected Poems*
(1970) was issued with an embarrassing memoir by Hugh
MacDiarmid and an evasive introduction by W. A. S. Keir.
The book occasioned little interest. But Singer is one of the
few original poets of his generation. Born two years before
Ted Hughes, his makes an interesting corrective to Hughes's
later vision. Anne Cluysenaar draws the distinction in
ethical terms. She quotes a passage from 'The Gentle
Engineer', written in 1951–2.

It is my own blood nips at every pore
And I myself the calcified treadmark of
Process towards me:
All of a million delicate engines whisper
Warm now, to go now
Through dragnets of tunnels forwards as my life.
I carry that which I am carried by.

She comments, 'This sense of being part of the universe, not
lost in it, allows for a more positive formulation than does
"wodwoism".' There is not the dissociation between man and

his environment, but rather continuity and interdependence. Singer was an accomplished scientist, while Hughes is a romantic anthropologist.

James Hyman Singer (he later adopted his mother's maiden name, Burns, as his middle name) was born in New York in 1928. His ne'er-do-well father and long-suffering mother returned to Scotland when the child was four. His background was insecure, unsettled. He could never claim a distinctive landscape, and nor had he any clear racial identity, being a mixture of Polish, Jewish, Irish, and other blood. He remained an American citizen, though he did not return to live in America.

Educated in Glasgow, he spent two terms studying English at the University, but left it and Scotland in disgust, choosing to avoid the university experience which he felt was inimical to creative work. He went to London and, aged seventeen, taught mathematics at a 'dubious private school'. He went from there to Cornwall where he came 'under the tutelage' of W. S. Graham, from whose mature work he learned basic lessons. He spent two years in Europe, then returned to Glasgow University, this time to read Biology. He told his Professor he wanted to 'write poems about animals'. In fact necessity – his father's poverty and his mother's suicide – drew him back, and though he did not finish the course, he became a marine biologist, entering the Scottish Home Department's Marine Laboratory in Aberdeen. After four largely unhappy years, he returned to London as a freelance. He wrote literary essays for *Encounter* and the *Times Literary Supplement*, scripted documentaries about the sea, wrote *Living Silver*, a popular book about marine life, and collaborated in a major anthology of Polish poetry in translation. All this time he was writing poems as well. He married the black American psychologist and painter, Marie Battle, and lived in brief security with her in Cambridge, but 'the caterwauling insecurity of my belief in myself' never left him. He died of natural causes in Plymouth, while engaged in marine research. Behind him he left a wealth of unpublished material: poems, notebooks, diaries, and other writings.

Only one large collection of his poems, *Still and All* (1957), appeared in his lifetime.

During his life he elected certain 'tutelary spirits' or teachers, and acknowledged his debt to them. W. S. Graham, and in Paris the painter Wols, at Glasgow the biologist Professor C. M. Yonge, and Hugh MacDiarmid drew him. Later he became fascinated with the writings of Wittgenstein, and the cerebral quality of some of his work is due to this allegiance.

MacDiarmid finds Singer obscure. If this is the case, the obscurity lies not in vocabulary, allusion, private reference or symbolism: it is a subtlety inherent in the intellectual agility and intensity of the poet. He was more than what MacDiarmid called 'a rootless cosmopolitan'. In some ways he is as rooted a poet as MacDiarmid, though he avoids dialect and does not celebrate a particular nation. His roots are in a world which science has clarified and made luminously mysterious through its limited definitions. This is one aspect of his originality.

It was the discipline of science and later philosophy that saved him from the easier practice of the poets he admired – Barker, Graham, and to some extent, MacDiarmid. As a poet, he remained an outsider. Drawn towards the literary power centre – London – he could not abide the 'literary gatherings'. He made a number of enemies as a result.

The title poem of *Still and All* develops the analogy between personal language and personal identity. Language is, too, a place in which to move. It impresses its own natural disciplines, but is flexible to a degree. It has laws of growth, like a natural organism; and the voice that carries it is also carried *by* it:

These words run vertical in their slim green tunnels
Without any turning away. They turn into
The first flower and speak from a silent bell.
But underneath it is always still
Truly awakening, slowly and slowly turning
About a shadow scribbled down by sunlight
And turning about my name. I am in my
Survival's hands. I am my shadow's theme.

The repetition of phrases and words which, in varied contexts, acquire different shades of relationship, is typical of Singer's style. In this poem certain phrases and images change places and in different constructions relate in analogous ways: the 'shadow' image, the tunnels, the word 'turn', the word 'green'. Despite the abstract manner, the poem has the consistent hardness of particularized images, even if they are unasserted; and more important, it has the authority of Singer's voice rhythms. He creates a complex of organic relationships, linked by analogy.

The poet suffers when the analogies and connections fail – usually at the apprehension of death which disrupts the harmony of his vision. In the poem '18IIIXSG' language ceases to unite: it disrupts, separates:

> I'm renegade
> To what I am. Between us language roars
> Its floods to drown me in. My death is sure:
> Though safe to watch me going down we stand
> Beside ourselves with horror on dry land.

The deployment of simple rhymes, a simple vocabulary, a clear syntax in measured rhythms, with carefully worked enjambments, is belied by the completeness of the wit with which the language is used. The originality is in fitting extreme experiences into such limpid forms, which heighten rather than temper the power of the experience. Singer does not choose an extreme rhetoric: his suffering is in measure, and without indulgence.

Time is the great enemy and the great healer: in other words, it is itself neutral, and the clock's 'empty precision' gains meaning only in particular contexts. Time is explored exhaustively in the narrative poems. Singer normally takes the story more or less for granted, concentrating on relationships or conditions and the ideas implicit in them. 'Marcus Antoninus' is one such poem, but a better one – perhaps Singer's best long poem – is 'The Transparent Prisoner'. Power is the dominant theme: power of men, forms, and language. The man with power ('Marcus Antoninus') and

the man who is the victim of that power ('The Transparent
Prisoner'): both are portrayed. 'The Transparent Prisoner',
a Second World War captured soldier, suffers first starvation
and then slave labour. That is the plot. His escape and recovery are treated briefly in the closing stanzas. Singer is
interested in the effect of extreme experience on the man's
mind – not in the physical details of suffering or in the adven-
ture. The prisoner is made to mine for coal. Eventually:

My hands against the coal would grow transparent,
Then, like a match felt softly by its flame,
My arms would char into a wandering current;
Warm radiance crept up them till the same
Vivid transparence flooded every part
And I could see the beating of my heart.

The prisoner gazes up through the roof of his working tomb
and 'sees' the grasses' roots, the blades, the air, the sky, the
sun. The vision – for it is vision – is intensely realized. The
poem 'Tree' develops the idea: the tree wishes to become a
man; the man wishes for some of the qualities of the tree. In
apprehending the wish itself, the poet achieves half his desire.
So, too, the prisoner. Acute suffering reduces the world to a
point of 'now', and in that 'now' vision develops. It is a vision
of unity.

The fifty 'Sonnets for a Dying Man' dwell, sometimes with
a wilful obscurity, on the *process* of dying. Death is seen at
work in all aspects – even the most vital – of life and relationship. There are thematic analogies with Hughes's *Crow*. But
the subject matter and the tone are more varied. The 'Dying
Man' of the title is 'everyman', including the poet himself, as
well – no doubt – as a particular person. Death becomes
synonymous with doubt. 'What they almost know' – the final
knowledge, death – obsesses the sonnets, which argue with
and around it. This is philosophical poetry with, at its best, a
vivid imagistic edge to it.

'Biography of an Idealist' is among Singer's outstanding
poems. It is subtitled 'The Crystal and the Shadow'. Here he
contrasts symmetry, perfection, and the idea of divine order,

with power, hierarchy, and the implicit imperfection in the
human order: chill light against living shadow, saint against
king. The king, shortly before his execution, says:

'If I believed at all
I believed in the small mistake
In judgement or behaviour
That only men can make,
The perfect limitation
Breached by imperfect power.'

When the saints take power, it is not God's order they
implement:

God is beyond belief:
His image everywhere
Half made of shape, half light,
Establishes despair.
The saints are counting money
Because the saints are men.

The ideal proves impotent in practice. Ideas, finished
thoughts, are valueless: they are alive only *as* they are
thought or enacted, not as abstractions.

   In 'Oracle Engraved on the Back of a Mirror', language is
a place, as in Graham's poems, but here continuous with
individual identity and the common world. The pertinent
lines occur: 'For thought is always and only thought: / The
thinking's different: thinking's in the blood.' A 'thought' is
incomplete when abstracted from its source in thinking, and
therefore in experience. The process of arriving at it reveals
its limits and its potential. Anne Cluysenaar quotes a passage
from Singer's uncollected prose which illuminates his view of
the ethical function of poetry – a view he shares, in different
terms, with Donald Davie: 'When a poet presents a series of
logical thoughts in a poem, it is not to express the logic of his
thoughts and thus to allow the reader to draw their logical
corollaries in other mnemonics – rather, it is to force the
reader through the thinking of these thoughts, since the process of thinking them is an essential part of the experience

which he wishes to re-create in the reader. It does not matter therefore if one logical series is placed alongside another with which it is logically irreconcilable, provided that both series properly belong to the experience in which they are involved.'

In 'Corner Boy's Farewell' Singer's argumentative 'thinking' is best observed. The argument is carried in an extended rhapsodic syntax, moving with authority from particulars into more abstract cogitations. It is a generalized love poem, including elegiac elements and satire in the manner of Pound's 'Commission'. Relationship gives him the power to set out in quest of himself and beyond himself:

Let my poems have bees' blood in them,
Let them be sharp but sensitive to honey.
For I still think of life as once of mist in Cornwall
Man-high and from the sea subsiding gently
Over the ploughed fields, brown, with scarce green growth,
But hidden under field-grey all that day,
Woven in one opacity.
Then on my eyesight the slant light broke
Of a single mist-drop narrowly slung to a cobweb
And each, the mist, through which my senses travelled
Broke at the sun-reflecting signal to its own:
The watered air grew bright with single claws:
So on the fine web spun from something stronger
One man can hold, precarious, complete
His own self's light that never is repeated
But acts as orrery to all the lights of others:
And that same web grows finer with its function,
More beautiful to praise with each drop held
In that peculiar tension once forever.

Thom Gunn (born 1929)

The sniff of the real, that's
what I'd want to get

Thom Gunn was born in 1929, the son of a successful Fleet
Street journalist. He studied at University College School in
London and at Cambridge University. While still an undergraduate he published with the Fantasy Press a pamphlet
collection. In the year he left Cambridge, his first book,
Fighting Terms (1954), appeared. Later in the same year he
went to Stanford University in California as a student and
teacher. There he came under the influence of Yvor Winters,
the distinguished critic and poet. His poem 'To Yvor
Winters, 1955' is a tribute to the teacher who helped free him
from prescriptive forms, first into experimentation with
syllabics, and finally into free verse. Winters showed Gunn
that the intensity of a poem is intrinsic in the rhythm and the
tone of the speaking voice. Gunn writes of Winters, 'You keep
both Rule and Energy in view, / Much power in each, most
in the balanced two.' In Gunn's early poems Rule had been
imposed on Energy, the fluid subject matter out of which he
pulled experiences and made meanings. In his later work, the
energy has come more to the surface, the poetry occurs in the
language, while the world to which it refers seems to have
become less fluid, more static, with inherent powers the poet
tries to tap.

In 1957 *A Sense of Movement* was published, and Gunn
returned to England to receive the Somerset Maugham
Award, on the proceeds of which he travelled to Italy. Out of

this experience came one of Gunn's best poems of his early style, 'In Santa Maria del Popolo'. He waits in the church for the afternoon sunlight to illuminate Caravaggio's painting of the Conversion of St Paul. It gradually appears. From the painting his mind turns to the painter's life and tragic death, and then to the old women praying, too weary to participate in the painted gesture of St Paul: 'the large gesture of a solitary man, / Resisting, by embracing, nothingness.' Gunn relates the work of art to the artist's life and then to lives in general. St Paul's isolation and his gesture, which – by accepting and defining 'nothingness' (one of Gunn's favourite words) – manages to keep him free of that nothingness, are typical of Gunn's approach to characterization. Few of the poems attain the fine integration of this one, where the meanings rise naturally out of the careful collocation of imagery. Normally a poet of intellect and willed meanings in his early work, here he releases the themes of isolation, self-sufficiency, and energy almost effortlessly.

My Sad Captains (1961) included some of Gunn's syllabic poetry and the culmination – not altogether triumphant – of his early prescriptively formal style. *Positives* (1966) was an attractive matching of poems with his brother's photographs, but the poems added little to the Gunn canon. With *Touch* (1967) he took a large step towards the resolution of his formal indecision, and *Moly* (1971), a less positive achievement in terms of finished poems, reveals Gunn increasing the number of choices open to him. Critics have perhaps underestimated the difficulty a poet experiences in adapting to an entirely new environment and, to a large degree, a new language. Gunn's adjustment to the United States has been gradual. *Jack Straw's Castle* appeared in 1976.

G. S. Fraser compares Gunn's early poems with Larkin's, contrasting Larkin's emotional economy – the feeling that it's silly to waste emotion where it can't do any good – with Gunn's lavishness, his often trumped-up effects. Larkin's mature poems have had the ring of middle age and acceptance about them. Gunn's, despite the rigorous forms of his early work, have had sometimes a wilful adolescence about their subject matter and their conclusions. Fraser reports that, in an early poem, 'Gunn insisted . . . that the heroic attitude, which he sees as behind all notable poetry, should be stimulated, not quenched, by a threatening age.' 'A Mirror for Poets' is one of several examples of this. Gunn depicts the Elizabethan society and its writers; violence, social forms imposed on a fluid experience, the fear and certainty of change, war, torture and death. He develops the paradox between imposed form and fluid content: 'Here moved the Forms, flooding like moonlight, / In which the act or thought perceived its error'. The forms are insubstantial, yet necessary. The poet senses the fluidity of what underlies the forms; he offers not explanations but moments of formed experience.

His 'Sartrean existentialism' is always invoked by the critics: man is self-creating; by his choices, some of them unconscious and arbitrary, he makes him*self*, without foreknowledge, but advancing in the belief that he may find. What and how are not known. Martin Dodsworth writes of his 'voluntary commitment to the irrational'. In a world without intrinsic meanings, Gunn's imagination finds or asserts analogies in a constructed and provisional 'plot'. Predictably, the least achieved of his early poems have the woodenness of arbitrary symbolism. The meanings do not adhere to the subject matter.

'On the Move' is an example of his existentialism. The blue jay 'follows / some hidden purpose', other birds are 'Seeking their instinct, or their poise, or both'. So too the motorcycle 'Boys', who 'almost hear a meaning in their noise'. They are unwilling and unable to keep still. The strict form and literary idiom of the poem are in tension with the subject matter. Extreme articulateness, a poetic bravado, are incongruous with 'the boys' who have replaced language with noise and pursue their 'hidden purpose' forward. The rhetoric borders on exhortation, praising what is itself an antithesis to the form the poem takes. The powerful tension in this incongruity between form and subject matter is found in many of the poems, notably in the mysterious 'The Allegory of Wolf Boy'.

'My Sad Captains', a later syllabic poem, develops the philosophical theme. The title from *Antony and Cleopatra* leaves Gunn (like MacNeice in 'The Sunlight on the Garden') posing unironically as Antony, besieged, living for the present, and without the company of a Cleopatra, with only defeat to look forward to.

Movement, choice, risk – and eventually touch. Charles Tomlinson wrote that Gunn 'resolved to seek out the heroic in the experience of nihilism'. This is the essence of his work: the *experience*, not the idea. In his later poems, particularly those written under the influence of hallucinogenic drugs, he has abandoned 'ideas' at last and concentrated entirely on the experience; those ideas that rise from the experience refer back to it. Ceasing to moralize content, he engages it fully, in the present.

Gunn's is a poetry of isolation. In the early work he needs isolation, self-sufficiency, wholeness. But isolation becomes a burden. He feels – as he expresses it in 'The Corridor' – that he is being watched even as he watches. He plots his amorous exploits in 'The Beach Head' with military precision, gauging the moment for the embrace. Because of the competitive nature of human relationships, sexual love cannot break down this isolation. And Gunn, with Yeats as his early mentor, is always to be found posing, assuming an attitude if not a voice, individuating himself. In his least successful poems it is his personality that detains us. Even in the recent poems, when he submits himself to experience, there is a touch of attitudinizing which often deflects the poem.

Eliot, Auden and Donne were early mentors as well as Yeats. Donne helped him develop extended analogies. Even in so unmetaphysical a poem as 'The Wound', presenting a personal experience in terms of physical phenomena and legend, it is Donne we think of, though the language owes little to him. Yvor Winters weaned Gunn off his early models, and the later influences – Marianne Moore and William Carlos Williams, for example – are not nearly so closely followed as the models of his youth.

'Vox Humana' was his first notable syllabic poem and

marks the beginning of his development away from the early style. He employs a seven-syllable line and a six-line stanza, rhyming (or slant-rhyming) *abccba*. The form is exacting, but Gunn approaches speech rhythms. Syllabics are dangerous, however – unless carefully used, the hesitancy of the rhythms and the pointed line endings, often on weak words, give the wrong emphasis and dissipate the effect. In the form Gunn chose for 'Vox Humana' the rhyme, effective in the four central lines of each stanza, is merely mechanical in the first and sixth lines because of the distance between them: there is no echo. Elements of the form are simply schematic and force on the poet certain mannerisms, making him condense in one place and expand in another. Another syllabic poem, 'Flying above California', is entirely successful in its overall condensation and careful word choice.

The poem 'Touch' is in short-lined free verse, dramatic, rhythmically varied and mimetic. It is not limited to a specific setting, though the experience is vividly evoked. The defensive, isolating patterns and strictures of the earlier style are not visible here, the situation suggests meanings which are left powerfully implicit. The poem marks a decisive beginning for Gunn's new manner.

'Confessions of a Life Artist' has attracted less attention than it merits. The poem is in ten eleven-line sections, each line of seven syllables. Each section is differently divided, like ten views of the same model. The third section includes the lines, 'Circling over a city, / to reject the thousand, and / to select the one.' The fourth section pursues the idea: 'But what of those unchosen? // They are as if dead. Their deaths, / now, validate the chosen.' The life artist affects life as he practises his art. The artist of the poem becomes a brothel keeper: an artist with lives. His amorality is in his coldness to his subjects – a necessary coldness from which he derives his power. Gradually he succumbs to sympathy and then empathy. He becomes one of them. The breaking down of the artist's amoral integrity, his evolving humanity, is convincing perhaps because Gunn's subject matter answers a personal development.

Gunn's most sustained long poem is 'Misanthropos' in *Touch*, in seventeen sections of great technical versatility. 'Misanthropos' is, as far as he knows, the last survivor of a holocaust. In the poem he gradually releases his past, experiences the total isolation of creatures and objects in nature, meets with some other survivors and, by an act not of will but instinctive sympathy, comes out of hiding to treat an injured man. In the first section Gunn describes Misanthropos:

If he preserves himself in nature,
it is as a lived caricature

of the race he happens to survive.
He is clothed in dirt. He lacks motive.
He is wholly representative.

Each experience Misanthropos has, each section of the poem, is in a suitable form, whether effectively contrasting with the experience or dramatically suited to it. The 'echo' technique, asking questions which the last word or syllables of the question answer, is used to express his unhope. One part is in terza rima, another in syllabics, another in blank verse. In part XII the poem reaches its inhuman climax: the separate dust particles are blown together back and forth. They never merge: they are hard, individual, purposeless. The poetic form chosen for the section is particularly apt: couplets, the first line of ten or eleven syllables, the second of eight syllables. There is a constant sense, as the couplets resolve on a seemingly premature rhyme, of contraction.

In *Moly* Gunn is attracted – not by legends, with their inviolable particulars – but by myths with which he can tinker, myth creatures, centaurs, or the mythical-seeming beast in 'Tom-Dobbin'. In 'Rites of Passage' he turns into a satyr. The process of metamorphosis fascinates him, leading him to Circe's cave or to his local pusher. He seems free to take the form he will, free in a dangerously malleable, Protean way. But he submits himself to each experience and lets it make of him what it will. 'For Signs' is an obscurely powerful poem in which metamorphoses are experienced but no specific meaning limits them. They are not arbitrary – apparently – but the poem exists unparaphrasably in them. He seems to find rather than impose meanings, though in 'Three', a throwback to his earlier style, his meanings are developed in the old way without the earlier formal skill.

Among the most recent poems Gunn seems to be trying to get at the immediately real, at the moment in its intensity. Surrendering time perspective and prescriptive form, he is in danger of giving us raw moments which are not poems, which are merely notes, irrelevant because not intense in the way they are communicated. Indeed, he has already done this in some of the prose poems in *Moly*. But Gunn, while moving forward, does not burn his bridges. He knows where he has been, and if – for a time – he wanders into the woods, he has the resources to change course, to come out again, not retreating, by a different path.

Ted Hughes (born 1930)

His wings are the stiff back of his only book,
Himself the only page – of solid ink.

Ted Hughes is a restless writer, hurrying from verse to short
stories, preparing libretti, translations, experiments with
'Orghast' or 'talking without words'. His work is impelled by
a single passion and repeats the same processes in different
forms; but his restlessness does not impede his craft. He seldom leaves a work unfinished. Indeed, his worst vice has
always been over-writing. His poems have apparent flaws in
the text; but the off-rhymes, the heaped alliterations, the
larded adjectives are usually intentionally set down. Hughes
can write with elegance when he wishes – as in 'October
Dawn'. But he frequently employs elegance only to betray it,
as in 'Crow and the Birds'. Or he chooses another idiom
altogether.

Ted Hughes was born in Mytholmroyd, Yorkshire, in
1930. The landscape of his poems – austere and sparsely inhabited – is there, and in the area of Mexborough where his
family moved when he was seven and where he attended the
local grammar school. His older brother hunted and fished
and finally became a gamekeeper. His example fascinated
Hughes. His father's experiences of the First World War were
another fascination. When Hughes was fifteen, he was
writing poems.

Before going up to Cambridge, he did two years' National
Service. In the fastnesses of East Yorkshire, engaged as an
RAF ground wireless mechanic, he found time to read and

re-read Shakespeare. At Cambridge, he began studying English, but changed to a course in Archaeology and Anthropology. The academic syllabus seemed to him contrived to stifle creative interest in literature. He came down in 1954.

At Cambridge he met Sylvia Plath, whom he married in 1956. In 1957 his first collection of poems, *Hawk in the Rain*, was published. In the same year, he and Sylvia Plath went to the United States, where they lived until 1959. In 1960, his second book, *Lupercal*, appeared. It attests to the rapid development of his skills. The relationship with Sylvia Plath was creatively fruitful for five years, but in 1962 they separated.

Hughes has published two collections of children's poems, *Meet my Folks!* (1961) and *Earth Owl and Other Moon People* (1963). Since then Ted Hughes has published *Wodwo* (1967), *Crow* (1970), *Season Songs* (1974), *Gaudete* (1977) and *Cave Birds* (1978). His principal critical writings have appeared in the same period, introductions and brief essays. Hughes conveys somewhat single-minded critical insights with power, and one wishes he would exercise himself in this area more regularly. His most important critical work has been advocacy: of Keith Douglas, whose *Selected Poems* he edited (1964); of Emily Dickinson (*Selected Poems* 1968); of Vasko Popa, the Yugoslav poet (1967); and too few others. With Daniel Weissbort Hughes founded *Modern Poetry in Translation*, a magazine which set the pattern for poetry translation in the 1960s. Hughes is selective in what he chooses to champion. His major critical essays have been self-critical as well.

Two experiences seem to have determined Hughes's frame of poetic reference: what Charles Tomlinson has called 'the mythos of World War I' and the European dislocations it brought about, cultural, historical and psychological; and an 'awareness of nature' and a fascination with the animal world. The study of anthropology was a further determinant, affecting even the early poems. Implicit in these experiences was a sense of the inadequacy of humanism, the bankruptcy of the old symbols, and a gradual recognition of the bankruptcy of the old forms. The human and animal worlds of violence dominate – but not *as* violence. As Calvin Bedient commented, 'His weakness is not violence but the absolute egotism of survival. It is the victor he loves, not war.'

There is an analogy with Lawrence: 'man cannot live in chaos,' Lawrence wrote. 'The animals can. To the animal all is chaos, only there are a few recurring motions and aspects within the surge.' The violence in the natural world is not, however, absolute for Lawrence. He warns against the exaggerated vision, suggesting that 'the yearning for chaos becomes a nostalgia'. At a certain point violence becomes sentimental – if we take sentimental to mean that final blurring of issues, simplification rather than clarification, that resolving of a poem in gesture, wilfully ascribing significance to an image. Many of Hughes's early poems and several of the *Crow* poems are facile in their resolutions. The word 'horizon', for instance, does overtime, sending the early poems vaguely out in search of resonance.

His early work echoes Hopkins, Dylan Thomas, Owen, Lawrence, and sometimes Eliot. His was a clear break with the curtailed ambitions of The Movement, a passionate belief in the scope of poetry. It is worth noting that his subject matter and range of experience, unchecked by irony and taken to greater depths than the doctrinaire Movementeer would have dared, is rigidly circumscribed.

A quality of all the poems is a Wordsworthian solitariness and a sense of choicelessness reminiscent of Keith Douglas. Creatures are sealed within their instinctive natures. They are often seen as mechanical. Theirs is a cruel 'stability'. A recurrent process in the poems is 'the replaced brain' – the brain of the protagonist taken over by some power, single impulse, alien force: a bullet, a rat's body, a bird's mind. Hughes bases his fascinating study of Shakespeare on this theme: the characters become tragic or comic when they are reduced to a single humour, a single mind.

Hughes is hardly an animal poet. His animals, sometimes accurately portrayed, are usually out of focus, or rather, re-focused to illuminate some specific metaphorical rather than complex natural truth. They are emblems, analogues, images, the quintessence of the poetic fallacy. In the best poems the private world Hughes explores and the animals' world are held apart and in balance. The animals are used for exorcism, not confession. It is his subtle infidelity to fact, or the incompleteness of the facts he gives, that makes the animals particular and affective. He is entirely in his own element when he begins projecting pseudo-creatures – his Crow, his Wodwo. But with them he is in most danger of sentimentalizing, for there is no background of facts against which he can project his macabre imaginings. His characteristic authority is in the tentative balance he maintains between a real and a nightmare world, revealing himself and what he observes at once. In *Crow* the odds is gone, and if he achieves individual successes in that sequence, the sequence as a whole is disappointing.

As one would expect from his dominant themes, Hughes is a manly poet, and his attitude to women in the poems – infrequently voiced – is often tinged with fear and revulsion. Isolation seems synonymous with independence. The poet avoids ensnaring relationships. In *Crow* (where one must allow for the hyperbolic treatment of his material) he conjures up a decapitating vulva, and sex becomes a vivid correlative of death.

'The Thought-Fox', included in *Hawk in the Rain*, was one of his first animal poems. In effect it defines his early poetic process: not to describe but to evoke. His loneliness above a blank sheet of paper is, like the night, empty, habitable. As the snow settles into the night, so the image of the fox settles into his solitude, its 'sharp hot stink' is sensed, it 'enters the dark hole of the head'. The poem is not formally regular, the tentative imperfect rhymes follow no fixed pattern. The rhythm is quietly varied. The first line echoes Hopkins's 'The Windhover', but the echo is forgotten in what follows. Hughes achieves a surprising fusion between the image of the natural, nocturnal world and the receptive, creative mind. The verse mimes the quiet curiosity and cunning of the fox quickly and effectively, with few details.

In 'Egg Head' Hughes scornfully expresses the aesthetic, the weakly humanist, or the intellectual response to extreme experience. He contrasts courage and openness with what he sees as willed blindness. The verse is dramatic, though its meanings stay unclear:

So many a one has dared to be struck dead
Peeping through his fingers at the world's ends,
    Or at an ant's head.

In one respect his attitude is Lawrentian. But where Lawrence would have us open to be filled and fulfilled, Hughes sometimes would have us open to be hurt. Lawrence's lush rhetoric might almost convince the egg head to hatch out, but Hughes's rhetoric makes him fortify his shell. In *Hawk in the Rain* Hughes is himself one of the egg heads, a watcher rather than a participator. He witnesses violence but is himself untouched. In poems such as 'Wind', where he is threatened and indeed implicated in his vision, his best effects are achieved. Nature rattles against frail certainties.

But the war poems – 'Bayonet Charge' for instance – are not witnessings but re-creations, revellings in documentary detail. They are not experienced. 'Six Young Men', a better poem, possesses after the vivid opening stanzas something of the sentimentality of violence noted earlier – a lingering relish which disturbs us on the poet's behalf. This quality also informs 'The Martyrdom of Bishop Farrar', which dwells on the organ by organ incineration of that unfortunate man.

In *Lupercal* the vicarious delight in violence has begun to subside. We are in a more responsible world. Hughes indulges in less over-writing, fewer stylistic affectations, and the themes are developed more clearly. He examines the single-minded creatures. 'Hawk Roosting' is a dramatic monologue. The notion of this particular beast soliloquizing is a contradiction in terms, but the poem is effective. As in Douglas's 'How to Kill', a brutal nature without conscience reveals itself:

There is no sophistry in my body:
My manners are tearing off heads—

The allotment of death.
For the one path of my flight is direct
Through the bones of the living.

So, too, 'The Bull Moses', observed by the child, has the sole function of a seed bull. Single-minded, vital, undeterred by conscience or self-consciousness, violent . . . the moral overtones of Hughes's vision are unsettling.

It is not only that he chooses single-minded animals, nor that the chosen animals – like the men he admires – breathe a different air from the general, that from time to time worries the reader; it is the particular quality of single-mindedness he is drawn to: not the bee, for instance, but the blood-beasts. His attraction for those qualities is as disturbing as his subtle infidelity to his subject.

'Thrushes', one of Hughes's most anthologized poems, is perhaps the clearest example of this. The opening, 'Terrifying are the attent sleek thrushes on the lawn', carries conviction – the choice of 'attent' – reminiscent of Emily Dickinson – is typical of the poems in *Lupercal*. Hughes proceeds to record the virtually automatic function – 'a start, a bounce, a stab' – with which the thrush goes about its business: 'a ravening second'. It is when he describes its 'single-mind-sized skull' and draws analogies with Mozart's and a shark's brain that we feel Hughes's single-mindedness reducing everything to its solving formula. His point is that the nature incapable of doubt is undeflected. To deny conscience, self-consciousness, and thought to animals is one thing; to deny them to Mozart is another, a rhetorical sleight of hand. The error mars the poem: for as his Mozart is faked, so too is his thrush. He has made absolute one aspect of the bird. He has forgotten that thrushes sing as well as stab. This would not matter had he not built a moral edifice on an incomplete foundation. He has used, not served, his subject.

'Pike', on the other hand, is a more complete and powerful poem. It sets fish and fisherman in a natural and historical context. The meanings complement one another. The *poem* is not single-minded. 'View of a Pig' is similarly powerful, the description of the dead animal carried out almost entirely in monosyllables. The poet is a dispassionate witness. He brings in no extraneous matter. Also startling in the best poems in *Lupercal* is the authority with which Hughes uses the verb 'to be' – with the power of a transitive verb.

The poet who writes *Wodwo* has come a long way from *Lupercal*. He is less sure of himself, the book is more experimental. The early relish for violence is now turned to dread and a sense of inevitability. He no longer witnesses to violence: it acts on him. 'Cadenza' and 'Ghost Crabs' are nightmarish poems. God begins to play a prominent, ambiguous role. He is Rosenberg's God taken a step further: for in *Wodwo* and later in *Crow* his cruelty is in his indecision. We suffer in his indecision. *He* is not single-minded, and we are in his image. But Hughes does not elegize, he celebrates endurance and survival. Suffering and loss are seen as crude forms of gain.

The war poems and the attempts at confessional verse are unsuccessful because Hughes fails to generalize the experience – his own or his father's. In poems such as 'Skylarks', however, we are near again to the world of *Lupercal*, that single-minded world explored finally in *Crow*. In 'Skylarks' as elsewhere there is Lawrence's rhetoric but none of his sensuousness. Hughes is all angles while Lawrence is all curves.

In *Wodwo* Hughes attempts to evoke not creatures only, but their driving impulse. 'Pibroch' and 'The Howling of Wolves' play with the heart of the experience, leaving the phenomenal details to suggest themselves. In 'Kafka' Hughes writes, 'He is a man in hopeless feathers.' The line is a key to the deft short-circuiting Hughes achieves in *Wodwo*, fusing subject and metaphor so they emerge as one. In 'Wodwo' itself – not a successful poem – Hughes defines the character which cannot define itself, 'but I'll go on looking'. Wodwos are creatures found in *Sir Gawain and the Green Knight*. Scholars can't agree on their actual nature – they are neither finally human nor animal, neither legendary nor monstrous – wood-dwellers, perhaps. The speaker of 'Wodwo' is such a creature, trying to forge relationships with others and with itself. In evoking this creature on the edge of our common world, Hughes was already preparing to say goodbye to earth and step off into myth.

In 1963 Leonard Baskin, the American artist, asked Hughes to write some poems to illustrate his engravings of anthropoid crows. Gradually the poems 'wrote themselves'.

Crow is the creature of a very particular nightmare. It is presented as God's nightmare. He tests it, and it survives. The book is not provided with a narrative. It is presented as fragments of an unfinished epic, burdened with various elements of primitive song and anthropological overtones.

What makes Crow more than merely a buffeted pawn is his intelligence. He has a conscience stirring. But given his nature – a grating songster, a carrion eater, sometimes a killer, a black bird – he is always eating death, witnessing or perpetrating or surviving violence. He may aspire to be a man, but he is doomed to being a crow. He is almost exclusively a creature of extremity, unlovable and unloving, solitary and yet surviving. The violence he suffers and causes is not repulsive because it is so exaggerated that it is incredible. The poem is more like a cartoon than a fable.

The language of the poem is colloquial and varied, moving from comic levity and violence to grotesque surrealism. It is primitive in its mimetic, repetitive style, irregular, incantatory, full of lists, breaking into didactic passages, rants and songs. Since it has no over-all structure, Crow's character changes frequently so that – like Wodwo – he does not finally exist – or rather, not yet.

In the first fourteen lines of the poem the word 'black' appears eleven times, contrasting with light, sun, and sight. The crow's emblematic colour and nature are evoked. The mock-Biblical constructions and rhythms give the poem some of its satirically religious authority. We hear odd echoes of other writers. 'Examination of the Womb-door' painfully recalls Eliot's 'Marina', for example. Crow's claws are in everything. His mind is torn by the simple, consuming will to survive and the less powerful desire to define himself, to stop and look. Everything is reversed in his world, however. 'A Kill' is about childbirth, for instance. Much of the poem is spent developing the fruitless equation of birth = death, sex = death. Only a creature such as Crow, isolated, mateless, childless, can survive in the world of *Crow*.

To make matters more complex, early in the poem the human body is divided up. Its limbs become plants and objects, the torso becomes a world. Crow inhabits and soils it. The myth is sexual, the refrain is guilt. In 'Crow Alights', one of the two outstanding poems in the volume, the violence remains implicit. Crow witnesses, and what he sees is, in this poem, more powerful than what he does or has done to him elsewhere. In 'Crow Tyranosaurus', the other outstanding *Crow* poem, he almost develops an active conscience, but like the thrush earlier, he is automatic. His will is weaker than his nature: 'But his eye saw a grub. And his head, trapsprung, stabbed.' The drama and comical exaggerations are in the language as much as in the action. We forget Crow is a crow – much as we forget Othello is black – until his supposed nature overcomes his will, and he is brutally reduced to himself.

In the poem Hughes achieves some of his best writing – as in 'Crow and the Birds'. But the passages exist to be soiled by Crow. In this poem the lyricism modulates into satire; the flowing opening cadences are followed by shorter ones; the rhythm begins to hobble and finally Crow's clumsiness reduces the poem to his own terms. When, in 'Crow Goes Hunting', his prey manages to elude him, he is delighted: he has found something he cannot render down to himself.

Despite the odd Crow pieces that have appeared since *Crow* was published, Hughes seems to have stepped beyond him. His most recent verse implies a recantation of materialism and its world of death, suffering and woe, a conscious abandonment of 'fate', even if, in halting and questioning one's destiny, one may be subject to profound loss. The man born running across an endless desert at last manages to arrest himself, wrenching himself free by act of will. Free for what?

Jon Silkin (born 1930)

Lie together, grin, creep, pant, assemble;
convene the kingdom.

Jon Silkin has never with complete success finished a poem; yet his partial successes with difficult themes and his attempt to develop an adequate style sometimes reward the reader as well as the perfected literary artefacts of poets with smaller ambitions do. Despite his often clumsily 'literary' use of language, his insistence on teasing out and elucidating the ambiguities implicit in his imagery and themes, his poems are provisional: they do not aspire to literary perfection.

Jon Silkin was born in London in 1930. During the War he was evacuated to Wales, an experience that left a vivid impression on him. Educated at Wycliffe and Dulwich Colleges, he did not take a university degree until 1962, when he received his BA from Leeds. Ten years earlier he founded the quarterly magazine *Stand*, a forum for new verse, fiction and criticism. In 1966 he moved to Newcastle upon Tyne where he has lived since. He has done some translation, edited a *Stand* anthology, and written an extended study of the poets of the First World War. He has travelled widely as well on academic and reading tours.

Without roots in any particular landscape, he frequently focuses in his poems on a place – a graveyard in Iowa, a kibbutz in Israel, a mill-wheel in Northumberland – and attempts to relate to it through its history and how that history acts in the present. He is a poet of 'commitment', particularly to persecuted minorities, whether the exploited workers of a nineteenth-century mill or the Jews of York in

1190 or the Jews of Europe in the Second World War. In an interview he describes his perspective: 'I am a Jew, and . . . largely because of this, being a European Jew, I have for better or for worse got something of this rootless cosmopolitan or European attitude.'

His first collection, *The Portrait and Other Poems*, appeared when he was twenty, and *The Peaceable Kingdom* (1954) and *The Two Freedoms* (1958) established his early reputation. The book which set the pattern Silkin has followed in his later poetry is *The Re-ordering of the Stones* (1961). The poet who emerges from this collection, and who dominates *Nature with Man* (1965), *Poems New & Selected* (1966), *Amana Grass* (1971) and *The Principle of Water* (1974) has lost much of the charm and fluency of the younger man. In the later poems the vocabulary is at times 'heightened', the syntax often so convoluted as to be insoluble. They possess a greater thematic and formal complexity. The chief virtue of his mature poetry is his ability, within a single image, to contain the paradoxes of his world – not resolved, but held in tension: whether in a flower, a graveyard, or a human relationship. The flaw in much of his later work is his naïve faith in the mimetic power of syntax, a belief that artificially complicated word order, dense onomatopoeia, and frequent syntactical obscurity, can reproduce the complexities of an image, emotion or idea.

Anne Cluysenaar speaks of Silkin's view of 'life as quest, as a constant probing of its own conditions', a probing in which – seeing what *is* – he suggests what should be, or should have been. In the early poems the combating forces of Good and Evil are separate, while in the later work they are contained in single images, as in 'The Centre' – 'where choice flickers, but does not choose'. In *The Two Freedoms* the vulnerable 'Peaceable Kingdom' is contrasted with the actual kingdom, for example in 'Hymn to the Solid World':

And I turned from the inner heart having no further cause
To look there, to pursue what lay inside,
And moved to the world not as I would have world
But as it lay before me . . .

'The world not as I would have world' – Silkin's later poems try to move away from the archetypal and visionary towards the literal. When he attempts to 're-order' the world his verse becomes assertive, losing the early tentative quality. He changes his forms in preparation for the later style. In *The Re-ordering of the Stones* itself there is an engaging simplicity in the syntax, short lines are deployed with skill, and there are few stanza breaks. His vision of nature becomes ambivalent, the organic images contain paradoxes. In 'Asleep' as in the best of the later poems the verse is dramatic *and* ruminative:

> everything that is
> Is agony, in this sense:
> That things war to survive.
> Pain is complex, something akin
> To a stone with veins of colour
> In it, that cross and cross
> But never reconcile
> Into one swab of colour
> Or the stone that contains them.

As Anne Cluysenaar indicates, the centrality of this passage to Silkin's work is undeniable. He portrays relationships, intimate or social, as 'symbiotic' – one individual feeding on another. 'Astringencies', 'The Malabestia', 'Amana Grass' and many other poems explore the theme. Only in Silkin's latest work, particularly in his long verse drama 'The People', is some resolution suggested, for there the relationship between Kye and Finn, a young couple with a mentally handicapped baby, is qualified and enriched by the presence of Stein, a survivor of the concentration camps, who is a giver and a healer. From suffering he has learned a humanity that runs counter to Silkin's general view of human nature. In 'Defence', an earlier poem, he had written, 'The whole of nature / Is a preying upon.'

An image which occurs first in *The Peaceable Kingdom* is that of the mentally handicapped child. It comes again in 'The Child's Life', 'Burying', 'The Child', 'The Continuance', and 'The People'. The image won't go away – it is Silkin's own child. Its birth and death lead to the breakdown of a relationship, evoked in 'Something has been Teased from Me'. The outstanding poem in this obsessive sequence is an early one, 'Death of a Son':

> Something has ceased to come along with me.
> Something like a person: something very like one.
>> And there is no nobility in it
>> Or anything like that.

The image of the child is fused with the image of the house: its stillness is his stillness. 'He did not forsake silence.' The simplicity of the language, the ruminative development of the imagery, make this a memorable elegy.

In *Nature with Man*, man has become a treacherous creature almost by definition. The God of these poems is malevolent. Nature and man are creations and victims of the same mind and reflect its qualities of power, beauty, isolation and treachery. Some of the poems in this collection attempt to treat images objectively, the poems ostensibly depend on close definition; but the meanings, intended to rise out of the images, are in fact separate from them. The image is merely a pretext; it does not contain the ideas Silkin tries to tease out of it. This is particularly clear in the sequence of 'Flower Poems'. Significance is meant to be implicit in the terms in which the flowers are described. They are erotic, or malevolent, or victimized. 'Milkmaids' and 'The Strawberry Plant' are notably successful, and in their success point up the failure of the sequence as a whole.

In most of these poems, the objectivity is irresolute: the flowers waver between real and emblematic. Silkin explains that 'the method' – a chilly, mechanical word describing a mechanical approach – 'is to take one particular species of flower and to look at the flower quite closely. I also try to characterize the life and process of the flower and, in making all these substantial, to suggest certain correspondences with human types and situations.' The attempt is to 'draw human life' towards organic symbols. The trouble is that, where poets such as Hughes contrast the animal and human worlds,

Silkin takes a more artificial course, attempting to draw continuous analogies. The poems demand that we gloss them.

In *Amana Grass* he explores new territory. The poems are set in Iowa, Israel and the North of England. He comes to see his role as distinctly political. But his social convictions do not find expression in politicizing. His interest is in exploring the implications of basic relationships. He cannot handle dialogue, whatever his skill with monologue, and the title poem of *Amana Grass* is far from successful. But the exploration of a relationship at once destructive and strangely natural and fulfilling has moments of clarity. Solitude is another of his themes, and the solitude induced by suffering he expresses best:

Nothing weeps here that does not weep, for itself, alone,
the tough small disc of grief
shuddering the body . . .

The Principle of Water, his most extensive collection, reveals the range of his mature style. In the 'Killhope Wheel' sequence and others of the short poems there is a sense that the chosen images begin to *contain* the meanings he attributes to them. There are still the flaws of overwriting. In one poem, for example, 'cuneiform voices' are heard 'wedging praise'. The implicit shape of the adjective 'cuneiform' is relentlessly beaten out by the participle – the element of suggestion is exiled. This contributes to the flatness of some passages, almost a sense that the poet distrusts his medium or his audience. But the overwriting apart, the varied rhythms – with a new psalmodic rhythm in 'Isaiah's Thread' – and the closer approximation to his subject matter show that he is nearing the world 'as it lay before me'.

Most of the poems are flawed by obscurities of diction, excessive punctuation, blurred syntactical line, or poetic wilfulness in ascribing meaning to his subject matter. But what is flawed in Silkin is not insubstantial. The poems' concern with situations of relationship, suffering, and death, and the strong tone of voice, with an 'I' not self-assertive but perceptive, redeem the frequent clumsiness. Silkin is always a poet coming to terms: with history, with nature, with people, and with himself. Few poets are so willing to let us into the confidence of their processes of thought and feeling, to observe, as if with them, the images struggling.

Geoffrey Hill (born 1932)

> When we chant
> 'Ora, ora pro nobis' it is not
> Seraphs who descend to pity but ourselves.

Geoffrey Hill has published, at discrete intervals, only four books: *For the Unfallen* (1959), *King Log* (1968), *Mercian Hymns* (1971) and *Tenebrae* (1978). His reputation has grown slowly, but now he is generally recognized as the outstanding poet of his generation. He has adapted the lessons of modernism to his own ends and made a poetry of integrity, acerbity, and power. He now has imitators, an ambiguous tribute.

He was born in Bromsgrove, Worcester, in 1932, and attended Bromsgrove Grammar School. In 1950 he went to Oxford to read English. He studied for a B.Litt and began teaching at Leeds University, where he has remained, combining full-time academic work with an attempt to maintain the poetic vocation.

In 1952, when he was twenty, the Fantasy Press issued a pamphlet containing five of his early poems, two of which – 'To William Dunbar' and 'For Isaac Rosenberg' – have not been collected in his subsequent books. The other poems became part of his first collection seven years later. His debt to the poets of the First and Second World Wars is evident. 'To William Dunbar' recalls Keith Douglas in its fine modulation from image into thought, though it bears thematic affinities with Rosenberg – the problems of power and of faith.

'God's Little Mountain' – with its archaic use of 'engraven' – recalls Rosenberg's use of intensive forms, and there is an

analogy between Rosenberg's early idea of God and Hill's –
seen as a 'pure force', not malignant but neutrally present.
The poem also acknowledges the difficulty of expressing
suffering. Judging from the Fantasy Press pamphlet, Hill
chose exacting masters from the outset, poets who 'knew the
clear / Fulness of vision' – Dunbar, Smart, Blake, Rosenberg,
Chaucer. And the example of the Metaphysicals was never
far away.

'Genesis' – one of his most remarkable poems – originally
bore the dedication, 'A Ballad to Christopher Smart'. There
is an element of balladic metre and rhyme, but no balladic
regularity. By the insistence on rhyme and rhythm, the
forced recurrences in a cruelly ordered world are expressed
in the form itself. The poem is in five sections and follows a
seven-day development. On the first day: 'the waves
flourished at my prayer, / The rivers spawned their sand'. His
vision is of the natural processes, of the salmon heading up-
river to spawn. Water, the sea, is living, against the 'dead
weight of the land'. The speaker is full of wonder. But in the
second section, on the second day, he perceives the process of
cruelty: 'The osprey plunge with triggered claw / ... / To lay
the living sinew bare.' And on the third day (also in the
second section) he ceases to celebrate and calls out in fear,
'Beware / The soft voiced owl, the ferret's smile.' The sudden
change of tone is the best achieved in the poem.

In the third section the speaker moves beyond fear and
revulsion to a renunciation of 'This fierce and unregenerate
day'. He begins 'Building as a huge myth for man / The
watery Leviathan'. He creates a sea-world, a false, projected
vision – 'A brooding immortality— / Such as the charmèd
phoenix has / In the unwithering tree.' It is apposite that the
poem falls into mild archaism as the speaker consoles himself
with poetic fantasies. But in the fourth section, on the fifth
day, he is compelled to turn to 'flesh and blood and the blood's
pain'. He is a member of the family of suffering. And on the
sixth day he accepts, becomes a part of the scheme; a rider
'in haste about the works of God, / With spurs I plucked the
horse's blood'. 'Plucked' implies the pluck of courage,
plucking a dead bird, and plucking a stringed instrument,

here with the suggestion of veins. The only vital myths, the speaker realizes, are the blood myths, and supremely the blood of Christ which frees even the dead. The seventh day of the week is left unspoken. Implicitly it is the day of judgement that will raise the dead from under land and sea. *That* is the 'Genesis' – but the poem also expresses the 'genesis' of faith, an apprehension of the reality of the Christian myth.

'Genesis', included in the pamphlet and in his first book, stylistically and thematically prefigures the later poems. The impersonal 'I', conveying experience and not an obtrusive 'self', is characteristic. The religious themes here and elsewhere are developed with passion but without final commitment, the poet aware always of the paradox and unable to surrender to it. Here, too, we find the technique of fusing various plains of reference, where several meanings seem to choose one word or word complex, as in the phrase, 'I plucked the horse's blood'. And cruelty and love, cruelty and faith, are even here inseparable. There is the extraordinary intensity of a mind witnessing to basic causes – the prophetic element, but a prophecy relating to that which occurs in every present time. Few of Hill's poems go by without the word 'death' or 'dead' in them, and 'Genesis' is no exception. It is the beginning of an apprehension of reality based on the observation of cruelty and ephemerality.

When *For the Unfallen* appeared, Hill had developed his technique through attending to the Metaphysical poets. The 'unfallen' in the title are those unslain in battle, in the extermination camps, in other words, survivors; those who, though dead, still have a presence, such as martyrs; and those not yet fallen from grace. The phrase is taken from the last poem in the collection, 'To the (Supposed) Patron', and there refers to those who have not yet experienced nature's inherent cruelty and 'the blood's pain':

For the unfallen – the firstborn, or wise
Councillor – prepared vistas extend
As far as harvest; and idyllic death
Where fish at dawn ignite the powdery lake.

The speaker is not himself among those unfallen.

In 'Merlin' he writes: 'I will consider the outnumbering dead: / For they are the husks of what was rich seed.' Looking back from Merlin's perspective – a variation on which is the perspective in the later *Mercian Hymns* – he senses universal death and rebirth. The heroes were seed and are husks, gone, 'Among the raftered galleries of bone'. Yet, 'Over their city stands the pinnacled corn'. Merlin senses the continuity, seeds growing from the perishing of other seeds; the allegory is strong, for the corn is 'pinnacled' – suggesting as much the ears of wheat as the growth of towns, palaces, and political orders.

'The Bidden Guest', a poem in elegiac tones, expressing the speaker's inability to be touched by the sacrament, accents the importance and the paradox of religious ritual. He must speak, since he cannot feel. So too, love or passion that are frustrated require speech; and a love that requires speech to assert its reality is either dead, and language replaces the form of relationship; or unreciprocated, and language is the unwilled but inevitable distillation, as in 'The Songbook of Sebastian Arrurruz'.

In the first and second books, there is considerable variety of form: quatrains, quasi-sonnets, 'coplas', and so on. But most of the poems are elegiac, addressed to individuals, historical figures, relationships, the victims of war. There is always an imbalance to be lamented, usually the imbalance of some form of love or power. Imbalance leads to changes of form, attempts to renew the balance. Metamorphoses, alterations which reveal more clearly as they progress the actual nature of the imbalance, are a key process in Hill's poetry.

What must strike every reader of the poems is the integrity of the whole work produced to date, the fact that the same themes are taken further, that forms evolve, that the poems illuminate one another. In 'Picture of a Nativity' the 'dumb child-king' emerges into the world of 'Genesis', among 'beasts / With claws flesh-buttered', and serpents. Those who contemplate, like the mourners presented in 'For Isaac Rosenberg' and in 'To a (Supposed) Patron', tend to distance, aestheticize, and neutralize perception, failing to apprehend it. They only 'appear to worship / And fall down', but they 'believe their own eyes / Above the marvel' – and because of their solipsistic response, the liberating Nativity casts them as dead.

The language of many of the poems – 'Canticle for Good Friday', for instance – is spat out. The tough phrases carry the weight of literary usage and yet are crude and new. The lines are effectively bitten off at the rhymes, and yet the breaks are unexpected, miming pain, struggle or disgust. In the 'Canticle' the poet deploys descriptive monosyllables, alternating with abrupt Latinate polysyllables, and the poem is carefully organized in sound effects, with the recurrent hard 'c', 'ch', 'd', 'p' and 'g'. Hill is careful in his use of consonants. One sometimes feels the vowels are not as well-chosen. The paradoxes in the poem are characteristically deft. Thomas stands 'At such near distance'. We read of 'a slight miracle', of 'carrion-sustenance'. There is the brutal pun, 'The cross staggered him'. The poem is about the miraculous paradox: the Son of Man and the son of Mary.

For the Unfallen and King Log include many poems developing the image of music. The titles suggest this: Canticle, Hymn, Requiem, Song, 'Funeral Music', Fantasia, 'Songbook'. In a sense the poems are attempting to transcend their forms into some liturgical function, but they remain poems because the faith is not intact. The titles reflect an aspiration rather than an achievement. Another image which recurs especially in the first book is that of water, the underwater world, death and birth by water. The Tempest must be one of the powers behind Hill's vision, with its firm irresolution, its mixture of cruelty and regeneration, its patterns of recurrence.

'On Commerce and Society' describes the recurrent processes in history, and the sequence of six poems reveals the cruel futility, yet the universal compulsion, of profit. Saint Sebastian makes his first appearance here. His presence is more acutely felt in the person of 'Sebastian Arrurruz', a fictitious Spanish poet who 'lived' between 1868 and 1927, and to whom 'The Songbook of Sebastian Arrurruz' is attributed.

The 'Songbook' opens with bitter matter-of-factness, a tone which recalls another poem in *King Log*, 'September Song', Hill's most ravaging elegy, and closely related to the 'Songbook' love sequence. 'September Song' develops the theme suggested in the poem before it: "That which is taken from me is not mine', a summary of the dominant issue in *King Log*, with its recurrent lament for victims. It is a poem of grim wit and absolute economy. 'Economy' is an apposite word, for the poem describes the extermination of human beings in terms of calculation, profit, loss. The inhumanity of the language, 'proper time', 'estimated', 'thing', 'marched', 'sufficient', 'patented / terror', and the irony of the title, are suddenly interrupted by an assumption, sudden and tentative, of complicity – with the murderer and the victim – by the speaker:

(I have made
an elegy for mysel
it is true)

He steps back from the concentration camps into his own garden, he tends his own bonfires. The analogy is clear. The poem ends: 'This is plenty. This is more than enough.' There is no evasion – he confronts the paradox in which he is implicated. The subtitle of the poem, 'born 19.6.32 – deported 24.9.42', makes it Hill's own elegy.

The 'Songbook' opens with the line, 'Ten years without you. For so it happens'. There is the same stress as in 'September Song' on routine, economy, discipline, those patterns that sublimate passion, conscience, commitment, that make survival in a cruelly paradoxical world possible. The lover falls into words at last. Sublimation has failed. Yet even here he tries to establish 'true sequences of pain'. The words 'proper' and 'value' are telling:

For so it is proper to find value
In a bleak skill, as in the thing restored:
The long-lost words of choice and valediction.

Equal power informs the 'Coplas', a sequence of four three-line poems:

'One cannot lose what one has not possessed'.
So much for that abrasive gem.
I can lose what I want. I want you.

The play with the words 'possess' and 'want' and the irony of 'gem' enhance this brilliantly colloquial and at once perfectly precise statement. The experience of want becomes an image which, in combination with a pithy aphorism, or a sudden experience which the poet cannot share, release the general significance of the particular experience. The image here, as elsewhere in Hill, is verbal, not natural – there is a linguistic imagism at work, the principle of juxtaposition taken deeper. He does not merely set objects or references side by side: he juxtaposes experiences, or a thought and a contrasting experience, the one betraying the other into meaning, without explanation.

Throughout *King Log* the principal theme is power – in various guises – and the individual's relationship to it. In the 'Songbook' it is the power a particular passion, a particular woman, has over another life. Elsewhere the poems explore social and natural tyranny. In *Mercian Hymns* the poet approaches the subject from another angle, from the point of view of the empowered. But *King Log* begins with 'Ovid in the Third Reich', expressing a desire to be left untouched by the terrible facts about him. A professed innocence of evil is an inadequate defence:

I have learned one thing: not to look down
So much upon the damned. They, in their sphere,
Harmonise strangely with the divine
Love. I, in mine, celebrate the love-choir.

'Funeral Music' is an historical foretaste of *Mercian Hymns* – eight unrhymed sonnets, continuous in their development. The poem recounts incidents from the Wars of the Roses with the authority of something *remembered* rather than something imagined, revealing Hill's remarkable historical sense. The theme suggests contemporary analogies without forfeiting its historical particularity. What makes the experience resonant is that it is unfinished; and as we have seen, what is unfinished or flawed is for Hill haunting and generative. He does not go in quest of what might have been but seeks out the durable elements in what was. Martyrs' truncated lives are therefore of great moment, for their meaning is in their incompleteness, they endure because they were cut short.

It would be wrong to speak of Hill's poems – even those credited to specific speakers – as dramatic monologues. They are soliloquies rather than expository set speeches, ruminations from within an experience, not *about* experience. The speakers do not set out to evoke themselves. Sebastian Arrurruz is a voice. It is wrong, too, to consider Hill a baroque poet in his approach to subject matter. The baroque element is in the language, where each word demands attention and relates to its neighbours on several different planes. Hill's poems are almost inexhaustibly generous in their meanings.

The principal flaw in all the poems is Hill's willingness to place too much trust in gritty, immediately effective words. They tend at times to neutralize each other. The tone, too, can become monotonous, as though the poet feels the poem can exist at only one pitch and use one register of language with effect; as though certain experiences, ideas, emotions, have no place, and the scope of the poetry is restricted. These limitations are an aspect of his integrity, however. One feels that he is delineating the areas in which his poetry will exist, but that the best poetry from within those frontiers has yet to come, and will come only when he takes his territory for granted.

Mercian Hymns was written in what Hill has called 'an alarmingly short time' – three years. Thirty poems comprise the sequence. They follow an ostensibly prose form, but it is better to regard the 'paragraphs' as long lines instead, opening as they do with a line set to full type measure, followed by other lines evenly indented. The poem is rigorously phrased rather than cadenced: that is, the through rhythm is replaced by short rhythmic runs; the phrases are juxtaposed. *Mercian Hymns* is formally Hill's most original, if not his most approachable, achievement.

The second poem in the sequence, to take one example from the integrated whole, explores the name 'Offa'. The tone changes from phrase to phrase. The wit which takes us through the complexities of the name – as a pun, as letters, as sound, as significance on a private and social level – reveals the multiple nature of the name and person of Offa, 'a presiding genius of the West Midlands', a person of legend and history with a traditional presence through a span of centuries. This justifies the anachronisms which are carefully handled:

A pet-name, a common name. Best-selling brand, curt
   graffito. A laugh; a cough. A syndicate. A specious
   gift. Scoffed-at horned phonograph.

The starting-cry of a race. A name to conjure with.

The full stops indicate modulations of tone. The movement is that of an Old English riddle. And yet, with brevity, the name acquires its full burden of significance. With the irony of tone Hill adopts with aphorisms, trite expressions, and the frequent religious images, we may be unsure of the specific weight of the last line. 'A name to conjure with' at once undercuts the portentousness of the phrase before, and confirms it by taking the power of the name further, into magic, into the very conjuration Hill is performing.

Mercian Hymns attempts to explore the analogy between the 'objects and justifications' of the 'conduct of government' and 'the conduct of private persons' (the epigraph is taken from C. H. Sisson's *Essays*). Though government and individual differ in technical and methodological aspects, beneath the differences there is an area of identity. Offa is the ideal vehicle to explore this, combining in one person the functions of king (embodiment of the objects and justifications of government) and individual person, and at the same time possessing a legend which Hill exploits skilfully.

There is little doubt that Hill has profited indirectly – through the Modernist writers – from Henri Bergson's ideas about time which Sartre summarized in these terms: 'On going into the past an event does not cease to be; it merely ceases to act and remains "in its place" at its date for eternity. In this way being has been restored to the past, and it is very well done; we even affirm that duration is a multiplicity of interpenetration, and that the past is continually organized with the present.' Hill might question whether the past fact 'ceases to act' – but in *Mercian Hymns* he seems to be tolerably in agreement with the rest of the idea.

The personal element in *Mercian Hymns* can be felt in the occasional affinity between the poet's and Offa's lives. Both are men set apart – not embattled against anything, but rather chosen by circumstance for weighty responsibility, a cultural and *therefore* a social responsibility. King and poet must interpret, act, and speak from a positive relationship with a wide social and historical context.

Since *Mercian Hymns* was published, Hill has advanced on his earlier course. *Mercian Hymns* was, for the time being at least, a detour from his natural course. A recent poem, 'Ecce Tempus', has the intensity of the *King Log* poems, and in terms of sound organization is less jagged, more cadential. It concludes with a juxtaposition similar to that noted in 'Merlin' – death, and the recurrences it feeds. The rhetoric of the *ubi sunt* motif is answered:

The towers of Cluny what are they?
The flowers of Cluny as they are.

Bibliographies

The bibliographies supplied are selective. In general, they direct the reader to the most accessible editions of the poets' works in print, to a few significant critical books or essays on individual writers, to biographies and (by abbreviation) to basic anthologies, critical surveys, or magazines that feature the poets' work or supply critical comment. The word 'collections' is used to refer to verse and prose texts, where relevant.

ANTHOLOGIES

Alvarez, A. *The New Poetry*, Harmondsworth, 1962 (TNP)

Hamilton, I. *The Poetry of War 1939–45*, London, 1965

Heath-Stubbs, J., and David Wright *The Faber Book of Twentieth Century Verse*, London, 1965 (FB)

Jones, P. *Imagist Poetry*, Harmondsworth, 1972 (IP)

Larkin, P. *The Oxford Book of Twentieth Century English Verse*, Oxford, 1973 (OB)

Lucie-Smith, E. *British Poetry since 1945*, Harmondsworth, 1970 (BP)

Reeves, J. *Georgian Verse*, Harmondsworth, 1962 (GP)

Roberts, M. *The Faber Book of Modern Verse*, London, 1965 (FBMV)

Skelton, R. *Poetry of the Thirties*, Harmondsworth, 1964

Skelton, R. *Poetry of the Forties*, Harmondsworth, 1968

Wright, D. *The Mid-Century: English Poetry 1940–1960*, Harmondsworth, 1965 (TMC)

Wright, D. *Longer Contemporary Poems*, Harmondsworth, 1966 (LCP)

Penguin Modern Poets Series (PMP)

GENERAL CRITICAL WORKS

Alvarez, A. *The Shaping Spirit*, London, 1958

Bedient, C. *Eight Contemporary Poets*, London, 1974 (8CP)

Bergonzi, B. (ed) *The Twentieth Century*, London, 1970

Davie, D. *Thomas Hardy and British Poetry*, London, 1972

Dodsworth, M. (ed) *The Survival of Poetry*, London, 1970 (TSP)

Dunn, D. (ed) *Two Decades of Irish Writing*, Manchester, 1975 (2DIW)

Fraser, G. S. *The Modern Writer and his World*, Harmondsworth, 1968

Fraser, G. S. *Vision and Rhetoric*, London, 1959

Hamburger, M. *The Truth of Poetry*, Harmondsworth, 1972

Hamilton, I. (ed) *The Modern Poet*, London, 1968

Leavis, F. R. *New Bearings in English Poetry*, London, 1961

Maxwell, D. E. S. *Poets of the Thirties*, London, 1969

Press, J. *A Map of Modern English Verse*, London, 1969

Schmidt, M., and Grevel Lindop (eds) *British Poetry since 1960*, Manchester, 1972 (BPS1960)

Sisson, C. H. *English Poetry 1900–1950*, London, 1971 (EP)

Stead, C. K. *The New Poetic*, Harmondsworth, 1967

Symons, J. *The Thirties, a Dream Revolved*, London, 1975

Thurley, G. *The Ironic Harvest: English Poetry in the Twentieth Century*, London, 1974

PERIODICALS

Agenda, London (A)

Critical Quarterly, Manchester (CQ)

London Magazine, London (LM)

The New Review, London (TNR)

PN Review, Manchester (PN)

The Review, London (TR)

Stand, Newcastle upon Tyne (S)

The Poets

Thomas Hardy

Anthologies: OB, FB

Periodicals: A, CQ

Collections:

Collected Poems, London, 1930

The Dynasts, London, 1965

Selected Poems, ed P. N. Furbank, London, 1966

Selected Shorter Poems, ed J. Wain, London, 1966

Stories and Poems, ed D. J. Morrison, London, 1971

Complete Poems, ed J. Gibson, London, 1978

Poems: A New Selection, ed T. R. M. Creighton, London, 1978

Criticism and Biography:
Hardy, F. E. *The Life of Thomas Hardy*, London, 1962
Cox, R. G. *Thomas Hardy* (Critical Heritage), London, 1970
Davie, D. *Thomas Hardy and British Poetry*, London, 1972
Lawrence, D. H. *A Study of Thomas Hardy*, London, 1973
Marsden, K. *The Poems of Thomas Hardy: a Critical Introduction*, London, 1969
Paulin, T. *Thomas Hardy: the Poetry of Perception*, London, 1975
EP

A. E. Housman

Anthologies: OB, FB, GP

Collections:
Collected Poems, London, 1967
Poetry and Prose, a Selection, London, 1971
A Shropshire Lad, London, 1972
Last Poems (Little Treasury Series), London, 1974

Criticism:
Ricks, C. (ed) *A. E. Housman: A Collection of Critical Essays*, Englewood Cliffs, 1969
EP

Rudyard Kipling

Anthologies: OB, FB

Collections:
Verse: Definitive Edition, London, 1940
A Choice of Kipling's Verse, ed T. S. Eliot, London, 1941
Stories and Poems, London, 1970
Complete Barrack Room Ballads, ed C. E. Carrington, London, 1973
Selected Verse, ed J. Cochrane, Harmondsworth, 1977

Criticism:
Carrington, C. E. (ed) *Rudyard Kipling*, Harmondsworth, 1970
Green, R. L. (ed) *Rudyard Kipling* (Critical Heritage), London, 1971
Rutherford, A. *Some Aspects of Kipling's Verse* (British Academy Lecture), London, 1967

W. B. Yeats

Anthologies: OB, FB, FBMV
Periodicals: A, CQ, PN

Collections:
(ed) *Oxford Book of Modern Verse*, Oxford, 1936
Collected Poems, London, 1950
Poems, ed P. Allt and R. K. Alspach (Variorum), London, 1957
Essays and Introductions, London, 1961
Poems, ed A. N. Jeffares, London, 1962
Selected Plays, ed A. N. Jeffares, London, 1964
Selected Prose, ed A. N. Jeffares, London, 1964
Selected Criticism, ed A. N. Jeffares, London, 1965
Letters on Poetry to Dorothy Wellesley, London
Memoirs, ed D. Donoghue, London, 1973

Criticism:
Bloom, H. *Yeats*, New York, 1970
Donoghue, D. *W. B. Yeats*, London, 1971
Ellmann, R. *W. B. Yeats: the Man and the Masks*, London, 1961
Hone, J. W. *W. B. Yeats*, Harmondsworth, 1971
Jeffares, A. N. *W. B. Yeats*, London, 1971
Jeffares, A. N. *Commentary on the Collected Poems*, London, 1968
MacNeice, L. *The Poetry of W. B. Yeats*, London, 1967
Stallworthy, J. *Yeats's 'Last Poems'* (Casebook Series), London, 1968
Stock, N. *W. B. Yeats, His Poetry and Thought*, London, 1961
Young, D. *Out of Ireland*, Manchester, 1975
EP, 2 DIW

Charlotte Mew
Anthologies: OB
Periodicals: PN
Collections:
Collected Poems (with a Memoir by Alida Monro), London, 1953
Collected Poems and Prose (ed Val Warner), Manchester, 1979

Walter de la Mare
Anthologies: OB, FB, GP
Collections:
Complete Poems, London, 1969
Collected Rhymes and Verses, London, 1970
Come Hither, Harmondsworth, 1973
Selected Poems, London, 1973
Collected Poems, London, 1978

Criticism:
Cecil, Lord David, *Walter de la Mare*, London, 1973
Hopkins, K. *Walter de la Mare* (Writers and their Work), London, 1973
EP

Edward Thomas
Anthologies: OB, FB, GP
Periodicals: TNR
Collections:
Collected Poems, London, 1949
Selected Poems, London, 1964
Letters to Gordon Bottomley, ed R. G. Thomas, London, 1968
Poems and Last Poems, ed E. Longley, London, 1973
Criticism and Biography:
As it Was and *World without End*, by Helen Thomas, London, 1956
Time and Again: Memoirs and Letters, by Helen Thomas, Manchester, 1978
Cooke, W. *Edward Thomas: A Critical Biography*, London, 1970
Coombes, H: *Edward Thomas*, London, 1973
EP

Wyndham Lewis
Anthologies: OB, FB
Periodicals: A, PN
Collections:
Unlucky for Pringle: Unpublished and other stories, ed C. J. Fox, London, 1973
Enemy Salvoes: Selected Literary Criticism, ed C. J. Fox, London, 1976
Collected Poems and Plays, ed A. Munton, Manchester, 1979
Criticism:
Chapman, R. *Wyndham Lewis, Fictions and Satires*, London, 1973
Pritchard, G. *Wyndham Lewis* (Profiles in Literature), London, 1972
EP
Tomlin, E. W. F. *Wyndham Lewis* (Writers and their Work), London, 1973

T. E. Hulme
Anthologies: OB, FBMV, IP
Collections:
Speculations, ed H. Read, London, 1936

Criticism:
EP, IP

D. H. Lawrence

Anthologies: OB, FB, FBMV, IP

Collections:

Complete Poems (3 vols), London, 1957

Selected Poems, ed James Reeves, London, 1967

Selected Poetry, ed Keith Sagar, Harmondsworth, 1972

Complete Poems, ed V. de Sola Pinto and F. W. Roberts, London, 1976

Criticism:

Beal, A. *D. H. Lawrence*, Edinburgh, 1961

Sagar, K. *The Art of D. H. Lawrence*, London, 1966

Spilka, M. (ed) *D. H. Lawrence* (Twentieth Century Views), Englewood Cliffs (nd)

EP, IP

Edwin Muir

Anthologies: OB, FB, PMP 23, FBMV, BP, TMC

Collections:

The Estate of Poetry, London, 1962

Collected Poems, London, 1964

Essays on Literature and Society, London, 1965

Selected Poems, London, 1965

Autobiography, London, 1968

Criticism:

Butter, P. H. *Edwin Muir* (Writers and Critics), Edinburgh, 1962

Butter, P. H. *Edwin Muir: Man and Poet*, Edinburgh, 1966

Gardner, H. *Edwin Muir* (W. D. Thomas Memorial Lecture), University of Wales, 1961

Edith Sitwell

Anthologies: OB, FB, FBMV

Collections:

Selected Poems, ed J. Lehmann, London, 1965

Letters, ed J. Lehmann, London, 1970

Façade and Other Poems 1920–35, London, 1971

The Poet's Notebook, Greenwood Press, 1972

Criticism:

Lehmann, J. *Edith Sitwell* (Writers and Their Work), London

Elizabeth Daryush

Periodicals: PN

Collections:
Selected Poems, Manchester, 1972
Collected Poems, with an introduction by Donald Davie, Manchester, 1977

Criticism:
Fuller, R. *Owls and Artificers*, London, 1974
Winters, Y. *The Uncollected Essays and Reviews*, Chicago, 1973

T. S. Eliot

Anthologies: OB, FB, FBMV

Periodicals: CQ

Collections:
Four Quartets, London, 1944
Collected Plays, London, 1962
Collected Poems, London, 1963
Selected Poems, London, 1964
Poems Written in Early Youth, London, 1967
Complete Poems and Plays, London, 1969
Selected Essays, London, 1973
Collected Poems, London, 1974
The Waste Land : Facsimile and Transcript of the Original Draft, ed V. Eliot,
London, 1974

Criticism:
Gardner, H. *The Art of T. S. Eliot*, London, 1968
Gardner, H. *The Composition of the Four Quartets*, London, 1978
Maxwell, D. E. S. *The Poetry of T. S. Eliot*, London, 1972
Southam, B. C. *Student's Guide to the Selected Poems of T. S. Eliot*, London,
1969
EP

Isaac Rosenberg

Anthologies: OB, FB, FBMV

Periodicals: A, PN, S

Collections:
Poems, ed D. W. Harding, London, 1972

Criticism and Biography:
Cohen, J. M. *Journey to the Trenches : the Life of Isaac Rosenberg 1890–1918*,
London, 1975
Liddiard, J. *A Half Used Life*, London, 1975

Hugh MacDiarmid (C. M. Grieve)
Anthologies: OB, FB, FBMV, BP, LCP, TMC
Periodicals: A
Collections:
In Memoriam James Joyce, Edinburgh, 1955
Clyack-sheaf, London, 1969
Selected Essays, ed D. Glen, London, 1969
More Collected Poems, London, 1970
Selected Poems, ed D. Craig and J. Manson, Harmondsworth, 1970
The Hugh MacDiarmid Anthology, ed M. Grieve and A. Scott, London, 1972
Criticism:
Buthlay, K. *Hugh MacDiarmid* (Writers and Critics), Edinburgh, 1964
Duval, K. D., and S. G. Smith (eds) *Hugh MacDiarmid: a Festschrift*, Edinburgh, 1962
Glen, D. (ed) *Hugh MacDiarmid and the Scottish Renaissance*, Edinburgh, 1964
EP

Wilfred Owen
Anthologies: OB, FB, FBMV, GP
Periodicals: CQ, S
Collections:
Collected Letters, ed H. Owen, London, 1967
Collected Poems, ed C. Day Lewis, London, 1967
Poems, ed E. Blunden, London, 1968
War Poems and Others: A Selection, ed D. Hibberd, London, 1973
Criticism and Biography:
Owen, H. *Journey from Obscurity: Wilfred Owen 1893–1919*, 3 vols, London, 1965
Stallworthy, J. *A Biography*, London, 1974
Welland, D. *Wilfred Owen: A Critical Study*, London, 1976
EP

David Jones
Anthologies: FB, FBMV, BP
Collections:
In Parenthesis, London, 1969
Anathemata, London, 1972
Epoch and Artist, London, 1973

The Sleeping Lord and Other Fragments, London, 1974
The Dying Gaul, London, 1978
Criticism:
Blamires, D. *David Jones, Artist and Writer*, Manchester, 1971
Cookson, W. *Agenda* (two special issues devoted to Jones's poetic, prose, and graphic work)
Hooker, J. *David Jones : An Exploratory Study of His Writings*, London, 1975
Matthias, J. (ed) *David Jones*, Aberystwyth, 1976

Robert Graves
Anthologies: OB, FB, FBMV, GP, BP, TMC
Collections:
New Poems 1962, London, 1962
Poems About Love, London, 1964
Poetic Craft and Principle, London, 1967
Selected Poems, Harmondsworth, 1968
Good-bye to All That, Harmondsworth, 1969
Poems 1968–70, London, 1970
Timeless Meeting, London, 1973
Collected Poems, London, 1975
Criticism:
Cohen, J. M. *Robert Graves* (Writers and Critics), Edinburgh, 1960
Kirkham, M. *The Poetry of Robert Graves*, London, 1969
Seymour-Smith, M. *Robert Graves* (Writers and their Work), London
Slade, G. *Robert Graves* (Essays on Modern Writers), Col. U. P., 1967
EP

Austin Clarke
Anthologies: OB
Periodicals: PN
Collections:
Collected Plays, Dublin, 1963
Old Fashioned Pilgrimage and Other Poems, Dublin, 1967
Echo at Coole and Other Poems, Dublin, 1968
Collected Poems, Dublin, 1974
Poems 1917–38, ed Liam Miller; *Poems 1955–66*, ed Liam Miller; *Poems 1967–74*, ed Liam Miller, all Dublin, 1975
Criticism:
Halpern, S. *Austin Clarke : His Life and Works*, Dublin, 1975

Montague, J. and L. Miller (eds) *Tribute to Austin Clarke on his Seventieth Birthday*, Dublin, 1966
2DIW

Edmund Blunden
Anthologies: OB, FB, GP
Criticism:
Hardie, A. M. *Edmund Blunden* (Writers and their Work), London
Thorp, R. *The Poetry of Edmund Blunden*, Maidstone, 1971

Edgell Rickword
Anthologies: OB, FB
Periodicals: PN, TNR
Collections:
Fifty Poems, A Selection, with a preface by Roy Fuller, London, 1970
Essays and Opinions 1921–31, ed Alan Young, Manchester, 1974
Collected Poems and Translations, Manchester, 1976
Literature in Society: Essays and Opinions 1931–1978, ed Alan Young, Manchester, 1978
Criticism:
EP

Basil Bunting
Anthologies: OB, BP
Periodicals: A, PN
Collections:
Briggflatts, London, 1966
Collected Poems, London, 1968
Collected Poems, London, 1978

Stevie Smith
Anthologies: OB, FB, PMP 8, BP, TMC
Collections:
Two in One, London, 1971
Novel on Yellow Paper, Harmondsworth, 1972
Collected Poems, London, 1975
Criticism:
8CP

Patrick Kavanagh

Anthologies: OB, FB, LCP, TMC

Collections:
The Green Fool, London, 1971
Collected Poems, London, 1972
Tarry Flynn, London, 1972
Self Portrait, Dublin, 1975

Criticism:
Warner, A. *Patrick Kavanagh, 1904–67 : 'Clay is the Word'*, Dublin, 1974
EP, 8CP, 2DIW

William Empson

Anthologies: OB, FB, FBMV, TMC

Periodicals: TR

Collections:
Collected Poems, London, 1962
Some Versions of Pastoral, Harmondsworth, 1966
Seven Types of Ambiguity, Harmondsworth, 1973

Criticism:
Gill, R. (ed) *William Empson : The Man and his Works*, London, 1974
Willis, J. R. *William Empson* (Essays on Modern Writers), Col. U. P., 1969
EP

John Betjeman

Anthologies: OB, FB, BP, TMC

Collections:
Ring of Bells : Poems, London, 1964
High and Low, London, 1966
First and Last Loves, London, 1969
Summoned by Bells, London, 1969
Collected Poems, London, 1970
A Nip in the Air, London, 1974
Ten Late Chrysanthemums, London, 1975

Criticism:
Stapleton, M. L. *Sir John Betjeman : A Bibliography of Writings by and about him*, London, 1975

Louis MacNeice

Anthologies: OB, FB, FBMV, BP, TMC

Collections:
The Dark Tower, London, 1964
Selected Poems, ed W. H. Auden, London, 1964
Collected Poems, London, 1966
The Poetry of William Butler Yeats, (ed) London, 1967
Modern Poetry: A Personal Essay, London, 1969

Criticism:
Brown, T. *Sceptical Vision*, London, 1975
McKinnon, R. *Apollo's Blended Dream*, London, 1971
Moore, D. B. *The Poetry of Louis MacNeice*, Leicester, 1972
EP, 2DIW

W. H. Auden

Anthologies: OB, FB, FBMV, LCP, TMC

Periodicals: TR

Collections:
The Dyer's Hand, London, 1963
About the House, London, 1966
Collected Shorter Poems, London, 1966
Collected Longer Poems, London, 1968
Secondary Worlds, London, 1968
City Without Walls, London, 1969
Selected Poems, Harmondsworth, 1970
Epistle to a Godson, London, 1972
Forewords and Afterwords, London, 1973
Thank You, Fog, London, 1974
Collected Poems, London, 1976
The English Auden, London, 1977

Criticism:
Davison, D. *W. H. Auden* (Literature in Perspective), London, 1970
Duchene, F. *The Case of the Helmeted Airman*, London, 1970
Everett, B. *Auden*, Edinburgh, 1964
Fuller, J. *Reader's Guide to W. H. Auden*, London, 1970
Spears, M. K. *Disenchanted Island*, New York, 1963
Spears, M. K. (ed) *W. H. Auden* (Twentieth Century Views), Englewood Cliffs, 1964
Spender, S. (ed) *W. H. Auden: A Tribute*, London, 1975
EP

Roy Fuller
Anthologies: OB, PMP 18, BP, TMC

Periodicals: LM, PN

Collections:
Brutus's Orchard, London, 1957
Collected Poems 1936–1961, London, 1962
New Poems, London, 1968
Off Course, London, 1969
Owls and Artificers, London, 1971
Tiny Tears, London, 1973
From the Joke Shop, London, 1975
Professors and Gods, London, 1977

George Barker

Anthologies: OB, FB, PMP 3, FBMV, BP, LCP, TMC

Collections:
Collected Poems, London, 1957
To Aylsham Fair, London, 1970
Essays, London, 1970
Poems of Places and People, London, 1971
In Memoriam David Archer, London, 1973
Dialogues, etc., London, 1976

Criticism:
Stubbs, J. H. (ed) *Homage to George Barker on his Sixtieth Birthday*, London, 1973
EP

R. S. Thomas

Anthologies: OB, FB, PMP 1, FBMV, TNP, BP

Periodicals: CQ

Collections:
Pieta, London, 1966
Not that He Brought Flowers, London, 1968
H'm, London, 1972
Selected Poems 1946–1968, London, 1973
Laboratories of the Spirit, London, 1975
Frequencies, London, 1978

Criticism:
8CP

C. H. Sisson

Anthologies: OB, FB, TMC

Periodicals: CQ, PN, A

Collections:

English Poetry 1900–1950, London, 1971
In the Trojan Ditch: Collected Poems and Selected Translations, Manchester, 1974
Art and Action, Manchester, 1975
Christopher Homm: A Novel, Manchester, 1975
The Poetic Art (Horace), Manchester, 1975
Anchises: New Poems, Manchester, 1976
The Poem about Nature (Lucretius), Manchester, 1976
The Avoidance of Literature: Collected Essays, ed M. Schmidt, Manchester, 1978

Dylan Thomas

Anthologies: OB, FB, FBMV, BP, TMC

Collections:

Portrait of the Artist as a Young Dog, London, 1940
Deaths and Entrances, London, 1946
Under Milk Wood, London, 1954
Adventures in the Skin Trade, London, 1965
Selected Letters, ed C. Fitzgibbon, London, 1966
Collected Poems 1934–53, London, 1966
A Child's Christmas in Wales, London, 1968
Selected Poems, ed W. Davies, London, 1975

Criticism and Biography:

The Life of Dylan Thomas by C. Fitzgibbon, London, 1965
Cox, C. B. (ed) *Dylan Thomas: A Collection of Critical Essays*, Englewood Cliffs, 1966
Fraser, G. S. *Dylan Thomas* (Writers and their Work), London
Holbrook, D. *The Code of Night*, London, 1972

David Gascoyne

Anthologies: OB, FB, PMP 17, FBMV, BP, TMC

Collections:

Night Thoughts, London, 1956
Collected Poems, ed R. Skelton, London, 1970
Collected Verse Translations, ed A. Clodd and R. Skelton, London, 1970
Sun at Midnight, London, 1970
A Short Survey of Surrealism, London, 1971

Criticism:

EP

Charles Causley
Anthologies: OB, FB, PMP 3, BP, TMC
Collections:
Underneath the Water, London, 1968
Figure of Eight, London, 1969
Figgie Hobbin, Poems for Children, London, 1971
Collected Poems, London, 1975

W. S. Graham
Anthologies: OB, FB, PMP 17, FBMV, BP, LCP, TMC
Periodicals: PN
Collections:
Malcolm Mooney's Land, London, 1970
Implements in their Places, London, 1977
Criticism:
8CP, BPS 1960

Keith Douglas
Anthologies: OB, FB, FBMV, TMC
Collections:
Selected Poems, London, 1964
Collected Poems, ed J. Waller et al., London, 1966
Alamein to Zem Zem, London, 1967
Complete Poems, ed Desmond Graham, London, 1978
Criticism and Biography:
Keith Douglas: A Biography, by D. Graham, London, 1974
Fraser, G. S. *Keith Douglas* (Chatterton Lecture), Brit. Academy, 1956

Edwin Morgan
Anthologies: PMP 15, BP
Collections:
The Second Life: Selected Poems, Edinburgh, 1968
Wi the Haill Voice (Mayakovsky), Manchester, 1972
From Glasgow to Saturn, Manchester, 1973
Essays, Manchester, 1974
The New Divan, Manchester, 1976
Rites of Passage: Selected Translations, Manchester, 1976

Donald Davie
Anthologies: OB, FB, FBMV, TNP, BP, TMC

Periodicals: A, CQ, PN, TR

Collections:

Events and Wisdoms: Poems 1957–63, London, 1964

Ezra Pound: Poet as Sculptor, London, 1965

Articulate Energy, London, 1966

Purity of Diction in English Verse, London, 1967

Six Epistles to Eva Hesse, London, 1970

Collected Poems 1950–1970, London, 1972

Thomas Hardy and British Poetry, London, 1972

The Shires, London, 1975

The Poet in the Imaginary Museum: Essays, ed B. Alpert, Manchester, 1977

In the Stopping Train and Other Poems, Manchester, 1977

Criticism:

8CP

Philip Larkin

Anthologies: OB, FB, FBMV, TNP, BP, TMC

Periodicals: CQ, PN, TR

Collections:

Jill, London, 1964

The Whitsun Weddings, London, 1964

Oxford Book of Twentieth Century English Verse (ed), London, 1973

High Windows, London, 1974

The Less Deceived, London, 1974

The North Ship, London, 1974

Criticism:

Timms, D. *Philip Larkin*, Edinburgh, 1973

8CP, TSP

Michael Hamburger

Anthologies: OB, PMP 14, TNP, BP, TMC

Periodicals: A, PN, TR, S

Collections:

The Truth of Poetry, Harmondsworth, 1972

East German Poetry, Manchester, 1972

A Mug's Game: Intermittent Memoirs, Manchester, 1973

Ownerless Earth: New and Selected Poems, Manchester, 1973

Art as Second Nature, Manchester, 1975

German Poetry 1910–1975, Manchester, 1977

Real Estate, Manchester, 1977

424   Bibliographies

Elizabeth Jennings
Anthologies: OB, PMP 1, BP, TMC
Periodicals: CQ, PN
Collections:
Every Changing Shape, London, 1961
Collected Poems, London, 1967
The Animals' Arrival, London, 1969
Lucidities, London, 1970
Relationships, London, 1972
Growing-Points, Manchester, 1975
Consequently I Rejoice, Manchester, 1977
Criticism:
BPS 1960

Christopher Middleton
Anthologies: PMP 4, FBMV, TNP, BP
Periodicals: A, PN
Collections:
Our Flowers & Nice Bones, London, 1970
The Lonely Suppers of W. V. Balloon, Manchester, 1975
Pataxanadu, Manchester, 1976
Bolshevism in Art and other expository writings, Manchester, 1978

Charles Tomlinson
Anthologies: OB, PMP 14, FBMV, TNP, TMC
Periodicals: CQ, TNR, PN, TR
Collections:
American Scenes and Other Poems, London, 1966
Seeing is Believing, London, 1969
A Peopled Landscape, London, 1970
Written on Water, London, 1972
The Way In, London, 1974
In Black and White: The Graphics of Charles Tomlinson, with an Introduction
by Octavio Paz, Manchester, 1975
Criticism:
8CP, BPS 1960

Burns Singer
Periodicals: PN

Collections:
Collected Poems, ed W. A. S. Keir, Manchester, 1975
Selected Poems, ed Anne Cluysenaar, Manchester, 1977

Criticism:
BPS1960

Thom Gunn

Anthologies: OB, FB, FBMV, TNP, BP, TMC

Periodicals: CQ, PN

Collections:
A Sense of Movement, London, 1957
Thom Gunn and Ted Hughes: Selected Poems, London, 1962
Fighting Terms, London, 1970
Moly, London, 1971
My Sad Captains, London, 1974
Poems 1950–66: A Selection, London, 1974
Jack Straw's Castle, London, 1976
Criticism:
TSP

Ted Hughes

Anthologies: OB, FB, FBMV, TNP, BP, TMC

Periodicals: CQ, PN

Collections:
Hawk in the Rain, London, 1957
Lupercal, London, 1960
Thom Gunn and Ted Hughes: Selected Poems, London, 1962
Earth Owl and Other Moon People, London, 1963
Wodwo, London, 1967
Selected Poems 1957–67, London, 1972
Crow, London, 1973
Selected Poems of Janos Pilinszky, Manchester, 1976
Gandete, London, 1977
Criticism:
Sagar, K. *Ted Hughes* (Writers and their Work), London, 1972
8CP, TSP, BPS1960

Jon Silkin
Anthologies: OB, PMP 7, TNP, BP

Periodicals: S

Collections:
Nature with Man, London, 1965
Amana Grass, London, 1971
Killhope Wheel, Ashington, 1971
Air that Pricks Earth, London, 1973
Poetry and the Committed Individual, Harmondsworth, 1973
The Principle of Water, Manchester, 1974
The Little Time-Keeper, Manchester, 1976

Criticism:
BPS 1960

Geoffrey Hill

Anthologies: OB, FB, PMP 8, FBMV, TNP, BP, TMC

Periodicals: A, PN, S

Collections:
King Log, London, 1970
For the Unfallen, London, 1971
Mercian Hymns, London, 1971
Tenebrae, London, 1978

Criticism:
BPS 1960

Index

About the House 237, 238
Acre of Land, An 260
'Air and Variations' 116–17
Amana Grass 393, 396
American Scenes 361, 364
'Among School Children' 56, 112
Anathemata 161–5
'Ancestral Homes' 55–6
*Ancient Lights: Poems and Satires,
   First Series* 177–8
Another Time 236
Ascent of F6, The 236
Ash Wednesday 124, 126, 132–3
'Asleep' 154
'At the Grave of John Clare' 291
Auden, W. H. 25, 233–43
'Autumn' 92, 93
Autumn Journal 230
Autumn Sequel 231–2

'Ballad of East and West, The' 42
'Ballad of Hector in Hades' 107
Barker, George 251–9, 287
'Barn, The' 183
Barrack Room Ballads 36, 40
'Bavarian Gentians' 100, 101
'Before I Knocked' 281
'Before the Anaesthetic' 222
Betjeman, Sir John 220–24, 260
'Biography of an Idealist' 373–4
'Birthday Ruminations' 191

Blind Fireworks 229
'Blind Lead the Blind, The' 185
Blunden, Edmund 67–8, 181–5
Bread of Truth, The 260
Brides of Reason 322
Briggflatts 195, 197–8
Brutus's Orchard 245
Buff 245
Bunting, Basil 193–9
'Burning Glass, The' 67
Burning Perch, The 232
Burnt Norton 125
'Byzantium' 56, 112

Cage without Grievance 298
Calamiterror 251–2, 253, 254–6
Cattledrive in Connaught, The 175
Causley, Charles 290–96
Certain World, A 239
'Chomei at Toyoma' 199
'Circus Animals' Desertion, The'
   56
City without Walls 242
Clarke, Austin 173–80, 209
'Cloak, The' 167
'Colonel Fantock' 109–10
Come Dance with Kitty Stobbling 208
Continual Dew 221
'Cool Web, The' 171, 282
'Corner Boy's Farewell' 375
Counterparts 245

'Counting the Beats' 171
'Coward, The' 37
'Cromlech, The' 228
Crossways 51
Crow 384–6, 389–91
'Crystals like Blood' 146

Dance of Death, The 236
'Daphne' 273–4
'Dark Ireland' 208
Daryush, Elizabeth 30–31, 115–20
Davie, Donald 24, 269, 321–9
'Day of Renewal' 231–2
'Dead Heroes, The' 138
Deaths and Entrances 279
De la Mare, Walter 64–8, 75
Departmental Ditties 36
'De Profundis' 289
'Discarnation, The' 274
'Discord in Childhood' 95
Dog Beneath the Skin, The 236
'Donkey, The' 202
Douglas, Keith 153, 184, 305–13
Dreams of a Summer Night 252
Drunk Man Looks at the Thistle, A
    143–5
Dry Salvages, The 125
Dual Site, The 314, 342
Dynasts, The 22–3

Earth Compels, The 229
East Coker 125
'Easter 1916' 55
Eliot, T. S. 25, 39, 79, 88, 121–33,
    147
Empson, William 92–3, 213–19
'Engine Fight Talk' 84, 85
'Envoy, The' 84, 87
Epitaphs and Occasions 245, 249
Eros in Dogma 252
'Especially when the October
    Wind' 279–80

Essex Poems 323, 324
Events and Wisdoms 323

Façade 110, 112–14
Fairies and Fusiliers 168
'Fall, The' 104, 106
Farewell, Aggie Weston 292
'Farmer's Bride, The' 58
Feeding the Chickadees 341
'Fête, The' 61
Figgie Hobbin 292
'Fisherman, The' 54–5
Flight to Africa 177
'Florestan to Leonora' 247
Flowering Cactus 340
Forests of Lithuania, The 322
Forget Me Not 179
'Forgotten the Red Leaves'
    309–10
For the Unfallen 398, 400–402
Four Quartets 125, 126, 133
'Fox, The' 364
Frog Prince, The 202
From Glasgow to Saturn 317–18
Fuller, Roy 244–50
Full Moon in March, A 56

Gascoyne, David 285–90
'Gerontion' 127, 128
'Glasgow Sonnets' 314, 319
Gold Coast Customs 110–11, 113
Golden Chains, The 252
Goliath and David 168
Good Time Was Had By All, A 201
Graham, W. S. 297–304
Graves, Robert 26, 166–72, 282
Great Hunger, The 208, 210–11
Green Helmet and Other Poems, The
    52
'Green Hills of Africa, The' 246
'Grignolles (Brittany)' 80
Growing Points 350–52

Gunn, Thom 376–82

Hamburger, Michael 339–45
Hands to Dance 292
Hardy, Thomas 13–26, 27, 30, 31,
   37, 43, 79
Harold's Leap 201–2
Hawk in the Rain, 384, 386–7
'He' 265
'Hebrides, The' 229–30
High Windows 332, 335, 337–8
Hill, Geoffrey 398–407
H'm 261, 264
Hölderlin's Madness 286, 289
Holes in the Sky 231
Hollow Men, The 124
'Homo Sapiens is of No
   Importance' 276–7
Horse Eaters, The 178
'Hospital Barge at Cérisy' 154–5
'House of Mercy, A' 200–201
'House on a Cliff' 232
Houseman, A. E. 25, 27–34
'How Do You See?' 202
'How Duke Valentine Contrived'
   198–9
Hughes, Ted 306–7, 383–91
Hulme, T. E. 88–93
'Human Fold, The' 108
'Humoresque' 123

'Idiot Boy, The' 40
'I Have Been Taught' 105–6
'Images' 92
'In Insula Avalonia' 269–70
In Memoriam David Archer 252, 258
In Memoriam James Joyce 140, 142,
   147
'In Memory of Major Robert
   Gregory' 51, 54
'Innumerable Christ, The' 143
Instamatic Poems 315–16

In the Seven Woods 52
*In the Trojan Ditch: Collected Poems
   and Selected Translations* 271
'Invocation' 111
'In Westminster Abbey' 223
'I Saw a Shot-Down Angel' 292–3
'I See the Boys of Summer' 280–81

Jennings, Elizabeth 346–52
'Jewels, The' 177
Johnny Alleluia 292
Jones, David 156–65
'Journey Back, The' 104
Journey to a War 236

Kavanagh, Patrick 207–12
King Log 398, 402, 403–4, 407
Kipling, Rudyard 22, 27, 35–43

Lament and Triumph 252
Larkin, Philip 31, 330–38
'Late Wasp, The' 108
Lawrence, D. H. 83, 94–101
Less Deceived, The 332, 335–6
Letters from Iceland 229
Lewis, Wyndham 79–87, 90
'Lines to Yeats' 208
'Listeners, The' 66–7
Little Gidding 125
London Zoo, The 267, 270
*Lonely Suppers of W. V. Balloon,
   The* 354, 358, 359
Look Stranger 236
Loquitur 195
Lost Season, A 245, 248–9
'Love Song of J. Alfred Prufrock,
   The' 123, 126, 127–8
Lupercal 384, 387–9

'McAndrew's Hymn' 40–41
MacDiarmid, Hugh 102, 140–47
MacNeice, Louis 225–32, 254–5

'Madeleine in Church' 61–3
'Malcolm Mooney's Land' 301–3
'Man He Killed, The' 15, 23
Man's Life Is His Meat 285
Map of Love, The 279
'Marina' 132–3
'Marvel, The' 310, 311
Mercian Hymns 398, 401, 404–7
Metamorphoses 270–71, 272
Mew, Charlotte 57–63
Michael Robartes and the Dancer 55
Middle of a War, The 245, 248
Middleton, Christopher 353–9
'Midnight Skaters, The' 183
Mind Has Mountains, The 347
Miserere 287
'Mnemosyne Lay in Dust' 179
Moly 377, 381–2
Morgan, Edwin 314–20
Mother, What is Man 201
Mount Zion 221
'Mr Over' 206
Muir, Edward 102–8, 139
Murder in the Cathedral 130
Muse Among the Motors, The 39–40
My Sad Captains 377, 379
'Myth, The' 102–3, 106

Nature with Man 393, 395–6
Necklace, The 360–61
News of the World 252, 258
'New Year Greeting, A' 242–3
Night and Morning 176–7
Nightfishing, The 297–301
Night Thoughts 286, 288
Nonsequences/Selfpoems 254, 357
North Ship, The 331, 333, 335, 337
Not that he Brought Flowers 261
'Not Waving but Drowning' 204–5
'Now It's Happened' 99–100
Numbers 270

'Obituary of R. Fuller' 249–50
Old Bats in New Belfries 221
Old Fashioned Pilgrimage and Other Poems 180
'Old Man' 74, 76
'On a Raised Beach' 146
One Way Song 80, 81–4
On the Frontier 236
Orators, The 236
Our Flowers and Nice Bones 354, 357
Out of the Picture 229
Over the Brazier 168
Owen, Wilfred 148–55
Ownerless Earth 341, 344

'Paddiad, The' 211, 212
Paid on Both Sides: A Charade 236
Pansies 99
'Parable of the Old Man and the Young, The' 153
Pataxanadu 354, 358
Peaceable Kingdom, The 393–5
Peopled Landscape, A 361, 363
Pieta 261, 263–4
Pilgrimage and other Poems 176
Plants and Phantoms 231
Ploughman and Other Poems 207
'Poem in October' 284
'Poem from France' 61
Poems of Dr Zhivago, The 323
Poetry for Supper 260, 261, 264
'Poor Man's Pig, The' 183
'Portrait of a Lady' 123, 128
'Prayer for my Daughter, A' 50, 55
Principle of Water, The 393, 396–7
'Prisoner, The' 307
'Prologue at Sixty' 238

'Quick and the Dead, The' 184
'Quiet House, The' 63

Recoveries 347
'Recovery, The' 184
Redimiculum Matellarum 195
Re-ordering of the Stones, The 393, 394
'Report on Experience' 183, 185, 312
Responsibilities 52–3
Rickword, Edgell 186–92
'Rolling the Lawn' 217
Roman Balcony 285
'Rope, The' 273
Rose, The 51–2
Rosenberg, Isaac 134–9, 153

Satires of Circumstance 17, 38
Schoolboy Lyrics 35
Scorpion 202
'Seamless Garment, The' 146
'Sea Voyage' 216
'Second Coming, The' 55
Second Hymn to Lenin 142, 146
Second Life, The 316, 317–18
Seeing is Believing 361, 363
'Senex' 222–3
Sense of the World, A 347
'September 1913' 53
Sequence for Francis Parkman, A 323
'Serenade: Any Man to Any Woman' 112
'Sermon on Swift, A' 180
'Sestina of the Tramp-Royal' 40
Seven Journeys, The 298
'Seven Sages, The' 53
'Seven Seals' 94
'Shadwell Stair' 153
'Shadow' 66
'Shadow by the Barn, A' 184–5
'Shancoduff' 210
'Shelley's Skylark' 20
'Ship of Death, The' 99, 101

Shires, The 323
Shropshire Lad, A 28
Silkin, Jon 392–7
Singer, Burns 369–75
Sisson, C. H. 38, 79, 83, 224, 266–77
Sitwell, Dame Edith 109–14
Six Epistles to Eva Hesse 323, 324, 326–7
'Sleep' 66
Sleeping Beauty, The 110
Sleeping Lord, The 165
'Slough' 223
Smith, Stevie 200–206
'Snake' 94, 100
'Snap Dragon' 99
'Snow' 229
'Soldier Addresses his Body, The' 192
'Solomon and the Witch' 55
Solstices 232
Some More Human than Others 202
Song at the Year's Turning 260
Song for a Birth or a Death 347, 349–50
'Song of Shadows, The' 68
'Song of the English, A' 42
Song of Childhood 64
Soul for Sale, A 208
Spain 236
Spoils, The 195, 196–7
Springboard 231
Still and All 371–2
'Still Falls the Rain' 111–12
Stones of the Field, The 260
'Strange Meeting' 154
'Straying Student, The' 177
Summoned by Bells 221
'Sunken Garden, The' 67
Survivor's Leave 292
Sweeney Agonistes 124, 126, 127, 129–30, 131

'Swimming Chenango Lake' 365, 368

Tares 260, 263
Ten Burnt Offerings 231
Tender Only to One 201
Thank You, Fog 242
'That Girl's Clear Eyes' 73
'Thaw' 75
Thomas, Dylan 278–84
Thomas, Edward 69–78
Thomas, R. S. 260–65
'Three Poems about Children' 178
Tiny Tears 245, 250
'To an Old Lady' 217
'To Carry the Child' 203
Tomlinson, Charles 360–68
Too Great a Vine 178
Torse 3: Poems 1949–61 353, 354
'Tortoise Family Connections' 100–101
Touch 377, 380, 381
Tower, The 47, 50, 55, 56
'Train to Dublin' 229
'Transformations' 18–20
'Translation' 246–7
'Transparent Prisoner, The' 372–3
Travelling 341, 344–5
'Trench Poets' 192
'Troy' 107–8
True Confessions of George Barker The 252, 258–9
'Twittingpan' 188
Two Freedoms, The 393–4

Underneath the Water 292
Union Street 292
'Usk, The' 269

Vagrant, A 286
Values' 184

'Variations on a Time Theme' 107
'Vengenance of Fionn, The' 174–5
View from a Blind I, The 252
'Villon' 195–6
'Virgini Senescens' 274–5
'Virgin Youth' 96
Vision of Beasts and Gods, A 252
Visitations 232
'Voice, The' 17

Wagoner and Other Poems, The 182
War Requiem 148
Waste Land, The 123–7, 129–32
'Watcher, The' 75
Way In, The 361, 367–8
Way of a World, The 361, 365
Way of Looking, A 347
'Way Through the Woods, The' 37
Weather and Season 314
'We Have Gone Too Far' 101
'Welsh History' 262–3
'Welsh Landscape' 263
Wessex Poems 14
'White Goddess, The' 170
White Threshold, The 298, 299
Whitsun Weddings, The 336–8
Wild Swans at Coole, The 53–4
Winding Stair and Other Poems, The 56
'Winter's Tale, A' 284
Winter Talent and Other Poems, A 322
'Witnesses, The' 241
Wodwo 384, 389–90
'Words for Music Perhaps' 56, 331
Written on Water 361, 366–7

Yeats, W. B. 30, 44–56
'Young Woman of Beare, The' 176, 177